Adjustment and Beyond

This is IEA conference volume no. 128

Adjustment and Beyond

The Reform Experience in South Asia

Proceedings of the IEA Conference held in Dhaka, Bangladesh

Edited by

Wahiduddin Mahmud
Professor of Economics
University of Dhaka

palgrave in association with
International Economic Association

First published 2001 by
PALGRAVE
Houndmills, Basingstoke, Hampshire RG21 6XS and
175 Fifth Avenue, New York, N. Y. 10010
Companies and representatives throughout the world

PALGRAVE is the new global academic imprint of St. Martin's Press LLC Scholarly and Reference Division and Palgrave Publishers Ltd (formerly Macmillan Press Ltd).

Outside North America
ISBN 0–333–74768–2

In North America
ISBN 0–312–23330–2

This book is printed on paper suitable for recycling and made from fully managed and sustained forest sources.

A catalogue record for this book is available from the British Library.

Library of Congress Cataloging-in-Publication Data
Adjustment and beyond : the reform experience in South Asia : proceedings of the IEA Conference held in Dhaka, Bangladesh / edited by Wahiduddin Mahmud.
p. cm. — (IEA conference volume ; no. 128)
"This book comprises papers presented at the Conference on 'Adjustment and beyond: the reform experience in South Asia' held in Dhaka, Bangladesh, between 30 March and 1 April 1998"—Preface.
"In association with International Economic Association".
Includes bibliographical references and index.
ISBN 0–312–23330–2 (cloth)
1. South Asia—Economic policy—Congresses. 2. Structural adjustment (Economic policy)—South Asia—Congresses. I. Mahmud, Wahiduddin. II. International Economic Association. III. I.E.A. conference volume ; no. 128.

HC430.6 .A65 2000
338.954—dc21

99–086152

10 9 8 7 6 5 4 3 2 1
10 09 08 07 06 05 04 03 02 01

Printed in Great Britain by Antony Rowe Ltd, Chippenham, Wiltshire

Contents

The International Economic Association

A non-profit organization with purely scientific aims, the International Economic Association (IEA) was founded in 1950. It is a federation of some sixty national economic associations in all parts of the world. Its basic purpose is the development of economics as an intellectual discipline, recognizing a diversity of problems, systems and values in the world and taking note of methodological diversities.

The IEA has, since its creation, sought to fulfil that purpose by promoting mutual understanding among economists through the organization of scientific meetings and common research programmes, and by means of publications on problems of fundamental as well as of current importance. Deriving from its long concern to assure professional contacts between East and West and North and South, the IEA pays special attention to issues of economics in systemic transition and in the course of development. During its fifty years of existence, it has organized over a hundred round-table conferences for specialists on topics ranging from fundamental theories to methods and tools of analysis and major problems of the present-day world. Participation in round tables is at the invitation of a specialist programme committee, but eleven triennial World Congresses have regularly attracted the participation of individual economists from all over the world.

The Association is governed by a Council, composed of representatives of all member associations, and by a fifteen-member Executive Committee which is elected by the Council. The Executive Committee (1995–98) at the time of this Conference was:

President:	Professor Jacques H. Drèze, Belgium
Vice-President:	Professor Anne Krueger, USA
Treasurer:	Professor Erich Streissler, Austria
Past President:	Professor Michael Bruno, Israel
Other Members:	Professor Anthony B. Atkinson, UK
	Professor Vittorio Corbo, Chile
	Professor Karel Dyba, Czech Republic
	Professor Jean-Michel Grandmont, France
	Professor Yujiro Hayami, Japan
	Professor Seppo Honkapohja, Finland
	Professor Valeri Makarov, Russia,
	Professor Luigi Pasinetti, Italy
	Professor Hans Werner Sinn, Germany

Sir Austin Robinson was an active Adviser on the publication of IEA conference proceedings from 1954 until his final short illness in 1993.

The Association has also been fortunate in having secured many outstanding economists to serve as President:

Gottfried Haberler (1950–53), Howard S. Ellis (1953–56), Erik Lindahl (1956–59), E. A. G. Robinson (1959–62) G. Ugo Papi (1962–65), Paul A. Samuelson (1965–68), Erik Lundberg (1968–71), Fritz Machlup (1971–74), Edmond Malinvaud (1974–77), Shigeto Tsuru (1977–80), Victor L. Urquidi (1980–83), Kenneth J. Arrow (1983–86), Amartya Sen (1986–89), Anthony B. Atkinson (1989–92) and Michael Bruno (1992–95).

The activities of the Association are mainly funded from the subscriptions of members and grants from a number of organizations, including continuing support from UNESCO, through the International Social Science Council.

Preface

This book comprises papers presented at the Conference on 'Adjustment and Beyond: the Reform Experience in South Asia' held in Dhaka, Bangladesh, between 30 March and 1 April 1998. The Conference was organized by the Bangladesh Economic Association under the auspices of the International Economic Association. This was the second IEA conference to be held in Dhaka; the first was held in 1973 under the initiative of the late Professor E. A. G. Robinson to discuss the development problems of the newly-independent Bangladesh.

The 1998 Dhaka conference was a timely one. It was held against the backdrop of the ongoing financial crisis in East Asia and provided an opportunity to try to understand the crisis and draw lessons for South Asia. Not surprisingly, the discussions at the Conference, as well as the contents of this book, are heavily concentrated on the issue of how to cope with global capital flows and their volatility.

Academics and policy-makers, from within and outside South Asia, participated at the Conference, which provided an opportunity for the exchange of ideas on the current state of debate on macroeconomic reform and the policy choices facing the economies of the region. There is a growing consensus that South Asia has the potential to achieve more rapid growth and even emerge as a global growth pole in the early decades of the next century. However, the identification of a reform agenda for realizing that potential and the political feasibility of its implementation are still subjects of considerable debate.

In planning the Conference and this book, care has been taken to achieve a balance of opposing views on the reform debate. In order to present a broad selection of views it has been necessary to shorten several chapters for inclusion here. The reader will thus be exposed to a whole spectrum of viewpoints and be able to make his own judgement on the issues discussed.

The essays in the book provide country overviews of reform experience as well as discussion of specific issues of particular interest to South Asia. The volume is arranged in six sections as follows:

I Country Overviews
II Globalization and Development Economics
III Adjustment and Poverty
IV Sustainability of Reforms
V Lessons from the East Asian Crisis
VI Comments: Beyond Adjustment and Emerging Issues

The South Asian reform experience needs also to be assessed in the light of the recent shift in development thinking in favour of a development strategy that goes beyond the orthodox neo-liberal agenda to accommodate some of the earlier concerns regarding the developmental role of the state. The reform debate has now covered new ground around such concepts as governance, institution building, participation and human capital development. The emphasis is on evidence and not ideology, and on research that is closer to the ground. The reform experience across the South Asian countries, with their distinctive socio-economic settings and public cultures, may thus provide fresh perspectives on the emerging development paradigms. The Dhaka Conference was indeed based on the premise that Development Economics and South Asia have a lot to learn from each other.

Acknowledgements

The Dhaka Conference and the published proceedings were made possible by the support and assistance of a number of individuals and organizations, both within Bangladesh and outside. Rehman Sobhan conceived the original idea for the Conference and promoted it assiduously. He acted as the Chairman of the Programme Committee, which also included Amartya Sen, Yujiro Hayami and Mustapha K. Nabli. Wahiduddin Mahmud and Debapriya Bhattacharya were responsible for the planning and organization of the conference on behalf of the Bangladesh Economic Association.

Most of the financial support came from a UNDP grant made available through the Ministry of Finance of the Government of Bangladesh. The British Council also generously shared a part of the cost. In particular, we would like to thank David Lockwood, Resident Representative of UNDP in Dhaka, Simon Kay of the British Council's Dhaka Office and Masihur Rahman, Secretary, Economic Relations Division, Government of Bangladesh, for their help in raising the funds. We thank Maureen Hadfield for help in preparing the volume for publication.

We are particularly grateful to Sheikh Hasina, Prime Minister of Bangladesh and S. A. M. S. Kibria, Minister for Finance, for their overall support for the Conference, the International Social Science Council for finance under its Project R3a, and to UNESCO for continuing collaboration.

List of Participants and Contributors

***Professor Abu Abdullah**, Bangladesh Institute of Development Studies, Dhaka
***Dr Isher Judge Ahluwalia**, Indian Council for Research on International Economic Relations, New Delhi
Professor Muzaffer Ahmad, University of Dhaka, Bangladesh
Dr Mohiuddin Khan Alamgir, State Minister for Planning, Bangladesh
***Professor Amiya Bagchi**, Centre for Studies in Social Sciences, Calcutta, India
***Professor Debapriya Bhattacharya**, Bangladesh Institute of Development Studies, Dhaka, Bangladesh
***Dr Mansoor Dailami**, World Bank, Washington DC, USA
Professor Meghnad Desai, London School of Economics and Politics, UK
Dr Paul Dorosh, International Food Policy Research Institute, Washington DC, USA
***Dr E. V. K. FitzGerald**. Queen Elizabeth House, University of Oxford, UK
***Dr Willem van der Geest**, European Institute for Asian Studies, Brussels, Belgium
Professor Dharam Ghai, Former Director, UNRISD, Geneva, Switzerland
Dr K. K. Guru-Gharana, National Planning Commission, Nepal
***Professor Koichi Hamada**, Yale University, USA
***Dr Nadeem Ul Haque**, IMF, Washington DC, USA
Dr Parvez Hasan, formerly World Bank, Washington DC, USA
Dr Mahbub ul Huq, Human Development Centre, Islamabad, Pakistan
***Dr Azizul Islam**, UN-ESCAP, Bangkok, Thailand
***Dr Nurul Islam**, International Food Policy Research Institute, Washington DC, USA
Dr Vijay Joshi, Merton College, University of Oxford, UK
***Dr A. R. Kemal**, Planning Commission, Pakistan
Dr Reza Kibria, University of Dhaka, Bangladesh
Mr S. A. M. S. Kibria, Minister of Finance, Bangladesh
***Professor Deepak Lal**, University of California, Los Angeles, USA
***Professor Wahiduddin Mahmud**, University of Dhaka, Bangladesh
***Professor Deepak Nayyar**, Jawaharlal Nehru University, New Delhi, India
***Dr Peter Nunnenkamp**, Kiel Institute of World Economics, Germany
***Professor S. R. Osmani**, University of Ulster at Jordanstown, Northern Ireland
***Dr Sheila Page**, Overseas Development Institute, London, UK
***Professor Prabhat Patnaik**, Jawaharlal Nehru University, New Delhi, India
Dr M. G. Quibria, Asian Development Bank, Manila, Philippines

Mr Saifur Rahman, Former Minister of Finance, Bangladesh
Professor Anisur Rahman, formerly of ILO, Geneva
Professor Mihir Rakshit, formerly Presidency College, Calcutta, India
Dr Narhari Rao, Asian Development Bank, Manila, Philippines
Professor Abhijit Sen, Commission for Agricultural Costs and Prices, India
Professor Rehman Sobhan, Centre for Policy Dialogue, Dhaka, Bangladesh
***Professor Frances Stewart**, Queen Elizabeth House, University of Oxford, UK
Mr M. Syeduzzaman, former Finance Minister, Bangladesh
Dr Min Tang, Asian Development Bank, Manila, Philippines
***Professor John Toye**, Institute of Development Studies, University of Sussex, UK, and ILO
***Dr G. Uswatte-Aratchi**, Marga Institute, Colombo, Sri Lanka
***Dr John Williamson**, The World Bank, Washington DC, USA
Professor Muhammad Yunus, Grameen Bank, Dhaka, Bangladesh

* Authors of chapters or comments

Abbreviations and Acronyms

ACP	African, Caribbean and Pacific
ADB	Asian Development Bank
ADMARC	Malawi parastatal marketing board
ADP	Adjustment Development Programme
AMS	aggregate measure of support
APEC	Asian and Pacific Economic Cooperation
ASEAN	Association of South East Asian Nations
BBS	Bangladesh Bureau of Statistics
BIBF	Bangkok International Banking Facility
BIDS	Bangladesh Industrial Development Service
BJP	Bharatiya Janata Party (India)
BKK	Bank Kredit Kecamatan (Indonesia)
CAC	capital account convertibility
CAP	Common Agricultural Policy
CFA	Communauté Financière Africain (franc)
CGE	computable general equilibrium (model)
CIS	Commonwealth of Independent States
CPA	critical path analysis
CPI	consumer price index
DC	developing country
DFI	direct foreign investment
ERTI	European Round Table of Industrialists
EPZ	export processing zones
ESAF	Enhanced Structural Adjustment Fund
EU	European Union
FAO	Food and Agriculture Organization of the United Nations
FDI	foreign direct investment
FTA	free trade area
GATT	General Agreement on Tariffs and Trade
GDP	gross domestic product
GDDS	General Data Dissemination System
GNP	gross national product
GOB	Government of Bangladesh
GOI	Government of India
GSP	generalized system of preferences
IFI	international financial institution
IFPRI	International Food Policy Research Institute
ILO	International Labour Organization

IMR	Infant mortality rates
ITC	International Trade Classification
IMF	International Monetary Fund
LDC	less developed country
LIBOR	London Inter-Bank Offer Rate
LTTE	Liberation Tigers of Tamil Eelam
MAI	Multilateral Agreement on Investment
MERCOSUR	South American Regional Organisation
MFA	Multi-Fibre Arrangement
MFN	most favoured nation
MIGA	Multilateral Investment Guarantee Agreement
NAFTA	North American Free Trade Agreement
NCBs	nationalized Bangladesh banks
NDP	net domestic product
NEDLAC	National Economic Development and Labour Administration Council
NGO	non-government organisation
NIC	newly industrializing country
NT	non-tradables
ODA	official development assistance
ODI	Overseas Development Institute
OECD	Organization for Economic Cooperation and Development
PCBs	commercial Bangladesh banks
PIP	private income poverty
PFP	Policy Framework Paper
PRC	People's Republic of China
PSP	phyto-sanitary standards
RBI	Reserve Bank of India
REER	real effective exchange rate
SAARC	South Asian Association for Regional Cooperation
SADC	South Asia Development Commission
SAF	Structural Adjustment Fund
SAL	structural adjustment loan
SAP	structural adjustment programme
SAPTA	South Asia Preferential Trade Agreement
SDDS	Special Data Dissemination System
SIP	social income poverty
SOE	state-owned enterprise
TNC	transnational corporation
TRIMs	trade-related investment measures
TRIPs	trade-related (aspects of) intellectual property rights
UNCTAD	UN Conference on Trade and Development
UNDP	United Nations Development Programme

UN-ESCAP	United Nations Economic and Social Commission for Asia and the Pacific
UNIDO	UN Industrial Development Organization
UNICEF	UN Children's Fund
UR	Uruguay Round
VAT	value added tax
WTO	World Trade Organization
ZCTU	Zimbabwe Congress of Trade Unions

Introduction

Wahiduddin Mahmud

South Asia faces the challenge of realizing its potential of achieving accelerated economic growth and alleviating the massive poverty that afflicts a large proportion of its 1.3 billion population. Strategies for meeting this challenge have shifted in recent years, away from state-bureaucratic controls and industrial autarky towards market-oriented liberalizing policy reforms known as structural adjustment. Given the considerable experience in implementing these policy reforms in the countries of this region, it is possible to attempt an assessment. With the initial phases of economic liberalization and integration into the global economy already completed, the reforms have now entered a stage of learning-by-doing, where looking at the actual reform outcomes is at least as important for policy makers as understanding the *ex ante* rationale for reform.

While the implementation of structural adjustment in the South Asian economies remains incomplete in varying degrees, why is there a need also to look *beyond* adjustment? First, the move towards economic liberalization has to some extent been overtaken by recent events in the global capital markets. In the wake of the East Asian financial crisis, there is a sudden realization that the pro-market reforms have to cope with a market of a very different kind – in Wall Street and the City of London. Second, and more important, there seems to have been a shift in development thinking in favour of a development strategy that goes far beyond the orthodox adjustment-stabilization package of reforms. The new emphasis on governance and institution-building, for example, has significantly broadened the scope of the reform agenda; it also brings back many of the old structuralist development concerns such as regarding the so-called institutional constraints to supply responses. The stage is perhaps set for a synthesis of the neo-classical development paradigms of the 1980s with the earlier ones emphasizing the developmental roles of the state.

It remains to be seen whether these new directions in development thinking can lead to a broader consensus than that originally reached within the precincts of the 18th and 19th Streets of Washington DC! While it may be agreed that the choice of an appropriate state–market mix should be based not on ideology but on evidence regarding market failure *vis-à-vis* government failure, there will be much less agreement on what that evidence is. Again, while it is agreed that economic liberalization alone is not sufficient for achieving equitable and sustainable growth, there is controversy regarding whether a broader strategy will be entirely compatible with the tenets of orthodox structural adjustment or will involve some compromise. There is also a general agreement that economic liberalization alone will not yield the desired results unless the institutional infrastructure is appropriate for the functioning of a market economy. Some would argue, therefore, that liberalization should be done gradually and cautiously since institution-building takes time. Others may, however, argue that institutional weaknesses should not be used as an excuse for delaying the reforms and that the process of liberalization itself creates pressures for institutional changes.

The spectrum of views in the reform debate is well-represented by the contributions included in this volume. Some of the contributions provide overviews of the reform experience in individual South Asian countries, while others deal with the specific issues of the reform debate that are of particular interest to South Asia. The volume has been deliberately designed so as to achieve a balance of opposing views; however, what may strike some as surprising is the extent of agreement and common ground that emerges from these apparently divergent viewpoints.

Among the South Asian countries, Sri Lanka was the first to move markedly towards economic liberalization during the late 1970s, followed by Pakistan and Bangladesh in the late 1980s and India at the beginning of the 1990s. In spite of the differences in the timing and the extent of the reforms (with India still lagging significantly behind), the country overviews in Part I bring out some common features of the South Asian reform experience. In none of the countries is there evidence of any sustained increase in the investment–GDP ratio (this is so even after discounting the expected initial investment squeeze needed for achieving economic stabilization). This largely explains why any improvement in growth performance has been rather modest or could not be sustained. While the sphere of public investment was curtailed, the response of private investment to the reforms was mostly lacking. Apart from the desire-to-invest factors, the domestic saving rate could not be sufficiently increased while net external assistance as a proportion of GDP declined continually. Another common feature is that the fiscal deficit has been reduced by curtailing the development part of the budget, and not by reducing current expenditure or by mobilizing more revenue (the only exception was a once-and-for-all increase in the tax–GDP ratio in Bangladesh following the introduction of value added tax in the early 1990s). As a result, public saving as a proportion of GDP has increased very little, or has in fact declined, and remains much too low by East Asian standards.

Improving the quality of fiscal adjustment and making provision for a better institutional and policy environment for private investment appear to be the common challenges facing South Asian economies. In fiscal adjustment, there will be controversy about the desired level of public investment, since such investment can, in some contexts, both 'crowd in' and 'crowd out' private investment. The key requirements for improving the investment climate include adequate infrastructure provision, strengthening of the financial and legal systems, and a general improvement in the quality of governance that can help to reduce the so-called transaction costs of doing business. Evidence from Pakistan cited by Kemal (Chapter 4) suggests that if privatization is not accompanied by improvements in the functioning of markets, there may not be any gains in production efficiency. The experience of Bangladesh (Chapter 3) highlights the risks of going for financial liberalization without providing for adequate regulation and supervision. India has, however, moved more cautiously towards economic liberalization. There are still in place many quantitative trade restrictions, agricultural and food subsidies, directed credits and a variety of investment restrictions; privatization also has not yet figured prominently in the Indian reform agenda. Are further liberalization, privatization and the opening of markets the way forward for India? On this question there is a wide range of viewpoints, as can be seen from the contributions by Ahluwalia in Chapter 1, Nayyar in Chapter 2, Patnaik in Chapter 7 and the comments by Bagchi in Part VI.

The lessons to be learnt from the East Asian financial crisis are of great interest to the South Asian economies aspiring to attract more foreign capital. In Part V, both Williamson and Azizul Islam make an attempt to understand this crisis in terms of certain common characteristics, notwithstanding many important differences in the country-specific situations. A general conclusion is that the crisis originated from the interaction between international capital market imperfections and institutional weaknesses in managing domestic financial liberalization. It is also noted that the crisis occurred only after these economies opted for full liberalization of external capital account transactions in the early 1990s and were subsequently exposed to large short-term foreign debts. The lessons for South Asia seem to be that external financial liberalization should be gradual and selective, accompanied or preceded by the development of efficient domestic financial institutions and adequate capacity for their regulation and supervision. At the same time, South Asia must learn the positive lessons of the erstwhile East Asian miracle, although there will remain controversy regarding the role of the various contributing factors that made the miracle possible. An interestingly different perspective on the East Asian lessons is, however, provided by Deepak Lal, who in his comments in Part VI points to a 'systemic flaw' in the 'Asian' model of development

The episodes of crisis in the global capital markets also bring home the inadequacies of standard Bretton Woods macroeconomics in dealing with the problem of deregulated capital markets. In this context, Chapter 6 by Nadeem Ul Haque and Dailami discusses the problems of devising sound macroeconomic policies for developing countries exposed to risks of volatility in international capital flows, while Nunnenkamp in Chapter 9 emphasizes the importance of policy consistency and credibility. There are clearly many unresolved issues, such as how to deal with large capital inflows and the associated problems of asset market bubbles and exchange rate management. In Chapter 8, FitzGerald attempts to analyse yet another important, but relatively unexplored, aspect of short-term capital flows, namely the transmission mechanisms through which the instability of such flows affects the 'real economy' variables including investment, production and employment. An understanding of these mechanisms is necessary for assessing the social returns from such capital flows as distinct from their private profitability.

The trade-related issues of globalization, although relatively neglected in this volume, are of great importance to South Asia's development prospects. In Chapter 10, Sheila Page discusses the constraints and opportunities faced by developing countries in the context of the evolving world trading system, while Nurul Islam, in his comments in Part VI, looks at the particular challenges facing South Asia. These challenges include coping with the new rules and conventions governing the global system and responding to the dual trends towards globalization and regionalism. The role of the public management of external economic policies will be significant but will change in character and content compared with successful policies in the past – such as those of the high-performing East Asian economies – and will require not less but greater skill and expertise.

In Part III, Frances Stewart draws on the evidence from Asia, and Osmani from Africa, for an update of the debate on the poverty impacts of structural adjustment. The weight of evidence suggests that the most important determinant of the impact of adjustment on poverty is what happens to the GDP growth rate. The effect on income distribution is less clear and may vary according to the structure of the economy – for example, whether the labour-intensive sectors of the economy are likely to benefit from reforms. In this respect, the Asian region as a whole may be in a better position to secure poverty-reducing adjustment than other regions. However, evidence from all countries seems to support the view that achieving sustained growth and accelerated poverty reduction will require public policies and strategies that may extend far beyond the conventional structural adjustment reforms.

The political economy aspects of reform are discussed by John Toye in Chapter 13 in the context of the sustainability of India's reforms, but several other authors also touch upon these aspects. Some measures of reform are clearly vote-losing, such as the withdrawal of agricultural and food subsidies which affects large sections of the population. Others may antagonize militant groups who have very little voting power but can create serious short-term disruption, such as the privatization of state enterprises resisted by trade unions. There are further reforms that will hurt only the small group of rent-seeking political-bureaucratic elite, but that are likely to get general public support; these would include institutional reforms, such as legislation for dealing with wilful default of bank loans, tax evasion or corruption in high places that subverts the effectiveness of the government's regulatory functions. Clearly, the degree of resistance to these different types of reform depends on the nature of prevailing political cultures. It is noteworthy that the politically-blocked reforms in India belong to all three types above. In Bangladesh and Pakistan, on the other hand, the reforms of the first type have met with little political resistance, and even those of the second type have, to a large extent, been implemented. It is the implementation of the last category of reforms that has so far lacked political feasibility – and not only in Bangladesh and Pakistan.

Part I
Country Overviews

1
The Indian Economy: Looking Ahead

Isher Judge Ahluwalia
Indian Council for Research on International Economic Relations, Delhi

1 Introduction

When India as a newly independent nation set out on the path of rapid economic development within a democratic political framework, it aroused great expectations. Today, 50 years later, the record is a mixed one. India's greatest achievement has been in building a working democracy in exceptionally difficult circumstances, thereby making her the largest 'free' market in the world. The economic achievements have been modest with some distinct disappointments. India has developed an impressive scientific and technological capability, but 45 per cent of the population is still illiterate. Again, while India avoided the worst fears of the Club of Rome in the early 1970s, that of being unable to feed her growing population, the progress in reducing poverty has been less than desirable.

The record of economic development in India is far less impressive than that of the East Asian economies and also well below its own potential. The Indian economy grew slowly in the first 35 years following independence, but at a more respectable pace in the past 15. The rapidly growing population further eroded the modest gains of growth. Until 1980, India was a slow-growing economy recording annual growth rates of gross domestic product (GDP) of 4.1 per cent, 3.8 per cent and 3.3 per cent in the three decades of the 1950s, 1960s and 1970s respectively as shown in Table 1.1. In the 1980s, India's annual economic growth accelerated to 5.6 per cent – a better record than in other developing countries.[1]

This slow growth in the earlier period constrained India's ability to deal with the long-standing problem of poverty. The percentage of the population below the poverty line fluctuated around 50 per cent between 1950 and 1980. By contrast, the decade of the 1980s witnessed a substantial decline in poverty, to less than 33 per cent[2] by 1993–4. This improved growth performance, however, became a victim of the internal contradictions that were emerging. The import intensity of the process of industrialization was not matched by export growth to finance these imports. When prudent fiscal

Table 1.1 Macroeconomic indicators: growth rates

	GDP			Prices		Foreign trade	
	Total	*Industry*	*Agriculture*	*WPI*	*CPI*	*Exports*	*Imports*
1950–1 to 1960–1	4.1	6.3	3.0	1.7	4.5	1.1	7.9
1960–1 to 1970–1	3.8	5.0	1.8	7.1	7.2	4.4	–0.5
1970–1 to 1980–1	3.3	4.8	2.1	9.1	7.8	15.6	23.8
1980–1 to 1990–1	5.6	7.1	3.2	6.6	8.5	8.3	4.5
1990–1	5.4	7.0	4.2	10.3	11.2	9.2	13.5
1991–2	0.8	–1.7	–2.0	13.7	13.5	–1.5	–19.4
1992–3	5.3	4.4	5.8	10.1	9.9	3.8	12.7
1993–4	6.2	6.9	3.6	8.4	7.3	20.0	6.5
1994–5	7.8	10.8	5.2	10.9	10.3	18.4	22.9
1995–6	7.2	12.7	–2.3	7.6	10.0	20.8	28.0
1996–7	7.5	6.8	7.3	6.3	9.4	4.1	5.1
1997–8[e]	5.5	5.7	–2.0	na	na	3.3*	7.4*

Notes: WPI is the wholesale price index; CPI consumer price index; [e] = estimate; na = not available; * is for April–December.
Source: Economic Surveys, Ministry of Finance, Government of India (various years).

policies gave way to rising fiscal deficits resulting in growing macroeconomic imbalances, the higher growth of the 1980s could not be sustained. The result was the balance of payments crisis of 1990–1 and the economic reforms that followed.

The Indian economy weathered the storm through good crisis management in the initial years of reforms and good agricultural fortune from 1992–3 to 1994–5. However, the zeal with which the policy-makers launched medium-term reforms in 1991 failed to survive the crisis. The economy responded a little too well for its own good, moving from less than 1 per cent GDP growth in the first year of adjustment to over 5 per cent and 6 per cent in the next two years, respectively, and to over 7 per cent per annum in the succeeding three.[3] The internal monetary squeeze and the unfavourable external trade environment of 1996–8 further compounded the problems arising for the infrastructural constraints. As a result, there has been a distinct slowing down of growth in 1997–8. For a relatively more open and faster growing economy a bold approach is needed to meet the new challenges as India proceeds towards liberalization as a means to increase employment opportunities and better standards of living.

This chapter considers the state of the Indian economy 50 years after political independence and seven years after the launching of the wide-ranging economic reforms, and analyses its economic prospects. The next section presents a brief sketch of the evolution of India's development strategy and the major indicators of economic performance from 1950 to

1990. This is followed in section 3 by a discussion of the reforms of 1991–6, while the remaining sections spell out the challenges ahead.

2 Strategy and performance: 1950–90

India's development strategy after independence was rooted in the recognition of industrialization as a means of achieving rapid growth and prosperity. The expectation was that growing employment opportunities would be created with rapid rates of economic growth, which in turn would provide a durable solution to the poverty problem.

The strategy was characterized by an inward orientation through import substitution with extensive import licensing and high tariffs, a crucial role for central planning and the public sector, and emphasis on heavy industry. While major policy attention was focused on the public sector, the private sector was expected to play an important complementary role in Indian industrialization. In particular, the private sector was expected to meet the growing demand for consumer goods. The industrial and regulatory policies were also designed to promote the development of the small-scale sector and help bring about industrial dispersal.[4]

Emphasis on import substitution was the dominant intellectual thinking in the developing world in the 1950s, supported by evidence of a long-term decline in the terms of trade in developing economies and expectations of a slowdown in world trade. In fact, world trade grew faster than expected during the 1960s and the 1970s, and while many developing economies adapted their policies to take advantage of the growing opportunities of trade and development, India persisted with heavily protectionist policies and combined these with strong domestic regulation in an effort to influence the pattern of growth.

Agriculture was the dominant sector, both in terms of contribution to total value added and as a support base for the majority of the labour force. Unlike industry, where the public sector had a significant presence, agriculture remained in private hands. The share of agriculture in GDP declined from over 57 per cent in 1951 at the start of central planning to less than one-third in 1995, although agriculture still provides employment to two-thirds of the labour force. The major part of public investment in agriculture (which ranged between 20 and 23 per cent of total plan outlays) went into irrigation.

The growing demand for food grains in the early phase of industrialization (from 1950 to the mid-1960s) was met by increasing production through extensive cultivation and the import of PL-480 wheat from the USA, while price incentives for domestic producers were suppressed. Two successive droughts in the mid-1960s and the abrupt withdrawal of the PL-480 import facility forced policy-makers towards evolving a new strategy of intensive cultivation through the green revolution. In its preoccupation with gaining self-sufficiency in food grains, however, the domestic market for food grains was largely insulated from movements in world prices.

India's strategy has been largely successful in creating a diversified industrial base. Capital goods account for 16 per cent of the value added in the industrial sector, while intermediate goods and consumer goods account for 20 per cent and 23 per cent respectively. Mining, electricity and gas together accounted for the remaining 39 per cent of value added. The strong presence of the public sector can be seen in its share of total investment, which peaked in the mid-1970s at close to 50 per cent. Even though the rate of capital formation in the public sector stagnated during the 1980s, in 1989–90 public investment accounted for 40 per cent of total investment. Certain core strategic sectors were reserved for the public sector; infrastructure was the exclusive preserve of the public sector.

A major problem with India's industrial policy regime was that the heavy protection from foreign competition and the high degree of domestic regulation created a high-cost industrial structure. Cost and quality considerations were overridden by rent-seeking aspirations. Poor performance in the infrastructure sector created cost pressures on industry. From the late 1960s, policies to promote small-scale enterprise protected the small from the large within the economy. The result of this highly complex domestic regulatory regime with a strong protectionist bias was the emergence of a high-cost industrial structure. The erosion of India's international competitiveness was reflected in a steady decline in her share of world exports of manufactures, from 2 per cent in 1950 to less than 0.5 per cent in 1990.

By the late 1970s, it was becoming clear that the Indian industrial and trade policies were not achieving their objective of high industrial growth rates. While saving and investment rates more than doubled between 1950 and 1980, gains on resource mobilization were more than offset by losses in productivity. Total factor productivity in the organized manufacturing sector declined at the rate of 0.5 per cent a year between 1960 and 1980.[5] Industrial sickness increased. The public sector, far from being an instrument of 'socializing' profits for use in furthering economic development, was actually 'socializing' the losses of public sector enterprises.

During the 1980s, efforts were made to address this low industrial productivity. This was done by reducing domestic regulation, relaxing physical controls in favour of financial controls to encourage greater marketization and private sector participation. Trade policies were simplified to improve access to intermediate imports and, to some extent, even capital goods. But the loosening up of the import-licensing regime was combined with higher tariffs so that competition from imports remained highly restricted. If domestic deregulation and simplification of the trade policy regime was instrumental in raising the total factor productivity growth rate in the organized manufacturing sector to 2.8 per cent per annum,[6] the spread of the 'green revolution' to new regions was successful in generating higher productivity growth in agriculture. The result was an acceleration in GDP growth to 5.6 per cent per annum in the 1980s. The long-term growth in food grain production in the post-green revolution period has been about 2.7 per cent per year, with some acceleration in the late-1980s.

The better growth performance of the 1980s, however, was not sustainable because of the growing macroeconomic imbalances. Fiscal profligacy on the part of the government in the 1980s resulted in government consumption expenditures increasing rapidly, while investment slowed down. Rising interest payments as the government borrowed more and more was part of the problem. A sharp increase in defence expenditures and rising subsidies contributed to rising government consumption.

The anti-export bias of trade policy was to be offset by export subsidies. The value of export incentives net of tax increased from 2.3 per cent of the value of exports in 1960–1, to 11.1 per cent in 1989–90. Food subsidies on account of the public distribution system also imposed a growing burden. Subsidies on fertilizers were an integral part of government policy to encourage farmers to adopt the new technology. Thus, notwithstanding the rise in food prices and the increase in the cost of producing fertilizer, the farmer paid the same price for fertilizer at the end of the 1980s as at the beginning. While the food and fertilizer subsidy burden was explicitly borne by central government, the credit subsidy was provided by the banking system, and the implicit subsidy on irrigation and power incurred by the state government.

Total input subsidies into agriculture, discussed by Gulati and Sharma (1995), were estimated to have increased from about 51 per cent of the planned expenditure on agriculture (by the centre and the states together) in the early 1980s to about 142 per cent by the early 1990s. The subsidy burden could, therefore, only be met by cutting back on public investment in agriculture. Indeed, public investment in agriculture in real terms declined during the 1980s.

The fiscal current account position of the central government turned from an average surplus of 1.8 per cent of GDP in the second half of the 1970s to a small deficit in 1980–1 which deteriorated further through the decade to reach a level of 3.3 per cent of GDP in 1990–1. The gross fiscal deficit worsened from 6.2 per cent of GDP in 1980–1 to 8.3 per cent in 1990–1 as shown in Table 1.2.

The fiscal profligacy of the 1980s created a macroeconomic situation which could not withstand the shock of the Gulf War of 1990. Quite apart from the adverse effect of the war on India's balance of payments, the loss of faith in the government's ability to provide good macroeconomic management created a crisis of confidence. This resulted in a dwindling of the foreign exchange reserves to a little over US$1 billion, barely sufficient to finance 10 days normal import needs. In the summer of 1991, international default by India seemed a real possibility. It would be reasonable to say that

Table 1.2 Central government revenue and expenditure (per cent of GDP)

	1970–1	*1980–1*	*1990–1*	*1991–2*	*1992–3*	*1993–4*	*1994–5*	*1995–6*	*1996–7*[re]
1 Revenue	9.5	9.1	10.3	10.7	10.5	9.3	9.6	10.0	10.4
Tax revenue	5.7	6.9	8.0	8.1	7.7	6.6	7.1	7.5	7.8
Non-tax revenue	1.9	2.3	2.2	2.6	2.8	2.7	2.5	2.6	2.7
Recovery of loans	1.9	1.5	1.1	1.0	0.9	0.8	0.7	0.6	0.6
PSU disinvestment	0.0	0.0	0.0	0.5	0.3	0.0	0.6	0.1	0.0
2 Expenditure	12.5	16.8	19.7	18.1	17.4	17.5	16.9	16.2	16.2
Interest payments	1.4	1.9	4.0	4.3	4.4	4.5	4.6	4.6	4.7
Subsidies	0.1	1.4	2.3	2.0	1.7	1.6	1.4	1.2	1.3
Defence expenditure	2.8	2.9	2.9	2.7	2.5	2.7	2.4	2.4	2.4
Other non-plan	4.2	4.1	5.7	4.5	4.0	3.6	3.6	3.9	3.4
Budget support for plan of which:	4.0	6.6	5.3	5.0	5.2	5.4	5.0	4.2	4.4
social sectors	na	na	1.00	0.96	0.91	1.02	1.04	1.18	na
3 Fiscal deficit (2–1)	3.0	6.2	8.3	5.9	5.7	7.4	6.1	5.5	5.0

na: not available; [re] revised estimates.
Source: Ministry of Finance, Government of India.

the balance of payments crisis of 1991 was precipitated by the Gulf War, but the crisis had been brewing for some time.

3 Economic reform: 1990s

The balance of payments crisis of 1990–1 proved to be a major turning point for economic policy-making, and the opportunity was seized to initiate wide-ranging economic reforms. A two-pronged approach was adopted, first to fiscal adjustment with a view to macroeconomic stabilization and medium-term reform in the industrial and trade policy regime, and second to reform the financial sector so as to improve productivity. The experience of other economies and India's own in the 1980s showed that a stable macroeconomic environment was crucial to sustaining higher growth. Most significantly, the process of opening up the Indian economy to foreign trade and investment was begun in a determined and steady manner. Ironically, when the positive response to the reforms was becoming noticeable, the will to reform weakened, and after three years the pace of reform slowed. The Congress party was defeated in the general elections of 1996 and the coalition governments that came to power continued with reform, but at a slower pace. Indeed, reform seems to be moving, albeit in a haphazard manner, from the centre to the states.[7]

4 Fiscal stabilization

Serious efforts at fiscal stabilization were made in the first year of adjustment, but the resolve weakened significantly thereafter. The fiscal deficit of the Government of India was brought down from 8.3 per cent of GDP in 1990–1 to 5.9 per cent in the first year of adjustment 1991–2, as shown in Table 1.2, but there was little progress after that. Seven years after launching these reforms the fiscal deficit was still around 6 per cent in 1997–8.

Reform of the tax structure has been a key element in the strategy of economic reform. While a moderate tax-rate regime has been established for direct taxes, and direct tax revenue as a percentage of GDP has increased from 2 per cent in 1990–1 to 3.5 per cent in 1997–8, it still remains low because of the narrowness of the tax base and poor compliance. As regards customs revenue, the explicit objective of reducing levels of protection in the economy meant lower contributions from this source. The main weakness in tax revenues has been in the area of excise duties; their share of GDP declined from 4 per cent in 1990–1 to 3.4 per cent in 1997–8. Excise duties are the single largest source of revenue for central government, accounting for 40 per cent of total tax revenue. The government has refined and simplified the excise duty regime, although introducing a full value added tax would require a constitutional amendment, because the centre's powers are limited to manufacturing and do not extend to sales.

Reforms on the expenditure front were weak. Defence expenditure was contained at around 2.4 per cent GDP but more generally the government found it difficult to cut current expenditure. In particular, interest payments imposed a growing burden as the government continued to borrow large amounts at deregulated interest rates. There was little restructuring of government expenditure or cutting back of unproductive expenditure; and large increases in the salaries of government employees following the recommendations of the Fifth Pay Commission added to government expenditure. As state governments also increase pay, the government fiscal deficit will increase.

Poor rates of return on public investment added to the problem of resource constraints. Since little policy effort was made during the 1990s to address the issue of the low return from public sector enterprises, this source could not be tapped to mobilize resources. India's public saving ranged from 0.6 to 4.1 per cent during the period 1980 to 1995, in sharp contrast to the public saving rates of 10–18 per cent during the 1980s in the economies of Malaysia, Singapore and Thailand (see Table 1.3). The brunt of the fiscal stabilization measures was borne by capital formation from the budgetary resources. However, efforts were made to protect spending on social sectors including health, education and rural development, after some cuts in the first year of adjustment. Expenditure on poverty alleviation and rural development programmes was directed at protecting the poor from the impact of adjustment.

The picture with respect to state fiscal deficits has been more complex. Given the ceiling on what states can borrow from the capital market, the

Table 1.3 Public and private savings in India and selected East Asian economies

	Public savings	*Private savings*	*Total*
Indonesia, 1981–8	7.7	14.0	21.7
Japan, 1981–8	5.1	15.8	20.9
Malaysia, 1981–90	10.3	19.1	29.4
Singapore, 1981–90	18.5	24.0	42.5
Thailand, 1980–5	14.3	4.7	19.0
India			
1980–3	4.1	15.9	20.0
1986–9	2.3	18.1	20.4
1990–1	1.0	23.3	24.3
1991–2	1.9	21.0	22.9
1992–3	1.5	20.5	22.0
1993–4	0.6	22.1	22.7
1994–5	1.8	23.8	25.6
1995–6	2.3	23.0	25.3
1996–7	1.9	24.2	26.1

Source: Bajpai, Varshney and Sachs (1999).

states have not really been in a position to widen their fiscal deficits much. But they were unwilling to cut subsidies in the face of hard budget constraints, and in some states fresh populist promises were made while the budgetary resources could not even cover the existing subsidies. All this led to a collapse of state spending on social sectors. A major fiscal constraint for the states has been the burden imposed by the persistent losses of the irrigation system and the state electricity boards. The revenue from user-charges for irrigation typically does not even cover the maintenance cost of the system. As for the state electricity boards, low operational efficiency, widespread theft of power and a non-viable tariff structure, particularly for agriculture, created a situation where the cumulative losses of the state electricity boards alone reached US$70 billion by 1995–6. The deteriorating fiscal position of the states may be less visible, but it has significant implications for overall macroeconomic stability as well as the development potential of the Indian economy.

5 Structural adjustment

On the structural front, decisive moves were made to open up the Indian economy to foreign competition from imports and to combine this with a radical change in foreign investment policy. Thus, quantitative restrictions on imports were removed on most intermediate and capital goods. Consumer goods, however, remained under an import-licensing regime. A systematic reduction in tariffs meant a gradual exposure to foreign competition for Indian industry, but even after declining from 87 per cent in 1990–1 to 30 per cent in 1998–9, the import-weighted tariff was much higher than in major developing economies such as Korea, Mexico, Brazil and Indonesia, as Table 1.4 shows.

Table 1.4 Tariffs: international comparisons (per cent)

		Maximum tariff	*Import-weighted tariff*	*Collection rate*
India	1997–8	40	27	29[2]
	1990–1	250	87	47
Mexico	1990	20	10	5
Brazil	1993	35	14[1]	na
	1990	105	32	7
Korea	1985–92[3]	30	9	6
Indonesia	1989–91[4]	60	10	5

Notes: [1] For Brazil, the data refer to a simple average in 1990; [2] India: collection rate refers to 1995–6; [3] Korea: data for columns 1, 2 and 3 relate to year 1985, 1992 and 1990, respectively; [4] Indonesia: data for columns 1, 2 and 3 relate to year 1991, 1990 and 1989, respectively; na: not available.
Source: World Bank and Ministry of Finance, Government of India.

The reduction in industrial protection has also had a significant liberating effect on Indian agriculture through the improvement in the terms of trade for agriculture. The index of agricultural prices relative to industrial prices rose by over 5 per cent between 1990–1 and 1995–6, which is likely to generate a shift of resources towards agriculture. The importance assigned to the agro-processing industry in the new economic policy is also likely to have significant backward linkages to agriculture and to help boost productivity. But the question of reallocating budgetary resources from subsidies into investment, particularly in irrigation, needs to be addressed squarely.

Though the domestic terms of trade have improved for agriculture, estimates by Gulati and Sharma (1995) of the aggregate measure of support (AMS) to Indian agriculture in the early 1990s remains negative at –22 per cent of the value of agricultural output. This is the same figure as that estimated for the period 1986–8 for GATT negotiations. Apart from the remaining protection of the industrial sector, there is the fact that while agricultural inputs are subsidized, output agricultural prices remain controlled, most notably on exports/imports. This implies continuing disprotection of the agricultural sector. Restrictive trade policies also distort the effective incentives on different crops.

The foreign investment regime was liberalized by allowing foreign investment in virtually every sector of the economy. While majority foreign investment is now freely allowed in most industries, foreign investment of up to 100 per cent is allowed in export-oriented enterprises, power, electronics and technology parks. Even in other industries, foreign equity up to 100 per cent may be permitted. Infrastructure sectors were singled out to attract foreign investment. For example, up to 74 per cent of foreign investment in nine high-priority metallurgical and infrastructure sectors has been approved. The Foreign Investment Promotion Board was set up for speed clearances, while a Foreign Investment Promotion Council was set up to attract foreign investment into India. But the question is not merely of 'promoting' or 'approving' foreign investment, but of creating the absorptive capacity for such investment.

Industrial policy reforms in the 1990s have injected a substantial measure of domestic competition and market orientation into Indian industry, but more remains to be done. The process of domestic deregulation, begun in the 1980s, was further strengthened through dispensing with industrial licensing requirements for most industries and providing larger scope for the private sector in areas previously reserved for the public sector. In particular, infrastructure sectors such as power, petroleum and telecommunications were opened up to the private sector including foreign investors. The response, however, has been slow, because many of the infrastructure sectors still function within a maze of regulations. For example, in power there is an urgent need to reform the state electricity boards and evolve a rational pricing policy which at least covers the cost of production. In fact there remain real underlying constraints which make it difficult for foreign investors in power generation to start producing power, mainly because the power generating companies have to deal with an unreformed public sector. First there is the question of an assured fuel supply for power generation; second, there is the question of whether the state electricity boards are financially able to pay for the power; and, third, there is the problem of the foreign exchange risks borne by the foreign investor.

In order to increase foreign investment in the power sector, the Government of India agreed to provide counter guarantees on the agreement between the power producers and the state electricity board for the first eight 'fast-track' projects. Progress has been slow, partly because of a lack of transparency in dealing with these projects. In the absence of competitive bidding it was natural to question the basic parameters such as the capital cost of the project. A non-transparent environment made it possible for power projects such as the Enron project in Maharashtra to be politicized, although in the end the project was approved by the major political parties. Two other fast-track projects have obtained central government's counter-guarantee, although one of these is being renegotiated by the state government of Orissa. Only two of the eight projects have been commissioned.

The need for public sector reform was recognized twenty years ago, but the reforms of that period were inadequate and had only a marginal impact. The after-tax profit to net worth ratio in central public sector enterprises taken together improved from −1.6 per cent in 1980–1 to 3 per cent in 1990–1, and 4.2 per cent in 1993–4. The same ratio for the private corporate sector was at least 13 per cent.

A practical policy change was to allow public sector enterprises that performed well access to capital markets on the strength of their own performance, and to enjoy greater autonomy in shaping their future. The non-performing non-viable public sector enterprises, however, languished for want of budgetary support and/or the political will to close them down. Privatization was not pursued as a serious option, even though the Rangarajan Committee in 1993 had clearly recommended privatization by divesting up to 74 per cent of the equity of enterprises, except for a few sectors reserved for the public sector. Selective disinvestment of public sector equity was undertaken with a view to financing fiscal deficits, as opposed to improving the returns on the capital invested. A Disinvestment Commission was set up in 1996 to review privatization policy, but the pace of disinvestment and privatization lacks political will and is further constrained by the depressed state of the capital market.

Unfortunately, the system of reserving the production of many items to the small-scale sector continues. This is a major hurdle to fostering export capability in areas where India has a natural advantage, as for example in the production of light consumer goods. Some attempt has been made to dilute the effect of the reservation policy by substantially hiking the investment ceiling for small units and also lowering the export obligation from 75 per cent to 50 per cent for larger units making reserved items. Another hurdle to exploiting India's comparative advantage in these industries lies in the continuation of import licensing for consumer goods. As all other imports are delicensed and subject to lower tariffs, consumer goods are the only goods with infinite protection. Relatively high domestic profit margins in these industries not only attract more investment into consumer goods rather than priority industries such as infrastructure, but this investment is designed for the domestic market so that the scale of production is not geared to the global market.

An inflexible judicial system has also been a barrier to the effective restructuring of the industrial sector. For example, amendments in the Company Act would facilitate mergers, and amendments to the Industrial Disputes Act would allow retrenchment of labour without state government permission. Similarly, amendments in the Urban Land Ceiling Act would enable non-viable firms to sell their real estate to settle their creditors' claims and move to new areas of economic activity. In the absence of these reforms, it is not easy for resources to be moved into the more dynamic sectors.

A beginning was made with financial sector reform to encourage the modernization of the financial system to serve the liberalized economic regime efficiently. Important banking sector reforms included a reduction in the mandatory reserve requirements to more reasonable levels, thus freeing resources for investment with a commercial return; substantial interest rate deregulation; more liberal licensing of private sector banks; and more latitude for expansion of the branch networks of foreign banks. Efforts were also made to tighten the prudential norms with respect to provision for non-performing assets and raising of the requirement for capital adequacy in relation to risk-weighted assets. In the banking sector, resistance to reform came from the trade unions as well as the beneficiaries of the discretionary regime. Long overdue reform of the insurance sector has also been resisted by the trade unions.

More generally, financial sector reform suffered a setback from the securities scam of 1992, which occurred during the transition from a highly regulated financial system to a more competitive one. Nevertheless, substantial foundations have been laid by the setting up of the Securities and Exchange Board of India, the introduction of screen-based trading in shares, and the putting in place of a Central Depository for expediting settlements. The Indian capital market is gradually being opened to foreign capital inflows, but the domestic financial system is still not strong enough for financial integration with the rest of the world.

6 Economic performance: 1990s

When the reforms were launched, not only was there a great deal of scepticism about the effectiveness of these policies in dealing with the balance of payments crisis, but also apprehension about their adverse effect on the economy at large. There were fears that fiscal stabilization policies might reduce economic growth and create unemployment; that the withdrawal of protection from Indian industry might bring about deindustrialization; and that a flood of imports – in response to the removal of import licensing – might cause the collapse of the Indian rupee. There was concern over the inflationary impact of the new economic policies and whether the government could protect the poor from the incidence of inflation.

In fact, the production response of the economy was good, even unique by international standards. After absorbing the initial shock of the stabilization measures in 1991–2, the economy recovered quickly to grow at over 5 per cent in 1992–3 and 6 per cent in 1993–4. The subsequent three years witnessed growth rates of over 7 per cent per annum. To some extent this strong growth performance was due to consistently good agricultural growth. Industry took a little longer to recover from the shock of the crisis, but, even there, a sharp acceleration in growth took place after 1993 recording growth rates of 11 per cent and 13 per cent in 1994–5 and 1995–6 respectively. As the economy responded to the newly injected growth impulses of the policy reforms, the absence of fiscal restraint was offset by a tight monetary policy which restricted higher growth. External demand recession added to the problems of the industrial sector. At the same time, the slow pace of public sector reform meant that infrastructure performed poorly and could not attract private investment.

Manufacturing growth continued to grow at an annual rate of over 12 per cent between April and October 1996, but growth in mining and electricity slowed down greatly. Later, the slow-down spread to the manufacturing sector, and 1997–8 was marked by industrial recession – industrial growth having slowed to around 5 per cent – and less than 4 per cent in early 1998–9.

The opening up of the economy, as can be seen from Table 1.1, meant a faster growth of imports as well as exports until 1995–6. The growth in imports went hand in hand with industrial recovery rather than at the cost of it. Not only were the fears of deindustrialization unfounded, but access to inputs and modern capital goods provided by the import liberalization policies increased the efficient use of industrial capacity and generated stronger export growth. Notwithstanding the significant disruption in India's exports to the former Soviet Union, exports from India grew, on average, at close to 20 per cent annum during the three years ending 1995–6. India's exports financed about 85 per cent of her imports during the five years from 1991–6, compared to 60 per cent in the preceding five years. This trend was reversed in 1996–7 when exports measured in US$ grew at 5 per cent, while imports grew at about 6.5 per cent. Further slowing down was recorded in 1997–8 when exports and imports recorded growth rates of 2.6 per cent and 5.8 per cent, respectively. Prospects for export growth in 1998–9 are poor.

The response of foreign investment to the liberal regime has been quite favourable. From negligible levels in 1990–1, foreign direct investment has doubled virtually every year to reach US$2.7 billion in 1996–7 as shown in Table 1.5. In the first nine months of 1997–8 US$2.3 billion of foreign investment came into the economy, compared with US$1.7 billion in the same period of 1996–7. For the year as a whole, direct foreign investment inflow is expected to reach US$3 billion. While the foreign investment inflows are still much lower than in many East Asian economies, a new direction has been set. As a major emerging market India has also been able to attract greater portfolio investment; total foreign investment in India in 1997–8 is expected to be of the order of US$5 billion. Foreign exchange reserves have grown from US$1 billion to US$19 billion and the current account deficit is less than 2 per cent of GDP.

Even though the tight monetary policy succeeded in bringing the rate of inflation down to 7.6 per cent in 1995–6 and to 5.7 per cent in the first 10 months of 1996–7, inflationary expectations continued to be high as fiscal deficits remained high. The year 1998–9 has seen a significant increase in the rate of inflation. Numerous barriers in the way of effective restructuring of the industrial sector have slowed down the pace of adjustment, while agriculture continues to suffer from inadequate support and investment.

The most important contribution of the 1991–6 economic reforms has been the changing mindset in the country. A number of states in the Indian Federation were already moving towards market orientation. After the

Table 1.5 Foreign investment inflows, US$ billions

	Total	*Direct foreign investment*	*Foreign institutional investors*	*Euro issues*	*Offshore funds and other*
1990–1	0.10	0.10	0.00	0.00	0.00
1991–2	0.16	0.15	0.00	0.01	0.00
1992–3	0.43	0.34	0.00	0.09	0.00
1993–4	4.24	0.59	1.67	1.60	0.38
1994–5	5.14	1.31	1.50	2.08	0.24
1995–6	4.88	2.13	2.01	0.68	0.10
1996–7	6.01	2.70	1.93	1.37	0.02
1997–8	4.80	3.20	1.00	0.60	0.00

Note: totals may not tally due to rounding.
Source: Ministry of Finance, Government of India.

general elections of 1996 brought about the defeat of the Congress Party, the 13-party coalition continued with economic reform. The Common Minimum Programme put out by the United Front government was a broad endorsement of the policies of the earlier regime with some product differentiation. It stressed the need to reduce the fiscal deficit, attract foreign investment, open up the insurance sector, disinvest in the public sector and effect privatization where necessary. At the same time, it highlighted the importance of investing in education and protecting the poor from the incidence of inflation.

The BJP-led coalition government that followed is also moving, albeit slowly, in the direction of market orientation and economic reform. A durable achievement of the 1991–6 period has been the building of a consensus in favour of economic reform. As with the Congress government after 1993–4, the commitment in principle by successive coalition governments to these reforms has also been circumscribed by the soft policy options prompted by the political temptations of populist promises.

7 The challenges ahead

The most important challenge as the Indian economy adjusts to a higher growth path is to persevere in the task of improving the macroeconomic balance. The economy has shown robust growth of around 7 per cent a year in the past few years but the fiscal deficit remains far too high at over 8 per cent of GDP for the centre and states combined. This is the root cause of the persistent high interest rates. Unless the deficit is significantly reduced, the economy will not be able to sustain growth of 7 per cent, let alone accelerate it to 7.5–8 per cent a year.

Management of a more open economy also poses special challenges as the system moves to greater capital account convertibility. The liberalized exchange rate regime has responded well to variations in the trade balance. However, macro-management in an open economy requires that fiscal and monetary policy are not only coordinated with each other, but also with the exchange rate policy, recognizing the close interaction between the real economy, domestic money and credit markets and international capital markets. Policy interventions in one market can have unintended consequences through these linkages. In the last two years, for example, the inability of the Government of India to control its fiscal deficit and the resulting increase in interest rates and tight monetary policy has led to pressure on exchange rates. While the tight monetary policy and other measures were able to withstand major attacks on exchange rates, this has meant accepting lower real growth in the economy.

The quality of fiscal adjustment has a significant impact on the growth potential of the economy. The challenge lies in cutting unproductive consumption expenditure while protecting essential expenditure on social infrastructure, rural development and poverty alleviation. The states have an important role to play since they bear primary responsibility for these sectors. As the process of liberalization is inevitably leading to decentralization and a larger role for the states, a redefinition of the centre–state financial relations is called for. In fact, the process of financial devolution needs to be taken further down to local government. The 73rd and 74th Amendment to the Constitution has created a third tier of democracy in India with the mandatory requirement of elected *panchayats* and *nagar palikas*. These local bodies play a major role in the delivery of critical services. The question of financial devolution needs to be addressed in the light of these new developments.

Massive efforts are needed to strengthen India's infrastructure, that is, power, transport, ports, telecommunications and so on. This is necessary even to sustain the present growth, let alone prepare for accelerated growth; and these sectors have not received adequate attention in the reform process so far. The government has neither the resources to invest in these sectors, nor the political will to carry out the necessary reforms to make them self-financing. Lack of financial viability resulting from low tariffs makes it difficult to attract private investment in sectors such as power and roads. The problems in the power sector, discussed earlier, are illustrative of the problems occurring generally in the infrastructure sector. But some important lessons have been learnt in the past six years and the effort to attract private investment is beginning to bear fruit. The need for transparency in infrastructure contracts is extremely important. If there are risks to be borne by the investor, these risks need to be properly and fairly charged. Most important, if budgetary subsidies are not feasible, then infrastructure services have to adopt a pricing policy which covers costs and provides a reasonable return.

For long-term growth to be sustainable India will have to invest in the social sectors, especially health and education. Despite being, in many ways, a strong emerging market, India scores poorly on human development indicators and this backwardness is at the root of persistent poverty. As the government withdraws from other sectors, it will have to focus more on the social sectors. This means spending more money, but equally important it means spending it well. This will call for a major restructuring both of government's resource priorities and its administrative system with a greater focus on decentralization. Carrying the reforms further requires the will to take tough decisions. In its 50th year of independence, India seems to have evolved a political consensus on economic reform, but the political will to pay the price of real adjustment is not yet evident.

Notes

1 See Table 1.2 in *India Industrial Development Review* (1995), published jointly by UNIDO, Vienna, and Economist Intelligence Unit, London, p. 2.

2 The official estimates of poverty by the Planning Commission have aroused a great deal of controversy. The alternative estimates prepared by the Expert Group set up by the Planning Commission also show a substantial decline in the percentage of people below the poverty line, although the decline is to a level of 39 per cent rather than 30 per cent.
3 The estimates released in February 1998 place the growth rate for 1996–7 at 7.5 per cent.
4 For a detailed description of the policy regime, see Bhagwati and Desai (1970), and Bhagwati and Srinivasan (1975).
5 For estimates of total factor productivity growth at a detailed level of disaggregation of the manufacturing sector, see Ahluwalia (1992).
6 See tables 11.9 and 11.10 in the EIU/UNIDO *India Industrial Development Review* (1995).
7 For further documentation on the case for economic reforms, see Government of India (1993) 'Economic Reforms: Two years After and The Task Ahead', Discussion Paper, Ministry of Finance, Government of India. A more updated review of different aspects of India's Economic Reforms is provided in Ahluwalia and Little (1997).

References

Acharya, S. N. (1995) 'The Economic Consequences of Economic Reforms in India', Sir Purshotamdas Thakurdas Memorial Lecture, Bombay.

Ahluwalia, I. J. (1985) *Industrial Growth in India, Stagnation since the Mid-Sixties* (Delhi: Oxford University Press).

Ahluwalia, I. J. (1992) *Productivity and Growth in Indian Manufacturing* (Delhi: Oxford University Press).

Ahluwalia, I. J. and I. M. D. Little (1997) *India's Economic Reforms and Development: Essay's for Manmohan Singh* (Delhi: Oxford University Press).

Ahluwalia, M. S. (1995) 'Economic Reforms for the Nineties', First Raj Krishna Memorial Lecture, Jaipur, April.

Bajpai, N., A. Varshney and J. Sachs (1999) *India in the Era of Economic Reform* (Delhi: Oxford University Press).

Bhagwati J. and P. Desai (1970) *India: Planning for Industrialization. Industrialization and Trade Policies since 1951* (Delhi: Oxford University Press).

Bhagwati J. and T. N. Srinivasan (1975) *Foreign Trade Regimes and Economic Development* (Delhi: Macmillan).

Economist Intelligence Unit, and UNIDO, Vienna (1995) *India Industrial Development Review* (London: EIU).

Government of India, Ministry of Finance (1993) 'Economic Reform, Two Years After and the Task Ahead', discussion paper.

Government of India, Ministry of Finance (1993) 'Report of the Committee on Public Disinvestment', Chairman C. Rangarajan.

Gulati, A. and A. Sharma (1995) 'Subsidy Syndrome in Indian Agriculture', *Economic and Political Weekly, Review of Agriculture*, vol. xxx, no. 39, (September).

2

Macroeconomic Reforms in India: Short-term Effects and Long-run Implications

Deepak Nayyar
Jawaharlal Nehru University, New Delhi

1 Introduction

The external debt crisis, which surfaced in early 1991, brought India close to default in meeting its international obligations. The balance of payments situation was almost unmanageable. The fear of an acceleration in the rate of inflation loomed large. The underlying fiscal crisis was acute. It is important to recognize that the deep macroeconomic disequilibrium which plunged the economy into a crisis situation was not attributable to any endogenous shock, such as a bad monsoon, or any exogenous shock, such as a dramatic increase in world oil prices. It was the outcome of mounting macroeconomic imbalances that accumulated, and negligent macroeconomic policies that persisted, through the 1980s.[1] In response to the macroeconomic crisis, the government set in motion a process of stabilization combined with fiscal adjustment and structural reform. It needs to be said this was nothing new. It replicated broadly the response of several developing countries in Latin America and sub-Saharan Africa to the debt crisis in the 1980s, which was also guided by IMF programmes of stabilization and World Bank programmes of structural adjustment. The short-term compulsions were to manage the balance-of-payments situation and to restrain inflation. The medium-term imperative was to find a sustainable solution to the fiscal crisis, without imposing a disproportionate burden on the poor. The long-term need was to return the economy to a path of sustained growth, in part through an increase in efficiency and productivity.

The process of stabilization, adjustment and reform was initiated in mid-1991. The period since then is long enough to attempt an assessment. The object of this chapter is to analyse the short-term effects, the medium-term consequences and the long-term implications of macroeconomic reforms in India. In doing so, it seeks to focus on stabilization and adjustment at a macro level. It does not, however, attempt to evaluate structural reforms, for such an evaluation would perhaps require another essay.[2] The structure of the discussion is as follows. Section 2 sets out the evidence on stabilization to discuss the adjustment in the balance of payments. Section 3 examines the stabilization experience in terms of its record in restraining inflation. Section 4 analyses the nature and the quality of fiscal adjustment, to explore whether it provides a sustainable solution to the problem and what it means for the distribution of the burden of adjustment. Section 5 considers the economic impact of stabilization and adjustment at a macro level on employment and poverty. Section 6 reflects upon some implications of the macroeconomic adjustment in India for economic growth in the long run. Section 7 draws together the conclusions that emerge.

2 Balance of payments

It would seem that, in the wake of the external debt crisis, the balance of payments situation was transformed during the 1990s. The capital flight from repatriable deposits held by non-resident Indians, which was threateningly large during 1991–2, came to a stop. The exposure in terms of short-term debt, which became increasingly difficult to roll over and could have been called in by lenders for liquidation at any time, was substantially reduced. Most important, the level of foreign exchange reserves climbed from a meagre US $2.2 billion at end-March 1991, to US $15.1 billion at end-March 1994, and US $22.4 billion at end-March 1997. The stoppage of capital flight, the reduction in short-term debt and the accumulation of foreign exchange reserves should be rated as a success, in terms of stabilization, provided the underlying factors are sustainable. The available evidence on the nature of balance of payments adjustment, presented in Tables 2.1 and 2.2, suggests that, for the purpose of analysis, it is useful to distinguish between two phases in this period: 1991–2 to 1993–4 and 1994–5 to 1996–7.

The adjustment in the balance of payments, during the first phase from 1991–2 to 1993–4, was based on a substantial reduction in the balance of trade deficit not only in terms of dollar values but also as a proportion of GDP. Much of this, however, was attributable to import contraction rather than export expansion. Even though the petroleum import bill did not register any significant decline, the dollar value of total imports throughout this phase remained lower than it was in 1990–1. This was juxtaposed with a surge in remittances. The total remittance inflows in this phase were as much as US $12.9 billion. And, in 1993–4, remittances rose to US $5.3 billion (2 per cent of GDP) as compared with US $2.1 billion (0.7 per cent of GDP) in 1990–1. Consequently, the reduction in the current account deficit was greater than the reduction in the trade deficit.

The smaller current account deficits which reduced the financing need, combined with capital inflows, were responsible for the build-up of reserves. But financing was not available from the usual sources such as external

Table 2.1 Balance of payments, 1989–90 to 1996–7 (US$ millions)

	1989–90	*1990–1*	*1991–2*	*1992–3*	*1993–4*	*1994–5*	*1995–6*	*1996–7*
Foreign exchange reserves end-of-year	3368	2236	5631	6434	15068	20809	17044	22367
Exports	16955	18477	18266	18869	22683	26855	32311	34133
Imports	24411	27915	21064	24316	26739	35904	43670	48948
of which: petroleum	3768	6028	5364	6100	5753	5928	7526	10036
Balance of trade deficit	7456	9438	2798	5447	4056	9049	11359	14815
Remittances	2297	2083	3798	3864	5287	8112	8539	12435
Current account deficit	7269	8424	2135	3603	1158	3369	5899	4494
IMF net	–877	1214	786	1288	187	–1143	–1715	–975
Net capital inflows of which:	6036	6097	4922	4057	7948	7623	8142	13315
external assistance (net)	1856	2210	3037	1859	1901	1526	883	1109
commercial borrowing (net)	1777	2249	1456	–358	607	1030	1275	2848
non-resident deposits (net)	2403	1536	290	2001	1205	172	1103	3350
direct foreign investment		97	135	313	586	1314	2133	2696
portfolio investment		5	4	242	3649	3581	2748	3312
External debt of which:	64.8	70.9	74.2	79.4	82.6	89.4	84.7	85.9
short term	7.5	8.5	7.1	6.3	3.6	4.3	5.0	6.7
medium and long term	57.3	62.4	67.8	73.1	79.0	85.1	79.7	79.2
Memorandum item: rupee debt	11.0	12.8	10.4	10.6	10.1	9.6	8.2	7.5

Notes: 1 There is one exclusion from external debt in the above table. The rouble debt (civilian and defence) to the erstwhile USSR, now denominated in rupees and repayable in exports to Russia, is excluded; this is because it represents an accumulated debt from the past which has not changed in the period under review, but its US$ equivalent, at current exchange rates, is set out in parentheses as a memorandum item.

2 The figures on exports, imports, balance of trade, remittances, current account deficit, net capital inflows and external debt as a percentage of GDP have been calculated from the respective rupee values at current exchange rates and national accounts statistics on GDP at current market prices.

Source: Reserve Bank of India, *Annual Reports* and *Reports on Currency and Finance*. The data on petroleum imports are from the foreign trade statistics compiled by the Directorate General of Commercial Intelligence and Statistics, Calcutta.

Table 2.2 Balance of payments, 1989–90 to 1996–7 (percentage of GDP)

	1989–90	*1990–1*	*1991–2*	*1992–3*	*1993–4*	*1994–5*	*1995–6*	*1996–7*
Exports	6.2	6.2	7.3	7.8	8.8	8.8	9.7	9.5
Imports	8.9	9.4	8.3	10.2	10.4	11.7	13.1	13.6
of which: petroleum	1.4	2.0	2.1	2.4	2.2	2.0	2.2	2.8
Balance of trade deficit	2.7	3.2	1.0	2.4	1.6	2.9	3.4	4.1
Remittances	0.8	0.7	1.5	1.6	2.0	2.6	2.6	3.4
Current account deficit	2.7	3.2	0.8	2.2	0.4	1.1	1.8	1.2
Net capital Inflows	2.2	2.0	2.0	1.8	3.1	2.5	2.5	2.4
External debt	24.3	25.7	35.8	35.1	32.0	29.5	26.1	24.1
Memorandum item: rupee debt	4.2	4.7	5.2	4.7	3.9	3.2	2.6	2.1

Source: Reserve Bank of India, *Annual Reports* and *Reports on Currency and Finance*. The data on petroleum imports are from the foreign trade statistics compiled by the Directorate General of Commercial Intelligence and Statistics, Calcutta.

assistance where net resource inflows continued to decline, or commercial borrowing where access to international capital markets was virtually closed. During this phase, from 1991–2 to 1993–4, there were three main sources of external finance.[3] The first set was constituted by borrowing from the IMF, structural adjustment loans from the World Bank or the Asian Development Bank and special bilateral assistance from donor countries. Such exceptional financing provided US $5.8 billion. The second set was made up of capital flows that originated in non-resident Indians, induced by amnesties (where no questions were asked about the sources of foreign exchange) and by special deposits (which offered more attractive terms than elsewhere or earlier). Taken together, these yielded US $5.4 billion. The third set comprised of private foreign capital flows which added up to US $4.9 billion. Of this, direct investment was US $1 billion, while portfolio investment was US $3.9 billion; much of the latter came in 1993–4 alone.

It is clear that extraordinary capital flows in the form of borrowing from multilateral financial institutions or from non- residents were once-and-for-all in nature and could not provide a sustained access to external resources. What is more, much of this was in essence borrowing abroad to support the balance of payments, which led to a rapid accumulation of external debt. Consequently, between end-March 1991 and end-March 1994, the outstanding external debt (excluding short-term debt and rupee- debt) increased from US $62 billion to US $79 billion (and climbed further to US $85 billion in end-March 1995). And, external debt rose from one quarter at the end of 1990–1 to over one third of GDP throughout the first phase from 1991–2 to 1993–4.

The adjustment in the balance of payments during the second phase from 1994–5 to 1996–7 was significantly different. There was a rapid growth in exports which slowed down towards the end of this phase. But the growth in imports was much faster. As a result, the balance of trade deficit registered a sharp increase to US $9 billion (2.9 per cent of GDP) in 1994–5, which was almost the same as it had been in 1990–1. It rose further to US $11.4 billion (3.4 per cent of GDP) in 1995–6 and US $14.8 billion (4.1 per cent of GDP) in 1996–7. This would have led to a sharp deterioration in the current account deficit were it not for the continued surge in remittances, which rose to US $8.1 billion (2.6 per cent of GDP) in 1994–5 and US $12.4 billion (3.4 per cent of GDP) in 1996–7. As it turned out, current account deficits, although larger than in the first phase, remained at modest levels.

The limited financing need, combined with large capital inflows, contributed to the accumulation of reserves. It is worth noting that net capital inflows in the period from 1994–5 to 1996–7 added up to US $29.1 billion. This is both recognized and emphasized. But it is seldom noted that remittance inflows, which also added up to US $29.1 billion over this period, were exactly the same. Although the magnitude of capital inflows in this phase was much larger, the composition of capital inflows in this phase was very different as compared with that in the first phase. In the sphere of debt creating capital flows, net external assistance continued to decline, but there was a discernible increase in the net capital inflows attributable to commercial borrowing and non-resident deposits. The outstanding external debt registered a significant increase in 1994–5 and stabilized at a somewhat lower level thereafter. For it was non-debt creating capital flows at US $15.8 billion that contributed more than half the net capital inflows during this phase. These capital inflows, in turn, were made up of direct foreign investment which provided US $6.1 billion and portfolio investment which provided US $9.7 billion.

The changed composition of capital inflows may not have led to an increase in external debt but may have created a different kind of vulnerability. For problems arise when capital inflows such as portfolio investment become an important source of financing of current account deficits in the balance of payments. The economy then needs a high interest rate and a strong exchange rate regime to sustain portfolio investment inflows in terms of both profitability and confidence. This erodes the competitiveness of exports over time and enlarges the trade deficit. It is important to recognize the macroeconomic implications. Larger trade deficits and current account deficits require larger portfolio investment inflows which, beyond a point, undermine confidence and create adverse expectations even if the government keeps the exchange rate pegged. But when the stifling of exports does ultimately force an exchange rate depreciation, confidence may simply collapse and lead to capital flight. These problems have indeed surfaced in several Latin American economies, particularly Mexico, and more recently, in the South East Asian economies. This experience suggests that a reliance on portfolio investment or similar capital flows to finance current account deficits, or to build up reserves, is fraught with risk.

In this context, it is worth noting that the comfort implicit in the size of reserves may be more illusory than real. These foreign currency assets are more than matched by foreign exchange liabilities which have short maturities or can be withdrawn on demand. This is the maturity mismatch problem underlying liquidity crises around the world. Consider, for example, the situation in India in March 1997.[4] The level of foreign exchange reserves was US $22.4 billion. Short-term debt with a maturity of less than one year was US $6.7 billion. The par value of outstanding portfolio investment, without allowing for capital gains realizable and repatriable, was US $13.2 billion. These short-term liabilities in foreign exchange added up to US $19.9 billion which was the equivalent of almost 90 per cent of the foreign exchange reserves. But that is not all. The outstanding stock of repatriable deposits held in India, mostly by non-residents, with a maturity of more than one year and up to three years, was as much as US $11.1 billion. It must be recognized that such deposits can be withdrawn on demand and, past experience confirms, are susceptible to capital flight, should there be any crisis of confidence.[5] Thus, at the end of the fiscal year 1996–7, the total liabilities in foreign exchange, which could be called in at short notice, were US $31 billion compared with reserves of US $22.4 billion.

The preceding discussion suggests that the story of rags to riches in the external sector is not as much of a success as is made out. For some of the important factors underlying the transformation in the balance of payments situation are not quite sustainable. During the first phase, from 1991–2 to 1993–4, the stabilization in the balance of payments was attributable to a substantial reduction in the balance-of-trade deficit, despite the modest export performance, essentially because of the sluggish import demand. This was combined with a surge in remittances, which reduced the current account deficit further, and substantial (mostly once-and-for-all or extraordinary) capital inflows, which led to a rapid accumulation of external debt. Except for remittances, most of these underlying factors were not sustainable. During the second phase, from 1994–5 to 1996–7, there was a dramatic increase in the balance of trade deficit despite the robust export performance because of the rapid import expansion. Yet, the balance of payments situation remained comfortable, attributable, in part, to the continued surge in remittances which kept the current account deficit at a modest level and, in part, to the substantial increase in net capital inflows which led to a build- up of foreign exchange reserves. The large share of non-debt creating capital flows in these net inflows ensured that the external debt situation did not worsen but the dependence on portfolio investment flows may have created a new kind of vulnerability. The sustained growth in remittance inflows through the 1990s made a critical contribution that is seldom recognized. However, the process of adjustment in the balance of payments would not be complete until export growth is sufficient to reduce the balance of trade deficit and would not be sustainable in so far as the build-up of reserves is based on a further accumulation of external debt or a reliance on capital inflows that are footloose or volatile in nature.

3 Inflation

In India, as elsewhere, annual rates of inflation are measured in terms of the wholesale price index or the consumer price indices for different socio-economic groups such as industrial workers, urban non-manual employees and agricultural labourers. The wholesale price index covers all commodities whereas the consumer price indices are limited to representative consumption baskets for the specified consumer-groups. Thus, the measure of inflation depends upon the price index, since the basket of commodities and the weight of each commodity differ across groups. But that is not all. It is possible to measure inflation either on a point-to-point basis or on an average-of-period basis.[6] It is a matter of arithmetic that point-to-point rates are higher than average-of-period rates when there is an acceleration in the rate of inflation and lower when there is a deceleration in the rate of inflation.

The evidence available for the 1990s is presented in Table 2.3. It does not suggest a real turn-around. And it would seem that inflation remained in the range of 10 per cent per annum irrespective of how we measure it. This can be described as a success only if Latin American countries are our point of reference. It is close to a failure if India's past record is the norm. Indeed, the period from 1990–1 to 1996–7 is the longest period of sustained double-digit inflation in independent India. This persistent inflation is somewhat puzzling. For one, it has coincided, for most of the time, with a concerted attempt at stabilization. For another, it has coincided, entirely, with six good monsoons in a row. What is more, the economy has not witnessed any significant exogenous shock, such as an increase in petroleum prices, during this period.

It is, therefore, necessary to explain the persistence of inflation.[7] In principle, fiscal austerity and monetary discipline, which were an integral part of the stabilization programme, should have led to a contraction of aggregate demand and thus dampened demand-pull inflation. However, the impact may have been reduced in so far as supply-demand imbalances underlying inflationary pressures persisted. Some imbalances may have worsened. For instance, credit restrictions may have squeezed the availability of working capital, particularly for small firms. Thus, supply may have been reduced in some cases even more than the contraction in demand. Monetary discipline would then have widened the gap between supply and demand in some sectors to fuel inflation. Even more important, perhaps, was the nature of fiscal adjustment enforced by the stabilization programme. It was bound to fuel cost-push inflation, when subsidies were cut as on fertilizers, administered prices were raised as for petroleum products, or user-charges were hiked by public utilities as for electricity. The tariff reform, which reduced customs duties across the board, was sought to be made revenue neutral not through an increase in direct taxes that would reduce the disposable incomes of the rich and dampen inflation, but through increases in indirect taxes on commodities that would fuel inflation and squeeze the real incomes of the poor. The substantial depreciation of the rupee, explicit in exchange rate adjustments and implicit in the introduction of a dual exchange rate system followed by a unification of the exchange rate, obviously contributed to inflation by raising the cost of imported intermediates and the mark-ups on final goods. In the sphere of monetary policy, the higher interest rates, which were an integral part of the stabilization programme, probably contributed to cost-push inflation by raising the cost of borrowing for firms. However, despite the high rates of interest, liquidity was not tight enough, for the increase in money supply, defined as M3, was 17.4 per cent per annum through the first half of the 1990s, which was almost the same as the unbridled monetary expansion during the second half of the 1980s.

Table 2.3 Annual rates of inflation, 1989–90 to 1996–7: comparison of point-to-point and annual averages

	Wholesale price index		*Consumer price index industrial workers*		*Consumer price index: urban non-manual*		*Consumer price index: agricultural labourers*	
	1	*2*	*1*	*2*	*1*	*2*	*1*	*2*
1989–90	9.1	7.5	6.6	6.6	8.0	6.9	1.0	5.4
1990–1	12.1	10.3	13.6	11.2	13.4	11.0	16.6	7.6
1991–2	13.6	13.7	13.9	13.5	13.6	13.7	21.9	19.3
1992–3	7.0	10.0	6.1	9.9	6.8	10.5	0.7	12.4
1993–4	10.8	8.4	9.9	7.3	8.3	6.9	11.6	3.5
1994–5	10.4	10.9	9.7	10.3	9.9	9.5	10.6	11.9
1995–6	5.0	7.8	8.9	10.0	8.2	9.5	7.4	10.8
1996–7	6.9	6.3	10.0	9.4	10.2	9.3	10.5	9.1

Notes: 1 denotes point-to-point, and 2 annual averages.
Sources: Wholesale price index: Office of the Economic Adviser, Ministry of Industry; Consumer price indices for industrial workers and agricultural labourers: Labour Bureau; consumer price index for urban non-manual employees: Central Statistical Organisation.

It is almost certain that the rate of inflation would have been higher, were it not for the succession of good monsoons. The reason is simple. In the absence of exogenous shocks, the performance of the agricultural sector has always been a crucial determinant of price behaviour in India. Bad harvests fuel inflation and good harvests dampen inflation. Food prices, in particular, lead the general price level and influence inflationary expectations. In this context, it is worth noting that the bounty of the weather gods may have been neutralized, in part, by stabilization policies. The sharp reduction in fertilizer subsidies, reinforced by a politics of compromise, led to a more than compensatory increase in the procurement prices of foodgrains for producers. The objective of restraining food subsidies led to a sharp increase in the issue price of foodgrains for consumers in the public distribution system. Consequently, the procurement prices of common paddy and wheat, paid to producers, were raised by more than 50 per cent between 1990–1 and 1993–4. At the same time, issue prices in the public distribution system, charged to consumers, were raised even more, by 86 per cent for common rice and by 72 per cent for wheat between mid-1990 and early 1994. These increases exercised an important influence on market prices of foodgrains and, in turn, on inflation. The increase in procurement prices, paid to producers, continued in subsequent years. This was, probably, an important factor underlying the persistent inflation. And, in retrospect, it is clear that stabilization policies did not succeed in restraining inflation.

4 Fiscal adjustment

The quality of fiscal adjustment in the government sector, which constitutes the core of the attempted macroeconomic adjustment, leaves much to be desired particularly when situated in a medium- term perspective.[8] There are three underlying reasons. First, it cannot provide a sustainable solution to the fiscal crisis. Second, it is likely to constrain economic growth. Third, it is distributing the burden of adjustment in an unequal manner. Consider each proposition in turn.

The broad contours and dimensions of the fiscal adjustment on the part of the central government during the 1990s are set out in Table 2.4, which also compares the first half of the 1990s with the second half of the 1980s. The evidence presented suggests that there was a moderate reduction in the gross fiscal deficit of the central government, from 8.2 per cent of GDP during the period 1985–6 to 1989–90 to 6.1 per cent of GDP during the period 1991–2 to 1995–6. This was associated with a significant reduction in the magnetized deficit from 2.3 per cent of GDP to 0.7 per cent of GDP and a discernible increase in the revenue deficit from 2.6 per cent of GDP to 3.1 per cent of GDP.

The almost exclusive emphasis on reducing the fiscal deficit is both inappropriate and misplaced. The macroeconomic cause for concern lies

Table 2.4 Government deficits, public debt and monetary expansion 1985–6 to 1996–7 (percentage of GDP at market prices)

Year	*Gross fiscal deficit*	*Revenue deficit*	*Monetized deficit*	*Internal debt*	*Interest payments*	*Money supply (M3) annual growth %*
1990–1	8.3	3.5	2.1	52.9	4.0	17.6
1991–2	5.9	2.6	1.1	51.5	4.3	15.1
1992–3	5.7	2.6	1.7	50.9	4.4	18.5
1993–4	7.5	4.0	1.4	53.2	4.5	15.7
1994–5	6.1	3.3	0.1	51.1	4.6	18.2
1995–6	5.5	2.7	0.9	50.5	4.7	21.2
1996–7	5.2	2.6	0.2	48.7	4.7	13.6
Average of period:						
1985–6 – 1989–90	8.2	2.6	2.3	50.7	3.2	17.4
1991–2 – 1995–6	6.1	3.1	0.7	51.5	4.5	16.2

Source: Reserve Bank of India, *Annual Reports*.

elsewhere. The more serious problem is that the revenue deficit of the central government (the excess of consumption over income supported by borrowing) is much larger than it was earlier.[9] During the second half of the 1980s, the government borrowed as much as 2.6 per cent of GDP every year, to finance its consumption expenditure. During the first half of the 1990s, however, the Government borrowed even more, on average 3.1 per cent of GDP every year to finance its consumption expenditure. In an ideal world, there should be a revenue surplus large enough to finance capital expenditure on defence and on the social sectors, where there are no immediate or tangible returns. This would ensure that borrowing is used only to finance investment expenditure which yields a future income flow to the exchequer. So long as that income flow is greater than the burden of servicing accumulated debt, government borrowing remains sustainable. The reality in India, despite fiscal adjustment, is just the opposite. The present fiscal regime, which borrows to support consumption, is simply not sustainable over time.

It must also be stressed that the size of the fiscal deficit, or the amount of the borrowing, are the symptoms and not the disease. And there is nothing in macroeconomics which stipulates an optimum level to which the fiscal deficit must be reduced as a proportion of GDP. Indeed, it is possible that a fiscal deficit at 6 per cent of GDP is sustainable in one situation while a fiscal deficit at 4 per cent of GDP is not sustainable in another situation. The real issue is the use to which government expenditure is put in relation to the cost of borrowing by the government. Thus, government borrowing is always sustainable if it is used to finance investment and if the rate of return on such investment is greater than the interest rate payable. However, evidence available and simple macroeconomics suggest that the fiscal adjustment implemented in India cannot provide a sustainable solution to the fiscal crisis despite the reduction in the gross fiscal deficit as a proportion of GDP. For one, the cost of government borrowing has risen significantly during the 1990s. This is so for two reasons. First, the government has cut back sharply on its borrowing at low interest rates from the central bank. Second, compared with the past, the government is now borrowing much larger amounts, and at a significantly higher cost, from the commercial banking system and the domestic capital market because interest rates on government securities have been raised to market levels. For another, the use of the borrowing during the 1990s remains as unproductive as before. If anything, a much higher proportion of government borrowing is being used to finance consumption expenditure which yields no return. In this context, it needs to be stressed that the proportion of total borrowing by the central government which was used to support its consumption expenditure rose from less than one-third during the second half of the 1980s, which was a period of fiscal profligacy, to more than one-half during the first half of the 1990s, which was supposedly a period of fiscal austerity. At the same time, there is no evidence to suggest that there has been any increase in the productivity of public investment expenditure.

The evidence on the composition of fiscal adjustment by the central government during the 1990s, presented in Table 2.5, provides further confirmation that it is unsustainable. A comparison of the period 1985–6 to 1989–90 with the period 1991–2 to 1995–6 is instructive. It reveals that the revenue receipts of the central government, as a proportion of GDP, declined from 11.1 per cent to 10 per cent, essentially because tax revenue as a proportion of GDP declined from 8.3 per cent to 7.4 per cent. But revenue expenditure of the central government, as a proportion of GDP, declined somewhat less from 13.7 per cent to 13.1 per cent. Even this was possible only because expenditure on subsidies and defence, as a proportion of GDP, contracted to compensate for the significant increase in interest payments as a proportion of GDP. The increase in the revenue deficit, as a proportion of GDP, from 2.6 per cent to 3.1 per cent, was the inevitable consequence. In spite of this, the fiscal deficit, as a proportion of GDP, was reduced from 8.2 per cent to 6.1 per cent, essentially because capital expenditure of the central government, as a proportion of GDP, was cut back sharply from 6.8 per cent to 4.1 per cent. Some of this capital expenditure, of course, was net lending by the central government to state governments. The real cutback in capital expenditure was on investment in so far as plan expenditure, as a proportion of GDP, dropped from 4.3 per cent to 2.2 per cent.

It is obvious that the process of fiscal adjustment created a massive squeeze on public investment. And the impact on resources made available by the central government for public investment was, indeed, significant. In the

Table 2.5 Nature and composition of fiscal adjustment by the central government (percentage of GDP at market prices)

	1985–6 to 1989–90	*1990–1*	*1991–2*	*1992–3*	*1993–4*	*1994–5*	*1995–6*	*1991–2 to 1995–6*	*1996–7*
Revenue receipts of which:	11.1	10.3	10.7	10.5	9.3	9.6	10.0	10.0	9.9
tax revenue	8.3	8.1	8.1	7.7	6.6	7.1	7.4	7.4	7.3
non-tax revenue	2.8	2.2	2.6	2.8	2.7	2.5	2.6	2.6	2.6
Revenue expenditure of which:	13.7	13.7	13.3	13.1	13.4	12.8	12.7	13.1	12.5
interest payments	3.2	4.0	4.3	4.4	4.5	4.6	4.7	4.5	4.7
subsidies	2.0	2.3	2.0	1.7	1.6	1.4	1.2	1.6	1.3
defence	2.6	2.0	1.9	1.7	1.9	1.7	1.7	1.8	1.6
Revenue deficit	2.6	3.5	2.6	2.6	4.0	3.3	2.7	3.1	2.6
Capital expenditure of which:	6.8	5.9	4.7	4.2	4.2	4.1	3.4	4.1	3.3
capital plan expenditure	4.3	3.0	2.6	2.4	2.3	2.0	1.6	2.2	1.7
Capital receipts (exc. borrowing)	1.2	1.0	1.4	1.1	0.8	1.2	0.6	1.1	0.7
Fiscal deficit	8.2	8.3	5.9	5.7	7.5	6.1	5.5	6.1	5.2

Note: The percentages have been calculated from the absolute values of revenues and expenditures.
Source: Government of India, *Union Budget*, Documents and Central Statistical Organisation, *National Accounts Statistics*.

Union Budgets from 1991–2 to 1993–4, the provision for capital expenditure in the central plan and in central plan assistance for the states – perhaps the best aggregate measure of resources allocated to public investment – remained almost unchanged in nominal terms at about the same level as 1990–1. It is obvious that these budget provisions did not even compensate for inflation, let alone the substantial devaluation of the rupee, so that public investment financed by the central government declined sharply in real terms.[10] And there was no discernible change, in real terms, in the Union budgets from 1994–5 to 1996–7. The resource crunch was much more acute for public investment in infrastructure. Budget support provided by the central government for key infrastructure sectors – energy, transport and communications – dropped sharply during the 1990s. It is worth noting that, between 1989–90 and 1996–7, such budget support for infrastructure declined from 8.5 per cent to 3.6 per cent of total central government expenditure, from 1.75 per cent to 0.57 per cent of GDP, and from Rs. 39 billion to Rs. 18.5 billion at constant 1980–1 prices.[11]

These cuts in public investment, particularly those for infrastructure, are bound to constrain the supply response of the economy in the medium term and the long run. The problem may be accentuated because available evidence in India suggests that public investment crowds-in rather than crowds-out private investment. Such complementarity may have dampened private investment which might have been higher if public investment had not stagnated. But that is not all. The stagnation in public investment is also a cause for concern because the level of public investment is an important determinant of the sustainability of the fiscal regime.

The distribution of the burden of fiscal adjustment has also been unequal. In a situation where inflation could not be restrained, the government should have endeavoured to protect the consumption levels of the poor by increasing public expenditure destined for them. But this did not quite happen. The evidence presented in Table 2.6, on trends in central government expenditure on programmes for employment creation and poverty alleviation in rural India during the period 1989–90 to 1996–7, provides some confirmation. It is not sufficient to examine these trends in terms of nominal values because of inflation and as a proportion of total central government expenditure because of expenditure cuts. Therefore, the table also considers the trends in such expenditure at constant prices and as a proportion of GDP. It shows that expenditure on anti-poverty programmes in both 1991–2 and 1992–3, in real terms and as a proportion of GDP, was lower than it had been in 1989–90 and 1990–1. From 1993–4 to 1995–6, this expenditure rose in real terms but remained at the 1990–1 level as a proportion of GDP. In 1996–7, however, this expenditure registered a significant decline both in real terms and as a proportion of GDP.

It may not be entirely appropriate to consider central government expenditure on poverty alleviation programmes in isolation because some part of expenditure on anti-poverty programmes is financed by state governments. But if we wish to consider the impact of fiscal adjustment, a focus on central government expenditure is unavoidable. What is more, the same conclusion is borne out by evidence available on employment generated through poverty alleviation programmes in rural India. In terms of million man-days, such employment generation declined in 1991–2 and 1992–3, recovered in 1993–4, rose significantly in 1994–5 and 1995–6 but fell sharply in 1996–7. The important fact which emerges is that the real value of resources made available for poverty alleviation programmes diminished for some time and possibly did not register the necessary increase thereafter. What is worse, the recovery was followed by another contraction. In a period of stabilization and adjustment, more real resources should have been provided to support the poor who are particularly vulnerable in such periods.[12]

Table 2.6 Central government expenditure on rural employment and poverty alleviation programmes: 1989–90 to 1996–7

Year	*Rupees million (current prices)*	*Percentage of total central government expenditure*	*Percentage of GDP at market prices*	*At constant 1980–1 prices rupees million*	*Employment generated (million man-days)*
1989–90	25895	2.79	0.57	12766	864.4
1990–1	24945	2.37	0.47	11081	874.6
1991–2	23141	2.08	0.37	8953	809.2
1992–3	30655	2.50	0.43	10947	782.2
1993–4	45952	3.24	0.57	14994	1075.3
1994–5	55960	3.48	0.58	16615	1225.7
1995–6	63889	3.58	0.57	17531	1242.4
1996–7	59978	2.98	0.47	15492	803.6

Notes:
1 The expenditure-GDP ratios are calculated as a percentage of GDP at market prices. The data on GDP are from CSO *National Accounts Statistics*.
2 Expenditure at current prices has been converted into expenditure at constant 1980–1 prices by using the deflator for GDP at factor cost. The conversion factors are obtained from CSO *National Accounts Statistics*.

Source: Government of India, Ministry of Finance, Union Budget documents and Ministry of Rural Development, Annual Reports.

Similarly, during this period, the resources provided for public expenditure on social services and in social sectors should have been increased adequately, so as to ensure that levels of social consumption for the poor were maintained, if not raised, to compensate for the possible decline in the levels of private consumption among the poor. As it turned out, however, this experience was not different from that of poverty alleviation programmes. Fiscal adjustment squeezed allocations for the social sectors – education, health, housing, water, sanitation, nutrition and social welfare – not only in the central government but also in the state governments which were not immune from the consequences of macroeconomic reforms.[13]

It is clear that the fiscal adjustment should have come from a more appropriate mix of expenditure cuts and revenue-raising measures instead of relying exclusively on the former. In a period when the government imposed a substantial burden on the poor through expenditure adjustment and commodity taxation, the equity principle required that the rich in particular, and the non-poor in general, should have shared in this burden through their contribution to direct taxes. For this, it would have been essential to broaden the base for direct taxes by bringing a larger number of people into the tax net and to deepen the structure of direct taxation by increasing the average rates of tax. The fiscal adjustment and the tax reforms implemented so far appear to have moved in the opposite direction. The underlying philosophy, it would seem, is to provide comfort for the rich even if it means hardship for the poor. It is important to stress that such patterns of adjustment, which impose a burden on the poor, are nothing new, for they have been reproduced time after time in developing countries which have embarked on stabilization and adjustment.[14]

5 Employment and poverty

The data on trends in employment and unemployment during the 1990s are limited and sparse. It is only possible to put forward a plausible hypothesis about the impact of the stabilization and adjustment experience on growth in employment, supported wherever possible by available evidence.

It is reasonable to presume that growth in employment in the agricultural sector was not affected much, insofar as the increase in output was sustained entirely because of the sequence of good monsoons and, possibly, despite stabilization policies. In contrast, it is most likely that growth in employment in the industrial sector was dampened by the near-stagnation in output during the early 1990s. This plausible hypothesis is supported by available evidence. The rate of growth of employment in the organized sector of the economy, including both the public sector and the private sector, dropped from 1.7 per cent per annum in the late 1980s to 0.8 per cent per annum during the first half of the 1990s.[15] The contraction in public expenditure and the consequent reduction in aggregate demand could not but adversely affect employment in the unorganized sector, whether non-agricultural rural employment or urban informal sector employment, given the flexibility of labour markets in such employment. It is plausible to argue, though difficult to prove, that landless labourers in the rural sector and casual wage labour in the organized sector were probably the most adversely affected by the pressure of increasing underemployment or unemployment.

In this context, it is important to recognize that the growth of the labour force in India has always been higher than the growth in employment, so that the backlog of unemployment has grown steadily over time. What is more, employment growth has not even kept pace with output growth. Evidence available suggests that the already low employment elasticities registered a significant decline between the early 1970s and the late 1980s, for the economy as a whole as also for the agricultural sector and the industrial sector. It appears that this trend continued during the period from the late 1980s to the early 1990s. The employment elasticity for the economy as a whole declined from 0.61 during the period 1972–3 to 1977–8 to 0.55 during the period 1977–8 to 1983 and 0.39 during the period 1983 to 1987–8 but remained at 0.39 during the period 1987–8 to 1993–4. The corresponding figures were 0.66, 0.49, 0.45 and 0.43 respectively for the agricultural sector, and 0.55, 0.53, 0.43 and 0.29 respectively for the manufacturing sector.[16]

In considering the longer-term prospects, it is only possible to speculate about the implications of macroeconomic reforms for employment growth. In rural India, particularly in the agricultural sector, the potential for employment expansion is, in any case, limited. For one, agriculture already provides almost two-thirds of total employment in the economy although its contribution to total output is less than one third. For another, available research suggests that beyond a certain level of development employment creation per unit of output growth in agriculture declines. There are, of course, parts of India where agriculture is still extremely backward and agricultural growth would make a significant contribution to employment growth for some time to come but only in these areas. However, the constraint on employment creation in agriculture can be relaxed significantly through investment in agriculture, particularly in irrigation. But macroeconomic reforms which have cut fertilizer subsidies, reduced direct lending, raised interest rates and slashed public investment, may have made this more difficult.

The process of economic liberalization would directly affect employment growth in the industrial sector and in urban India. This impact would be positive if it leads to export expansion in labour-intensive manufacturing activities where India has a potential comparative advantage. This impact could be negative if import liberalization switches domestic demand away from home-produced goods to foreign goods, irrespective of whether it enforces efficiency or closures at a micro level, for it would have an adverse effect on output (hence employment) at a macro level, which would be magnified through the multiplier effect. Such a magnified contraction is most likely in the sphere of consumer goods, where import liberalization is on the cards. The consumer goods sector contributes about one-third of output and provides roughly two-thirds of employment in the manufacturing sector: much of it in the small-scale sector which is that much more vulnerable. The vulnerability to import liberalization would not be confined only to the reduction in employment due to direct substitution in favour of imported goods. This contraction in employment would multiply through the consequent decline in purchasing power, reducing output and employment elsewhere in the economy through successive rounds of the same multiplier mechanism.

There is another dimension to the problem of employment in the industrial sector which is worth noting. In so far as economic liberalization increases the average productivity of labour, through the use of capital-intensive or labour-saving foreign technologies or through a restructuring of firms which increases efficiency, it will reduce the contribution of any given rate of economic growth to employment growth. The only way out is to increase the rate of economic growth in proportion to, or more than, labour productivity growth.

The probable increase in unemployment among the vulnerable sections of the population, during the period of stabilization and adjustment, coincided with a definite increase in food prices. Existing research has established that, in India, rising food prices erode most the real incomes of these vulnerable sections. It would, therefore, be reasonable to infer that the increase in food prices probably led to some increase in the incidence of poverty in both rural and urban India.

The data base for poverty estimates is provided by National Sample Survey tables on consumer expenditure but these are now compiled only on a quinquennial basis and, during the 1990s, just one such round was conducted for 1993–4. The National Sample Survey does, however, collect data on consumer expenditure, by decile groups, on an annual basis. But this is based on thin samples. It is, therefore, not comparable with the quinquennial rounds in terms of either coverage or reliability. All the same, even such limited information is better than mere inference or assertion. Estimates of the proportion and the number living below the poverty line, based on the quinquennial rounds are presented in Table 2.7. It shows that the incidence of absolute poverty in both rural and urban India registered a steady and continuous decline from the early 1970s to the late 1980s. Thus, between 1973–4 and 1987–8, the proportion of the population living below the poverty line dropped from 54.9 per cent to 38.9 per cent, while the number living below the poverty line decreased from 321 million to 307 million. Evidence from the last quinquennial round conducted in 1993–4 shows that the proportion of the population living below the poverty line decreased to 36 per cent, while the number living below the poverty line increased to 320 million. The quinquennial rounds, however, do not convey anything about what happened during the period between 1987–8 and 1993–4 or thereafter.

It is possible to sketch a picture of trends in poverty during the late 1980s and the first half of the 1990s by considering the evidence based on thin samples which is set out in Table 2.8. It reveals that the incidence of poverty

Table 2.7 Incidence of poverty in India: 1973–4 to 1993–4 (estimates based on quinquennial rounds)

	1973–4	*1977–8*	*1983*	*1987–8*	*1993–4*
Percentage below the poverty line					
Rural	56.4	53.1	45.7	39.1	37.3
Urban	49.0	45.2	40.8	38.2	32.4
Total	54.9	51.3	44.5	38.9	36.0
Number below the poverty line (million)					
Rural	261.3	264.2	252.0	231.9	244.0
Urban	60.0	64.6	70.9	75.1	76.3
Total	321.3	329.0	323.0	307.0	320.4

Source: National Sample Survey and Planning Commission. These estimates are from a Press Note on Estimates of Poverty, Government of India, Planning Commission, March 1997, which are also reported in Government of India, Ministry of Finance, *Economic Survey, 1997–98*, p. 141.

Table 2.8 Estimates of poverty in India: 1988–9 to 1997 (based on thin samples)

	1988–9	*1989–90*	*1990–1*	*1991–2*	*1992–3*	*1994–5*	*1995–6*	*1997*
Percentage below the poverty line								
Rural	39.2	33.7	35.0	40.0	41.7	41.2	37.6	35.9
Urban	38.4	36.0	37.0	37.6	37.8	35.5	29.9	32.3
Total	39.0	34.3	35.5	39.4	40.7	39.7	35.5	34.9
Number below the poverty line (million)								
Rural	236.7	206.7	218.4	255.6	269.0	272.9	253.5	248.6
Urban	77.8	75.1	79.5	81.6	85.8	87.3	75.5	84.9
Total	314.5	281.8	297.9	337.2	354.8	360.2	329.0	333.5

Notes:

1 These estimates of poverty are based on the methodology suggested by the Expert Group on Estimation of Proportion and Number of Poor (Planning Commission, 1993).

2 The estimates of poverty for 1988–9, 1989–90, 1990–1, 1991–2 and 1992–3 are obtained from the *Draft Mid-Term Appraisal of the Eighth Five Year Plan: 1992–97*, Government of India, Planning Commission, New Delhi, September 1996, p. 60.

3 The estimates of poverty for 1994–5, 1995–6 and 1997 have been made by the author based on the all-India poverty line implicit in the methodology suggested by the Expert Group in Planning Commission (1993). The poverty line estimated by the Planning Commission for 1993–4, from the complete quinquennial round conducted by the National Sample Survey, was Rupees 205.84 per capita per month in rural India and Rupees 281.35 per capita per month in urban India. The poverty lines for 1994–5, 1995–6 and 1997 have been constructed using the Consumer Price Index for Agricultural Labourers for rural areas, and the Consumer Price Index for Industrial Workers for urban areas, as deflators. The proportion of the population living below these poverty lines has then been estimated from the National Sample Survey data on the distribution of consumer expenditure.

Source: National Sample Survey and Planning Commission.

in 1988–9 was almost the same as in 1987–8 but fell sharply in 1989–90. However, between 1989–90 and 1992–3, the proportion of the population living below the poverty line rose from 34.3 per cent to 40.7 per cent while the number of persons living below the poverty line rose from 282 million to 355 million. The incidence of poverty rose essentially in 1991–2 and 1992–3, and the increase was far more pronounced in rural India than it was in urban India. This trend provides a sharp contrast with the steady reduction in the percentage of the population below the poverty line over the period from 1973–4 to 1987–8. It also shows that the long-term trend of declining poverty, which began in 1973–4, continued beyond 1987–8. Absolute poverty declined further until 1989–90, but registered a significant increase during the early 1990s which coincided with the period of stabilization. Thus, while the incidence of absolute poverty in 1993–4 was lower than it had been in 1987–8, it was higher than in 1989–90. Evidence available from thin samples suggests that the incidence of poverty during the mid-1990s remained about the same as it was in 1993–4. The proportion of the population living below the poverty line was 39.7 per cent in 1994–5, 35.5 per cent in 1995–6 and 34.9 per cent in 1997, compared with 36 per cent in 1993–4 and 34.3 per cent in 1989–90.

There can be little doubt that the major factor underlying the increase in poverty during the early 1990s, and the persistence of poverty despite rapid economic growth during the mid-1990s, was inflation. The sharp increase in the prices of food and necessities was probably the single most important cause.[17] The prices of foodgrains experienced double-digit inflation despite the succession of good monsoons. This was induced, perhaps, by the substantial increases in the procurement prices for producers and a more than commensurate increase in the public distribution system prices for consumers, particularly in the period from 1990–1 to 1993–4. In subsequent years, from 1994–5 to 1996–7, the pressure on prices may have been accentuated, at the margin, by the trade liberalization which relaxed or removed quantitative restrictions on exports of agricultural commodities. The increase in food prices was juxtaposed with a stagnation and decline in the per capita availability of foodgrains. What is worse, over this period, there was no discernible increase in the allocation for the public distribution system while the sales through the public distribution system declined steadily as the difference between ration-shop prices and market prices narrowed to a small margin. Ironically enough, there was a steady accumulation in the stock of foodgrains at the same time. It would seem that the higher procurement prices for producers, to compensate for the cut in fertilizer subsidies, enabled the government to add to its stockpile of food. But the higher issue prices for consumers, dictated by the fiscal compulsions of macroeconomic reform, meant that these inventories could not be utilized so that the public distribution system failed to serve its intended purpose. Strange though it may seem, the budget provisions for subsidies on food may have ended up in supporting the cost of carrying stocks, which increased significantly because of higher interest rates, rather than providing cheap food. The price of food, not only in the market place but also in the ration shops, was simply too high for the poor. But that is not all. The inflation was just as high in other primary food articles (comprising of cereals, pulses, fruits, vegetables, eggs, fish, meat and spices) and manufactured food products (such as sugar, edible oils and processed foods). Between end-March 1990, and end-March 1997, the prices of foodgrains rose by 133 per cent, the prices of primary food articles rose by 114 per cent and the prices of manufactured food products rose by 83 per cent. Given such inflation in food and in the prices of necessities, it is not surprising that the incidence of poverty registered a significant increase in the early 1990s but did not register any notable decrease in spite of the rapid economic growth through the mid-1990s.

6 Adjustment and growth

The short-term impact of macroeconomic adjustment on output and growth has been almost uniformly adverse across countries. The stabilization experience in India was no exception. In real terms, GDP growth dropped to 0.8 per cent in 1991–2. This provided a sharp contrast with the second half of the 1980s when growth in GDP was 6.4 per cent per annum. However, there was a recovery in 1992–3 so that the slowdown in growth lasted just two years. Beginning in 1993–4, until 1996–7, GDP growth was comparable with what it had been during the 1980s. This was, in part, attributable to the succession of good monsoons and agricultural growth. But it was also attributable to a revival of growth in the industrial sector and in the services sector.

The slowdown in growth was juxtaposed with an acceleration in inflation. It hurt the poor and led to an increase in poverty. The revival of growth, however, did not lead to a decrease in poverty. This was not in conformity with the experience of the 1980s when similar rates of growth led to a substantial reduction in poverty. The persistence of inflation was perhaps the important underlying factor. Although public expenditure destined for the poor was squeezed by fiscal adjustment, at least for some time, the existing anti-poverty programmes did probably mitigate the adverse impact of inflation on the poor. The outcome would have been worse without these programmes and could have been better if more resources had been provided for these programmes. But the provision for basic education, health care and social security remained grossly inadequate. It is clear that rapid economic growth is necessary but cannot be sufficient to improve the living conditions of people. It is also clear that anti-poverty programmes are essential and may need to be strengthened during difficult periods of economic transition but cannot provide a permanent solution. Ultimately, the process of economic growth must create employment and incomes for the poor. There is no other sustainable means of eradicating poverty. Hence, in the long run, incomes for the poor, rather than transfer payments, should sustain their private consumption. But public expenditure that sustains social consumption of the poor is just as critical. For that is the only way in which economic development can create social opportunities for people at large.[18] In considering the long-run implications of macroeconomic reforms, employment creation and social opportunity need much more attention for rapid economic growth to translate into meaningful economic development.

All the same, sustained growth is critical. In retrospect, it is clear that the short-run effect of stabilization on growth in India was adverse but short-lived. And, a medium-term perspective suggests that India fared better than most economies in Latin America, sub-Saharan Africa or East Europe that embarked on stabilization and adjustment. Yet, the long-run implications of macroeconomic reforms in India, for the possibilities of sustained growth, provide some cause for concern. For any given productivity of investment, the impact of adjustment on growth depends upon what happens to the *level* of investment in real terms and the *rate* of investment as a proportion of GDP. On both these counts, the Indian experience is not quite as good as it appears on surface.

In the public sector as a whole, which is made up of the central government, the state governments and public enterprises, gross investment at constant 1980–1 prices experienced a stagnation at about Rs.200 billion during the period from 1991–2 to 1993–4 and did not even recover to the level attained in 1990–1. This was obviously attributable to the fiscal adjustment in the stabilization programme which axed public investment. In the private sector, which is made up of the household sector and the corporate sector, the trend was similar as gross domestic investment at constant 1980–81 prices fluctuated in the range of Rs.300–350 billion during the period from 1991–2 to 1993–4 but did not quite return to the level reached in 1990–1. It would seem that the squeeze on public investment induced by fiscal adjustment, combined with monetary discipline, had a dampening effect on private investment. In mid-1990s, the significant increase in the level of public investment was perhaps an important factor underlying the substantial increase in private investment. This experience suggests that, in India, public investment and private investment are complements rather than substitutes. And it is plausible to argue that private investment would have been higher if public investment had not stagnated. Thus, if the level of public investment continues to be constrained by the compulsion of macroeconomic reforms, it is likely to constrain the level of investment in the economy in the long run.

The discussion on the implications of adjustment for growth cannot be complete without reference to the mode of macroeconomic adjustment in India which could have adverse consequences for economic growth in the long run. This is borne out by the evidence presented in Table 2.9 on the rates of investment and saving as a proportion of GDP during the period from 1989–90 to 1996–7. As a proportion of GDP, gross domestic investment registered a sharp decline during the period of stabilization, possibly because of the said complementarity between public and private investment. In so far as investment determines aggregate demand and aggregate income, this was associated with a decline in gross domestic savings as a proportion of GDP. So much so that, between 1990–1 and 1993–4, the investment-GDP ratio dropped by more than four percentage points, from 27.7 per cent to 23.6 per cent. The decline in net domestic investment as a proportion of net domestic product, at almost five percentage points, from 19.9 per cent to 15.1 per cent, was even more pronounced. The rates of domestic investment, both gross and net as a proportion of GDP and NDP respectively, recovered in subsequent years but just about returned to 1990–1 levels only in 1995–6 and were no higher in 1996–7.

Table 2.9 Saving and investment rates in India (percentage of GDP/NDP at current market prices)

	1989–90	*1990–1*	*1991–2*	*1992–3*	*1993–4*	*1994–5*	*1995–6*	*1996–7*[1]
Gross domestic saving	24.0	24.3	22.8	22.1	23.1	24.9	25.3	26.1
Net domestic saving	15.7	16.1	14.0	13.1	14.4	16.7	17.0	18.0
Gross domestic investment	26.7	27.7	23.4	24.0	23.6	26.0	27.1	27.3
Net domestic investment	18.7	19.9	14.6	15.3	15.1	17.8	19.1	19.2

Note: 1 The data for 1996–7 are provisional and based on quick estimates, reported in the CSO Press Note on National Income, February 1998.
Source: Central Statistical Organisation, *National Accounts Statistics*, June 1997.

Economic growth can come, in part, from an increase in the productivity of investment. But only in part. Ultimately, sustained economic growth also requires an increase in the rate of investment. If the rate of investment was so much lower for three years, it would have required a corresponding increase in the productivity of investment just to maintain the earlier rate of economic growth. And, if the rate of investment was no higher even six years later, a return to earlier rates of growth suggests that the productivity of investment was about the same as earlier. This is simple arithmetic. It must also be recognized that the level and the productivity of investment are interdependent variables that tend to move together. Higher investments mean the realization of scale of economies and infrastructural capital formation, which raise the productivity of investment directly or indirectly. Lower levels of investment could dampen productivity growth.

It would appear that the process of macroeconomic adjustment in India has been based on an investment squeeze and in so far as investment still exceeds saving at a macro level, the corresponding excess of imports over exports is being financed by foreign capital inflows. This must have adverse implications for economic growth in the long run. For, ultimately, sustained economic growth requires an increase in the rate of investment as a proportion of GDP. Thus, macroeconomic adjustment that is conducive to growth needs to raise the investment-GDP ratio. And, in an ideal world, the strategy should be to sustain higher investment rates by raising the export-GDP ratio and the domestic-savings-GDP ratio and not by allowing a compensatory increase in the import-GDP ratio supported by foreign capital inflows. Some correctives at the macro level are, therefore, necessary to sustain economic growth in the long run.

7 Conclusion

It is time to draw together some conclusions that emerge from the preceding discussion on the experience of macroeconomic reforms in India. The short-term effects of stabilization present a mixed picture. The management of the balance-of-payments situation should not be seen as the success story it is made out to be, because some of the important factors underlying the transformation are not quite sustainable. Indeed, the process of adjustment would not be complete until export growth is sufficient to reduce the large balance of trade deficit and would not be sustainable in so far as the build-up of reserves is based on an accumulation of external debt or a reliance on capital inflows that are footloose and perhaps volatile. The record on inflation, also, does not suggest a real turn-around. The persistence of double-digit inflation for much of the period, despite the concerted attempt at stabilization, is striking. And, it is almost certain that the rate of inflation would have been higher were it not for the succession of good monsoons.

The medium-term consequences of macroeconomic reforms are worrisome. The real problem is that the quality of fiscal adjustment is poor. It cannot provide a sustainable solution to the fiscal crisis. It may only have postponed the day of reckoning. The size of the fiscal deficit is less important than the use and the cost of the borrowing. It is the revenue deficit, which requires borrowing to support the consumption expenditure of the government, that must be progressively reduced and rapidly eliminated. The fetishism about reducing the fiscal deficit despite a burgeoning revenue deficit, or eliminating the magnetized deficit despite the much higher cost of borrowing, is entirely misplaced. At the same time, the burden of adjustment is being distributed in an unequal manner. Macroeconomic reforms meant that the resources made available for anti-poverty programmes, as also for the social sectors, were squeezed for some time and were not increased adequately thereafter. The persistence of inflation, particularly in the prices of food, inevitably hurt the poor. There was a significant increase in the incidence of poverty during the early 1990s which coincided with the period of stabilization and the slowdown in growth. But the rapid economic growth through the mid-1990s did not lead to any notable decrease in the incidence of poverty. In a situation where incomes are low, the consumption levels of the poor need to be protected by restraining inflation and maintaining public expenditure destined for the poor. But that is not all. The process of economic growth must also create employment and social opportunities for the people.

Clearly, India fared much better than most countries in Latin America or sub-Saharan Africa in so far as the slowdown was short-lived and the economy returned to earlier rates of growth sooner than might have been expected. Yet, the long-run implications of macro-economic reforms for the possibilities of sustained growth are a cause of concern, primarily because the process of macroeconomic adjustment has been based on an investment squeeze. It is necessary to raise the level of investment in real terms. This, in turn, requires an increase in public investment, particularly in infrastructure where sufficient private investment, whether domestic or foreign, is not forthcoming. It is just as essential to raise the rate of investment in the economy. As far as possible, the higher investment-GDP ratio should be sustained by raising the export-GDP ratio and the domestic savings-GDP ratio rather than by allowing a compensatory increase in the import-GDP ratio. Some correctives are, therefore, necessary not only to sustain economic growth but also to avert another macroeconomic crisis.

Notes

1 For a discussion on the macroeconomic origins of the fiscal crisis and the debt crisis, see Nayyar (1996) and Bhaduri and Nayyar (1996). See also Joshi and Little (1994).

2 For an evaluation of structural reforms in India, see Nayyar (1996). See also, Bhaduri and Nayyar (1996). For a somewhat different perspective, see Joshi and Little (1996).

3 For a detailed discussion, as also for sources of evidence on the magnitudes of these capital inflows, see Nayyar (1996).

4 The evidence cited in this paragraph is obtained from the Reserve Bank of India, *Annual Report, 1996–97*.

5 The factors underlying the capital flight from non- resident deposits, which accentuated the balance of payment crisis in 1990–1 and 1991–2, and its macroeconomic implications are discussed, at some length in Nayyar (1994).

6 Point-to-point rates of inflation compare the price level on the last day of the fiscal year with the price level on the last day of the preceding fiscal year. Average-of-period rates of inflation compare the average price level during the 52 weeks of a fiscal year with the average price level during the 52 weeks of the preceding fiscal year.

7 For a discussion on problems that arise in the transition from crisis to stabilization, in particular the persistence of inflation, see Taylor (1988), Bhaduri (1992), Cooper (1992) and Nayyar (1996).

8 The discussion that follows draws upon earlier work of the author (Nayyar, 1996). Joshi and Little (1996) reach the same conclusion about the quality of fiscal adjustment.

9 The gross fiscal deficit measures the difference between revenue receipts plus grants and total expenditure plus net domestic lending where the latter exceeds the former. The revenue surplus or revenue deficit measures the difference between the revenue receipts (income) of the government (made up of tax revenues plus non-tax revenues) and the non-investment expenditure (consumption) of the government. The distinction between the revenue account and the capital account is most simply stated as follows: transactions which affect the income or expenditure of the central government enter into the revenue account, while transactions which affect the net wealth or debt position of the central government enter into the capital account.

10 It is possible to assess the implications for the level of public investment in real terms if these budget provisions for capital expenditure in the central plan and in central plan assistance to states and union territories (see Union Budget documents for respective years) are converted into constant prices using the GDP deflator (from National Accounts Statistics). This calculation reveals that, at 1980–1 prices, such budget support declined from Rs.70.8 billion in 1990–1 to Rs.62.3 billion in 1991–2, Rs.58.6 billion in 1992–3 and further to Rs.56.2 billion in 1993–4. It was Rs.59.6 billion in 1994–5, Rs.51.2 billion in 1995–6 and Rs.57.7 billion in 1996–7.

11 This expenditure from the Union Budgets includes both plan expenditure and non-plan expenditure. The expenditure-GDP ratios are calculated as a percentage of GDP at market prices. Expenditure at current prices has been converted into expenditure at constant 1980–1 prices by using the deflator for GDP at factor cost. The figures cited here are calculated from data in *Union Budget* documents and *National Accounts Statistics*.

12 For an assessment of the impact of fiscal adjustment on resources allocated for anti-poverty programmes, as also for social services, see Guhan (1995). He concludes that: '...economic reforms have been content to treat social expenditures as a residual (which) have been "protected" in a minimal sense in the central budget(s)' (p.1101).

13 The implications and consequences of fiscal adjustment for government expenditure on social sectors are discussed by Guhan (1995) who considers the evidence on the central government and Prabhu (1996) who considers the evidence on the state governments.

14 In periods of transition, stabilization almost always imposes a burden of adjustment that is distributed in an asymmetric manner. Without correctives, this burden is inevitably borne by the poor. For all the rhetoric about social safety nets, economies in crisis simply do not have resources for this purpose. Adjustment with a human face is then an illusion. For evidence on the adverse impact of structural adjustment on social sectors, health, nutrition and living standards in developing countries, see Cornia, Jolly and Stewart (1987).

15 The rate of growth of employment in the organized sector of the economy, including both the public sector and the private sector, was 1.7 per cent in 1989–90, 1.4 per cent in 1990–1, 1.2 per cent in 1991–2, 0.4 per cent in 1992–3, 0.7 per cent in 1993–4, 0.5 per cent in 1994–5 and 1.4 per cent in 1995–6 (see Ministry of Labour, *Annual Reports*).

16 The data base for trends in employment is provided by the National Sample Survey through its quinquennial rounds. The figures on employment elasticities cited here

are based on this primary source and estimated by the Planning Commission. For the periods 1972–3 to 1977–8 and 1977–8 to 1983, see Planning Commission (1990). For the periods 1983 to 1987–8 and 1987–8 to 1993–4, see *Ninth Five Year Plan: 1997–2002*, Draft, Volume I, Planning Commission, New Delhi, March 1998.

17 For a detailed discussion of the argument outlined in this paragraph, as also for supporting evidence, see Nayyar (1996).

18 This is the theme of an excellent book by Drèze and Sen (1995) which discusses this set of issues at some length.

References

Bhaduri, A. (1992) 'Conventional Stabilization and the East European Transition' in S. Richter, (ed.), *The Transition from Command to Market Economies in East-Central Europe* (San Francisco: Westview Press).

Bhaduri, A. and Nayyar, D. (1996) *The Intelligent Person's Guide to Liberalization* (New Delhi: Penguin Books).

Central Statistical Organisation (1997) *National Accounts Statistics 1997* (New Delhi: Government of India).

Cooper, R.N. (1992) *Economic Stabilization and Debt in Developing Countries* (Cambridge, Mass.: The MIT Press).

Cornia, G.A., Jolly, R. and Stewart, F. (1987) *Adjustment with a Human Face* (Oxford: Clarendon Press).

Drèze, J. and Sen, A. K. (1995) *India: Economic Development and Social Opportunity* (Oxford: Oxford University Press).

Government of India (1994, 1995) *Economic Survey 1993–94* and *Economic Survey 1994–95* (New Delhi: Government of India).

Guhan, S. (1995) 'Social Expenditures in the Union Budget: 1991–1996', *Economic and Political Weekly*, vol. xxx, nos. 18–19, pp. 1095–101.

Joshi, V. and Little, I.M.D. (1994) *India: Macroeconomics and Political Economy, 1964–1991* (Washington DC and New Delhi: World Bank and Oxford University Press).

Joshi, V. and Little, I.M.D. (1996) *India's Economic Reforms: 1991–2001* (New Delhi: Oxford University Press).

Nayyar, D. (1994) *Migration, Remittances and Capital Flows: The Indian Experience* (New Delhi: Oxford University Press).

Nayyar, D. (1996) *Economic Liberalization in India: Analytics, Experience and Lessons*, R.C. Dutt Lectures on Political Economy (Calcutta: Orient Longman).

Planning Commission (1990) *Employment: Past Trends and Prospects for the 1990s* (New Delhi: Government of India).

Planning Commission (1993) *Report of the Expert Group on Estimation of Proportion and Number of Poor* (New Delhi: Government of India).

Prabhu, K. S. (1996) 'The Impact of Structural Adjustment on Social Sector Expenditure: Evidence from Indian States', in C.H.H. Rao and H. Linneman (eds) *Economic Reforms and Poverty Alleviation in India* (New Delhi: Sage Publications).

Taylor, L. (1988) *Varieties of Stabilization Experience: Towards Sensible Macroeconomics in the Third World* (Oxford: Clarendon Press).

3

Bangladesh: Structural Adjustment and Beyond*

Wahiduddin Mahmud
University of Dhaka

1 The background

Bangladesh has now had considerable experience in the implementation of market-oriented liberalizing policy reforms. These reforms were initiated in the early 1980s against the backdrop of serious macroeconomic imbalances; the beginning of the 1990s saw the launching of a more comprehensive programme of macroeconomic reforms which coincided with a transition to parliamentary democracy. While the macroeconomic restructuring has had considerable success in stabilizing the economy, the long-awaited transition from stabilization to growth has yet to take place. It is widely believed that the economy now has the potential to move to an accelerated growth path – even to match the erstwhile performance of the so-called East Asian miracle economies – but the actual performance of the economy remains far below this potential.

Although in this chapter I focus mainly on the macroeconomic reforms and the outcomes in the 1990s, it may be useful to look at some of the historical trends. Perhaps the most serious macroeconomic weakness of the Bangladesh economy has been, and remains, the low growth in investment and domestic saving. Historically, there was only one short-lived episode of investment boom, from the late 1970s to the early 1980s, with investment in both public and private sectors growing at nearly 15 per cent annually in real terms (Mahmud, 1995). This was made possible by relying increasingly on foreign aid and by adopting a strategy of private-sector development based on direct government controls together with the lavish dispensation of cheap credit and other incentives, such as highly protected markets for domestic industries. To a large extent, the present-day problems

*This chapter draws heavily on the author's contribution to the previous three annual volumes of the Independent Review of Bangladesh's Development prepared at the Centre for Policy Dialogue, Dhaka, under the leadership of Professor Rehman Sobhan. The author is indebted to E. V. K. FitzGerald, K. Hamada and L. Squire for their helpful comments.

regarding the so-called 'sick industries' and the large-scale default of bank loans originated from this experiment with aid-dependent state-sponsored private capitalism.[1] There was hardly any mobilization of domestic savings, so that the investment boom ended abruptly when, in the beginning of the 1980s, the external aid climate severely deteriorated accompanied by a sharp decline in the country's terms of trade.

It was in response to such serious macroeconomic imbalances that the policy reforms for stabilization and structural adjustment were initiated along the guidelines of the World Bank and the IMF.[2] These reforms were aimed at reducing the fiscal and trade deficits to a sustainable level, consistent with the reduced level of aid availability. In the event, this was achieved by cutting back on investment (through reduced public development expenditures and through a credit squeeze on private investment), rather than by mobilizing larger domestic savings (such as through improved fiscal effort). The ratio of investment to GDP steadily declined, thus undermining the economy's growth potential. Throughout the 1980s, the contribution of the government's fiscal operations to domestic savings continously declined because of the rapid growth in current expenditures along with a stagnant revenue–GDP ratio. As a result, macroeconomic strains started to reappear towards the end of the decade.

The policy reforms of the 1980s, initiated under the Bank–IMF conditionalities, included the withdrawal of food and agricultural subsidies, privatization of state-owned enterprises, financial liberalization, and withdrawal of quantitative import restrictions. The reforms of the early 1990s were particularly aimed at moving towards an open economy – such as making the currency convertible on the current account, reducing import duties generally to much lower levels, and removing virtually all controls on the movements of foreign private capital. In addition, wide-ranging fiscal reforms were undertaken including the introduction of a value added tax (VAT)

2 From stabilization to growth

2.1 Trends in macroeconomic balances

The launching of these wide-ranging policy reforms in the beginning of the 1990s was followed by a turnaround in the macroeconomy. This was marked by a significant improvement in the government's budgetary position along with a sharp increase in the national saving rate (although, as will be discussed later, the extent of the increase in savings seems to have been grossly overestimated by the existing national income accounts, see Table 3.1). However, this increase in national savings was mostly matched by an equally marked decline in foreign savings (that is, external current account deficit) rather than by an increase in investment. The lagging growth of investment led to a situation showing symptoms of aggregate demand deficiency, such

Table 3.1 Trends in macroeconomic balances, 1980/1 and 1989/90 to 1996/7 (per cent of GDP at current market prices)

	1980/1	*1989/90*	*1991/2*	*1993/4*	*1994/5*	*1995/6*	*1996/7*
Balance of payments							
Trade deficit[1]	12.9	10.1	6.3	6.4	8.3	9.8	7.9
merchandise imports	18.4	16.8	14.6	16.3	20.0	21.4	21.8
merchandise exports	5.8	6.6	8.0	9.8	11.9	12.2	13.4
Net factor income[2]	2.5	3.0	3.7	4.7	4.8	4.8	5.1
Current account deficit[3]	10.3	7.1	2.5	1.7	3.7	5.1	2.8
(net capital receipts)[4]	(9.1)	(6.0)	(5.0)	(4.3)	(4.4)	(2.3)	(2.0)
Savings–investment balance							
Gross fixed investment	16.2	12.8	12.1	15.4	16.6	17.0	17.3
private	9.6	6.4	6.6	7.8	9.4	10.7	10.9
public	6.7	6.4	5.5	7.6	7.2	6.3	6.5
Gross national savings[5]	5.9	5.7	9.6	13.7	12.9	11.9	14.5
Gross domestic savings[6]	3.4	2.7	5.9	9.0	8.1	7.1	9.4
Fiscal balance							
Total revenue	9.3	9.3	10.9	12.2	12.1	11.5	11.7
tax revenue	7.7	7.8	8.8	9.3	9.6	9.2	9.5
Total expenditure	18.4	17.2	16.8	18.1	18.9	17.1	17.0
Current expenditure[7]	5.6	8.8	8.3	8.9	8.8	8.7	8.9
Overall budget deficit	9.0	7.9	5.9	6.0	6.8	5.7	5.3

Notes: [1] Includes net income from non-factor services; [2] includes private transfers (mainly remittances), interest payments on external public debt and other investment incomes; [3] equals trade deficit minus net factor income from abroad; [4] equals current account deficit plus increase in international reserves; includes foreign public loans and grants (net of amortization) and all other net capital receipts, but may be an underestimation for the most recent years because of containing large 'errors and omissions' of balance of payments; [5] equals gross investment minus current account deficit; [6] equals gross national savings minus net factor income from abroad; [7] excludes food subsidies.

Sources: Estimated from official national income accounts of the Bangladesh Bureau of Statistics and data from the Bangladesh Bank.

as a sharp fall in the inflation rate to a near-zero level and a huge build-up of international reserves. It is worth noting that the reserve build-up took place in spite of the fact that the net capital inflow, consisting almost entirely of official grants and concessional loans, had been declining as a proportion of GDP. Overall, these developments could be interpreted in part as evidence of successful stabilization through improved domestic resource mobilization, but also in part as symptoms of a feeble investment response to policy reforms.

Around 1994–5, however, the trends in the macroeconomic balances took a different turn. The current account deficit (also representing the savings–investment gap) began to widen rapidly; by 1995–6 it had become unsustainable resulting in a huge drawdown on foreign reserves.[3] How did such a change in the economy's aggregate resource balance come about? The explanation may lie mainly in the ending of the process of strong growth in domestic savings as shown in Tables 3.1 and 3.3. The subsequent decline, or stagnation, in the rate of domestic saving was accompanied by a further decline in net capital inflows.[4] Meanwhile, there were signs of an upturn in private investment associated with large growth in the import of capital goods and in bank credit to the private sector during 1994–5 and 1995–6 (Table 3.2). This investment dynamism was short-lived as it came up against an unsustainable resource gap. Although the external current account deficit had been brought down to a more sustainable level by 1997–8, this was only achieved through a stifling of the growth in manufacturing and investment.

There were other adverse developments that frustrated the prospects of an economic upturn. Successive bad harvests had a destabilizing effect on the economy. The political unrest during late 1995 and early 1996 greatly undermined business confidence and caused widespread economic disruptions leading to a slowdown in industrial and export growth. Again, because of

Table 3.2 Annual percentage change in selected macroeconomic indicators, 1990/1 to 1996/7

	1990/1	*1991/2*	*1992/3*	*1993/4*	*1994/5*	*1995/6*	*1996/7*
Real GDP	3.4	4.2	4.5	4.2	4.4	5.3	5.7
Crop agriculture	1.2	1.7	0.8	−1.6	−3.8	2.8	5.6
Manufacturing, large-scale[1]	4.2	10.5	13.2	10.2	11.2	5.9	3.0
Inflation index[2]	8.9	5.1	1.3	1.8	5.2	4.1	3.9
Private sector credit (net)[3]	11.4	7.3	11.3	8.5	23.6	22.6	12.6
Merchandise exports (US$)	12.7	16.0	19.6	6.3	37.1	11.8	13.8
Merchandise imports (US$)	−7.4	0.5	15.5	2.9	39.2	17.9	3.5
of which: capital goods	−5.0	4.7	4.4	−3.4	29.9	13.6	4.3
Exchange rate[4]	8.4	6.9	2.6	2.2	0.5	1.6	4.6
Real exchange rate[5]	1.2	6.7	0.4	0.6	−1.3	0.4	−4.9

Notes: [1] Based on the quantum index of medium and large-scale manufacturing industries. [2] Based on the Dhaka Middle-Class Cost of Living Index. [3] Growth of year-end net outstanding credit of commercial banks to private sector; figures for 1991/2 and 1992/3 are adjusted for loan write-offs in those years. [4] A positive change indicates depreciation of taka. [5] Based on the real effective exchange rate index as estimated by the IMF (refers to calender years with base: 1990 = 100).

Sources: Estimated from official data of the Bangladesh Bank and the Bangladesh Bureau of Statistics (BBS).

the inefficient and corruption-ridden banking system, there was apprehension that a large part of the increased credit flow might turn into bad loans. The surge in credit disbursements had therefore to be restrained, not only to keep monetary expansion within safe limits, but also to prevent a further deterioration in the banking discipline.

The most visible source of increased national savings in the early 1990s was the significant improvement in the government's budgetary position resulting in higher public savings. Revenue earnings as a proportion of GDP increased by about 3 percentage points of GDP between 1989–90 and 1992–3, while the proportion of current spending was contained. That was evidently a remarkable fiscal development representing a reversal of the earlier trends.[5] The impressive revenue growth, however, turned out to be a once-and-for-all phenomenon with the revenue–GDP ratio remaining nearly unchanged or even slightly declining since 1993–4. The behaviour of the domestic savings rate as discussed earlier can thus be explained, at least in part, by these budgetary developments.

As mentioned earlier, the official estimates of investment, and also of domestic savings derived indirectly from it, are highly suspect. There are grounds for believing that, while the *levels of* investment are generally underestimated in the official national income accounts, the extent of *growth* in investment since the early 1990s is overestimated.[6] A new national income series (BBS, 1998), currently under preparation and still only provisional, lends support to this suspicion. This can be seen from the estimates in Table 3.3, which are based on the new estimates of investment and GDP.[7] A clear implication of these revised estimates is that, while the investment–GDP ratio remained virtually stagnant during the 1990s, the domestic saving rate increased only modestly – by 2 to 3 percentage points instead of the spectacular 7 to 8 percentage points shown in the existing national income accounts. Moreover, the extent of the increase in the saving rate could now be explained almost entirely by the increase in public savings generated

Table 3.3 Trends in investment and savings based on provisional revised national income accounts, 1989/90–1995/6 (per cent of GDP at current market prices)

	1989/90	*1991/2*	*1993/4*	*1994/5*	*1995/6*
Gross fixed investment	19.2	18.7	18.6	19.8	20.4
private	11.8	11.7	12.0	13.0	14.1
public	7.4	7.0	6.5	6.7	6.3
Gross national savings	13.9	16.8	17.3	16.9	16.4
Gross domestic savings	11.7	14.0	13.7	13.2	12.7

Notes and *Sources*: The estimates in this table are based on the provisional revised series of investment and GDP and therefore differ from those in Table 3.1. The investment and GDP figures used here are those reported in BBS (1998).

through increased revenue surplus of the government (which increased from 0.5 per cent in 1989–90 to 3.3 per cent in 1993–4, with no further improvement since).

This reassessment of the investment–savings performance points to some important aspects of development prospects in Bangladesh. First, the problem of a weak or delayed response of investment to policy reforms has often been cited as a major weakness in Bangladesh's experience with macroeconomic reform. This problem now appears even more serious in the light of the reassessment of the investment estimates. Second, this reassessment leaves far less room for optimism regarding the prospects for achieving a high rate of growth of domestic savings. There seems to be little ground for expecting savings to grow spontaneously to match an increase in investment demand, once investment starts to respond to policy reforms. Such an expectation is often implicit in the projections, such as those made in the World Bank's country reports, involving high-growth scenarios for the Bangladesh economy under accelerated policy reforms. Lastly, the revised estimates also point to the importance of mobilization of public savings through an increased tax effort as an effective way of raising national savings – notwithstanding the well-known Ricardian equivalence hypothesis regarding the offsetting effect of public saving on private saving.

2.2 The growth performance

The trend rate of GDP growth since the early 1980s has remained around 4 per cent a year, as shown in Table 3.4; estimates for the more recent subperiods show only a slight improvement, if any. Agricultural growth at around 2 per cent a year has hardly exceeded the population growth rate; it is only manufacturing production that has shown some acceleration in growth. It should be noted, however, that the growth performance could be maintained or even improved in the face of a secular decline in the inflow of foreign capital.

Table 3.4 Trends in sectoral and GDP growth 1980/1–1996/7 (annual per cent)

	1980/1–1996/7	*1986/7–1996/7*	*1989/90–1996/7*
GDP at factor cost	4.16	4.40	4.50
Agriculture	2.20	2.58	2.13
Manufacturing	4.32	5.41	6.29
Construction	6.03	4.95	4.81
Services	5.46	5.34	5.66

Notes: The growth rates are estimated by fitting semilogarithmic trend lines to the official national income series at constant 1984–5 prices. Services include all remaining sectors.
Source: Calculated from BBS (various years)

The official production index for large-scale manufacturing shows that between the mid-1980s and the mid-1990s, growth in the ready-made garment industry alone accounted for over two-thirds of the overall growth in production (while another one-third of the growth was explained by that in fertilisers, drugs and the pharmaceutical industries). Production in nearly all other industries, including export-oriented ones such as fish and shrimp and leather, either declined or remained stagnant during this period. This is in contrast to the more diversified, though lower manufacturing growth of earlier periods.

Export trends show an even more marked departure from diversification in spite of an impressive growth in overall export earnings. The average annual growth of exports in real terms accelerated from about 6 per cent in the 1980s to more than 15 per cent in the first half of the 1990s. This growth, particularly in the later period, was almost entirely due to the growth in the export of ready-made garments. Recent trends are thus contrary to the envisaged development of a broader, more diversified industrial and export base – on which the success of the ongoing macroeconomic policy reforms were premised.[8]

The sectoral composition of growth over the years shows that a disproportionately large share of the increase in GDP originated in the service sectors, including trade, transport and all other services as shown in Table 3.4. For example, between the mid-1980s and the mid-1990s, the share of services in GDP increased from 41 to 47 per cent (accounting for nearly 60 per cent of the incremental GDP), while that of manufacturing increased only marginally to 12 per cent. Compared to the average figures for developing countries, these sectoral shares are decidedly high for services and far too low for manufacturing.[9] Given that the share of services in national income generally increases with economic development, Bangladesh appears to be one of the most prematurely service-oriented economies in the world.

Apart from the question of reliability of the national income accounts, this calls for an examination of the demand-related sources of growth in the Bangladesh economy. The relatively low share of manufacturing in GDP may be partly explained by the pattern of consumer demand at the prevailing low income levels. The fact that imports are financed to a large extent by foreign aid and workers' remittances (rather than by earnings from merchandise exports) also has a depressing effect on the demand for domestic production of tradables, especially manufacturing products (*vis-à-vis* nontradables such as services).

This structure of domestic production has important implications for Bangladesh's development prospects. First, given the narrow manufacturing base of the economy, it may be premature for Bangladesh to focus exclusively on a 'medium-term growth agenda that relies on an export-oriented, private, manufacturing sector' (quoted from a World Bank report; see Mahmud,

1995). While manufacturing exports can undoubtedly play an important role, the likely contribution to growth arising from other sectors of the economy (such as non-crop agriculture, rural industries and formal and informal services) must also be assessed. Second, given the narrow, non-diversified export base and the predominance of the production of non-tradables, external sector liberalization (through a combination of import tariff reductions and a real devaluation) may not help investment incentives over large parts of the economy.

3 External sector developments

3.1 Trade policy reforms: are industrial policies needed?

In respect of import liberalization, Bangladesh had already moved from the initial phase of liberalization of quantitative controls to the phase of tariff reductions by the end of the 1980s. The removal of import controls, especially in the late 1980s, resulted in the elimination of the very high 'implicit' tariffs (that is, the scarcity premia) that had characterized the earlier trade regime.[10] Trade reform in the 1990s was aimed at achieving further import liberalization by reducing import duty rates to significantly lower and more uniform levels. The impact of these reforms on the average rate of import tax and on the average nominal rate of protection can be seen from the estimates in Table 3.5 which show both the unweighted average and the import-weighted average of import-item-specific rates. The nominal rate of protection is estimated by excluding the import duties that have no protective effect, such as VAT introduced in 1991–2. VAT is imposed on all types of imports and on domestic production under its coverage; the assessment of tax on the latter is adjusted for the VAT paid on intermediate goods, imported or otherwise.

Table 3.5 Nominal protection and import tax rate, 1990/1–1994/5 (per cent of landed value of import)

	1990/1	*1991/2*	*1992/3*	*1993/4*	*1994/5*
Nominal protection rate[1]					
unweighted mean	89	59	50	40	30
import-weighted mean	42	40	30	28	na
Total import tax rate[2]					
unweighted mean	91	84	73	57	44
import-weighted mean	44	59	47	42	na

Notes: na = not available; [1] excludes taxes that have no protective effect such as VAT; allowance is made for the negative effect of taxes imposed on domestic production only; [2] includes all import taxes and fees.
Source: Estimates by World Bank reported in Mahmud (1995).

One important concern regarding tariff reforms is the likely adverse effect on the government's revenue, given the predominance of import taxes in total revenue. However, this revenue-reducing effect seems to have been compensated to a large extent by the introduction of VAT. This can be seen from the small decline in the import-weighted rate of the total import tax – from 44 per cent in 1990–1 to 42 per cent in 1993–4, although it must be remembered that the actual collection may be significantly lower than shown by these figures (Mahmud, 1997). VAT provided a larger source of revenue compared to the taxes it replaced – both in the case of import VAT and domestic VAT – and thus helped to protect revenue as tariffs were lowered to reduce protection. However, this was largely a once-and-for-all effect, as can be seen from the fact that the total import tax rate (import-weighted) declined substantially following an initial sizeable increase with the introduction of VAT in 1991–2. This highlights the importance of raising revenue from domestic sources in the face of continued import liberalization.

Another notable aspect regarding the estimates of the nominal protection rate and the total import tax rate is that the import-weighted estimate shows a much smaller decline in each of these rates compared to the unweighted estimate. This implies that the government sought to protect revenue by reducing tariffs on minor items rather than those with a large recorded import value. It thus appears that the government's revenue concerns, rather than any protectionist policy, was a stronger deterrent to faster import liberalization. Interestingly, the initial tariff structure of the late 1980s would seem to have been dictated more by the need to provide protection than raise revenue.[11]

The extent and the speed of further import liberalization remain a contentious issue in the economic reform agenda of the government. In the absence of any pre-announced target and timetable, tariff reforms in Bangladesh would seem to fall into the category of what can be called a 'learning-by-doing' approach (even if not consciously recognized to be so). In this approach, further tariff reforms are to be decided on the basis of a continuous assessment of the economy's capacity to absorb reforms, which in turn would require an assessment of the response of entrepreneurs to the reform-induced changes in the structure of industrial incentives. The credibility of such an approach must depend on the government's willingness and capacity to conduct trade policy reforms in an analytical and apolitical way. It will also be important to relate the effects of tariff reforms with those arising from policy reforms in other areas, such as tax administration, provision of infrastructural facilities and public utilities, and the functioning of financial and labour markets. It is increasingly being recognized that without complementary measures in these other areas, trade policy reforms in isolation are unlikely to be effective in increasing investment and exports.

Clearly, an active industrial policy thus has a key role to play at least in the transitional reform period as the impact of trade policy reforms is bound to vary considerably across industries. This is all the more so because tariff reforms have to cope with the many structural limitations of the existing tax system that often give rise to policy conflicts between efficiency, equity and revenue objectives of taxation. For example, the taxation on imported intermediate and capital goods, which is undesirable on grounds of production efficiency, is an important source of revenue and is often the only means of taxing a large part of domestic production. In the face of incomplete import liberalization there is thus a need to remove the discrimination against exports, often by selective intervention. The existing schemes of duty-drawback, bonded warehouses and selective cash incentives for exports are essentially means for providing exporters access to duty-free imports of production inputs (or for compensating for the payment of such duties). The selectivity of such intervention depends not only on economic criteria but also, of necessity, on their administrative feasibility and effectiveness.[12] Improvements in the administration of the above types of export facilitation schemes should therefore be an essential part of developing the capability for conducting an industrial policy as discussed above.

3.2 Real exchange rate: symptoms of a Dutch disease?

A remarkable aspect of Bangladesh's experience of trade policy reform since the mid-1980s relates to the observed trends in the real exchange rate. In spite of substantial import liberalization, achieved through a gradual relaxation of exchange controls along with tariff reductions, there has been no real devaluation of the taka to any large extent. This is all the more remarkable since, during this same time, the external deficits have been substantially reduced. The available estimates suggest that the extent of real devaluation since the late 1980s to the mid-1990s was no more than 12 to 15 per cent and could be even lower (depending on which indices of domestic and international inflation are used). If, for example, domestic inflation is measured by the domestic wage index (instead of the general price index), it would in fact imply an appreciation of the real exchange rate of the taka during this time.[13]

This experience in respect of the trends in the real exchange rate is widely different from that of many developing countries undergoing structural adjustment, including some South Asian countries. All these countries have experienced a much larger depreciation of the real exchange rate of their currencies.[14] This has put Bangladesh at a disadvantage in export competition with other developing countries and in promoting an export market within these countries, especially the neighbouring ones. With a flexibly managed exchange rate and domestic currency already convertible on the current account, the option is therefore to go for strengthening various non-price measures to support export growth and diversification.

In the case of trade with India, Bangladesh's bilateral real exchange rate with that country and the bilateral trade balance showed some remarkable trends. The real value of the Bangladesh taka against the Indian rupee is estimated to have appreciated by as much as 25 per cent or more between the late 1980s and mid-1990s. This, combined with the fact that Bangladesh pursued faster import liberalization as compared to India, resulted in a dramatic increase in Bangladesh's trade deficit with India. This is reflected in the fact that Bangladesh's exports to India can now pay for a meagre 4 per cent of its imports from that country compared to more than 15 per cent a decade ago.[15]

Even if the Bangladesh economy has in the past shown symptoms of the Dutch disease (in the sense of not experiencing enough real devaluation in response to import liberalization), it is, as Mahmud (1995) suggests, largely a reflection of low growth in investment and other import-intensive activities. Since industrial production and investment are highly dependent on imports, an upturn in these activities could easily change the situation. The trends in the real exchange rate also reflect the increasing flows of remittances and the strong growth in the export of ready-made garments. The fact that the growth in the country's foreign exchange earnings has been almost entirely due to these two items underlies the fragility of the country's external balances.

4 Reforms and governance

A careful review of the implementation of macroeconomic reforms and their outcomes in Bangladesh suggests that the future challenges are largely to do with improving the quality of governance in a wide range of areas. Lack of good governance is perhaps the major factor inhibiting the response of domestic and foreign investors to policy reforms. The factors responsible for adversely affecting investment incentives are well-known: the weakness of the financial institutions, poor infrastructure, corrupt and inefficient bureaucracy, and an inadequate legal system, to name a few. The politics of agitation and confrontation are also another important factor allegedly responsible for undermining investor confidence. Some of these governance-related issues are highlighted below.

4.1 Financial sector reforms: from liberalization to regulation

The manifestations of a non-performing regulatory framework are nowhere so evident in Bangladesh as in the generally prevailing malaise plaguing the financial sector. The reason for this malaise can be largely attributed to the fact that Bangladesh went for financial liberalization without adequate regulation and supervision. A notable example of this is provided by the recent upheaval in the country's stock market. Just when foreign portfolio funds were beginning to flow into Bangladesh, boosting the country's nascent stock market, the market went through an episode of phenomenal boom and bust that virtually destroyed any prospect of its further growth, at least in the near future.[16] This episode was mainly created by the machinations of some unscrupulous share traders who took advantage of the laxity in regulation.

In commercial banking, interest rate deregulation along with the setting up of banks in the private sector led to an increase in real lending rates. The widespread culture of loan default resulted in high costs of financial intermediation as reflected in the large spread between deposit and lending rates of interest (currently as high as 7–8 per cent).[17] The reasons for loan defaults on such a large scale are many, such as politically-influenced loans given by public sector banks, 'insider' loans given to owner-directors by private banks, and the weakness of legal provisions for loan recovery. Besides increasing the cost of financial intermediation, non-repayment of bank loans also creates problems for recycling loan funds to finance new investments. Moreover, the effectiveness of a given amount of investment loans is reduced by low equity participation and by the diversion of loan funds for non-investment purposes. The factors adversely affecting the quality of bank lending must therefore remain a prime concern for financial sector management.

4.2 Fiscal effort: coping with tax evasion

Huge tax evasion makes Bangladesh's tax–GDP ratio one of the lowest in the developing world. Agricultural income as well as income from other informal sectors are virtually excluded from direct taxation because of the weak tax administration. As a result, direct taxes currently contribute only 15 per cent to total tax revenue. After the impressive revenue growth in the early 1990s, the revenue–GDP ratio has remained almost stagnant and has even declined slightly (Table 3.1). As discussed earlier, the mobilization of public savings through increased revenue efforts is key to achieving growth in domestic savings.

In the past, the revenue–GDP ratio was increased, or prevented from falling, by expanding the tax base and increasing the tax rates (leaving aside the reductions in protective import duties). In fact, most of the revenue gains during the early 1990s were due to the introduction of VAT with its higher coverage and rates compared to the taxes it replaced. The scope for such discretionary tax measures, contributing to the so-called buoyancy of tax revenue, will diminish in future, so that the revenue effort will increasingly have to rely on better tax administration designed to combat tax evasion.[18] Poor tax administration not only deprives the government of revenue income, but also distorts incentives and vitiates the environment for the functioning of the market economy.

Besides improved tax administration, there are other important governance-related issues in fiscal management such as how to reduce the budgetary burden of losses incurred by the state-owned enterprises or arrest the growth of the size of government. As regards development expenditure, it is generally recognized that there has been a huge wastage of public resources in the past due to the poor quality of development projects, cost and time overruns and allegedly large leakage of funds. The management of development expenditure in Bangladesh suffers from the syndrome of 'donor dependence' that is manifest in the absence of sustainable institutional capacity to carry forward development policies and projects (or their rise and fall with donor-funded project cycles). The existing arrangements for the planning and implementation of development projects clearly needs a major overhaul.

4.3 Reforms and rent-seeking

It is noteworthy that the implementation of market-oriented liberalizing policy reforms in Bangladesh has not been matched by progress in institutional reforms such as administrative, legal and financial reforms as well as privatization-cum-reform of state enterprises. These latter reforms are necessary, first of all, to improve the government's capability for administering the basic rules and regulations guiding private-sector behaviour. Institutional developments are also needed to improve the environment for private-sector development – such as the delivery of key infrastructural and other support services, or to reduce the allegedly high 'transaction costs' that currently inhibit private investment.

It is true that compared to the economic policy reforms the above institutional reforms are administratively more difficult to implement, and attract resistance to their implementation. Many of these reforms were needed to combat the economic crimes that generate huge illegal incomes, whether from the wilful default of bank loans, corruption in tax administration, leakage in public development expenditure, or illegal financial deals in the running of state-owned enterprises. While the removal of direct government controls, such as those on imports and private investment, may have eliminated the scope for rent-seeking activities, the imposition and strengthening of a regulatory framework for the private sector will itself give considerable discretionary powers to government functionaries, particularly in a transition period when enforcement remains incomplete and, of necessity, selective.

It is likely that effective policy measures involving institutional and legal restraints on such rent-seeking activities will meet with strong popular support, except from the few beneficiaries of the system; yet resistance to such reforms has apparently proved quite insurmountable. In contrast, there was no serious political resistance to the earlier policy reforms, such as the withdrawal or reduction of subsidies on agricultural inputs, abolition of urban food rations or a lowering of industrial protection through import liberalization. As discussed earlier, the government's revenue concerns rather than protectionist appeals from the domestic producer groups, were a stronger deterrent to faster import liberalization.[19] Although the country has had its fair share of political agitation and unrest, the underlying reasons were generally not primarily about economic issues.

No one standard explanation would, perhaps, suffice to explain the political resistance to these institutional reforms (Mahmud, 1998). In part, it is a problem of vested interest groups bent on protecting their sources of income, legal or illegal, and the government's inability to resist their appeals. Political leaders may forge alliances with these groups to create and distribute rents as a necessary tool of political management. A proactive industrial policy, for example, can easily degenerate into a vehicle for patronage politics. This would of course lead to the broader issue of the prevailing patterns of political power and the nature of engagement of the civil society at large. An even more sinister aspect of the political–economic nexus can be seen in the growth of financial extortion (including the collection of illegal tolls and protection money) under political patronage. This phenomenon has become an increasing menace, contributing to the 'cost of doing business' in Bangladesh.[20] Overall, one could perhaps conclude that if there is a demand in the political system for rent-seeking and illegal incomes, economic policy reforms alone will not be the remedy. That is why economic reforms need to be accompanied by complementary improvements in the political environment.

Notes

1 The subsequent decline of the development financing institutions (DFIs) is also closely related to the failure of this round of privatization in Bangladesh.
2 For a discussion of these reforms and the macroeconomic developments in the 1980s, see Task Forces (1991).
3 Net international reserves fell by US$ 850 million during 1995–6. The reserves had earlier risen from about US$0.5 billion in the end-1980s to about US$3.5 billion by early 1995 (worth 7–8 months' imports).
4 There are large 'errors and omissions' shown in the capital account of the official balance of payments statistics, particularly for 1995/6 and 1996/7, which are suspected to have arisen from an overestimation of export receipts. Actual net capital receipts in these years may therefore be higher than shown in Table 3.1 by up to about 1 percentage point of GDP.
5 The public sector's contribution to national savings also depends on what happens to non-investment expenditures under the development budget and the surplus of state enterprises. The latter is only partly reflected in the government budget.
6 The growth in investment is not supported by other evidence such as the growth in the availability of machinery and construction materials. Moreover, the investment estimates imply an upsurge in domestic savings, the extent of which defies any plausible explanation; see Mahmud (1995, 1997).
7 The revised estimates of investment and saving rates make these rates more comparable to those of other South Asian countries.
8 In 1996–7, about two-thirds of total exports of about US$4.4 billion were acounted for by garment exports. This share was a negligible 5 per cent during the early 1980s. It may be noted however that not more than 25–30 per cent of the export earnings from garments represent domestic value-added.
9 For low-income economies, the average (weighted) sectoral share in GDP in 1990 was estimated at 27 for manufacturing and 35 per cent for services; these estimates

are based on World Development Indicators included in the World Bank's annual *World Development Report.*

10 For the estimates of 'implicit' tariffs, see, for example, S. H. Rahman (1994)

11 For example, according to World Bank estimates the average nominal protection rate in 1989 was much higher for final goods that were produced domestically compared to those that could not be so produced; see Mahmud (1995).

12 For example, the existing schemes generally exclude the so-called indirect exporters as well as firms who produce for both the domestic and export market, mainly for reasons of administrative difficulty.

13 See Mahmud (1995). A variant of the real exchange rate estimation based on a domestic wage index has been suggested in Dornbusch and Helmers (1988), Appendix C.

14 According to one estimate, for example, the extent of real devaluation (as measured by the real effective rate for export) between 1985 and 1993 was 40 per cent in Pakistan, 53 per cent in India compared to 18 per cent in Bangladesh; see the Statistical Appendix in Asian Development Bank (1994).

15 The latest figures (1996) show that up to 40 per cent of Bangladesh's global trade deficit is accounted for by the deficit with India. This proportion would be even much higher if the trade deficit in illegal trade were taken into account.

16 The average stock price index increased more than threefold in a matter of 2–3 months during late 1996; since then the price index has precipitously dropped far below the pre-boom level.

17 Nearly one-third of all loans from commercial banks are 'classified' as involving repayment defaults; of these, about three-quarters can be said to be 'bad' or 'lost' loans. For some banks in the private sector, the proportion of classified loans goes up to an incredible 50 per cent or more. The loan repayment position of specialized banks is even worse.

18 An analysis of the trends in tax yields in Bangladesh suggests that the tax system is income-inelastic, so the rate of growth of tax revenue tends to fall behind that of GDP unless 'discretionary' measures are taken to enhance the rate structure and/or expand the tax base. A large and increasing degree of tax evasion is alleged to be the major factor behind this tax inelasticity; see Task Forces (1991), vol. 1, chapter on Macroeconomic Policies.

19 This scenario, however, may now change as the impact of further import liberalization is felt more severely by a larger number of domestic industries and as industrial lobbies become stronger politically.

20 Illegal financial extortion, which pervades industrial production, construction, trade and transport services, has been rising markedly particularly since the early 1990s. Whether this has anything to do with the transition to parliamentary democracy is a worthy topic for research.

References

Asian Development Bank (1995) *Asian Development Outlook 1994*, Manila.

BBS (1998) *National Accounts Statistics of Bangladesh (Revised Estimates, 1989–90 to 1994–95)* (Dhaka: Bangladesh Bureau of Statistics).

Dornbusch, R. and C. H. Helmers (1988) *The Open Economy*. EDI Series in Economic Development (New York: Oxford University Press).

Mahmud, W. (1995) 'Recent Macroeconomic Developments' in *Experiences with Economic Reform: A Review of Bangladesh's Development 1995*, Centre for Policy Dialogue (Dhaka: University Press).

Mahmud, W. (1997) 'Macroeconomic Update' in *Growth or Stagnation? A Review of Bangladesh's Development 1996*, Centre for Policy Dialogue (Dhaka: University Press).
Mahmud, W. (1998) 'In Quest of Democracy and Development', in A. Bayes and A. Muhammad, (eds), *Bangladesh at 25: An Analytical Discourse on Development* (Dhaka: University Press).
Rahman, S. H. (1994) 'Impact of Trade and Exchange Rate Policies on Incentives in the Agricultural Sector', IFPRI Working Paper, Washington, DC.
Task Forces (1991) 'Macroeconomic Policies' in *Report of the Task Forces on the Bangladesh Development Strategies for the 1990s* (Dhaka: University Press).

4

Structural Adjustment, Employment and Poverty in Pakistan

A. R. Kemal
Ministry of Planning and Development, Pakistan

1 Introduction

The structural adjustment and stabilization programmes required by the IMF and World Bank revolved round the reduction of budgetary and balance of payments deficits and the pursuit of market-friendly policies. While these policies were designed to improve efficiency levels, their impact on employment levels and poverty alleviation was generally overlooked.

Pakistan implemented a number of programmes, the most recent of which relate to 1988–91, 1993–6 and 1997–2000. These programmes required various actions including the rationalization of the tariff structure; an increase in the sales tax; the privatization of certain public enterprises; and a reduction in subsidies and budgetary deficits. A number of studies on the impact of structural adjustment and stabilization programmes have been carried out which reached different conclusions. I cite in particular: Corbo and Suh (1992), Jain and Bongartz (1994), Zaidi (1995), Kemal (1994), Killick (1995), Zaman (1995), Cameron (1995), Park (1995), McGillivray *et al.* (1995), Morrissey (1995), Rieger (1995) and Tetzlaff (1995).

This chapter examines the main features of these programmes, their implementation and the performance of the Pakistan economy. In section 2 we analyse economic trends, with particular reference to the budgetary deficit, monetary expansion, public sector enterprise performance, economic growth, investment, inflation and poverty. Section 3 deals with the effects on employment and unemployment. Privatization, efficiency, output and pricing are examined in section 4. In section 5 we consider structural adjustment and poverty. Finally, the conclusions are summarized in section 6.

2 Budgetary deficits, taxation policy and public expenditure

In 1988, Pakistan agreed to implement the IMF Structural Adjustment Programme, which was endorsed by the World Bank and the Asian Development Bank. This focused on controlling the increasing budget deficit, which

Table 4.1 Budgetary deficit in Pakistan (per cent of GDP)

Year	Total revenues	Tax revenues	Surplus of autonomous revenue	Public expenditures			Budgetary deficit
				Total	Non-development	Development	
1980–1	16.9	14.0	0.7	22.9	13.7	9.3	5.3
1984–5	16.2	11.9	0.5	24.4	17.9	5.5	7.7
1987–8	17.3	13.8	0.9	26.7	19.8	6.9	8.5
1989–90	18.6	14.0	0.8	25.9	19.3	6.5	6.5
1990–1	16.1	12.7	0.8	25.6	19.2	6.4	8.7
1992–3	17.9	13.3	1.2	26.0	20.3	5.7	8.0
1996–7	15.3	13.1	–	21.7	18.3	4.3	6.2
1997–8	16.5	13.0	–	21.2	18.0	3.4	5.4
1998–9	16.6	13.1	–	21.8	18.3	3.5	4.6

Source: *Economic Survey*, Government of Pakistan, various issues.

in 1987–8 reached 8.5 per cent of the gross domestic product (GDP). While this was clearly unsustainable, the IMF's insistence that the deficit should be reduced to 4.8 per cent of GDP by 1990–1 was equally unrealistic. Although by 1989–90 the deficit had fallen to 6.5 per cent, by 1990–1 it had risen again to 8.7 per cent. The 1993–6 programme aimed at reducing the deficit to 4 per cent within three years, but unfortunately never brought it below 6 per cent of GDP. The most recent programme signed in 1997 also set a goal of 4 per cent, and in the first year the budget deficit was reduced to 5.4 per cent. It is projected to fall to 4.6 per cent of GDP in 1998–9. This reduction is almost entirely due to a fall in development expenditure[1] as shown in Table 4.1 above.

2.1 Taxation policy

The intention was that any loss of revenue from a reduction in tariff rates should be compensated by the revenues accruing from the imposition of a sales tax on the imported and domestic production of manufactures, eventually to be extended to the retail stage. Although the sales tax net has been widened, it has yet to be extended to the retail stage. Tariffs have been reduced and the maximum is now 45 per cent. The increase in sales tax revenue failed to compensate for the loss from import duty revenue.

Overall the share of indirect taxation increased from 80 per cent in 1980–1 to 87 per cent in 1989–90, while direct taxation fell as a result of concessions to investors. However, this trend was reversed and the share of indirect taxes went down to 70 per cent in 1998–9 as can be seen from Table 4.2. Indeed both tax and total revenue fell sharply during this period. In the short term, it was anticipated that tariff rationalization would lead to lower output as marginal firms were forced out of the market, particularly in those industries

Table 4.2 Tax structure of Pakistan (per cent of total tax revenue)

	Direct taxes	*Indirect taxes*			
		Total	*Tariffs*	*Sales*	*Excise duties*
1980–1	20.1	79.9	36.7	7.4	27.0
1984–5	17.4	82.6	41.2	8.4	27.6
1987–8	13.3	86.7	40.7	9.3	18.8
1988–9	13.2	86.8	38.4	13.3	18.3
1989–90	13.2	86.8	42.4	13.0	19.5
1990–1	16.0	84.0	39.0	13.0	19.3
1991–2	18.2	81.8	37.7	12.7	18.7
1992–3	21.0	79.0	35.1	13.0	19.8
1993–4	21.4	78.6	30.8	14.6	16.8
1994–5	24.5	75.5	30.1	16.9	17.2
1995–6	26.2	73.8	29.1	16.3	17.0
1996–7	26.8	73.2	26.5	17.1	17.3
1997–8	28.6	71.4	21.7	14.9	17.7
1998–9	29.9	70.1	21.6	17.0	16.9

Source: *Economic Survey*, Government of Pakistan, various issues.

in which the country lacked any comparative advantage. This would tend to depress employment prospects and per capita incomes. In the longer term, increased investment in efficient firms should lead to increased output and employment.

Initially, the imposition of a sales tax increased revenues, but when the rate was increased above 15 per cent there was a fall in demand and domestic production. This situation was exacerbated by the increased availability of cheaper, smuggled goods. To overcome this problem, the sales tax rates were reduced in the 1997–8 budget and manufacturing recovered.

2.2 Public expenditure

The reduction in development expenditure during the 1980s and 1990s has had serious implications for economic growth. The increased share of GDP going to the social sectors should have had a positive effect on growth. In fact as can be seen from Table 4.3, this had little impact on the quality of life, particularly of the poor.

The structural adjustment programme also required the elimination of subsidies. The elimination of development subsidies caused the prices of farm inputs – such as fertiliser, pesticides, tubewells – to rise; farmers were to be compensated by an increase in the price of agricultural produce, but unfortunately this did little to help small farmers whose output probably fell. While current subsidies had kept down the price of essentials, such as wheat, vegetables and ghee, their removal led to a rise in the price of these

Table 4.3 Pakistan social indicators

	1991	*1995*	*1996–7*
Primary enrolment (%)	73	75	72
Literacy rates (%)	35	39	39
Immunization (%)	70	78	82
Infant mortality (per 000)	na	101	105
Total fertility rates (births per woman)	6.3	5.6	5.4
Contraceptive prevalence (%)	na	14	17

Source: *Integrated Household Survey*, Government of Pakistan.

commodities. Between 1980–1 and 1987–8 total per capita subsidies increased from Rs 29.2 to Rs 64.4 at constant prices, but fell to Rs 24.7 in 1997–8. As a percentage of GDP, these subsidies rose from 0.8 to 1.5 and then fell to 0.4 over the same period.

2.3 Monetary expansion

It is not easy to pursue a monetary policy when the fiscal deficit is high, and even harder to contain inflation and ensure sufficient credit for investment. The growth in money supply has slowed in recent years after the high rates of the late 1980s and early 1990s. This was a reflection of a fall in foreign assets, although domestic credit continued to expand. Two-thirds of total monetary

Table 4.4 Investment and growth

	Annual growth of GDP (%)	*Fixed Investment (% of GDP)*			*Money supply (%)*	*Budgetary support as proportion of money supply (%)*	*Inflation rate (%)*
		Total	*Private*	*Public*			
1980–1	6.4	15.9	7.2	8.7	14.8	–	12.3
1984–5	8.7	15.3	7.0	8.2	12.3	46.4	5.7
1987–8	6.4	15.8	7.4	8.5	7.8	73.6	6.3
1988–9	4.8	16.7	8.0	8.7	17.5	26.7	10.4
1989–90	4.6	16.6	8.6	8.0	17.4	64.5	6.0
1990–1	5.6	17.1	8.7	8.3	26.2	59.6	12.7
1991–2	7.7	18.4	9.7	8.7	17.8	73.1	10.6
1992–3	2.3	19.0	10.0	9.0	18.1	21.4	9.8
1993–4	4.5	17.8	9.5	8.3	17.2	30.0	11.3
1994–5	5.2	16.8	8.6	8.2	13.8	45.4	11.3
1995–6	4.6	17.1	9.0	8.1	12.2	63.2	10.8
1996–7	1.3	15.9	9.0	6.9	12.2	63.2	11.8
1997–8	5.4	na	na	na	14.1	20.7	7.8

Source: *Economic Survey*, Government of Pakistan, various issues.

expansion was accounted for by budgetary support, which left little credit for private sector investment. When both public and private investment fall, economic growth is bound to suffer. Poor infrastructure, particularly energy and transport facilities, will impede growth, but coupled with reduced investment – both public and private – a fall in productive capacity was inevitable. Total investment which up to 1992–3 had been growing has since declined. These data are shown in Table 4.4.

2.4 Economic growth

A deflationary policy and lower level of investment, together with the rationalization of tariffs, increased smuggling and poor infrastructure, all contributed to the sharp fall in the growth of output during the 1990s – which averaged 4.5 per cent a year, or 1.5 per cent per capita. And, as the structural adjustment and stabilization programmes failed to bring down inflation, Pakistan experienced a period of stagflation.

3 Structural programmes and employment

The IMF programme envisaged a virtual ban on public sector recruitment, which the government implemented. Data on government employees do not exist, but a partial picture can be obtained from the Federal Government Civil Service Census Report. The rate of increase in employment is shown to have varied from a modest increase of 2.7 per cent a year in the mid-1970s to over 8 per cent a year in the early 1980s. Since 1989, recruitment has fallen by around 6 per cent a year. Between 1989 and 1993, federal government employment is estimated to have fallen by nearly 50 000 employees, over 20 per cent of total federal government employment. Data for recent years are not yet available, but the decline in employment may have continued. Given that the Pakistan government is a major employer this was bound to have serious social repercussions.

3.1 Employment in public industrial enterprises

Between 1985 and 1990 employment in public enterprises increased by under 2 per cent a year while output increased at over 6.5 per cent a year, which meant that employment elasticity was low at only 0.28 per cent. This slower rise in employment was the result of deliberate government policy aimed at restricting investment and curbing employment growth in these enterprises. Privatization compounded the problem of laid-off public sector employees. To protect against job losses, workers' representatives and employers reached an agreement that new employers would guarantee all jobs for one year. Nevertheless, there has been considerable job shedding. Naqvi and Kemal (1994) estimated that nearly half of affected workers opted for a 'golden handshake' instead of staying on. The effects of this policy have been to discourage workers from entering the labour market and while open unemployment may not have resulted, the level of underemployment certainly increased.

4 Privatization, productivity and wages

The privatization of public enterprises was aimed at improving efficiency and reducing the fiscal deficit. But privatization does not necessarily improve efficiency. Various studies, including de Walle (1989), Naqvi and Kemal (1991), Sen (1991), CIDA (1987), Sobhan and Mahmood (1986) and Kikeri, Nellis and Shirley (1992), have concluded that efficiency is more likely to be influenced by policy and the market structure than type of ownership. It is well known that a monopolist will try to maximize profits, through raising prices and restricting output, which could mean a lower level of efficiency. Regressions of the growth rate of output in industrial sectors post-privatization against growth pre-privatization, market concentration and/or level of protection showed a decline in the growth rate after privatization. While this decline cannot be wholly ascribed to privatization, as this was a period of sluggish economic activity, there is no doubt that it was a contributory factor as evidenced by the sharp increase in prices in the privatized industries.[2]

To test the extent of the increase in net profitability of privatized firms, the change in the return on equity and the return on fixed assets after privatization was regressed against returns in the pre-privatization period. The results suggest that there has been no change in either return on equity or fixed assets. In a perfect market with complete knowledge, the sale price of assets would exactly equal the discounted flow of net benefits over time, and would, therefore, have no impact on the fiscal deficit. To have a positive impact on the fiscal deficit, the private sector purchaser would have to pay above this price. The likelihood of this would depend on whether the purchaser expected the unit to become more profitable after privatization. While the sale of loss-making enterprises would definitely help reduce the budget deficit, finding a purchaser is likely to prove difficult in those circumstances.

5 Structural adjustment and poverty in Pakistan

Four effects of structural adjustment in Pakistan are striking:

- It has led to stagflation;
- The changes in the tax structure have been regressive;
- The reduction in both development and current subsidies led to increased prices of essential commodities; and
- The negative impact on employment and wages accentuated poverty.

Whichever poverty estimate is taken, irrespective of how poverty is defined, it appears to have declined during the mid-1980s; similarly all studies point to an increase in poverty after 1987–8, with the exception of the World Bank (1995) study which found a continued decline in consumption poverty – albeit at slower rate. Studies carried out after 1990–1 suggest that poverty may have increased further in both rural and urban areas. In 1990–1, estimates of poverty ranged from 14 to 41 per cent of the population.

5.1 Growth and income inequality trends

For poverty to be reduced, growth must be accompanied by a decline in income inequality. In the mid- and late 1980s, GDP increased at 6.2 per cent and 5.0 per cent a year respectively. Whereas the agricultural growth rate increased from 4.0 per cent to 4.9 per cent a year, the manufacturing growth rate declined from 8.3 to 5.3 per cent a year, reducing the output in both the forward and backward-linked sectors. While this may be attributed to many factors, there is no doubt that the structural adjustment programme, because of its deflationary effects, played a major part.

Meanwhile, the money supply which had increased by over 46 per cent between 1984–5 and 1987–8, slowed to 40.6 per cent in the years to 1990–1. Credit to the private sector in the same years also slowed down, increasing by 43 per cent in the latter compared 68 per cent in the earlier period. Trade was severely affected by the rationalization of tariffs combined with the liberalization of the import regime; the growth rate of exports slowed from 21.4 per cent to 11.2 per cent, with imports rising from under 3 per cent a year to 6 per cent. This had an adverse effect on the demand for domestic production. In the earlier period GDP growth was accompanied by improved income distribution; in the later period the slower growth of GDP was accompanied by rising income inequality. The gini coefficient fell from 0.369 in 1984–5 to 0.348 in 1987–8 but rose to 0.407 in 1990–1. Nearly all the change in the gini coefficient can be attributed to a change in rural areas.

Comparisons between urban and rural areas are revealing. Poverty in the rural areas declined in both periods when the higher poverty line as defined by the Federal Bureau of Statistics is taken, but increased only in the second period taking the lower poverty line. Even so, it should be noted that while the incomes of the very poor – that is the first quartile – decreased, the remaining quartiles all enjoyed higher incomes. This lack of income growth can be attributed to the removal of subsidies on agricultural inputs, because farmers with little marketable surplus could not benefit from higher prices. In urban areas poverty increased for some because of the lower wages of unskilled workers and fewer employment opportunities.

The World Bank prepared a breakdown of changes in consumption poverty for 1987–8 and 1990–1. These results are given in Table 4.5. The estimates show that unless growth is sufficiently high, it will not compensate for the poverty-inducing effect of increasing income inequality. In the first period, 1984–5 to 1987–8, consumption poverty was reduced by over 18 per cent, mainly due to growth but also improved income distribution. In the later

Table 4.5 Consumption poverty change due to changes in growth and inequality (percentage change)

	1984–5 to 1987–8	*1987–8 to 1990–1*
Total change in consumption poverty	−18.6	−9.1
Change due to:		
growth	−15.7	−16.4
inequality	−2.5	5.6
residual	−0.4	1.8

Source: World Bank (1995).

period, 1987–8 to 1990–1, the growth in poverty reduction was diminished by the greater growth in income inequality.

Employment growth also exhibits interesting differentials. In the period 1984–5 to 1987–8, employment grew at 2.5 per cent a year falling to under 1 per cent a year during 1987–8 to 1990–1. This decline reflected the employment elasticity, which fell from 0.325 to 0.211 over the same periods, as well as declining growth rates of output as GDP growth rates fell from 6 to 5 per cent respectively.

Wage rate changes were also important. During the first period, wages in large-scale manufacturing rose by 8.4 per cent a year; in the agricultural sector the increase was 5.4 per cent a year, compared to only 1.8 per cent a year for unskilled urban workers. In the later period the rate of increase fell to 5.6 per cent for large-scale manufacturing and 2.8 per cent for agriculture, without any increase in employment in either sector. The wages of unskilled workers, however, declined – and it is the unskilled who comprise the bulk of the poor.

During the same years, both total revenue and tax revenue fell as a percentage of GDP. The share of indirect taxation also fell. These trends should imply lower poverty levels. The increased tax rates applied to turnover taxes, withholding taxes on imports and exports and taxes imposed on contractors are supposed to be direct taxes, but they are essentially indirect taxes, and as such the conclusion that they might help in the reduction of poverty may well be misleading. In practice, as all these taxes resulted in higher prices, including the price of essential goods, they hit the poor hardest. Unfortunately, data on tax incidence are not available for recent years, but for 1987–8 to 1990–1 during which a stabilization programme followed a structural adjustment programme the increase in taxation had a greater adverse effect on the poorest. That is to say, no attempt was made to protect the poorest from the effects of tax increases required by the adjustment programme. Meanwhile, the incidence of higher tax rates on the highest income groups declined as their incomes increased faster. As Kemal (1994) shows, the tax burden on the poorest increased by 10 per cent compared to a fall of over 4 per cent on the richest section of the population. Clearly, when government policy is aimed only at improving efficiency, a mechanism should be in place to protect and redistribute income to the poorest. In fact, transfers on a voluntary basis did take place. According to the World Bank (1995), nearly half of the lowest income group received voluntary transfers of money which accounted for nearly half of their total consumption.

To aid the poor, Zakat, Ushr and Baitul-mal schemes were instituted at state level. However, these were quite inadequate. Zakat was a fund set up to provide every person with a monthly stipend of Rs225 and a rehabilitation grant of Rs3000 as a one-time transfer. In practice there were few beneficiaries, numerous complaints about mismanagement and the authorities failed to collect anything like the full Zakat revenue due. Had the government collected from all those liable to pay Zakat on fixed and savings accounts, it would have yielded Rs4762 million compared to the actual yield in 1993–4 of Rs2844 million – a shortfall of nearly 70 per cent. Baitul-mal, introduced in 1992, comprised a number of schemes of which the two most important were the Food Subsidy Scheme and the Individual Assistance Scheme. Any person who did not receive Zakat and had a monthly income of less than Rs1500 was eligible for Baitul-mal, which provided child benefit at Rs50 per child per month and a fixed sum of Rs500 for persons with shelter and Rs300 for those without. Yet again the schemes failed to alleviate poverty.

6 Conclusions

This chapter has concentrated on examining the effects of the structural adjustment and stabilization programmes during the 1980s and 1990s on output, employment, incomes and poverty in Pakistan. Comparisons on a 'before' and 'after' basis were made difficult by inadequate data.

The structural adjustment programmes implemented during the years 1988 to 1993 led to a fall in government employment of around 6 per cent a year, while employment in public-sector enterprises showed little change. Privatization of these public enterprises was encouraged, and to make this acceptable to employees they were guaranteed job security for one year together with various benefits. In spite of this, nearly half of all government employees opted for redundancy and a 'golden handshake'. It is unlikely that this privatization policy will encourage private-sector employment as government and public sector employment continues to fall.

The structural adjustment programmes clearly led to stagflation. The rate of increase in output fell to less than 5 per cent a year while inflation continued in most years at over 10 per cent. Privatization failed to improve the economic situation; indeed it contributed to a slowdown in output increase, lower levels of employment and higher prices, particularly on basic commodities.

Many factors, including the slowdown in growth, removal of subsidies, rising income inequality, slower employment generation and the consequent decline in wage rates contributed to the rise in poverty levels, both rural and urban, under the structural and stabilization programmes. Finally, it is considered essential that when structural adjustment and stabilization programmes are implemented they should be accompanied by effective schemes to protect the poorest sections of the community.

Notes

1 As a matter of fact, the decline in development expenditure is more than the decline in fiscal deficit.
2 While the prices of the products of privatized industries increased at a rate of 6.1 per cent in the pre-privatization period compared to the general inflation rate of 9.3 per cent, the prices in the post-privatization period increased by 16.3 per cent compared to the general inflation rate of 10.5 per cent.

References

Amjad, R. and A. R. Kemal (1998) 'Macroeconomic Policies and their Impact on Poverty Alleviation in Pakistan', *Pakistan Development Review*, vol. 36, no. 1 (Spring).

Banuri, T., S. Rafi Khan and M. Mahmood (eds) (1997) *Just Development – Beyond Adjustment with a Human Face* (Karachi: Oxford University Press).

Cameron, J. (1995) 'The impact of IMF and World Bank Policy Stances on the Economic Debates in India', *Pakistan Journal*.

Canadian International Development Agency (CIDA) (1987) *A Study of Divestment of Industries in Bangladesh*, vol. 1, Dhaka.

Corbo, V. and S.-M. Suh (eds) (1992) *Structural Adjustment in a Newly Industrialized Country – The Korean Experience* (Washington DC: The World Bank).

de Walle, N. van (1989) 'Privatization in Developing Countries: A Review of the Issues', *World Development* vol. 17, no. 5, pp. 601–15.

Jain, R. B. and H. Bongartz (eds) (1994) *Structural Adjustment Public Policy and Bureaucracy in Developing Societies* (Frankfurt/Main: Friedrich Ebert Stiftung).

Kemal, A. R. (1990) 'Fiscal Imbalances as an Obstacle to Privatization Effort', *Pakistan Development Review*, vol. 28, no. 4, (Winter).

Kemal, A. R. (1994) 'Structural Adjustment, Employment, Income Distribution and Poverty'. *The Pakistan Development Review*, vol. 32, no. 4.

Kemal, A. R. (1997) 'Why Regulate a Privatized Firm', *Pakistan Development Review*, vol. 35, no. 4 (Winter).

Kikeri, S., J. Nellis and M. Shirley (1992) *Privatization: The Lessons of Experience* (Washington DC.: The World Bank).

Killick, T. (1995) 'Conditionality and the Adjustment–Development Connection', *Pakistan Journal of Applied Economics*, vol. XI. nos 1 & 2.

McGillivray, M., M. White and A. Ahmad (1995) 'Evaluating the Effectiveness of Structural Adjustment Policies on Macro-economic Performance: A Review of the Evidence with Special Reference to Pakistan', *Pakistan Journal of Applied Economics*, vol. XI, nos 1 & 2.

Morrissey, O. (1995) 'The Political Economy of Trade Liberalization: A Framework and Application to Pakistan', *Pakistan Journal of Applied Economics*, vol. XI, nos 1 & 2.

Naqvi, S. N. H. and A. R. Kemal (1991) 'The Privatization Experience of Public Industrial Enterprises in Pakistan', *The Pakistan Development Review* (Summer).

Naqvi, S. N. H. and A. R. Kemal (1994) 'Structural Adjustment, Privatization and Employment in Pakistan' in I. Rizwanul, *Social Dimensions of Economic Reforms in Asia*. ILO, SAAT, New Delhi, India.

Park, S.-H. (1995) 'Major Issues in the Role of Trade and Industrial Policies in Developing Countries', *Pakistan Journal of Applied Economics*, vol. XI, nos 1 & 2.

Pasha, H. A. (1995) 'Political Economy of Tax Reforms: The Pakistan Experience', *Pakistan Journal of Applied Economics*, vol. XI, nos 1 & 2.

Rieger, H. C. (1995) 'Income Distribution, Poverty Alleviation and Human Development: The Structural Adjustment Experience of ASEAN Countries', *Pakistan Journal of Applied Economics*, vol. XI, nos 1 & 2.

Selim, R. (1988) 'Public and Private Enterprises in Bangladesh: A Case Study of the Jute Manufacturing and Textile Mills' (unpublished M.S. thesis submitted to the Postgraduate School of Studies in Planning, University of Bradford, UK).

Sen, B. (1991) 'Privatization in Bangladesh: Process, Dynamics and Implications', in *Privatization: Trends and Experiences in South Asia*, paper presented at an international seminar organized by CSCD, Colombo, Sri Lanka.

Sobhan, R. and S. A. Mahmood (1986) *The Economic Performance of Denationalised Industries in Bangladesh: The Case of the Jute and Cotton Textile Industries*, BIDS (Bangladesh Industrial Development Service), Dhaka.

Tetzlaff, R. (1995) 'Good Governance and Structural Adjustment Programmes – The World Bank's Experience in Africa South of Sahara', *Pakistan Journal of Applied Economics*, vol. XI, nos 1 & 2.

World Bank (1995) *Poverty Assessment, South Asia Region* (Washington DC: World Bank).

Zaidi, S. A. (1995) 'The Structural Adjustment Programme and Pakistan: External Influence or Internal Acquiescence?', *Pakistan Journal of Applied Economics*, vol. XI, nos 1 & 2.

Zaman, A. (1995) 'The Government's Present Agreement with the IMF: Misgovernment or Folly?', *Pakistan Journal of Applied Economics*, Karachi, vol. XI, nos 1 & 2.

5
Slow Adjustment and Faster Growth in Sri Lanka

G. Uswatte-Aratchi
Marga Institute, Colombo

1 Background

The stabilization and adjustment programme adopted by the newly-elected government in 1977 was designed mainly to open economic activity to market forces rather than to stabilize aggregate demand or the price level or adjust to a balance of payments crisis. What is characteristic of the programme of economic adjustment in Sri Lanka is its slow pace and incompleteness. By programme, I mean the set of measures adopted by the government in 1977 and thereafter. In adjustment I include both adjustment and stabilization. In addition, the programme from the beginning made a well-pronounced effort to continue to provide a 'social safety net', although somewhat different from the previous 25 years. Indeed, benefits from government intervention in the provision and delivery of social services continued to grow during these years. The programmes were buttressed by larger inflows of capital from abroad, including from the IMF and the World Bank. The adjustment process was greatly helped by the export of labour to West Asia, seriously hampered by a cessionist war in the northern part of the country, and rudely interrupted by an insurrection in the southern part of the country. The programme was incomplete in terms of the standard recipe. Rates of economic growth in the 20 years from 1977 were markedly higher than in the previous 20 years, from 1956 when policies of state ownership of the means of production and distribution and regulation were basic government economic policy. Yet, growth remained well below the rates in the fast-developing economies in East and Southeast Asia.

There was an instructive collaboration between the IMF and the World Bank, with the Fund advocating policies to rationalize prices by changing taxes and subsidies on commodities traded both domestically and internationally, improving the design of government taxation, reducing the budget deficit and Bank support for large government investment programmes. These, as ably discussed in Jayawardene, Maasland and Radhakrishnan (1987) were designed to enable the government to substitute employment income for the transfer payments, which were to be to cut in order to reduce the budget deficit.

2 The economy 1977

The coalition governments formed by the Sri Lanka Freedom Party, led by S.W.R.D. Bandaranaike from 1956 to 1959 and his widow, prime minister from 1961 to 1965 and again between 1970 and 1977, were disastrous for economic growth, as shown in Table 5.1. Income per person declined between 1956 and 1960 and grew at little over 1 per cent per year from 1961 to 1965 and 1971 to 1977. Egged on by a highly articulate group of Marxist politicians who controlled the powerful trade unions in critical areas of economic activity, these governments proceeded to take ownership and management of privately-owned enterprises, otherwise expand the state sector and subject the economy to greater regulation. These governments were fiercely antithetical to foreign investment and nationalized the foreign capital assets in the economy.

By 1976, the economy of Sri Lanka was one of the most state-controlled outside the Comecon countries, although formally governed democratically. The ratio of government expenditure to GDP was 29 per cent in 1976. There were several rates of exchange for the rupee: a black market rate; a tourist rupee rate; another for the import of essential foodstuffs and intermediate input into agriculture and selected industry; and several more effectively determined by the different rates of taxation on imports and exports. There was a bewildering array of subsidies both to producers and consumers, and the domestic prices of traded goods diverged widely from border prices. The major exports of tea, rubber and coconuts were taxed at the exit point. The major food items were subsidized at the point of delivery to the consumer. The production of rice, the staple food grain, was subsidized at many points with credit, fertilizer and other chemicals sold to the producer

Table 5.1 Annual growth rate of GDP and GDP per head (%)

	GDP	*GDP per head*
1951–5	4.3	1.6
1956–60	2.6	–0.2
1961–5	3.6	1.2
1966–70	5.3	2.9
1971–7	2.9	1.3
1978–88	5.0	3.3
1989–93	4.8	3.6
1994–7	5.2	3.9

Source: Central Bank of Sri Lanka (1998a).

at prices lower than in international markets, and water was supplied free of charge. Finally the output was bought by government at prices well above those in international markets. All imports were subject to government control. Foreign exchange was allocated by administrative decision, the annual fiscal budget, and accompanied by a foreign exchange budget. An Exchange Control Department kept account of the uses of foreign exchange.

Internally, there were pervasive interventions and regulation. To quote from the budget speech (1977) by Ronnie de Mel:

> The last seven years [1970–7] witnessed a rapid expansion in the role of the public sector in direct production and distribution. In the agricultural sector, through the implementation of the Land Reform Act 1972 and its subsequent amendment in 1975, the public sector now accounts for 63 per cent of the ownership of the acreage under tea, 32 per cent under rubber and 10.5 per cent of the coconut acreage. In manufacturing, the public sector accounts for 54 per cent of the value of production. State agencies also occupy a dominant place in wholesale, retail and foreign trade and in banking and insurance. (p. 15)

Earlier in his speech he had drawn attention to the fact that: 'A citizen of this country had to get a permit from his local Member of Parliament even to get one bag of cement or to get some cloth for a funeral ceremony' (p. 10). Of the total population some 85 per cent was served by cooperative societies which were, in fact, little but an extension of the government bureaucracy. Restaurants, including those serving foreign tourists, were directed by government on the pattern of meals they were to serve their customers.

Jayawardene, Maasland and Radhakrishnan (1987) point out that in 1977 there was extensive unused capacity: no more than 60 per cent of installed capacity of machinery and equipment was reported to be used in 1977, and open unemployment was estimated at 20 per cent. The balance of payments problem was of a structural nature with falling terms of trade against the principal export commodities: tea, rubber and coconut.

Whatever the government pundits made of these circumstances, the public would have none of it. At the general election in July 1977, despite all the propaganda, violence and the abuse of power for political party purposes, the people voted them out of power most ignominiously. Of the total electorate, an unprecedented 86.7 per cent voted. The two Marxist parties which had had 25 members of parliament from 1971 to 1977 were completely wiped out, and the major coalition partner was reduced from 91 seats in parliament to eight. The United National Party which promised liberal economic reforms and had had 17 seats in the 1970–7 parliament won 140 of 168 seats in the new parliament. The frustration of the people and the mandate for a change from them could not have been clearer.

3 The reforms

3.1 The exchange rate

Most importantly, the exchange rate was unified and the nominal value of the rupee fell, with temporary upsurges, from that time. The nominal value of the rupee was reduced to keep it close to the market value; the real value was reduced for exports to remain competitive. The value of the US$ rose from Rs8.87 at the end of 1977 to Rs15.61 in 1978 and Rs61.29 at the end of 1997. The float in the exchange rate was managed within a narrow band of 0.5 per cent between buying and selling prices until 1986, when it was widened to 1 per cent, followed by 1.5 per cent in 1989 and 2 per cent in 1994. Payments on current account were progressively liberalized, and in March 1994 the country entered Article VIII status with the IMF with all current account transactions free of control (Central Bank of Sri Lanka, 1998a and 1998b).

There was a marked shift of resources from domestic uses to export. The most telling instance was the rapid rise in the export of labour to West Asia. The number of people leaving for foreign employment (not necessarily for the first time) increased from 28 644 in 1980 to 162 572 in 1996. Private remittances increased from 0.2 per cent of GNP in 1975 to 6.1 per cent in 1996; from 1.3 per cent of total foreign exchange earnings to 16.7 per cent in 1996. The economy became more open to international trade as shown in Table 5.2, yet nowhere near as open as in 1950. Exports, measured in US$, grew at an annual rate of 10 per cent per annum from 1975 to 1995, still well below that of South East and East Asia.

3.2 International trade

International trade was liberalized, tariffs reduced and simplified and quantitative restrictions almost abolished. From a situation where all imports were subject to licence, less than 3 per cent of all imports remained under licence at the end of 1977. The number of duty rate bands was reduced from 19 to 10 in 1977, with a rate of 500 per cent on luxury items and zero per cent on essential consumer goods. In 1991, the number of bands was cut to four. A three-band tariff structure with 10 per cent, 20 per cent and 35 per cent was

Table 5.2 Trade dependency ratios

	1950	*1977*	*1996*
Exports – % GDP	40.4	18.2	29.5
Imports – % GDP	30.2	16.5	38.9
Total external trade – % GDP	70.6	34.7	68.4

Source: Central Bank of Sri Lanka (1998a).

Table 5.3 Composition of exports and imports (%)

	1951	*1977*	*1996*
Exports			
Agriculture and mining	93.7	81.0	25.8
Industry	–	14.2	73.4
Other	6.3	1.7	4.8
Imports			
Consumer goods	56.6	42.2	19.1
food	44.6	36.3	11.1
rice	15.2	15.3	1.7
Intermediate goods	17.5	44.1	54.9
Investment goods	25.7	12.4	22.3
Other	0.2	1.3	3.8

Source: Central Bank of Sri Lanka (1998a).

introduced in 1995. The proportionate value of all imports subject to import duty fell from 71.8 per cent in 1978 to 39.5 per cent in 1995 (Atukorale and Rajapatirana, 1998) However, some significant barriers remained intact. Administrative approval remained necessary for several items to qualify for low rates of duty; import licences were required for some 300 items. In some cases licences were required for health, security and regulatory reasons, in others for protective purposes (Report of the Presidential Tariff Commission, 1991, pp. 16–17). The permit raj had not been quite laid to rest as claimed by the Minister of Finance in 1977! (Budget Speech, p. 19).

The structure of exports and imports underwent massive change. Resource-intensive exports gave way to labour-intensive exports as shown in Table 5.3. Imports of consumer goods were replaced by intermediate and investment goods. Rice production remained highly protected with all sorts of subsidies and controls and that explains its strength in domestic production in contrast with other resource-intensive products.

3.3 Interest rates

Interest rates which were probably negative in real terms until 1976 rose substantially following the reforms. The objective was to reward savers with real rates of interest and to reduce the misallocation of resources prompted by these negative real rates of interest '... if adequate resources for development are to be generated, savers should be paid a return (which is the rate of interest) which is higher than the expected (or at least the current) rate of inflation' (Central Bank of Ceylon, 1979). Money rates of interest remained high because of high inflation and the high costs of financial intermediation. The costs of financial intermediation were high mainly because default was high, and because the costs of management in the two major banks, which were both government owned, were exceptionally high. The effect on the real economy was to reduce investment, and on the financial system the risk of attracting short-term foreign funds.

4 Size of government and composition of expenditure

The package of reforms failed to achieve one of its objectives as the government failed to balance revenue with expenditure. The overall budget deficit, before taking overseas grants into account, remained high throughout the 20 years as Table 5.4 shows. There has been a tendency for it to fall during this decade, as subsidies to government enterprises fell. The consequences of financing this high deficit can be seen from the growth of the public debt. In the last two years, some debt has been retired using the proceeds of the sale of public enterprises.

The size of the public sector, as measured by the ratio of government expenditure to GDP, has always been high in Sir Lanka, and the government's capacity to collect revenue had much to do with this. The ratio of government expenditure to GDP was 28.5 per cent during the 1960s; it rose even higher during the 1970s and increased further after the structural adjustment programmes began, reaching an average of 34 per cent in the 1980s. There has been some reduction since then. A similar picture emerges if one uses a different indicator: government employment. There has been no drop in the number of people employed in government ministries and departments; on the contrary. The drop in public sector employment occurred as a result of the transfer of ownership of enterprises from government to the private sector. The proportion of people employed in

Table 5.4 Government fiscal operations, selected indicators (% of GDP)

	1976	*1981*	*1986*	*1996*	*1997*
Total government expenditure	28.6	31.1	33.6	27.8	23.8
Current expenditure	18.4	17.2	18.9	22.8	20.7
Interest on the public debt	3.5	5.0	5.3	6.4	6.2
Pensions	1.6	1.2	1.7	2.0	2.0
Capital expenditure	9.0	13.9	14.4	4.9	5.0
Total revenue	19.0	17.4	20.7	19.0	18.5
Current account deficit	0.5	0.2	−3.9	3.8	2.2
Budget deficit (before grants and without proceeds from privatization)	9.6	15.6	12.2	7.8	4.5
				8.9	7.9
Government debt	58.5	76.1	86.8	92.2	85.0

Sources: Central Bank of Sri Lanka (1987; 1998a, b); Central Bank of Ceylon (1983).

government departments and statutory institutions (not including the northern and eastern provinces) fell from 39 per cent of the labour force in 1990 to 25 per cent in 1996 (Department of Census and Statistics, 1998).

The composition of government expenditure seems to have changed substantially as shown in Table 5.5, but there is less substantive change than meets the eye. Expenditure on social services fell dramatically from 62 per cent of total government expenditure in 1976 to 30 per cent in 1997, mainly on account of a change in policy regarding food subsidies. The drop of 32 percentage points was reallocated; 17 points were absorbed by defence and public safety expenditure, another 13 points by the interest on public debt, and the balance of two points by economic services. The higher expenditure on the war in the north was mainly paid out as wages to soldiers, the economic effects of which were similar to the transfers previously paid to households as food subsidies. The one difference was the destruction caused to persons and property by the soldiers. The change in the contribution to economic growth and social well-being was likely to be negative, if any. The extra 13 percentage points paid out as interest on the public debt was in some part the cost of the capital assets created under the Mahaveli Project, for which funds were borrowed from the private sector. That part of the funds borrowed to wage war cannot be counted as contributing to economic growth, at least in the short and medium term. There was also the question of whether the capital invested in the Mahaveli Project could have been used more productively had the resources been left in the private sector. Since government capital expenditure has often been less than the current account deficit, it is reasonable to assume that some of the borrowing was to finance the war. To that extent the higher interest payments were not payments for resources which increased production or productivity. The changes in the structure of government expenditure did not change in a fundamental sense so as to contribute to growth in output and productivity, which remain the basic problems of the economy.

Table 5.5 Composition of government expenditure (%)

	1976	*1981*	*1986*	*1996*	*1997*
General public services	9.9	11.3	16.5	25.8	26.5
of which: defence, public order and safety	2.2	3.5	10.2	20.3	19.0
Social services	61.6	52.9	22.7	31.5	30.1
Economic services	14.8	19.9	42.6	18.2	16.9
Other	10.1	16.9	18.2	24.5	26.5
of which: interest on public debt	9.7	14.1	14.6	22.1	3.4
Total	100.0	100.0	100.0	100.0	100.0

Source: Central Bank of Sri Lanka (1977, 1987, 1998b).

5 Adjustment with a human face

The process of structural adjustment is generally pictured as destructive of the provision of social services by the state and reductions in the quality of life. The standard measures of the quality of life are the death rate, infant mortality rate, malnutrition, the poverty ratio and similar indices. There is no evidence of a deterioration in these conditions in Sri Lanka, except for malnutrition as shown in Table 5.6. Some 24 per cent of all children under the age of five years were reported as malnourished in 1996. Infant mortality rates continued to decline during the years of adjustment, and in the country as a whole fell by half from 34 per thousand in 1980 to 17 per thousand in 1995. Literacy rates inched forward as they approached universal literacy among young people. Housing conditions, including the disposal of waste improved substantially. There is no evidence of a marked widening in the distribution of income.

There were major improvements in health conditions whether measured by input or outcome. Population per doctor fell from 6431 in 1977 to 3579 in 1996, and per paramedic from 2374 to 1351. The number of hospital beds and the number of doctors in the public sector rose from 39 879 and 2168 in 1977 to 49 264 and 4047 in 1994 respectively. Immunization programmes reduced the incidence of diphtheria, poliomyelitis and whooping cough, and death due to diarrhoea fell from 10.4 per 100 000 in 1984 to 1 per 100 000 in 1995. However, as Colombage (1998) points out, public expenditure on health as a percentage of GDP fell from 1.63 in 1977 to 1.56 in 1996. The proportion of households seeking medical treatment in government hospitals fell from 51.2 per cent in 1978–9 to 45 per cent in 1996–7.

Private-sector health services grew and partly filled the shortfall in public-sector provision. The process began in 1978 with the removal of restrictions

Table 5.6 Living standards 1978–9 and 1996–7

	1978–9	*1996–7*
GDP per capita (US$)	273	760
Literacy rate (% of population > 5 years old)	86.2	91.8
Households with electricity (%)	13.1	56.8
Houses with cement floors (%)	54.4	73.2
Piped water (% of households)	21.8	31.0
Households without toilets (%)	28.6	6.5
Households with one or more radio (%)	49.6	73.6
Households with television (%)	0	50.6
Share of income received by bottom 40% income receivers (%)	11	13
Share of income received by top 20% income receivers (%)	57	53

Source: S.S Colombage (1998).

on private-sector health activities; doctors employed in the public sector were permitted to work in the private sector outside their hours of work for government. The number of private hospital beds grew to 85 in 1996, mostly limited to obstetrics and gynaecology. About 1000 medical practitioners were working in the private sector in 1996; they provided services to about half the outpatients while most inpatient services were provided in government facilities. With the growth of private-sector employment in large establishments, arrangements were made to provide health insurance to these employees, which made the development of private-sector medicine possible.

As in health care services, adjustment policies did not stand in the way of continued expansion of educational services to the public. However, parallel to developments in the health sector, the provision of educational services in the private sector grew substantially. The number of students in government schools increased by 65 per cent and the number of students in universities more than two and a half times between 1976 and 1996 (see Table 5.7). However resources spent on education fell from 3.02 per cent in 1976 to 2.65 per cent in 1996 (Central Bank of Sri Lanka, 1998a).

Table 5.7 Students and teachers in schools and universities

	1976	*1981*	*1986*	*1991*	*1996*
General education					
Number of government schools	8655	9521	9657	9998	10280
Number of students (million)	2.6	3.5	3.8	4.2	4.1
boys			1.9	2.1	2.1
girls			1.9	2.1	2.0
Number of teachers	110563	135869	149039	177231	195203
Students per teacher	23.5	25.8	25.5	23.7	21.0
University education					
Number of students	12178	17656	18913	28260	33948
Number of teachers	1324	1609	1906	1811	2747
Students per teacher	9.2	11.0	9.5	15.6	12.4

Source: Central Bank of Sri Lanka (1988a).

A market for education in the private sector was created by two sets of forces. Private returns to education remained high despite some unemployment among university graduates. Students with financial resources were willing to buy more education than was provided in government schools. School teachers saw an opportunity to earn extra income by meeting that demand. They also had the power and incentive to persuade students to attend private tuition classes by withholding adequate instruction in regular schools. The consequent growth of private tuition classes created a severe dent in the long policy of creating rough equality of opportunity for education irrespective of parental income. One feature of the liberalized economy was a redistribution of opportunities for university education in favour of those with resources to buy education outside government schools.

The process of liberalization caused an even more severe dent in the equality of opportunity for education irrespective of family resources when private entrepreneurs set up schools outside the purview of the Ministry of Education. These schools, often euphemistically called International Schools, were set up under the Companies Act, like any other business enterprise. They charged students what the market would bear and secured the services of teachers at wages higher than those paid by government. Children of parents in high income brackets including politicians began to buy this fast track to prosperity denied to the rest of the population. From two such schools in 1976, the number grew to 36 in 1986 and 42 in 1996.

6 Income distribution

It is probable that the distribution of income became more uneven following the adoption of free-market policies but this is far from certain as can be seen from Table 5.8. There has been no marked change in the proportion of income received by the lowest 40 per cent of spenders since 1978–9 when reforms began. Although there has been some movement during the 20 years the changes are small and, given the reliability of these data, not entirely significant. Such widening of income differences as took place, occurred between 1973 and 1977, rather than during the 20 years of adjustment. One might question whether the effects of these reforms worked fast enough to show up in the income distribution of 1978–9. Snodgrass (1998) presents an interesting analysis of this phenomenon.

Table 5.8 Income distribution: percentage of income received by group

	Lowest 40%	*Middle 40%*	*Highest 20%*	*Gini ratio*
1973	19.29	37.76	42.95	0.35
1978–9	16.06	34.07	49.87	0.43
1981–2	15.25	32.79	51.96	0.45
1986–7	14.14	33.56	52.30	0.46
1996–7	15.30	34.80	49.90	0.43

Source: Central Bank of Sri Lanka (1998a).

The large increase in employment in West Asia began in the late 1970s with the rise in the rupee value of foreign wages, and women who sought employment in West Asia as housemaids and cooks often came from the poorest families. The higher value of foreign earnings in rupees was a direct result of the progressive devaluation of the rupee under adjustments programmes, and the transfer of these incomes from West Asia contributed in great measure to raise rural incomes and the incomes of those previously in the lower income bracket. To the extent that incomes earned abroad were not included in income/expenditure statistics, then the lower income brackets are likely to have been understated and income inequality overstated. The higher rupee wages in West Asia also raised domestic wages, especially at the lower end of the wage pyramid. That, again, is likely to have raised the incomes of those who were poor but found work in the domestic economy. A second source of income for the poor was employment in the armed forces, which expanded by about 100 000 between 1980 and 1997. Policies of income support implemented by successive governments, whether under the Janasaviya programme of the United National Party or the Samurdhi programme of the People's Alliance, also raised the incomes of those at the lower end of the income distribution. To summarize, it would appear that the distribution of income was not really adversely affected by the adjustment programmes. The two Lorenz curves showing the relationship between percentiles of income and spending units receiving incomes in 1986–7 and 1996–7 confirms that argument (Colombage, 1998).

7 Beyond adjustment

The adjusted exchange rate encouraged about 750 000 of the workforce to seek paid employment in West Asia. The armed forces, government, the Liberation Tigers of Tamil Eelam (LTTE) and the auxiliary armed services employ about 270 000 persons. Emigration from the country for various reasons including voluntary repatriation to India accounted for another 250 000 people. This total probably amounts to 12–15 per cent of the workforce that would otherwise have been seeking employment in 1994.

Employment in West Asia provided transfer incomes to families in Sri Lanka which, together with government transfers of various kinds, raised the reserve price of labour as well as of course, raising living standards. This rise in the reserve price of labour does create pressure on enterprises to raise productivity in order to remain in business. The historic evidence from nineteenth-century Europe and early-twentieth-century Japan strongly illustrates this phenomenon, as discussed by Maddison (1991) and Scott (1995). The primary agent for increasing productivity is the addition of capital for that labour to work with, since the labour force is literate and reasonably healthy. That process will also bring about major changes in the structure of the economy, with old industries and enterprises dying and new ones emerging. The means of creating employment opportunities for those currently unemployed and additions to the labour force consists of a process of investment in more productive industrial activity. Hitherto there is no evidence of a rapid growth in investment with total investment no more than 25 per cent of GDP in the 1990s.

There is some evidence from other economies that the elasticity of employment with respect to output has been falling over time and that tendency applied to exports with even greater force. In China, the elasticity of employment with respect to output in industry during 1984–94 was 0.27 and in Vietnam during 1990–5, 0.12 (Khan, 1997). It follows that the absorption of those without employment and annual additions to the labour force will require a rate of growth of 9 to 10 per cent rather than the 5 to 6 per cent evident during the years of best performance – 1977 to 1997. The net addition to the workforce will increase as more better-educated women seek paid employment outside the household. They have been doing so in the past and there is no reason why they should now discontinue until they hit a ceiling of about 50 per cent, which is common in developed countries. Historically, investment ratios have never exceeded 25 per cent, but providing employment to 50 per cent of women would imply an investment ratio of 35–40 per cent.

In considering the economy beyond adjustment, it is necessary to strengthen those forces which will raise incentives for investment, and above all encourage the cessation of the secessionist war in the north and the poor law-and-order situation in the rest of the country. Widespread random violence causing destruction to persons and property remains the strongest disincentive to enterprise and investment. High positive real rates of interest brought about by high default rates in the two state-owned banks – which between them own 60 per cent of all banking assets in the country – together with their high operating costs because of inefficiency remain a second powerful disincentive. Certain features of the labour market, including the many intermittent holidays, indiscipline in the workplace and long-disputed mechanisms for the settlement of disagreements between employee and employer remain a third disincentive. Discontinuation from employment would cease to become as disputatious as now as labour markets become tight, because employers will wish to retain labour, and employees could easily obtain alternative employment. Market forces which were expected to promote growth and development when they were introduced in 1977 will not function in that manner unless government policies go well-beyond past adjustment policies.

References

Atukorale, P. and S. Rajapatirana (1998) 'Economic Liberalization and Industrial Transformation in Sri Lanka', mimeo.

Central Bank of Ceylon (various issues, 1978–89) *Review of the Economy*.

Central Bank of Sri Lanka (1998a) *Economic Progress of Sri Lanka 1948–1998*.

Central Bank of Sri Lanka (1998b), *Annual Report for the Year 1997*.

Colombage, S. S. (1998) 'Socio-economic Development in Sri Lanka: Major Findings of the Consumer Finances and Socio-economic Survey 1996–97' Central Bank of Sri Lanka, mimeo.

de Mel., Budget Speech 1978 (Colombo: Government Printer).

Department of Census and Statistics (1993) *Household Income and Expenditure Survey 1990/1991, Final Report* (Colombo: Government Printer).

Department of Census and Statistics (1998) *Statistical Profile of Sri Lanka A Statistical Compendium to Commemorate the 50th Anniversary of Independence in Sri Lanka* (Colombo: Government Printer).

Gunatilleke, G. (1998) *The Cost of the War* (Colombo: National Peace Council of Sri Lanka).

Jayawardene, L., A. Maasland and P. N. Radhakrishnan (1987) *Stabilization and Adjustment Policies and Programmes, Country Study 15 Sri Lanka*, World Institute for Development Economic Research, Helsinki, mimeo.

Khan, A. R. (1997) 'Emerging Asia, Changes and Challenges, a Second Opinion', the Ministry of Foreign Affairs, Stockholm, mimeo.

Lakshman, W. D. (1995) 'Domestic and External Influences on Economic Policy Making: The Sri Lankan Experience', Colombo UC–ISS Project Working Paper Series, working paper no. GEA501.

Maddison, A. (1991) *Dynamic Forces in Capitalist Development, a Long-run Comparative View* (New York: Oxford University Press).

Report of the Presidental Tariff Commission (1991) (Colombo: Government Printer).

Scott, M. F. (1991) *A New View of Economic Growth* (Oxford: Clarendon Press).

Snodgrass, D. R. (1998) 'The Economic Development of Sri Lanka: a Tale of Missed Opportunities', Colombo, mimeo.

United Nations Development Programme (1990) *Human Development Report 1990* (New York: Oxford University Press).

Part II

Globalization and Development Macroeconomics

6
Which Macroeconomic Policies are Sound?

Mansoor Dailami
World Bank, Washington DC

Nadeem Ul Haque
IMF, Washington DC

1 Introduction

Most people will agree that 'sound policies' should be judged by their efficacy in fulfilling the socio-objectives of steady growth, full employment, price stability and a viable external payments situation. At this level of analysis the question 'Which macroeconomic policies are sound?' hinges on the role of the state within a particular economic structure and institutions, and will be sensitive to the degree of openness in the economy to international trade and finance.

Over the past half century, macroeconomics has both influenced and been influenced by the evolution of social consensus and the economic structure in a complex interactive manner in both developed and developing countries.[1] In the industrial countries, the postwar consensus – born out of the legacy of the Great Depression of the 1930s and the Second World War[2] – established the model of the mixed economy and welfare state, with the government committed to full employment.[3] The role envisaged for macroeconomic policy was one of short-term stabilization and fine-tuning of the economy, whether in the closed or open-economy paradigm. Implicit in this model was a general confidence in the ability of the government to manage effectively. Armed with the the Keynesian tool of demand management, the model yielded the *belle époque* performance of the 1950s and 1960s in the industrial countries, only to be succeeded by the high and volatile inflation of the 1970s which led to the re-emergence in the 1980s of a conservative ideology which set price stability above full employment. To quote Owen and Schultze (1976) 'Ten years ago the government was widely viewed as an instrument to solve problems; today, government itself is widely viewed as the problem'.

In developing countries, in response to the debt crisis of the early 1980s, the macroeconomic policy model assigned a dominant role to external balance and the restoration of confidence to improve creditworthiness. This association with external constraints focused undue attention on the relationship between domestic macro policy and external balance; macroeconomic policy was closely related to the availability and price of foreign capital, that is, the supply curve or constraint imposed by the balance of payments. The supply of capital to developing countries, however, tends to be strongly correlated with perceptions of that country's risk. This risk is assessed by ratings assigned by credit rating agencies to the country's foreign currency debt obligations, which takes account of numerous economic, social and political factors.[4]

Our focus on financial integration and capital mobility in the nexus of macroeconomic and economic structure is justified by virtue of the fact that macroeconomic policy affects the real economy largely through the credit and capital markets. Does financial integration make it more difficult to achieve macroeconomic stability?[5] On the whole, it would seem not, even though at times large-term capital flows can adversely affect macroeconomic stability, possibly resulting in a misalignment of asset prices, including exchange rates. What financial integration does do, is limit the scope for countries to pursue policies that are incompatible with medium-term financial stability. The disciplining effect of global financial and product markets applies not only to policy makers, via financial market pressures, but also to the private sector by making it more difficult to sustain unwarranted wage increases and price mark-ups.[6] If markets adopt too sanguine a view of a country's economic policies and prospects, however, this could relax policy discipline for a time and result in a high adjustment cost when market perceptions change. Globalization, rather than acting as a constraint on appropriate policies, can provide added leverage to such policies. It may also provide added flexibility. The greater international mobility of private capital, by easing financing constraints, can extend the time period in which countries can adjust. Markets will only extend this leeway, however, if they perceive that countries really are making adjustments that fundamentally address existing and prospective imbalances. Otherwise, markets will eventually exert their own discipline so that the time period for adjustment might be brutally shortened.

2 Longer-term macroeconomic policy considerations under increased financial integration

Financially integrated developing countries today operate in a macroeconomic environment in which capital movements are highly sensitive to changes in the prospective rates of return – both foreign and domestic. Indeed, volatility and excessive optimism and pessimism characterize the relationship of developing countries to international private finance. This cycle of investor euphoria and panic led to the currency crisis of the early 1980s, following two decades of expanded commercial bank lending. The resumption of capital flows to emerging market economies culminated in the currency crisis in Mexico in the winter of 1994–5. Dornbusch, Goldfajn and Valdes (1995) provide a detailed account of Mexico's peso crisis. The particular macroeconomic and external liability profile of Mexico, that is, its large concentration of short-term foreign, debt, pegged exchange rate regime, and the special political circumstances preceding the crisis gave support to the view that other countries were not likely to face the same fate as Mexico as long as their macroeconomic policies remained on track. This assumption has been challenged recently by the currency and financial crisis that engulfed East Asian countries (such as Thailand, Malaysia, Indonesia and Korea) with traditionally high domestic savings rates, robust growth, and seemingly prudent fiscal stances (see Dailami, 1998).

While falling short of a crisis situation, cross-border capital flows may exhibit substantial volatility – that is, temporary shocks resulting in above-normal values from changes in world economic conditions, or less extreme changes in portfolio managers' perceptions of domestic creditworthiness. Enhanced volatility may well be a longer-term fact of life facing developing countries as they become more integrated into international financial markets. The question then is how to frame macroeconomic policy in the presence of this volatility, and in particular to decide the broad principles that should guide policy in key areas of macroeconomic management. We assume that the objectives of macroeconomic policy should be to provide a stable non-inflationary environment that fosters economic growth. From the broader perspective, especially in a poor economy, the generation of quality growth – sustained increases in domestic incomes together with the sustained reduction in the absolute numbers living in poverty – is of paramount importance. Inflation and unsustainable indebtedness which lead to a slowdown in growth must, therefore, be avoided. Indeed, new growth literature stresses that the maintenance of low inflation and a reasonably conservative balance of payments scenario may be necessary for growth, but will not generate quality growth without an adequate institutional framework, well-functioning financial markets and good governance structures.

A preliminary cross-country examination of the relationship between growth and macroeconomic stability for a sample of 42 developing countries confirmed that countries with volatile inflation, frequently running a larger current account deficit (over 2 per cent of GDP) with a more volatile growth performance, on average experienced lower GDP growth between 1975 and 1995. Examination of the relationship between growth and balance of payments difficulties again confirmed the negative relationship. Perhaps the most interesting conclusion that can be drawn from the East Asian crisis as well as the South Asian experience is that without macro stability investment and growth will slow down.

2.1 The imperative of maintaining public-sector solvency

Fiscal policy has a fundamental role in the context of increased financial integration, as both the direction and magnitude of capital flows are likely to be sensitive to perceptions of domestic public-sector solvency. Potential insolvency may trigger large capital outflows and/or large interest rate premia, as creditors try to avoid the prospective taxation of domestic assets and demand compensation for exposing themselves to the risk of such taxation by continuing to lend in the domestic economy. This situation is aggravated when the government makes explicit guarantees to creditors, since the value of these guarantees will fluctuate with the government's perceived financial ability to back them. The upshot is that, in the context of high financial integration, the stock dimension of fiscal policy in the form of changes in the government's perceived net worth may itself represent an important source of shocks to the domestic economy, transmitted through the terms on which both domestic and foreign creditors are willing to hold claims on the domestic economy.

The stock and the flow dimension of fiscal policy are not independent. A critical link between them is created by the fact that what matters is the *perceived* solvency of the public sector. For a government whose long-run fiscal stance is uncertain, short-run policy changes will be scrutinized for any information about the government's longer-run intentions. Knowing this, governments may be reluctant to act in any way that could be perceived as sending the *wrong* signals to creditors; and this reluctance may limit the government's short-run policy flexibility. Thus, achieving a reputation for fiscal responsibility may maximize the government's short-run policy flexibility.

2.2 Signalling credibility

While public-sector solvency requires that the public sector's net worth be positive, preserving macroeconomic stability in a financially-integrated environment may impose stricter conditions on the public sector's balance sheet. The composition of assets and liabilities may also matter. Even a solvent public sector, that is one that can honour its obligations over time, may be vulnerable to short-run liquidity crises. Expectations of debt-servicing difficulties can turn out to be self-fulfilling. The likelihood of a 'debt run' depends on the maturity and currency composition of the public sector's liabilities relative to that of its assets, that is, dependent on the government's debt management policies.

In managing its debt composition, the government faces a difficult trade-off between enhancing its credibility and exposing itself to liquidity crises. Long-term (fixed interest) domestic-currency-denominated (nominal) debt, unlike short-term foreign currency debt, can effectively be repudiated through inflation and/or devaluation which will reduce its real value.

Given the nominal interest rate on the debt, it may indeed be sensible for a welfare-maximizing government to follow this course, especially in circumstances where productivity can be sustained or distortionary taxes reduced. However, the prospect of the government's following this course of action would increase nominal interest rates, making it expensive for the government to borrow long-term in nominal terms. Whatever policy is pursued, the possibility of time-inconsistency may not convince creditors of the government's honourable intentions. To reduce its borrowing costs, the government may therefore be induced to borrow short-term in foreign currency. By doing so it forfeits the option to gain from devaluation and/or inflation, but enhances the credibility of its promise to do neither. The problem, of course, is that it will have incurred liquid foreign-currency-denominated liabilities, and become vulnerable to debt runs. The Mexican Tesobono crisis is a case of such an event.

Creditors can rationally expect the government to forgo the option of inflating away the real value of their assets. Dailami and Leipziger (1998) showed that foreign creditors are particularly sensitive to local inflation rates in pricing their foreign currency loans. Further, not only was the risk premium attached to such loans positively related to the domestic inflation rate, but where this was above a benchmark rate it was further penalized by imposing a high-risk premium on infrastructure loans. To avoid such a situation, the government needs to create institutions that limit its discretion, for example by increasing the independence of the central bank; by establishing its reputation for non-discretionary behaviour; and by mobilizing sources of taxation that minimize distortions.[7] Under these circumstances, the option to borrow long-term in domestic currency remains, and the likelihood of macroeconomic stability being impaired through runs on government debt is minimized.

2.3 The need for fiscal flexibility

Consider the case of a 'pure' external shock in a country with well-integrated financial markets, no option of sterilized intervention, with only one independent monetary policy instrument. Faced by an external shock, the domestic monetary authorities can either select a value for the exchange rate or for the domestic money supply – including the domestic interest rate – but not both independently. Where both the level and composition of aggregate demand are important to the authorities, they will be short of one policy instrument. They may then be faced with choosing between, say, stabilizing domestic demand or safeguarding the competitiveness of exports.

This trade-off suggests an important role for short-run fiscal flexibility. To the extent that fiscal policy can be relied on to sustain the *level* of aggregate demand at the pre-shock value – by adopting a more or less expansionary policy – a more managed exchange regime policy would be needed. Then a monetary response could be chosen to achieve the desired composition of aggregate demand by adjusting the real exchange rate as appropriate. In the absence of short-run fiscal flexibility the nature of monetary response would depend on trade-offs between the level and composition of demand.

2.4 Taxation under globalization

Globalization has implications for a country's tax system, in addition to the conduct of monetary and fiscal policy. The origins of national tax systems and the structure of government spending can be traced back to a period of fewer open economies and lower factor mobility. Taxation is basically based on the 'territoriality principle', that is, the right to tax incomes and activities within the territory of jurisdiction. In an increasingly global environment, this principle loses efficiency and may be a source of conflict.

Globalization increasingly constrains governments' choices of tax structures and rates, especially in smaller countries. Internationally-mobile factors of production, financial capital and some highly trained sectors of the labour market can avoid the taxes of particular countries, and the scope for tax evasion by individuals and corporations has also been enhanced. Indeed, many countries have experienced an erosion of the capital tax base. Some countries have responded by establishing favourable tax regimes. This *tax competition* may affect the average tax level of some countries by compelling them to lower the rates of certain taxes. To the extent that the allocation of capital will be driven by tax considerations rather than pre-tax rates of return, the allocation of capital will be less efficient. Similarly, personal income taxes and expenditure policies related to social spending may become a more important factor in labour migration. Presumably, globalization will increasingly cause tax systems to converge, either through tax harmonization or via tax competition across jurisdictions.

2.5 Monetary and exchange rate regimes

In the past, countries relied on financial repression and direct controls, which often entailed the use of punitive measures that segmented their economies from the rest of the world. Partly in recognition of the inefficiencies caused by those policies, and in no small way because of a global trend towards openness (manifested in financial market integration and large capital flows), many countries have moved to more open and market-based policies and monetary management – with the dedicated aim of price stabilization in most cases. In the future, monetary management will, broadly speaking, have to be more cognizant of the constraints of the new environment of internal and external liberalization.

The 'price' of base money can be loosely viewed in three different ways: first, relative to domestic goods and services, that is, the inverse of the price level; second, relative to foreign monies, that is, the nominal exchange rate; third, relative to future domestic money, that is, the interest rate. These three prices are linked by important relationships that market forces will ensure:

- The principle of arbitrage suggests that the *ex-ante* risk-adjusted rates of return will be equalized across all assets. In the choice between instruments denominated in domestic and foreign currency, not only the prevailing interests in international markets matter, but also any change in valuation which might arise from exchange rate variations.
- In the long run, the domestic price level and the exchange rate are ultimately underpinned by purchasing power parity where the relative price of domestic goods to foreign goods is determined by the demand for the two goods.

Because of these linkages, there is the *impossible trinity*, that is, that monetary aggregates, exchange rates and interest rates cannot all be fixed by the monetary authorities.[8] The central bank can determine only one nominal variable: the level of the monetary aggregate M, the interest rate i or the exchange rate e. The choice of M as a policy variable corresponds to a flexible exchange rate regime where the exchange rate and interest rates adjust to equate aggregate supply and demand. The authorities, in that case, could also choose whether to set the interest rate to the exchange rate and money supply to be endogenously determined. When the exchange rate is chosen as a policy anchor, in the case for example of a fixed or pegged exchange rate regime, M and i are endogenous. With a fixed exchange rate, disequilibrium in the domestic money market would ultimately be eliminated through the balance of payments. Tanzi (1996) and Brookings Institution (1995) include a detailed discussion of these issues.

Where substantial, if not perfect capital mobility has been attained, either conspicuously through liberalization or less directly through erosion and the circumvention of exchange controls, the basic principle driving monetary and exchange rate management is that interest and exchange rates are two sides of the same coin. They are essentially the same instrument and it is not possible to use them to pursue two different goals at the same time. Nor would it generally be desirable to do so, as the pursuit of different short-term objectives, or even switching between objectives, is the crux of the time-inconsistency problem in monetary policy. There may be occasions when a shock is so severe that a temporary change of objective is imperative. In such situations some form of safety valve may well be needed in the monetary and exchange rate operating framework. A way needs to be found, however, to manage these shocks, minimize the damage to market confidence, and return to the basic policy as soon as possible.

The only qualification to this principle is in respect of the time-scale. In the short term, capital mobility may not be perfect. This may give additional, though limited, scope for policy flexibility. The success of this policy flexibility is predicated importantly on the markets' assessment of the credibility, coherence and consistency of monetary and exchange management over time, including the broader supporting economic policy framework. Several economic features will influence the choice of the monetary and exchange rate management framework. For instance, the more open the economy (the larger the traded-goods sector relative to the economy, and the stronger the effect of traded-goods prices on the overall domestic price level), the more likely the use of the exchange rate as one of the more important indicators or targets, or even an anchor. Conversely, if the economy is particularly vulnerable to large external shocks (partly depending on the composition and direction of trade, and the extent of specialization), it may not be desirable to manage the nominal exchange rate too closely as this could restrict the scope for more efficient real exchange rate adjustment.

When stabilization and liberalization programmes had advanced sufficiently, significant capital inflows were often incurred. It is, perhaps, ironic that what is essentially the markets' endorsement of an improved economic environment should later become a policy dilemma for many countries. At this point, faced with a choice between nominal appreciation, mounting interest costs from sterilized intervention, or money expansion and consequent inflation risks, the interlinkages and trade-offs inherent in money and exchange rate management become obvious – especially when fiscal measures (or outflows) are not readily available in the shorter term to ease the trade-offs. In many cases, the experience of large capital inflows has eventually forced central banks to move to more flexible exchange rate regimes. In other countries, the authorities resorted to capital controls and other regulatory measures to discourage inflows and avoid having to choose between appreciation, sterilization or inflation. How long such measures remain effective is debatable as they are inherently incentive-incompatible; at best such measures buy time until the implementation of a more coherent policy.

Relevant to the choice of money or exchange-market intervention is the relative stage of development of foreign exchange and the domestic money/securities market. To some extent, the volume and nature of a central bank's own transactions may stimulate development in the relevant market or related financial markets, and although market development will not be a central bank's objective, it might take market-development considerations into account in the details of the design and implementation of particular monetary and exchange instruments, since these will impinge on the nature and strength of market development. Many developing and transition economies are constrained by key markets or instruments that may be at a very early stage of development. Poorly linked markets may prevent a properly coordinated policy framework. For example, the effective operation of monetary policy by means of indirect instruments in these countries requires a reasonably efficient payments system and transmission of interest rate effects. Even so, there is growing evidence that indirect instruments appear to have enabled the authorities to manage monetary conditions more effectively. Thus, there is a clear incentive for countries to push forward with structural reforms.

Aside from these more technical factors, there are some broader aspects that may impact on the choice of operating framework. The magnitude of the fiscal deficit and outstanding public debt (including foreign currency debt) will affect the choice of operating regime as well as the monetary and exchange rate policy. For example, where the fiscal and public debt situation is such that confidence is lacking in the domestic financial policy framework generally, it may be impossible to maintain a fixed or pegged regime, and a flexible exchange rate regime may be preferable. Conversely, the type of monetary and exchange regime could impose an effective constraint on fiscal policy and encourage fiscal consolidation.

2.6 Managing the exchange rate

Managing the exchange rate seems the preferred strategy of most developing countries. The question is how to manage a float? The emergence of a perceived misalignment and/or lack of credibility of the commitment to the announced peg – both of which may happen in any managed exchange rate arrangement – could trigger such large capital flows that the peg has to be abandoned, as in the Mexico and ERM cases.[9] To the extent that they are actively managed, nominal exchange rates should succeed in tracking the fundamentals and so avoid speculative attacks. The pursuit by governments of a 'good policy' should achieve enough credibility to avoid speculative attacks driven by self-fulfilling expectations.

One approach to the problem is to consider the exchange rate regime as consisting of a band around a moving central parity. The decisions then are about how to adjust the parity, how wide to make the band and how to intervene within the band. Polar cases can be derived in the form of a fixed parity with narrow bands (amounting to a fixed exchange rate) and very wide bands with no intervention within the band (amounting to flexible rates). The closer the policy to a fixed exchange regime, the greater the burden on domestic interest rates and/or the money supply to adjust to shocks.

The desirability of an independent monetary policy for the domestic economy depends on two factors:

- The availability of alternative stabilization instruments (a flexible fiscal policy); and
- The sources of shocks to the economy.

With a flexible fiscal policy, domestic real shocks can be countered through fiscal adjustments, thereby diminishing the value of an independent monetary policy as a stabilization instrument. However, if fiscal policy is not an available tool in the short term, domestic real shocks would have to be countered by greater exchange rate flexibility.

Consider an alternative source of shocks – that is, external financial shocks, say in the form of fluctuations in world interest rates. In that case, exchange-market-intervention policy determines the form in which the shock is transmitted to the domestic economy. If world interest rates fall, for example, and active (unsterilized) intervention maintains the exchange rate fixed at its central parity, domestic monetary expansion and lower domestic interest rates will follow – an expansionary shock. However, if the central bank does not intervene, the domestic currency will appreciate in both nominal and real terms, inflation and output growth will slow, and the domestic real interest rate will rise – a contractionary shock. From the perspective of stabilizing aggregate domestic demand, the appropriate intervention policy must depend on the extent it is feasible to adjust fiscal policy. Where fiscal policy is inflexible, then the choice confronting the monetary authorities is to live with the prospect of real appreciation caused either by nominal exchange rate revaluation or by overheating and domestic inflation. Maintaining unchanged inflation targets, in this context, would probably mean a mixture of nominal (and real) exchange rate appreciation and lower interest rates. As embodied in the concept of a monetary conditions index, the contractionary effect of the appreciation would be offset against the expansionary effect of lower domestic interest rates. On the other hand, if additional fiscal contraction can be achieved, the need for a real currency appreciation to prevent overheating, should be reduced or eliminated.

Finally, developments in the real sector can affect monetary policy. For example, in a country with a nominal income target, real growth will influence how monetary policy is conducted. In the case of inflation targeting, real growth is highly relevant to an assessment of when capacity constraints will become binding, and therefore of future price and wage pressures. Central banks may not be totally oblivious to political pressure and will occasionally take real sector developments into account. To maintain export competitiveness, the policy might be to keep the nominal exchange rate so that the real exchange rate does not deviate too much from the value determined by fundamentals – always assuming this can be reasonably accurately identified. Where there is a high degree of capital mobility, competitiveness would be maintained within a setting constrained by the interest parity condition.

3 Short-run inflow considerations

3.1 Preventing overheating

While the large-scale capital inflows that many developing economies have experienced have been beneficial from the standpoint of external balance, they have created concern over their potential effects on macroeconomic stability and competitiveness of the external sector. A key concern has been the acceleration of inflation and any adverse movement in the real effective exchange rate as a result of an appreciation in the nominal exchange rate and/or widening of the inflation differential *vis-à-vis* trading partners. Policy-makers in developing countries, faced with macroeconomic turbulence in the wake of capital flows of varying maturity, have had to decide the extent to which adjustment should take place through higher domestic inflation and/or currency appreciation. We argue that the answer will depend on the policy objectives, the exchange regime, domestic institutional constraints, and, importantly, on the factors causing the inflows.

In practice, identification of these factors is difficult, and may depend on limited information. We focus on two policy questions: first, which indicators might be used to distinguish between possible causes of capital inflows? Second, depending on the answers to the first, what would be the appropriate nature, timing and sequencing of policy actions?

3.2 The macroeconomic effects of capital inflows

The causes of capital inflows can here be grouped into three major categories:

1. Inflows that reflect an autonomous increase in domestic money demand;
2. Inflows induced by an increase in the domestic productivity of capital; and
3. Inflows caused by external factors, such as a decrease in international interest rates, particularly US interest rates.

The first two categories are examples of the 'pull' factor and the last of the 'push' factor.[10] The main cause of the inflow and the prevailing exchange rate regime will determine the economic impact, and the need, if any, for policy intervention. Under a fully-flexible exchange rate system, capital inflows (regardless of cause) will lead to an appreciation of the exchange rate, a fall in the relative price of imported goods and a shift away from the consumption of non-tradables – which will reduce inflationary pressures. Therefore, all other things being equal, the higher the degree of exchange rate flexibility, the less likely it is that capital inflows will have an inflationary effect. Under a managed float or a fixed exchange rate system, the inflationary pressures created by capital inflows will depend on the underlying cause of the inflow. In general, if capital inflows are a response to an increase in the domestic demand for money, they will not be inflationary. If capital inflows increase because of the other factors – domestic productivity or external shocks – the accumulation of foreign exchange reserves will lead, in the absence of sterilization, to an expansion of the monetary base and result in inflationary pressure.

3.3 Identifying the causes of capital inflows

Table 6.1 lists indicators that might be used to determine which of the three factors above is the dominant cause of a particular inflow episode. These indicators are divided into four categories: asset prices; monetary and credit aggregates; balance of payments data; and key international variables. Clearly the usefulness of financial indicators will depend on the institutional structure of the economy, and the sophistication of the statistical data. In terms of time lags, both domestic and international asset prices will probably have the smallest time lags, whereas data on monetary and credit aggregates and the external accounts will have relatively longer lags. Because of reporting lags, detailed data on the balance of payments or national accounts cannot be employed as indicators here. Furthermore, in most developing and transition economies, GDP data are generally only available on an annual basis. Where monthly or quarterly industrial production statistics are available with a relatively short lag these might be used.

The behaviour of these indicators provides information that can be used to identify the cause of inflows, shown in Table 6.2. In countries with established financial and equity markets *relative asset price movements* can be used. Assuming less than perfect substitutability between assets and less than perfect mobility, an increase in money demand is likely to exert downward pressure on bond, equity and property prices as portfolios are reallocated, and inflows resulting from lower international rates will bid up the prices of real and financial assets. An increase in domestic productivity is likely to have the same effect on asset prices as a fall in international interest rates – upward pressure on equity prices and financial asset prices.

Interest rates can be useful in differentiating between 'push' and 'pull' factors. Other things being equal, pull factors tend to drive nominal interest rates up, while push factors tend to lower them. Returns to investors also provide useful information. Real returns to foreign investors, which depend on exchange rate movements – together with foreign rather the domestic inflation – are likely to be higher than in their own countries in the case of pull factors. Money demand-driven capital inflows that increase money balances without increasing inflation, increase *real money balances*. The impact of inflows generated by a decrease in international interest rates would be to increase nominal and real balances. The lag in the price response is likely to be longer in countries with low inflation than high. In the case of a positive shock to domestic productivity, interest rates will increase as well as domestic income, the net effect on money depending on the relevant elasticities. It is, however, likely that the holdings of real balances will be reduced because of higher returns from competing assets such as equities.

Foreign currency deposits in the banking system should decrease when the domestic demand for money increases and, possibly, when international

Table 6.1 Financial indicators of capital inflows

Indicator	*Typical data frequency*	*Availability, reliability and timing*
Asset prices		
Interest rates / yield curve	Daily / specified time intervals	Short-term rates available daily or weekly; longer-term rates generally on government paper available from primary market at time of offering; secondary markets likely to be thin and under-developed
Exchange rates	Daily	Market rates may be available with a small lag if they are different from official rates
Forward exchange rates	Available	Forward exchange market likely to be very thin
Inflation	Monthly	
Equity market index	Daily	Typically will display high volatility as a relatively thin market reacts to 'news'
Real estate prices	Available	Commercial real estate prices in the industrial and financial centres may be available; residential prices are likely to be more difficult to obtain
Monetary and credit aggregates		
Real money balances	Monthly	
Base money	Monthly	
International reserves	Monthly	
Bank credit	Available	There may be some delay depending on the reporting lags of commercial banks
Foreign currency deposits	Available	There may be some delay depending on the reporting lags of commercial banks
Balance of payments		
Foreign direct investment	Monthly, but more likely quarterly or lower frequency	Categorization into FDI and portfolio investment may be difficult; for FDI, information to distinguish between commitments and disbursements may be available only with some lag
Portfolio investment	Monthly	Categorization into FDI and portfolio investment may be difficult
Information on international trends		
International interest rates	Daily	Interest rate differentials may convey information on source of capital inflows and the credibility of policies
Investment Funds	Monthly	Data are now available from different sources

Table 6.2 Use of indicators for determining causes of capital inflows

Indicator	*Increase in domestic demand for money*	*Sustained inflows (increase in domestic productivity of capital)*	*Temporary inflows (fall in international interest rates)*
Asset prices			
Interest rates	Increase	Increase	Decrease
Yield curve	Flatter	?	Steeper
Exchange rate	Appreciation	Appreciation	Appreciation
Inflation	Decrease	Increase	Increase
Equity prices	Decrease	Increase	Increase
Real estate prices	Decrease	Increase	Increase
Monetary and credit aggregates			
Real money balances	Increase	Likely to decrease	Increase
Base money	Increase	Increase	Increase
International reserves	Increase	Increase	Increase
Bank credit	Likely to increase	Increase	Likely to increase
Foreign currency deposits	Decrease	?	May decrease
Balance of payments			
Foreign direct investment	?	Increase	?
Portfolio investment	Increase, especially in short-term flows	Increase, in both short-term and long-term flows	Increase, especially in short-term flows

interest rates decline. However, in the case of a domestic productivity shock the effect is ambiguous: an increase in the demand for domestic currency leads to a reduction while the income effect works in the opposite direction.

While examining the composition of capital inflows can potentially provide information about the causes of inflows, it is often difficult to distinguish between foreign direct investment flows and portfolio investment flows, especially in the short term. In general, an increase in money demand or a temporary fall in international interest rates will attract a relatively larger proportion of short-term flows; an increase in the domestic productivity of capital will attract a relatively larger proportion of foreign direct investment. Here, too, lags may be important and will depend *inter alia* on the regulatory environment as well as the absorptive capacity of the country. The initial response to higher domestic productivity of capital may be larger portfolio flows with direct investment taking longer to flow in.

Although the indicators described provide information for policy-makers, the problem of disentangling the effects of different factors from the observed indicators can be complex. The message from the indicators may be ambiguous. Additional complementary information may be available; for example, the views of market participants might provide useful insights. Broader changes in the economic framework, such as economic reforms that promote productivity and/or the efficiency of financial intermediation could be behind inflows. Finally, even when the indicators send a clear message, this needs to be evaluated against a counterfactual. In other words, the behaviour of the indicators has to be interpreted in relation to what might otherwise have happened – a very difficult thing.

3.4 Formulating a policy response

The appropriate policy response, will be determined by the degree of flexibility in the domestic institutional structure and prevailing policy stance as well as the causes of the capital inflows. Countries pursuing relatively balanced macroeconomic policies will be freer to fashion an appropriate policy response, while those pursuing unbalanced policies – for most an excessively expansionary fiscal policy – will be more constrained in handling disruptions caused by inflows.

In general, countries have three main instruments for dealing with inflationary effects of capital inflows: sterilization; exchange rate appreciation; fiscal policy. The mix of instruments used will depend on the institutional structure and past policy. The ability to sterilize the effects of a capital inflow on the monetary base could be constrained by the lack of suitable instruments at the central bank and the state of development of the financial markets. These operations could be further constrained where previous interventions had already led to a large quasi-fiscal deficit arising out of the difference between interest earned on foreign exchange reserves and the borrowing costs incurred to finance the sterilization operations. Although fiscal policy is an appropriate instrument for the medium term, the lags associated with its implementation make it unwieldy for short-term demand management. The use of exchange rate appreciation may be constrained by its negative effects on competition.

Temporary capital controls could provide an alternative instrument if the three mentioned above are inadequate. Capital controls, first, are only effective for a short time, and if kept in place for long are likely to have an adverse effect on the development of the financial system. Second, institutional factors may be crucial to selecting the appropriate response to capital inflows. With macroeconomic stabilization and economic deregulation, the returns on investment may rise sharply and attract capital flows, at a time when the banking system may still not have fully recovered from past financial repression and weak prudential supervision. In those circumstances, capital controls and supervision measures to direct the flow of capital into the purchase of relatively safe assets may be justified. As the quality of prudential supervision and the capacity of the banking system to handle flows improves capital controls can be relaxed.

Table 6.3 presents a matrix of the appropriate use of each instrument in a country with balanced macroeconomic policies. When the capital inflow is associated with a money demand shock (induced, say, by financial deregulation) no policy action is required and the expansion of the monetary base will be non-inflationary. However, intervention by the central bank in the money and foreign exchange markets may be needed to smooth fluctuations in the interest rates and exchange rate. A poorly supervised and weak banking system could potentially lead to excessive risk taking in lending and measures may be needed to restrict bank intermediation.

In the case of an inflow caused by a decrease in international interest rates or by a domestic productivity shock, one must distinguish between a sustained and a temporary increase in capital flows. For a sustained increase, resulting, say, from an increase in the domestic productivity of capital, policy-makers would have to decide how best to appreciate the real exchange rate. Price adjustment of goods, and factor and asset prices, will ultimately induce an exchange rate appreciation regardless of the exchange rate regime, and this should not be inhibited. Nevertheless, with a flexible exchange rate, the real exchange rate appreciation could be achieved through an increase in the nominal exchange rate rather than an inflationary increase in the price of non-traded goods. Over the medium term, a tightening of fiscal policies may be needed to control inflation and prevent excessive appreciation of the real effective exchange rate. Experience suggests that in countries facing concerted capital inflows a tighter fiscal stance is needed, particularly where the inflow has been large relative to the absorptive capacity.

For a temporary increase in capital flows, due for example to a fall in international interest rates, sterilized intervention, possibly with some exchange rate appreciation, could be used to limit the inflationary impact of inflows. If feasible, sterilization of the inflows is to be preferred as the intervention could be swiftly reversed to stem capital outflows, without any adverse effects on external competitiveness. Adjustments to fiscal policy are best avoided unless the constraints on sterilization were severe and the economy's competitive position were weak.

With *unbalanced* financial policies, the level of domestic interest rates and expected exchange rate movements are likely to be the dominant factors influencing speculative inflows. If the high real domestic interest rates provide an incentive for capital inflows due to a loose fiscal with tight monetary policy configuration, then the best policy is to make appropriate fiscal and monetary adjustments. However, the reduction in interest rates while reducing speculative inflows could stimulate domestic aggregate demand and inflationary pressures. Where controlling inflation is an overriding objective, and corrective action to the unbalanced policy mix is expected, the response should be similar to that for a temporary external shock, namely sterilized intervention and some exchange rate appreciation.

Table 6.3 Policy matrix for a country with balanced policies

Action	*Increase in domestic demand for money*	*Sustained inflows*: e.g. *increase in domestic productivity of capital*	*Temporary inflows*: e.g. *fall in international interest rates*
	No policy response is required; equilibrium real effective exchange rate (REER) does not change	Appreciation of the equilibrium real effective exchange rate; policy response aimed at containing effect on liquidity, orderly appreciation of the REER and facilitating the non-inflationary absorption of the inflows	The equilibrium real exchange rate need not change; policy response essentially attempts to limit the impact on liquidity
1 Sterilization	Central bank intervention may be needed to smooth fluctuations in the money market and the foreign exchange market	Some sterilization may be necessary to limit the effect on liquidity and smooth fluctuations in interest rates	Sterilization is appropriate for containing the impact on liquidity
2 Exchange rate appreciation	—	Depending on exchange rate flexibility the increase in the REER is achieved partly through nominal appreciation and partly through increase in price of non-traded goods; a step appreciation or a decrease in the rate of crawl in predetermined exchange rates should be considered	Some temporary appreciation of the nominal exchange rate may be warranted, if there are constraints on sterilization
3 Fiscal policy	—	Fiscal policy may need to be tightened over the medium-term, especially if the absorptive capacity of the economy is limited relative to the size of the inflows. Experience suggests that a tighter fiscal stance has been necessary in many countries faced with concerted flows	If the constraints on sterilization are too severe and competitive position is weak then some fiscal tightening may be considered. However, the time it takes to implement fiscal measures makes fiscal policy an unwieldy instrument in the short term
4 Capital controls	If the constraints on sterilization are too severe and competitive position is weak then temporary capital controls may have to be considered	Temporary capital controls may be useful if the management of liquidity cannot be adequately handled by sterilization and/or the domestic financial system is weak	If the constraints on sterilization are too severe and competitive position is weak then temporary capital controls may have to be considered

4 Conclusion

What does this mean for South Asia which has not accepted globalization to the same extent as other regions? It is still opening out, albeit at a relatively slow pace, and while this may have protected it from the vicissitudes of international financial markets it has prevented it from tapping those markets for its investment needs. It is worth noting the similar approach adopted by countries in this region. They have all relied on capital controls and high protective barriers to insulate their economies from external influences. These countries continue to adhere to planning and, despite deregulation, privatization and liberalization, need to reduce the size and role of government further. Inflation has been generally contained despite large fiscal deficits because of the financial repression in a closed economy. The unhappy consequence may have been a lower growth rate than would have happened in the counterfactual.

Compared to Latin America or even East Asia, South Asia has been fairly stable. There have been no major balance of payments crises or inflationary episodes. They have been quick to undertake adjustment programmes to stem potential inflation or debt service difficulties. Growth has been positive and mostly fairly steady, although not rapid enough to catch up with the rest of the world. Despite the obvious costs from controls in terms of growth foregone, these have been maintained ostensibly to avert a macroeconomic crisis or for some sociopolitical reason such as redistribution.

In recent years this has changed as South Asian countries have increasingly accepted openness. Macroeconomic policy regarding controls has mostly been dictated by the large fiscal deficits which the monetary regime had to finance mainly through repressive policies rather than through direct central bank financing. In the future, the points we have considered will increasingly become relevant to the conduct of macroeconomic policy. Recent empirical work on growth suggests that, with the acceptance of this new open environment together with appropriate macroeconomic policy choices outlined and the requisite structural changes to ensure sound governance, South Asia will be able to achieve higher growth of output in the future.

Notes

1 Macroeconomic stability is a prerequisite of credibility of a government's commitment to currency convertibility, which in turn is the key element to financial integration. For a description of the macroeconomic roots of post-Second World War currency inconvertibility see Sachs and Warner (1995).

2 For a description of the postwar consensus in the UK, see Skidelsky (1990) and Yergin and Stanislaw (1998).

3 This is enshrined for instance in the US Employment Act of 1946.

4 For a fascinating description of the interplay between these factors in the case of India, see Khilnani (1997).

5 For instance, India did not embrace the economic component of western liberal democracy after independence as it did the political aspect, and pursued a national agenda of import substitution and non-reliance on the outside world. The system became known as the 'licence raj'; many imports were subjected to a complicated regime of regulations and licensing and customs duties that reached over 300 per cent. This is in contrast to the outward-oriented, export-driven economies of East Asia.

6 The complexity and fragmentation of Indian society helped democracy; no one group was strong enough to 'capture' the state and direct the state's resources to itself. See Bardhan (1984).

7 When credibility problems become extreme, the government may need to adopt institutional devices that limit its freedom of action, such as adopting a currency board or joining a currency union.

8 Like any monopolist, the central bank can set either the price or the quantity of the product, but not both at the same time in a market-based regime. It can use one variable as a means to an end defined in terms of another variable; that is, it could use a base money or exchange rate target to achieve a domestic price inflation goal, or an interest rate or base money target to achieve an exchange rate objective.

9 The basic framework developed here outlines some useful guidelines for identifying the causes of capital inflows and defining the policy reaction. Capital inflows in a specific country are likely to have a combination of causes, which complicates the task of identification and policy formulation. Our categorization of causes and policy responses will need to be adapted to each situation.

10 These explanations have important implications for the sustainability of capital inflows and hence for policy design at both national and international level. For further discussion see Dailami and Leipziger (1998).

References

Bardhan, P. (1984) *The Political Economy of Development in India* (Oxford: Basil Blackwell).

Brookings Institution (1995) *Taxation in an Integrating World* (Washington, DC: Brookings Institution).

Dailami, M. (1998) 'Euphoria and Panic: Developing Countries' Relationship to International Private Finance', in *EDI Forum*, vol. 3, no.2, Fall.

Dailami, M. and D. Leipziger (1998) 'Infrastructure Project Finance and Capital Flows: A New Perspective', *World Development*, vol. 26, no. 7, pp. 1283–98.

Dornbusch, R., T. Goldfajn and R. Valdes (1995). 'Currency Crises and Collapses', *Brookings Papers on Economic Activity*, no. 2, Washington, DC.

Khilnani, S. (1997) *The Idea of India* (New York: Farrar, Straus, Giroux).

Owen, H. and C. Schultze (1976) *Setting National Priorities* (Washington, DC: Brookings Institution).

Sachs, J. and A. Warner (1995) 'Economic Reform and the Process of Global Integration', *Brookings Papers on Economic Activity*, no. 1 (Washington, DC: Brookings Institution).

Skidelsky, R. (1990) 'Britain: Mrs. Thatcher's Revolution', in D. P. Calleo and C. Morgenstern (eds), *Recasting Europe's Economies: National Strategies in the 1980s* (Lanham, Maryland: The University Press of America).

Tanzi, V. (1996) 'Globalization, Tax, Competition and the Future of Tax Systems', IMF Working Paper, no. 96/141, December.

Yergin, D. and J. Stanislaw (1998) *The Commanding Heights: The Battle Between Government and the Marketplace that is Remaking the Modern World* (New York: Simon & Schuster).

7

Theoretical Premises of Structural Adjustment: A Critique

Prabhat Patnaik[*]
Jawaharlal Nehru University, Delhi

1 Two concepts of equilibrium

Orthodox economic theory operates in terms of a concept of equilibrium, traceable to Walras, which is characterized by the property that if all transactions occurred at the equilibrium price configuration then all markets would clear. This equilibrium has well-known properties of optimality. But even assuming that all transactions occur at the equilibrium price configuration, the uniqueness and stability of this equilibrium require the satisfaction of certain stringent conditions (Mukherji, 1990). When transactions occur at prices other than the equilibrium price, there is no reason to expect stability. There is, however, an alternative conception of equilibrium which has been used by the different *genres* of heterodox economic theory, whether Keynesian, classical or Marxian, and which, though palpably different from the Walrasian conception, needs explicit characterization. Before doing so, however, some preliminary remarks are necessary.

The problems with the Walrasian concept have been much discussed, but, for our purposes, two problems in particular are relevant. First, the flexibility of prices, whether in terms of the numeraire money or in terms of some other particular commodity, may in fact be subject to limits, in which case the Walrasian equilibrium as a stylization of the functioning of a market economy would lose its rationale, even if we ignore all its other problems. Malinvaud, (1977) talked about a rationing equilibrium at fixed prices, but of course prices need not be fixed in all markets. In classical and Marxian economics, in the short run, all markets cleared to eliminate excess demand, except the labour market where the 'real wage', that is the price of labour-power relative to the price of some basket of wage goods, has a lower bound which may even change from one period to the next (Goodwin, 1967). (Over time – logical or historical – these 'market prices' would tend to 'gravitate' towards the 'prices

* I wish to thank Mausumi Das, Utsa Patnaik and Abhijit Sen for their helpful comments on an earlier draft.

of production', but that is a separate matter). In Keynes all markets clear except the labour market; the money wage rate was assumed to be given.

It does not follow, of course, that if these prices were perfectly flexible then unemployment would disappear in the classical or Keynesian systems. But insufficient flexibility undermines the relevance of the Walrasian stylization. This insufficient flexibility in turn may occur for any number of reasons: institutions such as a monopoly or a trade union characterizing the economic landscape, political compulsions, 'efficiency wages', 'subsistence wages' and so forth.

The second problem with the Walrasian concept of equilibrium arises because of the historicity of time, the fact that the present is sandwiched between an irrevocable past and an unknown future. The past leaves a legacy, not only of endowments as commonly recognized, but also of commitments in the form of payment obligations; the future, on the other hand, is something about which only expectations can be held which provide the basis for action today. One can think of a set of particular expectations on the basis of which a Walrasian 'temporary equilibrium' can be defined, but once we accept that these expectations change as the variables relating to the current period change, the concept of equilibrium presents serious problems. Owing to the existence of commitments from the past and expectations about the future, it becomes conceivable that no amount of price movement in a world of perfect price flexibility can eliminate excess demand (positive or negative) in particular markets (Keynes, 1936, ch. 19; Kalecki, 1967). The fact that such a world nonetheless experiences a state of rest somewhere, would then result not from any tendency towards a Walrasian equilibrium, but from the fact that there actually are bounds to price movements.

One interpretation of Keynes would hold; not that rigid money wages are a cause of unemployment equilibrium, but that there is no spontaneous tendency towards the removal of excess supply in the labour market through money wage movements, and that it is the sluggishness of money wage movements that prevents a free fall of money wages and provides a perch for prices to rest. If anything, the inelasticity of price expectations in asset markets, which is necessary for ensuring that excess demand moves inversely with the current price, can arise from the fact that certain prices have limited flexibility.[1] In other words, limited price flexibility acts to stabilize the system around some state of rest, even if this is not the Walrasian equilibrium. If such limits did not exist then there would be no anchor for price expectations whose elasticity might be too large to permit the usual shape of the excess demand curve that underlies Walrasian equilibrium.

If the first point mentioned above argues that limited price flexibility undermines the relevance of a Walrasian equilibrium, the second point argues that unlimited price flexibility, as assumed for a Walrasian equilibrium, can also undermine it, but for a different reason, namely by removing the basis for inelastic price expectations in particular asset markets. It follows then that an alternative concept of equilibrium is called for which would provide a more adequate stylization of the economic universe. Such a concept defines equilibrium merely as a state of rest for the economy where all markets do not clear, and it recognizes the existence of limited price flexibility in many markets, as well as the possible destabilizing role of expectations. In other words, if we do not burden the concept of equilibrium with the clearance of all markets and in the process deprive ourselves of the ability to cognize several real-life phenomena, then we could define equilibrium merely as a state of rest for the economy, and make our theory more open-ended. This is what Keynes did; and this also characterizes classical economics in its short-period version (which is the version comparable to Walras). Such a concept of equilibrium represents a better stylization of reality, and we shall use the term only in this sense.

2 The equilibrium concept underlying structural adjustment

The purpose of this preliminary disquisition is the following: the theory underlying structural adjustment is derived from the Walrasian concept, and its claim to validity is necessarily based on the presumption that the Walrasian stylization is an adequate representation of the real world.[2]

This may appear strange at first sight, as much of the argument in support of structural adjustment rarely invokes any high theory and is generally confined to swapping anecdotes about government 'inefficiency' from which the need for greater reliance on the market mechanism is supposed to follow as a self-evident proposition. But this impression is erroneous. Structural adjustment refers not to some minor administrative reorganization but to a systematic shift towards greater reliance on the market on the grounds that the market works. *Any* statement that the 'market works' must be backed by some theory, and in particular some notion of equilibrium; and no theoretical statement about the successful working of the market can be made unless it is believed that the market achieves full employment of all resources, that is that under the functioning of the market mechanism all individual markets clear as envisaged by the Walrasian equilibrium. Even propositions about the advisability of 'more use of the market' being better, that is propositions comparing two 'sub-optimal situations' (in Walrasian terms), if they are presented as being unambiguously valid, must logically entail an acceptance of the Walrasian stylization. In short, the advocates of structural adjustment have been using Walrasian equilibrium, without always knowing it,[3] in which case it follows from the inadequacy of the Walrasian equilibrium as a stylization of reality that the theory underlying structural adjustment is misleading.

To establish my point that structural adjustment does indeed rely on a Walrasian equilibrium, and is for that reason flawed, I give two illustrations. The first relates to the much-used concept of 'efficiency':[4]

- In any period, and we shall confine attention here only to the single period, 'efficiency' can be unambiguously and unexceptionably defined as follows. If on the basis of the same endowment of resources available for use, one activity bundle gives a larger vector of final goods than another activity bundle, then the first is more 'efficient' than the second.

This definition which is in terms of the *production outcome* is supposed to be achieved through a certain instrumentality which itself is therefore sometimes used as a second definition of 'efficiency'. This second definition can be seen as follows:

- Consider any actual position of production characterized by an activity-set. One can think of marginal rates of transformation/substitution of inputs into outputs, of outputs into outputs and of inputs into inputs associated with this activity-set. Now, if there exists some activity outside of this set whose inclusion at the expense of some activity inside the set 'improves' these rates of transformation/substitution, in the sense that one more unit of any input either gives more extra output in the alternative set than currently or saves more of some other input than currently, or that one more unit of any output necessitates a lower fall in some other output than currently, then the use of this alternative set instead of the current one entails an improvement in 'efficiency'.

This second proposition above can be stated in a different way: associated with any activity set is a set of implicit prices (whose ratios are nothing else but these rates of transformation/ substitution we have been talking about). If at these prices some other activity-set, formed by replacing a current activity by an activity outside the set, yields a profit, then a move to this set represents an improvement of 'efficiency'.

Now, these two definitions of 'efficiency' which are usually taken to be identical are not identical. The view that the market promotes 'efficiency', or that 'trade is efficient production', is based on the belief that the two definitions are identical: the market of course palpably promotes efficiency in the second sense, but this second sense is meaningful only as an instrument for achieving efficiency in the first, real sense. Thus if the two are not identical, then that makes the 'efficiency' argument in favour of the market untenable. And the lack of identity between the two arises because of the fact that greater recourse to trade *does not leave the level of employment*, that is the level of resource use, *unaffected*. In other words if the market while trying to promote, supposedly, the efficiency of resource use, actually makes resources unemployed, then by any objective criterion, such as our first unexceptionable definition of efficiency, it reduces, not promotes, efficiency. Those who believe in the proposition that the market promotes efficiency must *ipso facto* believe that unemployment, whether of the Keynesian or of the classical (Marxian) variety, does not occur, that is, the operation of the market ensures full employment exactly as in a Walrasian equilibrium. It follows that the proponents of structural adjustment who argue that the market would improve the efficiency of resource use must believe in the reality of the Walrasian equilibrium.

The second illustration relates to the effect of the so-called 'rent-seeking' activities (Krueger, 1974), and, more generally, of the 'directly unproductive expenditures' that Professor Bhagwati refers to. These, which it is taken for granted constitute an unmitigated evil, could well be instrumental in keeping the level of employment higher than it would otherwise have been if the system were demand-constrained (Ghosh, 1995). Certainly, it is better to achieve the same injection of demand through other, more 'productive', means than through unproductive expenditure; for example, if the resources devoted to unproductive expenditures could be used for investment, the economy would be much better off. But this is not the same as saying that the elimination of directly unproductive expenditures is *per se* an unmixed blessing. In fact if the system is demand-constrained, then, since a reduction in unproductive expenditures would not automatically lead to an increase in investment or in other worthwhile expenditure, there would be a reduction in the level of activity and employment through the multiplier. This may even have the effect of lowering the level of investment subsequently through the accelerator, so that far from stimulating growth the reduction in unproductive expenditures could have precisely the opposite effect. Indeed, Baran and Sweezy (1966) have shown how 'wasteful expenditure' of various kinds had played the role of boosting the level of employment, activity and investment in postwar American capitalism.

Moreover, even if the system is not demand-constrained to start with, if the elimination of unproductive expenditures would make it demand-constrained, then such elimination *per se* would lack justification. Those who argue that unproductive expenditures are unambiguously harmful for the economy under all circumstances and argue for a removal of *dirigisme* on this ground, must therefore believe that the introduction of more or less free markets would eliminate unproductive expenditures without there being any drop in employment and activity. They must, in other words, believe in the spontaneous ability of the market to eliminate deficiency of aggregate demand. This is tantamount to a belief in Walrasian equilibrium.

So far I have argued that the theory underlying structural adjustment, which assumes the spontaneous tendency of the market to eliminate involuntary unemployment, whether of the Keynesian or of the classical (Marxian) kind, is necessarily based on the belief that the Walrasian equilibrium is an adequate representation of the world. Since, for reasons discussed, it is not, the programme of structural adjustment lacks theoretical validity. I shall now try to show that its introduction in a third-world economy may even be pernicious. I propose a simple model which in my view gives a better stylization of the reality of third-world economies than the Walrasian one. The equilibrium we refer to is a heterodox one which recognizes involuntary unemployment.

3 A simple model

Consider an economy with just two sectors 'food' and 'manufacturing' where 'food' output is given in the short run (one of the specificities of agriculture which yields the bulk of food) but 'manufacturing' output is a function of labour alone with diminishing marginal productivity, since the equipment stock is given. (One can think in terms of a vintage model to make the story more credible, but the purpose of using the production function approach is precisely to remain as far as possible within the neoclassical paradigm).

Workers spend their entire wages on the consumption of 'food' while 'manufacturing' output is used for capitalists' consumption, government consumption and investment. The real wage rate of the workers is given, that is, their money wage rate is such as to give them some 'subsistence' amount of 'food' at the prevailing food price. We can express this through the following equations:

$$O_f = \bar{O}_f \tag{1}$$

$$O_m = g(L_m),\ g' > 0,\ g'' < 0 \tag{2}$$

$$p_f \bar{w} = p_m g' \tag{3}$$

where O denotes output, L employment, p price, $\bar{w}$ in equation (3) the (fixed) real wage, and subscripts f and m the corresponding sectors. The equations are self-explanatory.

Food is the export commodity (the general case of primary commodity exports will be discussed later), the magnitude of exports being fixed by the government through export quotas. The manufactured good is imported, the magnitude of imports being given by the excess of domestic absorption over production. The world prices of the two commodities are given and unaffected by the country's actions ('price-taker' assumption). The domestic prices (at the given price of foreign exchange) are different from these world prices, higher for the manufacturing sector and lower for the food sector. The difference between the world price of food and its domestic price is sustained through quantitative restrictions on food exports, and the difference between the world manufactured good price and the domestic price is mopped up by an import tariff. We thus have:

$$O_f - X = \bar{w}(L_f + L_m) \tag{4}$$

$$L_f = L(O_f) \ldots L' > 0 \tag{5}$$

$$p_m = \bar{p}_m e(1 + \tau) \tag{6}$$

$$M = D_m - O_m \tag{7}$$

where D_m denotes the quantity of the manufactured good demanded (and actually absorbed), e the price of foreign exchange, and τ the tariff rate; X the quantity of food exported; M the quantity of manufactured goods imported, and $\bar{p}$ the world price with subscripts denoting the commodities. All other symbols are self-explanatory. Now D_m, the magnitude of the manufactured good domestically absorbed depends on the demand of the government and of the capitalists operating domestically. We assume that the government's total demand is its current and investment expenditure which are given in the short period (we ignore here the complications arising from the fact that private propensity to spend out of government transfers such as interest payments may be less than unity). The government's fiscal deficit is simply the difference between this total expenditure and its revenue. This revenue consists of import tariff revenue and other (tax and non-tax) revenue which is some fixed proportion of the total surplus of the manufacturing sector (we avoid in this way, for the sake of simplicity, the need to draw any distinction between public and private sector enterprises). The investment by the capitalists of both sectors is given; the consumption of the 'manufacturing' capitalists is a fixed proportion of the manufacturing sector's surplus left over after the government has taken its share, and of the 'food' capitalists the same fixed proportion of their surplus (which is not taxed and which consists of export revenue[5] plus domestic sales proceeds minus the wage bill). On this basis we have:

$$D_m = G + I_g + I_p + cP(1 - t)/p_m + c[X \cdot \bar{p}_f \cdot e + (O_f - X - \bar{w}L_f)p_f]/p_m \tag{8}$$

$$p_m(G + I_g) = t \cdot P + \tau \bar{p}_m Me + D \tag{9}$$

$$P = p_m \cdot O_m - \bar{w}p_f L_m \tag{10}$$

$$F = X \cdot \bar{p}_f - M \cdot \bar{p}_m \tag{11}$$

where P denotes the manufacturing sector's surplus, t the proportion of it taken by the government, c the capitalists' propensity to consume, I_p their 'real' investment, I_g 'real' government investment, G 'real' government expenditure, D the fiscal deficit, and F the trade deficit in foreign exchange terms. Given G, I_g, I_p, τ, e, t and X (and parameters such as the world prices, the subsistence wage and the capitalists' propensity to consume) these 11 equations determine the 11 variables: $O_f, O_m, L_m, L_f, p_m, D_m, p_f$, M, P, D and F.

The essential point of the above model is the following: the domestic price ratio between more 'food' and more 'manufacturing' is more unfavourable for 'food' than the international price ratio in equilibrium. In other words, more manufactured goods can be obtained per unit of food through trade than through domestic production. But if the country does export food and import manufacturing, then there would be a net contraction of total domestic output and employment, a net reduction of per capita food availability and an unambiguous increase in poverty, for both these reasons, in the short run.

We now need to consider what happens *over time*, but before doing so let us establish the above propositions, by looking at the effects of 'stabilization' in such an economy.

4 The effects of 'stabilization'

Suppose in the above model, which can be seen as a simple representation of a *dirigiste* economy, there are insufficient capital inflows (including a possible running down of reserves) to finance F. The economy can pursue 'stabilization' through alternative routes. One would be to reduce its fiscal deficit through higher taxation of the surplus P or by widening the tax net to cover the agricultural capitalists, supplemented by some reduction in non-investment, non-welfare expenditure. The reduction in aggregate demand here would show itself in terms of a reduction in the fiscal deficit which occurs *via* a reduction in the current deficit of the government.

On the other hand, if the government is unwilling to raise a larger tax revenue, it might simply reduce government expenditure, and such a reduction if it is to carry the entire burden of 'stabilization' is likely to affect expenditure of all descriptions including investment and welfare expenditure. In this case the fiscal deficit would have been cut, but not necessarily through a cut in the current deficit alone. Both these routes are through a reduction in aggregate demand. But 'stabilization' associated with structural adjustment not only frowns on higher tax rates on the capitalists, but insists on bringing the domestic prices into closer alignment with world prices through the removal of export restrictions on 'food' and through a reduction in the tariff rate.

Now, let us denote the inter-sectoral terms of trade in the domestic market (that is p_m/p_f) by T, and in the world market (that is $\bar{p}_m/\bar{p}_f$) by R. It follows that:

$$T/R = (e \cdot \bar{p}_f/p_f)(1 + \tau)$$

To start with, since the tariff rate is positive and export restrictions keep the domestic food price below the world food price, T/R exceeds unity. But as the tariff rate is lowered and export restrictions are removed, T moves closer to R, that is it gets reduced. And this happens no matter what changes occur in the exchange rate. 'Structural adjustment' in other words invariably lowers T. Since from equation (3) it follows that in equilibrium:

$$\bar{w}/T = g' \dots \tag{12}$$

a lowering of T raises g', that is, reduces employment and output in 'manufacturing'. Since output and employment in the 'food' sector are given in this period, the overall output and employment are reduced by following 'stabilization-cum-structural adjustment'.

5 Intersectoral terms of trade and investment behaviour

It may be thought that even if this is true in the short period, matters would get rectified *over time* since investment would flow into the 'food' sector. Or, looking at it differently, as the domestic terms of trade are narrowed to come closer to the international terms of trade, while the 'manufacturing' sector would shrink in the face of competition from imports, the 'food' sector would expand to take advantage of the world market. This may not happen immediately in the single period in question but would certainly happen over time, as comparative advantage theory predicts.

What this argument misses is again the specificity of the act of investment. What governs investment differs from sector to sector. And food production has its own *sui generis* determinant of private investment. Here, while a certain minimum profitability constitutes a condition for investment, once this is ensured, raising profitability further does not have any positive effect on private investment (Mitra, 1977). What private investment depends on (once the minimum profitability is ensured) is the availability of complementary public investment in the form for example, of infrastructure, irrigation, extension and so on.[6] To say this is not to assert some unique relationship between public and private investment – since how much of private investment is stimulated would depend on a host of additional factors including land relations and the available technology. Nor can one deny the very significant time-lags that may elapse before a certain provision of public investment calls forth any response in the form of larger private investment. All that is being argued is that a mere increase in profitability, beyond the threshold level, does not *per se* lead to larger private investment.

Since structural adjustment entails a reduction in the role of the state as an investor, the resource crisis facing the state in such a regime, on account of the predilection for lower taxes, higher interest rates and reduced fiscal deficits (all dictated by the need to maintain 'investors' confidence') results inevitably in the curtailment of its investment, and the overall growth in food production remains constrained. In other words, even over time our 'food' sector does not necessarily grow at a rate higher than that which the economy would have experienced if it had been stabilized in a different way, as suggested above, without being drawn into structural adjustment. Hence, if structural adjustment in the short run entails an output and employment loss, and in the long run does not necessarily give any higher growth than would have happened on an alternative non-structural adjustment path, then clearly structural adjustment should be shunned in favour of an alternative path.[7]

6 The general case of primary commodity exports

Even when 'food' exports as such are insignificant, the relevance of the above argument remains. This is because as long as 'food' and non-food export crops compete for land, a shift of land use towards the latter associated with larger exports reduces *ceteris paribus* the 'food' availability in the economy exactly as in the above model. In other words, instead of 'food' being directly exported, structural adjustment which entails a reduction in T may have the effect of pushing up the exports of commodities that, from the production point of view, are substitutes for 'food', through a diversion of land use away from 'food'. It would simultaneously, however, cause a reduction in 'manufacturing' output ('de-industrialization') which makes this shift away from 'food' production at the prevailing real wages possible.

We mentioned above that the short-run decline in per capita food availability resulting from structural adjustment is not necessarily followed by a higher investment profile in food production, which would entail in the long run a higher employment profile than could have been sustained otherwise, because of the complementarity between public and private investment in food production. Once we consider non-food export crops, then, taking agricultural production as a whole, this complementarity may become less pronounced (as many have noticed in the Indian context of late), but that still makes no difference to the argument presented above, unless it can be shown that higher private investment in non-food production can somehow raise the profile of food availability, which is a far-fetched suggestion.

On the other hand, the spectre of an economy engaged in the export of non-food crops witnessing, as a consequence of the growth of such crops, a shift of acreage from food production of an order which entails a substantial absolute decline in per capita food availability, is by no means far-fetched. It is what characterized colonial India during the first five decades of this century. Blyn (1966) noted that between 1897 and 1947 cash crop production grew at an annual average rate of 1.3 per cent in 'British India' while food crop production grew at 0.11 per cent. Per capita food production declined by about 25 per cent between the turn of the century and 1947, and by over 28 per cent between the peak reached around the First World War and independence. For 'Greater Bengal' this figure was 38 per cent. Similarly, in the 1990s there are unmistakable signs of an acreage shift in India from food-grains to export-crop production, which, together with declining government capital formation in agriculture, underlies the slowdown in the growth of food-grain production. Even Government of India (1997) official publications have shown concern over these developments. These are some of the stylized facts underlying the above model.[8]

7 The vortex of speculative finance

There is a further major problem with structural adjustment, which arises from the capital account of the balance of payments. From equation (12) it is clear that the effect of the exchange rate on the overall level of activity of the economy is exercised through changes either in T or in the 'subsistence wage'. If T is kept constant, and in any case there is a fixed T equal to R which the economy would attain if it were fully 'opened up', then the only way that the exchange rate could make any difference to the real economy is by depressing real wages below the 'subsistence' level. If this cannot happen, which is our assumption here, then it cannot have any real effect. It follows that balance of payments problems would be handled essentially by varying the domestic level of activity. Now so far we have assumed that the only reason for adjustment is an unsustainable trade deficit, but structural adjustment opens the economy up to capital inflows including movements of speculative finance. These movements have an asymmetric effect in the following way.

When such short-term funds come in, they add to the country's reserves (we assume that the government is sensible enough to prevent an exchange rate appreciation that would gratuitously de-industrialize the economy and enlarge its current account deficit to accommodate capital inflows without adding to reserves). These additional reserves, however, cannot be used for productive purposes for at least two reasons: first, if capital formation is stepped up on the basis of short-term capital inflow, then the country is 'borrowing short to invest long' which exposes it to extreme illiquidity risks; second, even for doing this there has to be an agency. Since private investment is not undertaken simply because there are larger reserves (unless it was credit-rationed to start with, which is unrealistic, or unless the interest rate is lowered, which however the government would be loath to do for fear of triggering off capital flight), the only agency capable of responding to accumulated reserves through stepping up investment is the government. But structural adjustment discourages the role of the government as an investor (and in any case the larger fiscal deficit through which government investment is to be financed if it is to deplete reserves would frighten speculators and be opposed by the IMF). The upshot is that accumulating reserves on the basis of short-term capital inflows are of no help in stepping up productive investment.

On the other hand, when short-term funds flow out for whatever reason, the outflow cannot be met merely by running down reserves; the real economy inevitably gets affected. There are two reasons for this: first, if reserve depletion has been undertaken earlier to stimulate domestic luxury consumption, by credit financing of liberalized consumer goods imports (and consumption is more likely to have been credit-rationed than investment), then the sheer amount left over for meeting capital flight would be less. Second, exchange rate expectations are likely to turn elastic in such a situation, with an initial outflow giving rise to a torrent until some palpable measures for 'boosting confidence' are undertaken. And these typically take the form of deflation affecting real economic performance.

In short, while the inflow of short-term funds does not stimulate output, employment or investment in the economy, the outflow of short-term funds does lead to a contraction in these. What is more, the very fear of outflow in an economy that is open to the movement of short-term funds encourages a tendency towards the pursuit of contractionary policies with regard to the real sectors as a means of retaining the confidence of speculators in the domestic economy. Openness to movements of finance capital therefore has a dampening effect on growth even though such openness is advocated as being growth-stimulating via enhanced DFI inflows. While direct foreign investment (DFI) inflows for locating production domestically and meeting the international market[9] tend to be niggardly, the economy gets caught in the vortex of speculative finance to its detriment.

8 Concluding observations

Once we abandon the Walrasian stylization of the economic universe and reckon with the facts of rigid prices, of unemployment, of elastic expectations, of the structural constraints on resource movements from one sector to another which show themselves as specificities of investment behaviour, we have to work in terms of a heterodox concept of equilibrium. Both classical and Marxian economics as well as Keynesian economics operated in terms of such concepts. The point is not simply to take over one such concept but to set up a *sui generis* stylization of a heterodox kind which is more appropriate. And if we do so, then the detrimental consequences of structural adjustment emerge in bold relief.

Notes

1 According to Grandmont (1982) something akin to inelasticity of price expectations in commodity markets is necessary even for ensuring that there is a non-zero value of money as a form of holding wealth.

2 Frank Hahn (1984) has pointed out that monetarism, which incidentally is a component part of the theory of structural adjustment, is based on the belief that the real world corresponds to a Walrasian equilibrium.

3 Professor Jagdish Bhagwati in a recent interview in a popular Indian magazine accused the early Indian planners of committing the fallacy of believing that because the market is not perfect it does not work. Since the proof that the market can work is given only for the case where it is perfect (and that too under

exceedingly stringent assumptions), it would appear that the planners were right and Professor Bhagwati's argument is a *non sequitur.* In fact to argue from the proposition that the market works when it is perfect, the conclusion that it also works (more or less) even when it is not perfect, is rather like arguing from Voltaire's famous remark that 'you can always kill a person through incantations – plus a little poison' the conclusion that 'you can at least maim a person through incantations alone'.

4 The discussion which follows is based on Patnaik (1997).

5 Throughout this chapter, for simplicity we ignore freight charges.

6 The connection between irrigation and agricultural growth across regions in the pre-independence period in India is discussed in Bagchi (1976). For the post-independence period a similar argument is made by Rao (1971).

7 It may of course be argued that in a liberalized economy exports of manufactures would pick up and could even be the engine of growth. The counter-arguments to this are well-known and need not be repeated here. We would, however, have made some progress if it is at least conceded that exports of 'food', and, by implication primary commodities (see next section), *cannot* be the engine of growth.

8 For evidence on this question relating to Africa and India see U. Patnaik (1996).

9 This is the DFI that is clearly beneficial for the economy, since displacement of already-occurring exports is extremely unlikely. By contrast, DFI oriented towards the home market is likely to displace already-existing home producers with lower import content of production which has a contractionary effect on the domestic economy.

References

Arrow, K. J. and M. D. Intrilligator (1982) (eds) *Handbook of Mathematical Economics*, vol. 2 (Amsterdam: North Holland).

Bagchi, A. K. (1976) 'Reflections on Patterns of Regional Growth in India during the Period of British Rule', *Bengal Past and Present*, January–June.

Baran, P. A. and P. M. Sweezy (1966) *Monopoly Capital* (New York: MR Press).

Blyn, G. (1966) *Agricultural Trends in India 1891–1947* (Philadelphia, PA: University of Pennsylvania Press).

Ghosh, J. (1995) 'State Intervention in the Macroeconomy', in P. Patnaik (ed.), *Macro-economics* (Delhi: Oxford University Press).

Goodwin, R. M. (1967) 'A Growth Cycle', in C.H. Feinstein (ed.), *Socialism, Capitalism and Economic Growth* (Cambridge: Cambridge University Press).

Government of India (1997) *The Economic Survey 1996–97*, Ministry of Finance, New Delhi.

Grandmont, J. M. (1982) 'Temporary Equilibrium Theory', in K.J. Arrow and M.D. Intrilligator (eds), *Handbook of Mathematical Economics*, vol. 2 (Amsterdam: North Holland).

Hahn, F. H. (1984) *Equilibrium and Macroeconomics* (Oxford: Clarendon Press).

Kaldor, N. (1978) *Further Essays on Economic Theory* (London: Duckworth).

Kalecki, M. (1967) *Studies in the Theory of Business Cycles 1933–39* (Oxford: Blackwell).

Keynes, J. M. (1936) *The General Theory of Employment, Interest and Money* (London: Macmillan).

Krueger, A. (1974) 'The Political Economy of Rent-Seeking Socities', *American Economic Review*, vol. 64, no. 3.

Malinvaud, M. (1977) *The Theory of Unemployment Reconsidered* (Oxford: Blackwell).

Mitra, A (1977) *Terms of Trade and Class Relations* (Ilford: Frank Cass).

Mukherji, A. (1990) *Walrasian and Non-Walrasian Equilibria* (Oxford: Clarendon Press).
Patnaik, P. (ed.) (1995) *Macroeconomics* (Delhi: Oxford University Press).
Patnaik, P. (1997) 'On the Concept of Efficiency', *Economic and Political Weekly*, 25 October.
Patnaik, U. (1996) 'Export-Oriented Agriculture and Food Security in Developing Countries and in India', *Economic and Political Weekly* (special issue).
Rao, S. K. (1971) *Inter-Regional Variations in the Growth of Agriculture and Population in India 1951–1968*, unpublished PhD thesis, University of Cambridge, UK.

8

Capital Surges, Investment Instability and Income Distribution after Financial Liberalization

E. V. K. FitzGerald[*]
Queen Elizabeth House, Oxford

1 Introduction

The benefits to developing economies of their comparatively recent integration to international capital markets are clearly substantial: access to international savings allowing the rate of investment (and thus industrial progress and income growth) to be raised; the ability to dampen exogenous shocks by borrowing abroad; and efficiency gains from the transfers of competitive technology and financial skills by foreign banks. Nonetheless, there is increasing concern as to the destabilizing effect of short-term capital flows after financial liberalization, which can bring about sudden shifts in real exchange rates, domestic interest rates, asset values and domestic credit levels. National authorities are frequently forced to undertake large shifts in fiscal and monetary policy in order to offset such shocks, while international institutions become even further involved in policy conditionality and last-resort lending.

This concern about the impact of short-term capital movements clearly goes beyond the traditional concerns with systemic risk in the financial system arising from the differing maturity of assets and liabilities and the consequences of uncertain expectations being transmitted from one institution or market to others ('contagion'). It is often implied that the 'real economy' – that is production, investment, wages, social services and so on – is in some way negatively affected by these flows, but the transmission mechanisms involved are not fully specified. The stabilization policies recommended by the IMF under such circumstances are mainly based on fiscal retrenchment, high real interest rates and severe credit restrictions.

* The research of this chapter was supported by the MacArthur Foundation. I would like to thank Stephany Griffith-Jones and Rodrigo Cubero-Brealey for useful comments.

These measures are aimed at stabilizing the exchange rate and strengthening the foreign currency reserves of the central bank, but may well also have the effect of weakening the real economy. Again, the transmission mechanisms do not appear to be fully appreciated by policy-makers.

The design of institutional reform and macroeconomic policy required to reduce this instability is hotly debated, but not the economic consequences of the instability itself. However, unless these consequences are fully understood it is difficult to see how an appropriate policy might be designed. The purpose of this chapter is thus to explore these 'real effects' in greater depth.

The chapter opens (section 2) with a discussion of the macroeconomic consequences of short-term capital-flow instability arising from changes in investors' planned holdings of liquid assets in the face of uncertainty. The transmission mechanism towards the real economy consists of two elements: the price effect though variables such as the interest rate and the real exchange rate; and the volume effect through changes in bank deposits and government bonds sales. Section 3 examines the impact of short-term capital inflows and outflows on fiscal behaviour, demonstrating that the shifts in the primary budget deficit consistent with solvency can shift dramatically with investor sentiment, forcing large fluctuations in public investment expenditure. The impact of these capital surges on firms through the availability of bank credit is analysed in section 4, where it is shown that the impact on output and investment is not only considerable, but also asymmetric. This then creates financial vulnerability in domestic firms and has serious consequences not only for employment but also for long-term private investment as this is particularly sensitive to uncertainty. In section 5 the effect of these capital flows on employment and the real wage rate is shown to be transmitted through the fluctuations in the real exchange rate and aggregate output. However, the relative adjustment of employment and wages depends upon the macroeconomic stance adopted by the government in its attempts to restore monetary stability. Section 6 concludes with some tentative implications of the analytical results for national and international policy-makers concerned with mitigating the negative effects of short-term capital flows.

2 Capital market stability in open developing economies

'Short term capital flows' take a wide variety of forms: in this chapter they are assumed to include the purchases (or sales) by non-residents (including foreign banks) of corporate equities and government bonds on local capital markets, and their deposit (or withdrawal) of funds in or credits to domestic banks, with maturities of less than one year. This working definition could easily be extended to include changes in the net position of residents in foreign assets ('capital flight') without analytical difficulty, but this reduced definition makes the exposition clearer.

While resident financial investors evidently behave differently from non-residents, much of this difference arises from their respective portfolio compositions – resident investors have a much greater weighting of local assets ('home bias') – which leads to a different response to sovereign risk (Hallwood and MacDonald, 1994). Access to information and control over investment outcomes also seems to differ between residents and non-residents, although here the distinction may well be between large and small investors rather than their location. Moreover, as the result of decades of overseas asset acquisition by domestic wealth-holders ('capital flight') not only do their portfolios have a large foreign-exchange denominated component, but also much of what appears to be 'foreign' portfolio investment inflows is often in fact the reduction of external asset positions by domestic investors ('repatriation of flight capital').

Finally, annual fluctuations in flows conventionally regarded as 'long-term' such as foreign direct investment (FDI) and sovereign debt issues may also reflect short-term liquidity considerations. However, they are not considered here because the *stock* of such capital cannot be sold by non-residents to residents through the domestic capital market in the short run and thus the same destabilizing consequences for the domestic economy do not occur.

These fluctuations in short-term portfolio flows cannot sensibly be considered 'perverse'. Indeed the very attraction of these assets to non-resident investors is precisely their *liquidity*. This means that uncertainty as to future asset values can to some extent be controlled by the ability to dispose of these assets quickly to a local market-maker such as a commercial bank or the government treasury itself. In contrast, international banks involved in long-term government loans attempt to reduce uncertainty by inter-bank syndication, better information through their local branches and – in the last resort – by obtaining support from international financial institutions; because this debt is not traded locally. Again, a foreign corporation engaged in FDI can only reduce uncertainty about the future value of its assets in the local economy by direct participation in management and, again in the last resort, by appeals to international legal arrangements. In the absence of efficient insurance markets, liquidity thus becomes the best means of hedging against uncertainty.

High-risk emerging market assets with high returns have a positive attraction for global portfolio investors because the riskiness of their overall portfolio is considerably reduced by the low covariance between regional markets; but this does not prevent fund managers from switching frequently between markets in attempt to maximize short-term profitability. Although capital movements towards 'emerging markets' should depend upon 'fundamental valuation efficiency' on the part of international portfolio managers in assessing future income streams, in practice this is very difficult and relies to a great extent on observing the behaviour of other investors, so that misallocation, as Tobin (1984) notes, is widespread and sudden corrections are frequent.

The volatility of portfolio flows thus cannot be attributed to investor irrationality or even to 'speculation', except in the technical sense of international or intertemporal arbitrage (Hirschliefer and Riley, 1992). Rather it is the scale of these flows in relation to the size of the domestic capital market – in terms of both the proportion of the domestic capital stock that is effectively 'on the market' and the size of the local market in relation to the international market in which the non-resident investors operate – and the high covariance between asset prices within a given developing economy or even region, which renders them problematic. Further, since asset values themselves are the result of investor behaviour, the volatility of their investment decisions reflects the lack of coordination.

In this chapter the *changes* in the short-term asset holdings of non-residents are considered to be exogenous to fluctuations in the real economy – output, investment, employment and wages. It is widely agreed that the larger part of the fluctuations in short-term capital flows to any one developing country are caused by changes in global capital markets (IMF, 1997). As Stiglitz and Weiss (1992) note financial markets, particularly in developing countries, are supply-constrained so that they are in stable disequilibrium with adjustments determined by creditors rather than debtors because demand is, in effect, infinitely elastic at the equilibrium interest rate. In consequence, changes in the asset-demand pattern (reflecting international portfolio composition) of non-resident investors, rather than the supply of liabilities by residents, can be taken as the immediate cause of short-term capital flows.

The conventional view of the effect of capital flows in the policy literature derives from the presumed mechanics of the 'debt cycle'. External savings (that is, the acquisition of domestic financial assets by non-residents) raise domestic fixed capital formation and provide foreign exchange, and thus potential output expands. Subsequently, domestic saving rises too, which eventually permits the debt to be repaid through an increased domestic surplus available to the debtor through increased tax yields (if public) or company profits (if private). Simultaneously, the excess of new saving over new investment should be reflected in an increased surplus (or reduced deficit) on the current account of the balance of payments, which provides the foreign exchange required to complete the cycle.

These relationships are reflected in the 'accumulation balance' – the national accounting identity which relates the savings of the public sector (S_g) and the private sector (S_p) and investment in the two sectors (I_g, I_p) on the one hand, and the changes in the short-term asset position of non-residents (A), long-term external debt and foreign investment stocks (H) and the level of reserves (R) on the other – which must hold *ex-post* at all times:

$$(I_g - S_g) + (I_p - S_p) \equiv \Delta A + \Delta H - \Delta R \quad (1)$$

Public saving depends on fiscal revenue (T) and current expenditure (G), while private savings are disposable income ($Y - T$) less consumption (C) so we have

$$(I_g + G - T) + (I_p + C - Y + T) \equiv M - X \equiv \Delta A + \Delta H - \Delta R \quad (2)$$

Thus if short-term liabilities (A) rise *ex-ante* and the other capital account items (H, R) are given, then one of the left-hand variables must adjust *ex-post*: the key issue in evaluating the effect of short-term capital flows is to determine which variable or variables do adjust, and what the consequences of this adjustment are. However, if the central bank sterilizes the inflow (ΔR) this adjustment does not take place.

In effect, if the debt cycle is to end virtuously, this adjustment must involve increased rates of investment. Specifically: (1) capital inflows should increase investment rather than consumption ($dI/dA > dC/dA$); (2) the resulting investment should be efficient in the sense of leading to factor productivity growth ($dY/dA > 1$); (3) investment must be in tradeables to create the required trade surplus ($dX/dA > dM/dA$); (4) and marginal savings rates must exceed the average ($dS/dY > S/Y$).

This essentially optimistic picture has been modified by experience since private capital flows returned to developing countries in the early 1990s: the initial belief was that the virtuous circle could be guaranteed by eliminating the fiscal deficit (or at least the 'primary' deficit before interest payments) so as to prevent excess pressure on capital markets and the balance of payments. Subsequently, however, attention has been drawn to the need to strengthen the domestic financial system in order to prevent bank insolvency from poor asset management in the face of rising liquid liabilities. In addition, the danger is well-known of capital flows being skewed towards non-traded sectors through the so-called 'Dutch Disease' effect of exchange rate appreciation and speculative investment in sectors such as real estate. In either case, the foreign exchange subsequently required to service debt and repatriate dividends may not in fact be available and the debt cycle does not reach a virtuous conclusion.

Apart from the longer-term effects on saving and investment, capital inflows are generally regarded as being expansive in the sense of increasing domestic adsorption (Y), unless they are fully sterilized by increasing reserves (R). Thus the orthodox policy response to short-term capital flows is based on the need to maintain an external account target reflected in the maintenance of minimum and maximum reserves levels. For instance, in the IMF 'monetary programming model' set out in Khan and Ul Haque (1990), an autonomous inflow of capital will permit the government to relax monetary policy and increase growth; a subsequent outflow would lead to the opposite policy. However, this expansive process is not the same as an autonomous rise in government expenditure (or even an export-led boom) because a financial asset has been acquired from a domestic agent and much depends upon that domestic agent's consequent response – to consume, invest or acquire external assets in the case of private agents, or to spend, invest or reduce debt in the case of government. The different maturity of the assets and liabilities created in this process may also be crucial; a short-term deposit in a banking system may be converted into a medium-term loan to a firm, which acquires fixed capital. By the same token, a broad notion of the 'lifting of a foreign exchange constraint' as in the World Bank 'standard macroeconomic model' (*loc cit.*) does not seem very helpful unless we are considering an administered economy where the central bank assigns foreign exchange directly to producers. It is therefore necessary to define more clearly how more or cheaper imports affect the behaviour of governments, firms and households.

The conditions for a 'virtuous debt cycle' based on short-time flows have also been made more difficult due to the very financial liberalization that makes these flows possible. Unsterilized short-term capital inflows often lead to an unsustainable appreciation of the exchange rate, which prevents export promotion and generates an import boom, while the expansion of domestic credit tends to result in unsafe loans being made by banks at low rates of interest in the expectation of rapid growth in not only income but also asset prices. The subsequent outflow usually forces cutbacks in domestic adsorption to restore external balance, which lead in turn to a fall in current output levels to the extent that rigidities prevent resource reallocation, so that the contractionary disabsorption effects on non-traded sectors outweigh any expansionary substitution effects in traded sectors. The fragile banking system then often collapses under the pressure of bad debts and the fall of asset prices as interest rates rise and domestic activity declines (Rojas-Suarez and Weisbrod, 1994).

Financial deregulation can thus be regarded as a permanent shock to the banking sector which alters the environment in which the intermediation is carried out (Bachetta, 1992). Specifically, the lifting of regulations on asset portfolios and reserve ratios combined with privatization is designed to encourage better risk management and narrower margins, but may lead to excessive risk acquisition in the search for market share. Monetary policy becomes more difficult to implement as the behaviour of monetary variables becomes more volatile with the reduction in market segmentation and consequently increased elasticities of substitution between assets (Melitz and Bordes, 1991). The high real interest rates associated with financial liberalization can thus actually *increase* banking fragility.

As Minsky (1982) points out, a recession generally causes a deterioration in the asset quality of financial intermediaries due to bankruptcies in the real sector, although these problems are often seen as transitory by regulators reluctant to intervene in major institutions due to the risk of contagion.

Inflation and exchange rate instability has usually given large windfall profits to banks before liberalization; but lending skills (such as risk appraisal) are generally weak due to the previous experience of oligopolized credit markets. Banks cannot become efficient overnight as they have poor information on borrowers and depositors may believe banks to be more solvent than they really are. Real interest rates rise not because of an increase in real capital productivity but because of tight monetary policy and competition with domestic government bond issues. Regulators appear to underestimate the problems faced by an underdeveloped banking system with a weak domestic savings base; because high interest rates and rising asset prices attract foreign portfolio investors as well as generating large short-term profits and there are strong domestic pressures on regulators to permit the boom in asset values to continue. It takes a number of years for distress-lending to build up to the point where bad loans cannot be rolled over any more; during which time things seem to be going well and the reforms continue. The subsequent collapse of asset values becomes contagious, spreading from individual firms to entire sectors, and eventually affecting country-risk evaluations.

This experience underlines the fact that local capital markets do not clear according to textbook principles. The local interest rate does not perform the expected role of resource allocation for two fundamental reasons. On the one hand, capital market equilibrium is determined by quantity adjustment, due to the prevalence of asymetric information and agency problems, which require lenders to ration credit – and much the same is true of equity investors (Stiglitz and Weiss, 1992). On the other hand, financial intermediation involves the conversion of liquid into illiquid assets, and thus the assumption of risk which cannot be expressed in interest rates due to the adverse selection effect. In the face of incomplete financial markets – particularly for long-term assets – any large imbalance tends to be thrown onto the most liquid markets, those for quoted securities and foreign exchange.

Moreover, interest rates in small open economies exposed to the international capital market are not determined by the marginal productivity of capital or the intersection of the investment and savings schedules as textbook theory indicates. Rather the domestic interest rate (i) is determined by the international interest rate ($i_\$$), the expected depreciation of the exchange rate ($E_e - E$) and the country-risk proper (ρ):

$$i = i_\$ + (E_e - E)/E + \rho \tag{3}$$

Of these three terms, the first is clearly exogenous and fluctuates considerably in the short term; while the second depends not only on the current macroeconomic policy of the government but also on expected policy in the future and fluctuations in *other* currencies. The third term depends on foreign investors' perceptions of the country in the context of changing circumstances in the region and the world as a whole, and reflects the substitutibility of domestic and foreign assets (that is liquidity) as well as default risk proper. The domestic interest rate is thus a consequence of much the same domestic and external factors that determine short-term capital flows, rather than being a domestic capital market clearing mechanism as such.

In consequence, small open-market economies in general, and developing countries in particular, can be characterized as 'credit constrained' in the sense that firms require working capital in order to undertake production and that this is limited by banks' behaviour. Blinder (1987) sets out a complete exposition of a model of a credit-constrained economy where supply is constrained by an asymmetric-information type of bank-lending behaviour, which creates a category of 'effective supply'. Another approach to asymmetric shocks transmitted through the credit system – based on interest rate spreads rather than credit rationing – which produces similar results is suggested by Edwards and Vegh (1997). Interest rate changes are considered as essentially exogenous, with the exchange rate as the main instrument of government macroeconomic policy. Portfolio flows are regarded as affecting the real economy through their effect on bank credit: the purchase of an existing security by a non-resident from a bank makes more credit available, while purchase from an individual has much the same effect when the proceeds are deposited in a bank account. If a *new* security is issued by a firm and purchased by a non-resident, this can be seen as reducing the firm's use of bank credit and thus releasing this resource for other uses. Similarly, purchases of new government securities by non-residents increase the resources available to the public sector.

3 The impact on government borrowing and public investment

The main direct impact of short-term capital flows on the fiscal balance is through the conditions on the government bond market: in particular the ability to maintain or increase the planned public sector borrowing requirement at reasonable rates of interest. Therefore, the impact of short-term capital inflows and outflows on fiscal behaviour is mainly felt through the local securities market, the creation and expansion of which has been one of the main features of financial liberalization. However, the impact is not so much through the interest rate itself as through market perception of fiscal solvency, which is in effect a form of credit rationing.

There are three other ways in which short-term capital flows can affect the budgetary balance indirectly. First, any variations in the exchange rate caused by capital flows will have an effect on the budget, although the direction and scale depends upon the currency composition of income and expenditure: normally the main effect will be through the cost of external debt service, so capital inflows causing appreciation improve the budget balance; although in the case of primary exporters where revenues are dollar-based such appreciation may even cause a deterioration. Second, fluctuations in the domestic interest rate accompanying capital inflows will also impact on the cost of debt service: in theory inflows should cause interest rates to fall (and thus reduce the budget deficit) but in practice as these inflows are closely associated with financial liberalization involving high real interest rates. To the extent that these inflows are sterilized by the monetary authorities, interest rates will also remain high. However, outflows will generally be accompanied by further increases in interest rates. Third, to the extent that monetary policy has become less effective due to the integration of capital markets, or confined to a single target such as price stability, fiscal policy will have an increased role in the maintenance of macroeconomic stability and countering external shocks. In the face of revenue inflexibility and large fixed commitments to wagebills, transfers and debt service, capital expenditure may become the only macroeconomic instrument available to do this.

Formally fiscal solvency can be said to exist when the discounted sum of future income (T) and expenditure (G) at some discount rate (i) is greater than or equal to the present debt – in other words, that debt can eventually be paid off, rather than rising explosively:

$$\sum_{t=0}^{\infty} \frac{T_t - G_t}{(1+i_t)^t} \geq D_0 \tag{4}$$

Conventionally, fiscal solvency models assume that fiscal revenue and expenditure are constant proportions of GNP (r, g), that there is a fiscal surplus ($r > g$) and that the growth of output y and interest rate i are fixed to an infinite time horizon ($i > y$), so that the solvency condition is simply reduced to a critical debt-output ratio z:

$$z_0 = \frac{D_0}{Y_0} \leq \frac{r-g}{i-y} \tag{5}$$

In practice, such parameter stability does not occur and fiscal consolidation tends to lie in an uncertain future. It is more realistic to regard governments (and bond purchasers) as targeting a particular debt to GNP ratio (z^*) which reflects their assessment of the prospects of fiscal consolidation (r, g), output growth (y) and capital market conditions (i) without perfect foresight. At best, this ratio should fall over time and at worst should not rise. The level of the primary (that is, before interest payments) fiscal deficit as a proportion of GNP (c), is given by the *accounting* definitions that link the debt level (D), GNP (Y), the rate of amortization of the debt (d) and the gross borrowing requirement (B)

$$
\begin{aligned}
D_t &= D_{t-1}(1-d) + B_t \\
B_t &= i_t \cdot D_{t-1} + dD_{t-1} - c_t Y_t \\
Y_t &= Y_{t-1}(1+y_t) \\
z_t &= \frac{D_t}{Y_t} = \frac{D_{t-1}}{Y_{t-1}} \cdot \frac{1+i_t}{1+y_t} - c_t \\
&\approx z_{t-1}(1+i_t-y_t) - c_t
\end{aligned} \tag{6}
$$

From this accounting balance the rule for the minimum level of the primary fiscal balance consistent with fiscal solvency is derived, based on the requirement that the debt ratio (z) does not rise over time beyond its target level – in other words, an equilibrium solution

$$
\begin{aligned}
z_1 &= z_0 = z^* \\
c_1 &= z^*(i_1 - y_1)
\end{aligned} \tag{7}
$$

The corresponding fiscal deficit (f^*) consistent with debt solvency is then found to be:

$$
\begin{aligned}
f^* &= c^* + i\,z^* \\
&= z^* y
\end{aligned} \tag{8}
$$

However, in the case of large short-term capital flows into (and out of) a developing country we are considering by definition *disequilibrium* situations. In general the debt ratio desired by the government is larger than that which international investors regard as sustainable (due perhaps to asymmetric information but more probably to distinct incentives) so that the government is in effect rationed by not being able to place sufficient bonds on the local capital market under acceptable conditions to fund the programmes it desires to undertake. The circumstances of the inflow of short-term capital are characterized by a marked change in market perceptions as to the sustainable public debt ratio (z^*) due to improved expectations for economic growth, exchange rates and country risk in the future. These expectations are often reinforced by the effects of public enterprise privatization, even though the revenue is rarely used to write off debt.

Consider the situation where, as a result of these changes, the (apparently) sustainable level of the debt ratio (z^*), rises sharply between the initial level in one period (0) and the next period (1), this ratio being maintained in the following period (2). In consequence, not only does the permitted fiscal deficit (f), rise, but in the 'transition' period (1) this deficit can be very large in order to adsorb the sudden change in the debt ratio (from z_a to z_b)

in addition to the increased growth rate (y_a to y_b) arising from the demand expansion:

$$\begin{aligned} f_0 &= z_a y_a \\ f_1 &= (z_b - z_a) + z_a y_b \\ f_2 &= z_b y_b \\ f_1 &\gg f_2 > f_0 \end{aligned} \tag{9}$$

In practical terms, the effect is large. For quite modest changes in the parameters (z^*, y), the acceptable (that is, 'compatible with public debt solvency') primary fiscal balance can shift suddenly from a conservative primary balance ($c = 0$) to several percentage points of GNP in the period of transition; but thereafter, with the debt ratio stabilized at its new value, the primary balance should return towards zero again.

However, once foreign investors see the macroeconomic result of their individual decisions, sentiment shifts back suddenly, probably even to a lower solvency ratio (z^*) than before the shock. In consequence, the market demands that the government achieve a large fiscal *surplus* (that is, the previous exercise in reverse) in order to finance the repayment of enough of the *existing* debt stock to reduce the debt ratio sharply. This would presumably be followed by a new equilibrium in the medium term, but meanwhile panic selling of government bonds sets in when the foreign-exchange reserves are insufficient to permit them to be cashed in and the proceeds repatriated.

The government is obliged to adjust the remaining fiscal variables in order to allow for the exogenous fluctuations in its borrowing capacity. Tax revenue is difficult for developing countries to adjust in the short run, and in practice it appears that public investment takes the main brunt of the shock. On the one hand, the traditional rule is that budgetary borrowing should only be used for capital expenditure (Heller, 1975), so that the current expenditure and revenue budget can be kept in balance. In consequence, any fluctuation in the primary deficit would be fully reflected in public investment expenditure. On the other hand, when borrowing capacity rises, it is always politically attractive for governments to initiate new projects to gather political support. When there is a need to reduce the deficit, it is always politically easier to postpone promised investment programmes rather than lay off teachers and nurses.

The consequences of these sharp fluctuations in public investment (even if the mean is stable over the longer term) are clearly negative, due to the inability of public services such as transport, health and education to maintain an effective development programme. This leads to losses in efficiency both when new projects are implemented without proper planning in order to take advantage of unanticipated resources while they are available, and when ongoing projects are delayed or frozen during construction. Furthermore, reductions in public investment due to lack of access to capital markets have a negative multiplier effect on private investment and thus on employment levels in the economy as a whole (FitzGerald and Mavrotas, 1997).

4 The impact on firms, output and private investment

Short-term capital flows clearly have a marked effect on credit availability, because the inflows directly affect the deposit base of the banking system. This can occur through direct deposits of funds or purchases of bank paper, through the deposit of the proceeds of equity sales to non-residents, through the reduction of government credit requirements due to bond sales to non-residents, and through the general relaxation of monetary policy which tends to accompany them. The reverse will be true with outflows, exacerbated by bad debt accumulating in banks' asset portfolios.

In developing economies (and indeed in most developed ones too) firms do not depend on securities markets directly for their long-term funding requirements; rather, they rely on retained profits for the bulk of their investment funds, and on bank finance for much of their working capital. In addition, the control of companies in developing countries is usually retained by families, groups or foreign corporations; so securities markets do not act as a medium for 'disciplining' management, because a controlling shareholding cannot be obtained through the open market. Of course the control of domestic corporations is not the objective of non-resident portfolio investors, or even the receipt of dividends – but rather capital gains on the resale of the securities as the aggregate market index rises. In consequence, the long-run effect of portfolio capital inflows on private sector fixed capital formation in LDCs has been found to be insignificant (FitzGerald, Jansen and Vos, 1994; FitzGerald and Mavrotas, 1997).

This also explains why equity markets in developing countries are so narrow and shallow – and thus oscillate widely in response to changes in foreign investor interest. As equity markets in developing countries do not represent a significant source of fresh investment capital as a way of improving firms' efficiency, it might appear to follow that equity market fluctuations would not have a great effect on firms' behaviour. Unfortunately this is not the case, because the aggregate *macroeconomic* effect of stock-market fluctuations on expected variations in external reserves and monetary policy is considerable.

Firms' responses to changes in short-term capital flows can be conveniently analysed through the effect of changes in bank credit to them as a result of changes in bank deposits by non-residents. Consider a representative firm with a capital structure (C) made up of variable capital (V) in the form of cash balances (for wages and so forth) and inventories, fixed capital (K) which defines company assets, and bank credit (N) and own equity capital (Z) as liabilities. The balance sheet is then composed as follows:

$$V + K = C = N + Z \tag{10}$$

The level of output (Q) at a given level of prices is directly related to the amount of variable capital (V) committed to production, which is in turn constrained by the level of fixed capital:

$$Q = aV \leq bK \tag{11}$$

The firm has a desired ratio (α) between variable and fixed capital when there is also full utilization of capacity ($Q = bK$) so that

$$K/V = \alpha = a/b \tag{12}$$

This ratio, we assume, corresponds to the point of maximum efficiency in the sense of maximizing the net present value of profits accuring to the firm (Sen, 1994), so the firm will attempt to adjust towards this capital structure in the long run. The firm also has a desired balance (β) between bank debt (N) and its 'own' capital (Z) made up of equity and reserves – which can only be increased out of retained profits (we ignore dividend payments an new equity issues for convenience), themselves a constant proportion (s) of net output (Q) less debt service ($i.N$):

$$Z = Z_{-1} + sQ - iN \tag{13}$$

The firm has a *demand* for bank credit, expressed as a gearing ratio between debt and equity, based on its optimal exposure to creditors which in principle depends on interest rates and tax patterns. However, in a credit-constrained economy the level of debt desired by the firm is not met so loan capital (N) is exogenously set by the banks on the basis of collateral available in the form of assets which can be resold by the creditor.

In effect, banks define the level of credit which they are willing to extend to firms in terms of a collateral ratio (n) of fixed assets (K):

$$N \leq nK \tag{14}$$

The banks' opinion as to the desirable collateral ratio (n) varies in two senses. On the one hand, it rises or falls according to the level of business confidence or threats to the banks' own solvency; on the other hand, it varies between firms of different sizes – small firms have lower ratios due to information asymmetry, while larger firms may benefit from direct ownership links with banks, or in the case of multinational firms with implicit collateral in the form of headquarters backing. We assume that banks renew credit in each period, so that they can reduce as well as increase firms' debt levels at will. In consequence, at the credit-constrained equilibrium, the firm thus has a liability structure determined by its own past saving and its exogenously determined borrowing capacity:

$$C = S + D = Z_{-1} + sQ + (1 - i)nK \tag{15}$$

In order to maximize profits in long-run equilibrium, the firm will adjust its output, and thus its asset structure, so that capacity is fully used:

$$C = V + K = \frac{Q}{a} + \frac{Q}{b} \tag{16}$$

The firm's continual adjustment of the balance between assets and liabilities yields the level of output (Q) as a function of the banks' collateral ratio (n):

$$Q = \frac{Z_{-1} + (1 - i)nK}{\frac{1}{a} + \frac{1}{b} - s} \tag{17}$$

Note that the level of output (Q) will depend not only positively on the level of bank debt (N) and thus the collateral ratio (n) but also negatively on the interest rate (i) as this affects net retained profits and thus the ability to finance production from the firm's own resources. These credit restrictions will in turn constrain the fixed assets of the firm (K) and the level of investment ($I = \partial K$); assuming that the (unspecified) desired output and fixed capital of the firm is always greater than that realised.

We are interested in the consequence of fluctuation in short-term capital flows, which produce similar fluctuations in bank credit levels (N). To do this we assume that the banks are lending less to firms than they would wish, otherwise greater foreign deposits will not lead to further lending to firms but rather to the accumulation of liquidity in banks:

$$N < nK \tag{18}$$

while we still assume that firms receive less credit than they would wish, so that they take up the offered funds.

An increase in the credit ratio ($\partial N > 0$) allows output to rise proportionately by providing resources for working capital, but as the firm is already at full capacity fixed assets will have to rise (that is, investment be undertaken) as well. Specifically:

$$\partial Q = \frac{(1 - i)}{\theta}\partial N; \quad \text{where} \quad \theta = \frac{1}{a} + \frac{1}{b} - s \tag{19}$$

New fixed investment (I) is determined by:

$$I = \partial K = \frac{(1-i)}{b\theta}\partial N \tag{20}$$

Finally, if we assume that increased short-term deposits of foreign capital in the banks (∂A) are all passed on to firms in the form of bank credit (net of the banks' reserve requirement, r) then we have:

$$\partial A > 0; \quad \partial Q = \frac{1}{\theta}(1-i)(1-r)\partial A; \quad I = \frac{(1-i)(1-r)}{b\theta}\partial A \tag{21}$$

Now, if bank deposits and thus credit to firms *falls* ($\partial D < 0$) by the same amount, the effect is not 'equal but opposite'. Investment decisions are irreversible (Dixit and Pindyck, 1994) – in other words, fixed assets once installed cannot easily be sold, especially on a declining market, so it is not possible to adjust the fixed capital stock downwards to achieve the new (credit-constrained) desired capital structure. Because K is fixed, *all* the downward adjustment must be undertaken by reducing working capital (V) and thus output (Q), so that:

$$\partial Q = \frac{(1-i)}{\phi}\partial V; \quad \text{where} \quad \phi = \frac{1}{a} - s < \theta \tag{22}$$

In other words, the downward movement of firms' output following a given outflow of short-term capital will be much larger than the upward movement in output following an inflow of the same size, while fixed investment is zero:

$$\partial A < 0; \quad \partial Q = \frac{1}{\phi}(1-i)(1-r)\partial A; \quad I = 0 \tag{23}$$

As a consequence, the greater variability of capital flows and bank credit around the mean, the lower will be the average output level. In other words, volatile capital flows reduce both output and investment.

Unless the short-term capital flows are fully sterilized, there is presumably a close correlation between capital flows and the domestic rate of interest: either because perceived risk declines (rises) and stimulates greater inflows (outflows) at a given international interest rate; or because the international interest rate falls (rises) and there are greater inflows (outflows) for a given risk. This correlation will reinforce the asymmetric effect on output and investment: the capital inflow will drive down the interest rate (i) and thus stimulate output (Q) and investment (I) even more due to the increase in resources available to the firm; vice-versa for capital outflows. The fluctuations in domestic output and investment will thus be even larger than in our simple model; in other words, *local capital markets will have a pro-cyclical effect rather than buffering external shocks.*

5 The impact on households, employment and wages

Households are affected by real macroeconomic shocks through the level of employment and wages on the one hand, and the availability of government services and bank credit (particularly for residential construction and consumer durables purchases) on the other. To a great extent, therefore, the impact of short-term capital flows on households will reflect the consequence of the response of the fiscal and firms sectors to external shock in the way described above. First, the negative effect of these flows on public investment stability, and thus on the effective provision of social infrastructure leads to a reduced supply of and effectiveness in health and education services, public transport systems and urban services. Second, is the asymmetric effect of these flows on the volatility of corporate output and thus on the level of current 'formal sector' employment and, through the level of investment, on longer-term employment. Third, the negative effect of these flows on capital market and exchange rate volatility, and thus on the level of private investment has long-term consequences for the level of sustainable employment and thus income distribution.

Overall, the most significant negative consequence on welfare is probably – as in the case of trade liberalization – felt through the long-term consequences for private investment, because this (rather than low wage rates or even labour skilling) is the main source of sustainable long-term employment (FitzGerald and Perosino, 1999). Nonetheless, the broader effect of capital flows on the real exchange rate is of considerable interest, because this affects the level of aggregate employment in the economy as a whole (including the small-scale sector) and the level of real wages through relative prices.

Consider an economy with a current account composed of exports (X), imports (M), interest (i) on external debt (D) and short-term assets (A); which is balanced by changes in short-term assets held by non-residents, changes in external debt and changes in reserves (R):

$$M + i(D + A) - X = CAB = \Delta D + \Delta A - \Delta R \tag{24}$$

As in the case of fiscal solvency, external debt solvency relates to the long-term ability to repay external debt; and from this a sustainable debt-to-GNP, or debt-to-exports, ratio can be derived (World Bank, 1997b). On exactly the same basis as our analysis of fiscal debt solvency set out in section 3 above, the level of current account deficit (b) as a proportion of GNP consistent with a stable external debt to GNP ratio (π) and a given GNP growth rate (y) is given by:

$$b^* = \pi y \tag{25}$$

Again, as in the case of the fiscal deficit, when asset demand constrains the international capital market a small change in the perceived creditworthiness of a particular country permits a large increase in the current account deficit that foreign investors will finance, but this is a transitory feature:

$$\begin{aligned} b_0 &= \pi_a y_a \\ b_1 &= (\pi_b - \pi_a) + \pi_a y_b \\ b_2 &= \pi_b y_b \end{aligned} \tag{26}$$

Therefore a relatively small shift in non-resident investors' view of creditworthiness (that is, π) generates a large current account deficit financed from short-term inflows during the transition period. This in turn permits an 'import boom' with imports rising considerably even though GNP growth rates have only risen slightly, if the authorities take no compensatory action. The mechanics of this boom often take the form of banks extending consumer credit backed by the short-term capital inflows, rather than extending it to companies as in our earlier model. This boom is not sustainable, however, and to remain consistent with market expectations of solvency the current account should be closed again in the subsequent period and imports should fall sharply again *even if the capital inflow is not reversed.*

In practice, halting an import-and-credit boom generated by short-term capital inflows is very difficult: partly for the technical reason that reducing credit levels to consumers implies rapid repayment of debt which cannot be achieved by selling the corresponding household assets (such as, houses or consumer durables); and partly for the political reason that the euphoric sense of economic success is difficult to abandon. In consequence, it is not surprising that the authorities seek to sustain the boom in the hope that *further* short-term capital inflows can be attracted. However, when foreign investors reach the conclusion that the deficit is unsustainable, the reverse process starts. Capital outflows require that the domestic economy generate a large *surplus* on the current account of the balance of payments; and when drastic reductions in domestic demand have caused widespread bankruptcy and household distress, to borrow heavily from international financial institutions in order to – in effect – acquire the domestic assets of non-resident investors.

The macroeconomic consequences depend on the policy response of the authorities to the capital inflow, whether to adjust the real exchange rate or the level of activity. Consider the situation where external trade is a function of the real exchange rate (e) and the demand (world output, W) for exports and domestic output (Y) for imports, respectively. So

$$M = m_1 Y + m_2 e; \quad X = x_1 W + x_2 e \tag{27}$$

Policy-makers can, in principle at least, achieve any current account balance (*CAB*) in response to an external capital flow; which then determines how much the reserves change (that is, how much of the inflow is sterilized) if long-term debt is taken as given:

$$\Delta R = CAB - \Delta A \tag{28}$$

The desired current account deficit can be attained by adjusting either the real exchange rate (e) or the level of domestic output (Y) – or both – by an appropriate monetary and fiscal stance in the familiar way. As we shall see, the employment and wage effect of short-term capital flows depends crucially on which stance is adopted.

Consider two scenarios. First, if output is held stable (conventionally by fiscal means) then

$$\frac{\partial e}{\partial A} = \frac{1}{-x_2 + m_2} < 0; \quad \frac{\partial Y}{\partial A} = 0 \tag{29}$$

Second, if the real exchange rate is held stable (conventionally by monetary means) then

$$\frac{\partial Y}{\partial A} = \frac{1}{m_1}; \quad \frac{\partial e}{\partial A} = 0 \tag{30}$$

In the case of a capital inflow, an active monetary policy would involve some domestic inflation in order to force up, that is, devalue, the real exchange rate and allow output to rise, which may well be politically unattractive. On the outflow of short capital, exactly the reverse situation should hold; but as nominal prices are more or less rigid downwards in practice, it is much more difficult to devalue the real exchange rate than to revalue it, so that a forced reduction in output (Y) is much more likely. In sum, an inflow followed by an equal outflow is likely to have an asymmetric character: the real exchange rate falling, that is, appreciating, with the inflow, and output falling on the outflow.

We can now go on to analyse the employment and wage effects of this cycle. In LDCs there is widespread unemployment and surplus labour held in the informal sector, so that employment can rise without inflationary consequences if output rises unconstrained by the balance of payments. The employment effect can thus be seen as the effect of the increase (or decrease) in aggregate demand if the real exchange rate (and thus real wages, as we shall see) is held steady. Consider an aggregate production function that has the familiar form:

$$Y = K^{\alpha}L^{\beta} \tag{31}$$

Then under these circumstances we can simply derive

$$\frac{\partial L}{\partial A} = \frac{\partial L}{\partial Y}\frac{\partial Y}{\partial A} = \frac{\beta}{m_1}\frac{L}{Y} > 0 \tag{32}$$

The impact on real wages is a little more complicated, but may be derived using the approach set out in Dornbusch (1980). The real exchange rate is defined in terms of the relationship between the nominal exchange rate (E), domestic prices (P) and world prices (P); and the real wage rate (w) as the ratio between the nominal wage rate (W) and domestic prices:

$$e = \frac{E_p}{P}; \quad w = \frac{W}{P} \tag{33}$$

World prices are of course exogenous, but domestic prices are formed by a markup (r) on costs composed of labour inputs (u) and imported inputs (m) so that:

$$P = (1 + r)(uW + mpE) \tag{34}$$

These three relationships yield a simple expression of the real wage in terms of the real exchange rate, where the higher (that is, more depreciated) the real exchange rate, the lower will be the real wage:

$$w = \frac{1}{u}[\frac{1}{1+r} - me] \tag{35}$$

In the case where output (Y) does not vary, we can derive a relationship between short-term capital flows and the real wage rate, where an inflow causes the real wage to rise and vice versa:

$$\frac{\partial w}{\partial A} = \frac{\partial w}{\partial e}\frac{\partial e}{\partial A} = (m_2 + x_2)\frac{m}{u} > 0 \tag{36}$$

This analysis of the response of the real exchange rate and aggregate demand to short-term capital inflows and outflows also reveals asymmetric implications for wages and employment. The real exchange rate had risen on the inflow. This is because real wages rise with the inflow, but employment remains the same; while with the outflow, real wages do not fall but employment declines. As a key problem of income distribution is the balance between the incomes of the employed and those of the un- (or under-) employed, fluctuations in external capital flows can be expected to have a negative effect on income distribution.

6 Conclusions: volatile capital flows, private investment and public policy

In this chapter the following general propositions have been established with respect to the impact of exogenous changes in short-term capital flows:

1. The main direct transmission effects on the real economy are through variations in credit available to firms and in the demand for government bonds; the main indirect effects are through variations in the real exchange rate and the level of economic activity;
2. The impact on the fiscal sector is mainly seen in sudden shifts in the perceived solvency of the public sector, and thus upon the level of debt believed by foreign investors to be sustainable; the effect of these fluctuations is felt in volatile levels of public investment, which reduce the efficiency of public provision of infrastructure and social services;
3. The impact on the firms sector is mainly through the supply of working capital, which generates asymmetric responses in terms of investment and output due to the impact on firms' balance sheets; the volatility of expected profits resulting from this has a strong depressive effect on private investment;
4. The impact on the household sector is the result of the employment and wage effects; these occur both directly through firms' responses to short-term capital flows, and as a result of the consequences of fiscal instability; and also indirectly through the effects of real exchange rate variations on real wages and aggregate employment levels.

Although financial liberalization and integration to international capital markets clearly have important longer-term implications for sustainable growth and income distribution (Dutt, 1995; FitzGerald, 1996), we have focused here on the short to medium term.

However, there is a further and potentially even greater consequence of volatile short-term capital flows for private investment, and thus for the growth of employment and productivity in the longer run. This is derived from the effect of this volatility on the expectations of firms about the profitability of investment through the impact of macroeconomic variables such as the real exchange rate as well as the credit conditions for the firm itself.

Most investment expenditures are largely irreversible – sunk costs that cannot be recovered if market conditions turn out to be worse than expected. In an open developing economy these conditions are as much the consequence of macroeconomic conditions as they are of the circumstances of a particular sector. As firms can delay investments until more information arrives, there exists an opportunity cost of investing now rather than waiting. In consequence, the value of a unit of investment must *exceed* the purchase and installation cost, by an amount equal to the value of keeping the investment option alive – which will increase with the level of uncertainty (Dixit and Pindyck, 1994). Increased uncertainty will reduce the level of private investment: for reasonable parameter values, a standard deviation as low as 20 per cent in annual profit expectations can generate an option value of twice the original investment cost – requiring a far higher expected rate of return in order to justify investment. In consequence, the literature on irreversible investment suggests that if the goal of macroeconomic policy is to stimulate investment (and thus growth), stability and credibility may be much more important than particular levels of taxes or interest rates (Pindyck and Solimano, 1993). What is more, policy reforms such as tax incentives designed to stimulate investment may themselves have very little effect if there is a probability that the policy will be reversed. These findings would apply *a fortiori* to short-term capital flows.

Moreover, firms are not in fact a homogeneous group in LDCs, and in practice react in quite different ways to similar macroeconomic shocks (FitzGerald, 1995). The affiliates of multinational corporations will not face the same liquidity constraints as local firms as they can always rely on their headquarters as 'lender of last resort', or raise credit from international banks with the international assets of the corporation as implicit collateral. Large domestic firms, often organized as 'groups', have preferential access to bank credit at any one time (often because they have a bank within the group) and thus should suffer less from capital market fluctuations. Indeed, it is often the case that banks are vulnerable to the non-financial firms in the group rather than the other way around. In contrast, independent domestic firms are the most vulnerable to shifts in bank credit. Small enterprises outside the formal credit system are also vulnerable to the business cycle because they rely on sub-contracts from larger firms or the expenditure of wages by their employees.

The policy implications of the argument set out in this chapter are considerable. The design of the appropriate macroeconomic policy should logically be preceded by an identification of the causes of the original fluctuation in short-term capital flows – and indeed a judgement as to whether this represents a temporary or a permanent shock (Reisen, 1996). Flows which will soon be reversed would presumably be handled through compensatory reserve management, while permanent flows require some form of macroeconomic adjustment. In the absence of any clear basis for such a judgment, the proverbial admonition to 'treat all positive shocks as temporary and all negative shocks as permanent' is a good guide. Nonetheless, the source of fluctuations in short-term capital flows varies widely: alterations in local conditions (both structural such as banking liberalization and privatization, and policy shifts such as in interest rates), changes in international capital markets (such as variations in prudential regulation or in domestic asset yields), or perhaps – and most importantly, as we have seen – shifts in the perceived risk associated with a particular market. Each source implies a distinct policy response: for instance, increased demand for money domestically can be countered by monetary accommodation, while a change in international perceptions of risk may be best handled by sterilization of capital flows, particularly if the policy objective is to maintain a stable real exchange rate in order to promote exports. However, the overriding goal should presumably be to maintain high rates of private investment in traded sectors through macroeconomic stability and low real interest rates.

Such 'fine tuning' is not easy, particularly since much of its effect depends upon the reputation of the economic authorities. Indeed, Obstfeldt (1995) suggests that because of the international integration of capital markets the only way to reduce the shocks arising from external capital flows is either a completely clean float or an irrevocable currency union. However, a pure float is probably unworkable in most developing countries due to the fact that monetary aggregates do not provide a reliable policy anchor, particularly in a period of financial liberalization. In any case, the resulting fluctuations in real exchange rates would have the negative real-economy effects we have discussed above. Monetary union is not a feasible option for most developing countries – and for those for which it is a real prospect (such as Mexico) the fiscal implications for the central economy of the region (for example, the USA) are probably unacceptable. In practice, therefore, the options appear to be: the design of fiscal policy to reduce the pressure on domestic debt markets; sterilized intervention as the basis of monetary policy, combined with a strong reserve level and low real interest rates; high but flexible marginal reserve requirements on banks in order to mitigate the effects of capital flows on credit provision; and active management of the nominal exchange rate in order to maintain a stable, competitive real exchange rate.

The implications for longer-term financial policies are as follows:

1 Sustain public investment programmes by avoiding the use of short-term debt as a source of funds; undertake a tax reform sufficiently extensive to generate a structural fiscal balance; and avoid the refinancing of long-term external debt with short-term internal debt.
2 Avoid high real rates of interest, which do little to stimulate aggregate savings, but clearly depress private investment and in this context, attract volatile capital flows while increasing the budgetary cost and also the vulnerability of domestic firms.
3 Ensure that long-term credit is available to firms in order to sustain private investment through the cycles caused by short-term capital flows; possibly by the provision of rediscount facilities at the central bank and tax incentives to long-term profit retention.
4 Protect small firms and homebuilding from the effect of credit restrictions by dedicated loan schemes; and restrict the capacity of larger firms and

banks to borrow abroad if this makes their capital structures vulnerable to exchange rate fluctuations.

5 Maintain a stable real exchange rate in order to avoid excessive fluctuations in real wages resulting from capital inflows and outflows; using capital flows sterilization and variable reserves requirements on banks in order to avoid fluctuations in employment.

Insofar as domestic capital markets form part of a global capital market, the stabilizing measures listed above would be greatly strengthened by appropriate action at an international level. In particular, international taxation and regulatory arrangements could provide the incentives to foreign investors to support longer-term investment in tradable production and human capital formation in developing countries (FitzGerald, 1997). Insistence by international financial institutions, such as the World Bank (1997a), on financial deregulation and capital account liberalization alone as ends in themselves, without a clear view of the implications for the 'real economy', is not generally consistent with sustainable economic development.

References

Bachetta, P. (1992) 'Liberalization of Capital Movements and the Domestic Financial System' *Economica*, pp. 465–7.

Blinder, A. S. (1987) 'Credit Rationing and Effective Supply Failures', *Economic Journal*, vol. 97, pp. 327–52.

Dixit, A. K. and R. S. Pindyck (1994) *Investment under Uncertainty* (Princeton NJ: Princeton University Press).

Dornbusch, R. (1980) *Open Economy Macroeconomics* (New York: Basic Books).

Dutt, A. K. (1995) 'Interest Rate Policy, Growth and Distribution in an Open Less-developed Economy: A Theoretical Analysis', in P. Arestis and V. Chick (eds), *Finance, Development and Structural Change* (Cheltenham, Glos: Edward Elgar).

Edwards, S. and C. A. Vegh (1997) 'Banks and Macroeconomic Disturbances under Predetermined Exchange Rates', *Working Paper Series 5977*, NBER, Cambridge MA.

FitzGerald, E. V. K. (1995) 'Hamlet without the Prince: Structural Adjustment, Firm Behaviour and Private Investment in Semi-industrialized Economies, in P. Arestis and V. Chick (eds), *Finance, Development and Structural Change* (Cheltenham, Glos: Edward Elgar).

FitzGerald, E. V. K. (1996) 'International Capital Markets and Open-economy Macroeconomics' *Oxford Development Studies*, vol. 24, no. 1, pp. 79–92.

FitzGerald, E. V. K. (1997) 'Intervention versus Regulation: The Role of the IMF in Crisis Prevention and Management', *UNCTAD Review 1996* (Geneva: United Nations).

FitzGerald, E. V. K., K. Jansen and R. Vos (1994) 'External Constraints on Private Investment Decisions in Developing Countries' in J-W. Gunning (ed.) ,*Trade, Growth and Development* (London: Macmillan).

FitzGerald, E. V. K. and G. Mavrotas (1997) *International Capital Flows, Investment and Employment in Developing Countries* (Geneva: International Labour Organization).

FitzGerald, E. V. K. and G. Perosino (1999) 'Trade Liberalization, Employment and Wages: A Critical Approach', in G.B. Navaretti, R. Faini and G. Zanalda (eds), *Labour Markets, Poverty, and Development* (Oxford: Clarendon Press).

Hallwood, C. P. and R. MacDonald (1994) *International Money and Finance*, 2nd edn (Oxford: Blackwell).
Heller, P. S. (1975) 'A Model of Public Fiscal Behaviour in Developing Countries: Aid, Investment and Taxation', *American Economic Review*, vol. 65, no. 3, pp. 429–45
Hirschliefer, J. and J. G. Riley (1992) *The Analytics of Uncertainty and Information* (Cambridge: Cambridge University Press).
IMF (1997) *World Economic Outlook, May 1997* (Washington DC: International Monetary Fund).
Khan, M. S. and N. Ul Haque (1990) 'Adjustment with Growth: Relating the Analytical Approaches of the IMF and the World Bank', *Journal of Development Economics*, vol. 32, pp. 155–79.
Mathieson, D. and L. Rojas-Suarez (1993) 'Liberalization of the Capital Account: Experience and Issues', *IMF Occasional Series*, no. 103.
Melitz, J. and C. Bordes (1991) 'The Macroeconomic Implications of Financial Deregulation', *European Economic Review*, pp. 155–78.
Minsky, H. P. (1982) 'The Financial-instability Hypothesis', in C.P. Kindelberger and J.-P. Laffarge (eds), *Financial Crises* (Cambridge: Cambridge University Press).
Obstfeldt, M. (1995) 'International Currency Experience: New Lessons and Lessons Relearned', *Brookings Papers on Economic Activity*, no. 1, pp. 119–220 (Brookings Institution, Washington DC).
Pindyck, R. S. and A. Solimano (1993) 'Economic Instability and Aggregate Investment', *Working Paper 4380*, NBER, Cambridge MA.
Reisen, H. (1996) 'Managing Volatile Capital Inflows: The Experience of the 1990s' *Asian Development Review*, vol. 14, no. 1, pp. 72–96
Rojas-Suarez, L. and S. R. Weisbrod (1994) 'Financial Market Fragilities in Latin America', *IMF Working Paper no. 117*, International Monetary Fund, Washington DC.
Sen, P. (1994) 'Saving, Investment and the Current Account', in F. van der Ploeg (ed.), *The Handbook of International Economics* (Oxford: Blackwell).
Stiglitz, J. E. and A. Weiss (1992) 'Asymmetric Information in Credit Markets and its Implications for Macroeconomics', *Oxford Economic Papers*, no. 44, pp. 694–724.
Tobin, J. (1984) 'On the Efficiency of the Financial System', *Lloyds Bank Review*, no. 153, London, UK.
World Bank (1997a) *Private Capital Flows to Developing Countries: The Road to Financial Integration* (New York, NY: Oxford University Press).
World Bank (1997b) *Global Development Finance 1997* (Washington DC: World Bank).

9

Boom and Bust in Capital Flows to Developing Countries

Peter Nunnenkamp
Kiel Institute of World Economics

1 Introduction

According to Malaysia's Prime Minister, Mahathir Bin Mohamad, the verdict on foreign investors in developing countries (DCs) is clear: DCs

> can be suddenly manipulated and forced to bow to the great fund managers who have now come to be the people to decide who should prosper and who shouldn't... Quite a few people who are... in control of the big money seem to want to see these South East Asian countries and in particular Malaysia stop trying to catch up with their superiors and to know their place. If they don't then they will just have to be made to do so and these people have the means and the wherewithal to force their will on these upstarts. (Mahathir, 1997)

You may ask, of course, why these 'hostile elements' were so eager to participate in the previous economic boom by investing in East Asia and until recently lending money. You may wonder why foreign investors were allowed to engage in Malaysia in the first place, and why Asian leaders did not complain when they received huge inflows of capital. In an interview with the *Times of India* (31 December 1997), a prominent economist, Jagdish Bhagwati, suggested an answer:

> Wall Street has become a very powerful influence in terms of seeking markets everywhere. Morgan Stanley and all these gigantic firms want to be able to get into other markets and essentially see capital account convertibility as what will enable them to operate everywhere... Wall Street views are very dominant in terms of the kind of world you want to see. They want the ability to take capital in and out freely.
> (Quoted in Wade and Veneroso, 1998)

This seems to imply that DCs which complied with Wall Street demands by opening up towards international capital markets have acted against their own interest. Wade and Veneroso (1998) draw the logical conclusion and argue that high-saving Asian economies do not need foreign savings, and advise Asian governments to close the capital account so that mobile capital cannot move freely in and out. Once again, Bhagwati provides support. Capital markets 'are very volatile. Suddenly expectations can turn around. You may be very healthy but suddenly you can catch pneumonia . . . Markets may do something when you have done nothing wrong . . . I would put off capital account convertibility for quite a while'. Bhagwati's assertions on volatility and changing expectations in international capital markets are plain truth. Yet, much of the above reasoning amounts to shooting the messenger of bad news. Moreover, it would become more difficult for DCs in South Asia and in other regions to catch up economically with more advanced economies if DCs were to reverse the course of opening up towards international capital markets.

I will expand on this proposition. First, I portray recent trends in capital flows to DCs. Second, I present a more balanced account on opportunities and risks of increased capital mobility for DCs. Third, I consider volatility in international capital flows to be a symptom, rather than the cause of recent financial turbulence in Latin America and East Asia and show that crises were caused by inconsistent economic policies, lack of credibility and government-induced incentive problems. Fourth, by reviewing the experience of South Asia, I argue that openness has been instrumental to economic catching up. Finally, I discuss ways of limiting the risk of sudden capital outflows and stress the role of foreign direct investment (FDI) in sustaining external financing and in overcoming financial crises.

2 Foreign capital flows to DCs

Foreign capital inflows are of increasing importance in DCs. Relative to GDP, net resource flows to all DCs doubled during the 1970s as shown in Figure 9.1. The subsequent decline in this ratio can be attributed to the foreign debt crisis that particularly hit Latin American countries in the first half of the 1980s. In 1996, however, the ratio of net resource flows to GDP reached an unprecedented level of almost 5 per cent. FDI data stress the increased appeal of DCs to foreign capital. In 1994/5, FDI inflows accounted for 8 per cent of gross fixed capital formation in DCs, about twice as much as in industrial countries (UNCTAD, 1997). The share of DCs in worldwide FDI flows doubled from 17 per cent in 1985–90 to 35 per cent in 1994–6.

Figure 9.2 portrays the development of capital flows from 1980 to 1996 to DCs from three major sources, the data indicating that:[1]

- External financing of DCs shifted from debt to equity finance. FDI inflows into the 14 DCs considered in Figure 9.2 increased tenfold between 1980 and 1996. FDI became the most important source of external

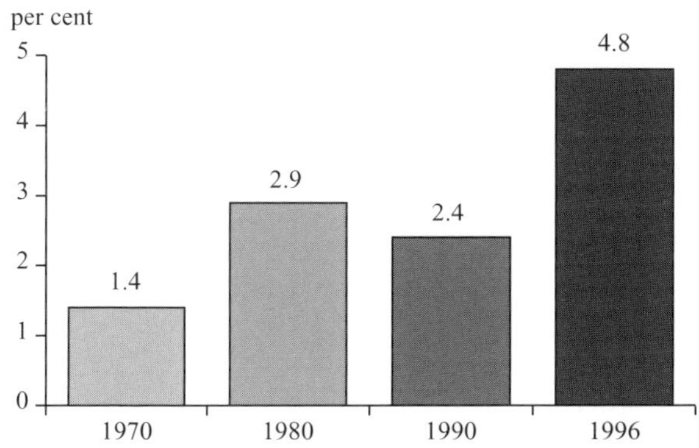

Figure 9.1 Net resource flows to DCs, 1970–96 (per cent of GDP)
Note: 1996 figures are preliminary.
Source: World Bank (1997a).

financing in the mid-1990s. Furthermore, the steadily rising trend suggests that FDI was least affected by turbulence in international capital markets.

- Portfolio investment in DCs remained marginal throughout the 1980s. It soared from US$ 0.6 billion in 1989 to US$90 billion in 1993. In contrast to FDI, however, portfolio investment proved to be extremely volatile. The Mexican peso crisis of 1994/5 was associated with a sharp fall in portfolio investment. The sudden reversal of portfolio investment was most pronounced in Mexico, but several Latin American economies, notably Argentina, suffered from contagion.
- External financing through debt instruments (other investment liabilities in Figure 9.2) turned negative in the second half of the 1980s. This was probably due to both supply and demand factors. Foreign banks refused further loans to debt-ridden DCs, and various DCs preferred equity over debt finance. The situation changed in the 1990s when the significance of debt instruments fluctuated heavily. The booming other investment liabilities in 1995 are attributable to steeply increasing debt inflows into Brazil and some Asian DCs. The latter financed rising current account deficits by short-term borrowing abroad (see section 4).

Most recent data on foreign capital flows to DCs underline various of the above findings.[2] Compared to 1996, net private capital flows to leading emerging markets declined by one-third to about US$200 billion in 1997. This decline is to be attributed to financial turbulence in East Asia. The five major problem countries in this region (Indonesia, Malaysia, Philippines, South Korea and Thailand), which had received capital inflows of more than

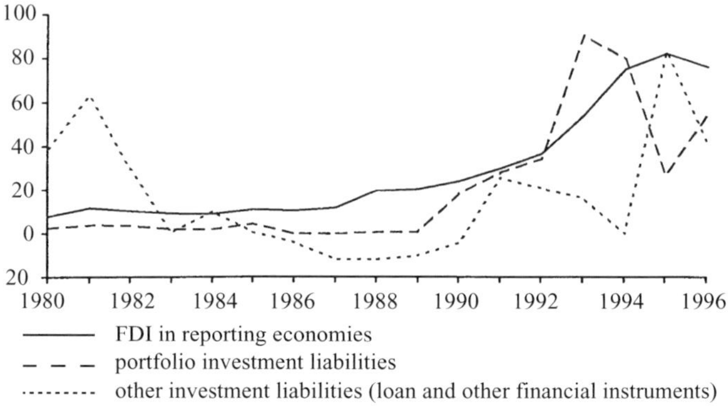

Figure 9.2 Capital flows to DCs. (FDI, portfolio investment and other investment liabilities, 1980–96 (US$ billion))
Notes: 1 Flows to a group of 14 DCs (Argentina, Brazil, Chile, China, Colombia, Egypt, Indonesia, Malaysia, Mexico, Philippines, Singapore, South Korea, Thailand and Venezuela); 2 1980 without China and Indonesia; 3 1981 without China; portfolio investment liabilities without Chile in 1980–5; 4 1996 without Brazil, Indonesia, Malaysia and Philippines. The group of 14 DCs accounted for 65 per cent of FDI, portfolio investment and other investment in all DCs in 1993–5.
Source: IMF (b).

US$90 billion in 1996, suffered capital outflows of US$12 billion in 1997. The East Asian crisis did not cause a sudden reversal of capital flows to emerging markets in other regions, which reported stagnating or even increasing inflows in 1997.[3]

The reaction to the East Asian crisis differed significantly between major types of foreign finance. FDI remained unaffected; FDI flows to all emerging markets continued to grow by about 20 per cent per annum, exceeding US$114 billion in 1997. By contrast, portfolio investment and bank lending was volatile. Portfolio *equity* investment in emerging markets was reduced by some 40 per cent to less than US$ 20 billion in 1997.[4] This sudden shift was even more pronounced with regard to commercial bank lending to emerging markets, which was practically zero in 1997. Not surprisingly, this turnaround particularly affected East Asian economies. The previous lending boom came to an abrupt end, and these economies suffered debt-related capital outflows of US$21 billion in 1997.

3 Increased capital mobility: catching up under policy constraints

International capital mobility appears extremely high when looking at cross-border financial flows. By contrast, *real* capital mobility is revealed by the difference between investment and domestic savings, that is, the current account balance. Current account deficits rarely exceeded 5 per cent of DCs' GDP over longer time periods. In the 1960s and 1970s econometric analyses pointed to *de facto* segmentation of capital markets (Feldstein and Horioka, 1980). In the 1990s, domestic savings have remained the key to investment. However, real capital mobility has increased over time. Feldstein (1994) showed that the correlation coefficient between domestic saving rates and investment rates declined from over 0.8 in the 1960s to about 0.6 in the 1980s.

Relaxation of capital controls in various emerging markets is one important factor underlying increased capital mobility. The European Round Table of Industrialists (ERTI, 1996, p. 7) identified a 'general deregulation and liberalisation since the mid-80s in a tide of movement in many countries to make themselves more attractive to foreign investment'. Likewise, the IMF (1997a: box 9) reported a significant decline in an index of capital controls in emerging markets, especially since the early 1990s. The negative correlation between this index and capital inflows 'provides some simple corroboration for the claim that liberalization of external transactions has been instrumental in attracting foreign capital' (*ibid.*, p. 242).

Furthermore, recent analyses at the Kiel Institute of World Economics point to a strikingly strong correlation between DCs' attractiveness to foreign capital and their economic growth performance. Gundlach and Nunnenkamp (1996) argue that globalized capital markets improved the prospects of DCs to catch up economically with industrial countries. This view is supported by the following observations:

- DCs attracted more than a third of worldwide FDI in the mid-1990s. Regional distribution of FDI flows to DCs showed significant shifts between 1980 and 1996 as shown in Figure 9.3. Most notably, Latin America lost its top position to East Asia in attracting FDI.[5] The *intra*-regional distribution of FDI flows also changed. In Latin America, for instance, Brazil suffered a decrease, while Argentina, Chile, Mexico and some smaller economies increased their share in total Latin American FDI inflows (Nunnenkamp, 1997).
- FDI shifts between and within regions are clearly related to economic policies pursued by DC governments. Typically, early reformers with a favourable record on macroeconomic stability, investment and human capital formation gained FDI shares, whereas latecomers in reform, such as Brazil, lost FDI shares.[6]
- DCs which proved to be attractive to foreign capital were successful in catching up with industrial countries. The different experience of East Asia and Latin America is most striking; per capita income growth in the latter region lagged considerably behind per capita income growth in industrial countries, compared to an outstandingly favourable growth performance in East Asia (Figure 9.4). South Asia, too, caught up

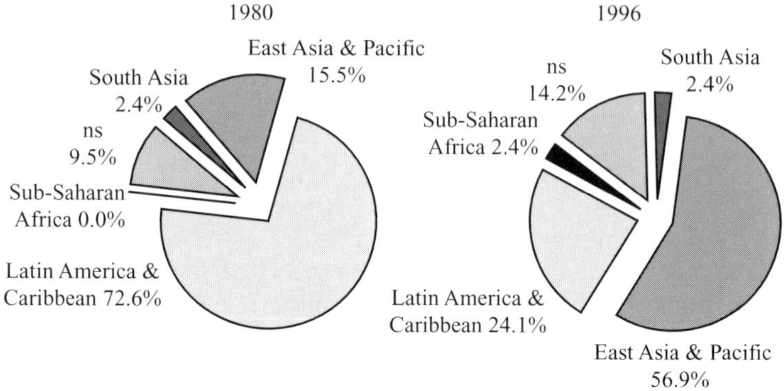

Figure 9.3 Regional distribution of net FDI flows to DCs, 1980 and 1996
Notes: ns = not specified; 1. percentage share of FDI flows to DCs except Middle East and North Africa; this region is excluded because of negative (net) FDI flows in 1980; 2. 1996 preliminary figures.
Source: World Bank (1997a).

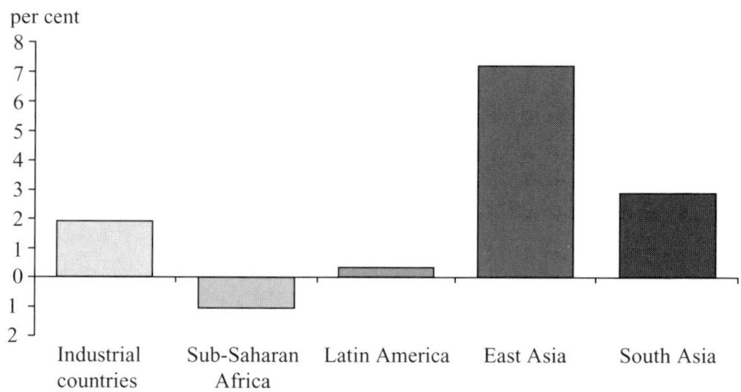

Figure 9.4 International comparison of per capita income growth, 1985–95 (annual average change)
Note: 1 Industrial countries includes some newly industrializing economies with a high per capita income.
Source: World Bank (1997b).

somewhat with industrial countries, though with less speed and from a fairly low level of per capita income. Similarly, the intra-Latin American pattern of attractiveness to foreign capital is reflected in intra-regional growth differences. Chile, the region's frontrunner in economic reform, was most successful in catching up (Nunnenkamp, 1997).

I have dealt with correlations so far, and one may object that causation can run both ways when considering attractiveness to foreign capital and economic catching up. For example, various empirical investigations identified economic growth as an important determinant of FDI. Yet, there is reason to believe that openness towards international capital markets renders it easier to catch up economically. Openness implies that investment in DCs is no longer constrained by domestic savings. Higher investment, in turn, promotes labour productivity growth and, thereby, allows for higher per capita income, particularly as certain types of foreign capital inflows, notably FDI, offer more than just capital. FDI tends to provide for managerial knowhow, easier access to foreign markets and, most importantly, access to internationally available technologies. Technology transfers reduce the risk for DCs, which are still playing a marginal role in generating technical progress, of falling behind technologically leading economies.

Recent analyses support the view that openness is instrumental in achieving high economic growth (Sachs and Warner, 1995; Gundlach 1997). According to Gundlach's regression results, open DCs converge to the steady-state at a rate of about 5 per cent, whereas closed DCs converge at a rate of about 1.5 per cent. This confirms theoretical predictions according to which convergence rates for open and closed economies should differ by a factor of about 2.5. Openness is defined as in Montiel (1994), who used the Feldstein–Horioka approach of measuring international capital mobility in a time-series context: DCs for which the correlation between the investment rate and the domestic saving rate turned out to be lower (higher) than 0.6 are considered to be open (closed).

These findings contradict the notion that, when opening up towards international capital markets, DCs are complying with Wall Street demands and acting against their own interest. However, openness involves risk. The risk of drawing on foreign capital, in order to supplement domestic savings, is twofold. First, an open capital account increases the impact of changes in world-market conditions on DCs. High capital flows to Latin America in the early 1990s, for example, were partly explained by external economic conditions, such as recession in the USA and low international interest rates (Calvo, Leiderman and Reinhart, 1992). The perceived 'hot money' character of inflows caused concern at that time. Capital inflows may adversely affect the international competitiveness of exports if they result in undesired real exchange rate appreciation, and deficient financial intermediation in recipient countries may cause misallocation of capital inflows. Such risks are revealed once world capital-market conditions change. Rising international interest rates may lead to reduced inflows, or even capital outflows. Hence, access to foreign capital comes at the cost of higher macroeconomic vulnerability of recipient countries.

Second, even if capital flows to all DCs as a group are sustained, individual DCs with an open capital account may become the target of speculative attacks (IMF, 1997a, pp. 33–5). Increased capital mobility constrains economic policy choices in recipient countries. Policy failures have more serious consequences if capital can move freely in and out. Especially if exchange rate flexibility is limited, individual DCs may be 'tested' through a speculative attack on their exchange rate, combined with an abrupt loss of market access, whenever international capital markets are concerned about inconsistent macroeconomic policies and structural weaknesses. Relatively high inflation and a weak fiscal position can cause over-valuation of the domestic currency, which undermines the government's credibility in defending the nominal exchange rate. Government credibility is particularly low if short-term foreign indebtedness is high in relation to international reserves. A weak domestic financial system adds to the risk of changing expectations, particularly if financial institutions are heavily engaged in financing long-term investment projects of dubious viability by drawing on short-term foreign loans.

4 The role of DC governments in sustaining external financing: victims or culprits?

Increased capital mobility has brought with it financial turbulence and currency crises in Asia, Europe and Latin America. The subsequent short account of the Mexican peso crisis in 1994/5 and recent turbulence in East Asia reveals that international capital markets tend to overshoot. Nevertheless, these episodes do not confirm Bhagwati's notion that 'markets may do something when you have done nothing wrong'. Rather, these episodes support the view that policy inconsistency and lack of government credibility are the cause of financial distress, while international capital mobility can multiply the social costs of government failure.

4.1 The 'tequila' crisis

Mexico offers a telling example of boom and bust in capital flows. Far-reaching stabilization and structural reform measures in the late 1980s encouraged huge inflows of FDI, portfolio investment and debt finance as shown in Table 9.1. Overall capital inflows peaked in 1993 at US$ 37 billion. The crisis erupted one year later. Overall capital flows turned negative in 1995 and recovered in 1996.

Volatility in overall capital flows to Mexico disguises different developments for specific sources of external finance. FDI flows proved to be relatively stable; and FDI inflows in 1995 and 1996 remained significantly above inflows in the pre-crisis year 1993. By contrast, portfolio investment that had contributed 77 per cent to overall capital inflows in 1993 turned negative in 1995. Even portfolio investment comprises relatively stable elements, such as investment by pension funds and life insurance companies; volatility in portfolio investment is mainly due to the short-term profit orientation of

Table 9.1 Mexico: foreign capital flows, 1987–96 (US$ billion)

	1987	*1988*	*1989*	*1990*	*1991*	*1992*	*1993*	*1994*	*1995*	*1996*
Foreign direct investment (gross)	1.2	2.0	2.8	2.5	4.7	4.4	4.4	11.0	9.5	7.6
Portfolio investment liabilities	−1.0	1.0	0.4	3.4	12.7	18.0	28.9	8.2	−9.7	14.2
Other investment liabilities[1]	1.5	−5.8	−0.9	11.2	8.7	−0.9	4.1	2.3	−2.9	−11.2

Notes: [1] Loans and other financial liabilities.
Source: IMF (b).

managed investment funds (country funds and mutual funds) (Langhammer and Schweickert, 1995, p. 22).

It is plausible to argue that factors beyond the control of Mexican authorities contributed to volatility. In 1991–3, economic recession and low interest rates in major industrial countries stimulated capital inflows into Mexico and other DCs. Subsequently, economic recovery in industrial countries and rising interest rates in USA may have led portfolio investors to withdraw from Mexico. Strikingly, however, portfolio investment in Asian DCs remained almost as high in 1995 as in 1993 (IMF a).[7] Hence, something specific must have triggered the 'tequila' crisis.

It is by now widely accepted that internal factors played a prominent role in causing the crisis of 1994/5, which falls into the category of failed attempts at exchange rate-based stabilization.[8] The reversal of capital flows was related to rising concern about the sustainability of large current account deficits. Real exchange-rate appreciation impaired the international competitiveness of Mexican industry.[9] Capital inflows had been used mainly to finance a private consumption boom, that is, they replaced domestic savings rather than supporting sustainable economic growth. Hence, real exchange-rate appreciation was in conflict with economic fundamentals.

The government's attempt to stabilize the nominal exchange rate was not credible, even though Mexico implemented an impressive fiscal consolidation programme. Nominal devaluation was kept low while inflation inertia was quite substantial. Policy inconsistency can be traced back to 1990, when the rate of the crawl was lowered while monetary policy became more expansionary and the labour market remained regulated. In early 1994, the Mexican peso was considered to be overvalued by 20–35 per cent. Rumours were that the government would have to revise its exchange-rate policy sooner or later. Such rumours tend to be self-fulfilling since investors withdrawing their funds in anticipation of depreciation add to pressure on the local currency. The speculative attack occurred in December 1994, and the peso lost about half its value within a few weeks.

4.2 The East Asian crisis

Various East Asian currencies plummeted in 1997/8. East Asian governments, too, had adopted a fixed or quasi-fixed exchange rate regime. They were forced to give this up, although economic fundamentals had seemed consistent with fixed exchange rates until recently. Throughout the 1980s and the first half of the 1990s, East Asia was given credit for high economic growth, sustained macroeconomic stability, outstandingly high saving and investment rates, and favourable export performance. At first sight, the contention that DCs are the victims of panicking world capital markets appears to be more reasonable in the case of East Asia than that of Mexico.

On closer inspection, however, the East Asian crisis resembles previous crises in that government failure was the cause of overshooting market reactions.[10] The risk of speculative attacks on East Asian currencies increased when (trade-weighted) effective real exchange rates appreciated by about 10 per cent between early 1995 and mid-1997. An exogenous event, namely the strengthening of the anchor currency the US$, against the yen and European currencies, occurred during this time. Asian governments failed to respond by allowing for more exchange rate flexibility. Rising current account deficits, and drastically reduced export growth rates in Malaysia and Thailand in 1996 fuelled market concern about over-valuation. Current account deficits were financed largely by short-term foreign borrowing. Mounting short-term debt, which exceeded the international reserves held by Indonesia, South Korea and Thailand in mid-1997, undermined governments' credibility with regard to sustaining the fixed exchange rate regime.

The outbreak of the crisis might have been postponed if governments had taken timely measures to correct external imbalances. It is unlikely, however, that such measures would have been sufficient to sustain economic growth and financial stability in East Asia in the longer run. Serious *internal* financial problems were ignored within and outside the region until recently. With hindsight, today's problem countries were prone to crisis mainly because of the fragility of their domestic financial systems (Krugman, 1998b).

Weak financial institutions extended credit without sound risk evaluation. Excessive lending at high risk took different forms in the afflicted countries. In Thailand, essentially unregulated finance companies borrowed short-term, often in US dollars, for long-term onlending to speculative investors. In this way, finance companies incited booming real-estate investment, which later proved to be a huge speculative bubble. In South Korea, public authorities directed banks to continue lending to industrial conglomerates for investment projects of dubious viability. The common feature was that the risk exposure of financial institutions was not effectively controlled by supervising banks and enforcing prudential standards according to international best practice. On the contrary, financial institutions perceived their liabilities to be guaranteed implicitly by the government.

It may be tempting to blame local financial institutions for causing the crisis by taking excessive risks, as well as foreign banks and investors for supporting the financing of an unsustainable boom. However, government failure lay behind the institutional weaknesses and incentive problems that induced moral hazard of financial institutions. Implicit government guarantees encouraged risky lending until they had to be honoured. The crisis deepened as soon as the financial institutions realized that the guarantees were not credible. In fact honouring guarantees would have been too costly for the government when asset prices started to decline and vacancy rates in the real-estate sector increased.

Consequently, the failure of some large investors, who saw their profit expectations frustrated, triggered a downward spiral. Financial intermediaries stopped lending and tried to collect their claims, thereby reinforcing the decline in asset prices. It was only then that East Asian currencies came under serious pressure. Foreign banks refused to roll over outstanding loans or demanded higher risk premiums, which added to the calamity of local enterprises and intermediaries. The latter tried to hedge their liabilities by purchasing foreign exchange at the spot market. As in previous crises, the expectation of depreciation proved to be self-fulfilling. The brakes that could have prevented the crisis had already been removed long before, namely when the governments' failure in ensuring prudent financial intermediation induced an unsustainable boom.

5 South Asia: recent experience and current challenges

5.1 Openness, capital inflows, and economic performance

According to a survey (ERTI, 1996) on improvements in investment conditions in the developing world, South Asian economies have become considerably more open since the mid-1980s. In 1987–92, India and Pakistan were among the six DCs which 'stood at the forefront with their high speed of opening'. India remained on a 'very fast track of opening' in 1993–96, and was considered to be 'moderately open' at the end of 1996. The degree of openness achieved by Bangladesh and Pakistan at that time was regarded as somewhat higher than that of India. Among South Asian economies, Sri Lanka ranked highest with regard to the degree of openness ('quite open'), although the speed of opening in 1993–96 was 'somewhat lower' in Sri Lanka (and in Bangladesh).

More welcoming attitudes towards FDI were part of 'the broadly based liberalization of South-Asian economies' (UNIDO 1996, p. 30). Major policy changes were initiated in Sri Lanka in the late 1970s. Bangladesh and Pakistan represent intermediate cases with regard to the timing of reforms in South Asia. India was a latecomer to reform; some adjustment measures were launched in the mid-1980s, but major reforms only started in 1991.

The process of economic opening was associated with a closer integration of South Asia into the international division of labour, and with improved attractiveness to foreign capital. The ratio of South Asian exports to GNP increased from 5.4 per cent in 1970 to 10.5 and 13.6 per cent in 1990 and 1996 respectively (World Bank 1997a). The ratio of net FDI inflows to South Asian exports quadrupled from 0.8 per cent in 1980 to 3.4 per cent in 1996. Net resource inflows (excluding grants) increased sixfold between 1970 and 1990, and further doubled until 1996 (Figure 9.5). Relative to South Asia's GNP, net resource inflows reached 2.6 per cent in 1996.

Net resource flows to the four major South Asian economies seem to be related to the timing of economic liberalization. Comparing net resource inflows in 1970 with average annual inflows in 1994/5, the increase was most pronounced in Sri Lanka, the frontrunner in reform (World Bank, 1997a). Moreover, Sri Lanka reported the highest ratio of net resource inflows to GNP in 1980 and 1990 (6.6 and 4.5 per cent respectively). Bangladesh, the next reformer (in 1983–6), ranked second with 5.2 and 4.2 per cent respectively. By contrast, net resource inflows stagnated at about 1–1.5 per cent of GNP in India until 1990; this ratio increased to 2.5 per cent in 1994, exactly when economic reforms gathered momentum in India.[11]

FDI data provide further evidence for the link between economic liberalization and attractiveness to foreign capital. Traditionally, South Asia was a minor host of FDI (UNIDO, 1996, p. 29). The region enhanced its attractiveness to FDI when major countries opened their economies. Average annual FDI inflows in 1987–91 were twice as high as in 1980–6 as shown in Table 9.2. FDI inflows increased steadily from US$0.5 billion in 1991 to US$2.5 billion in 1995, mainly because of rising FDI flows to reforming India.

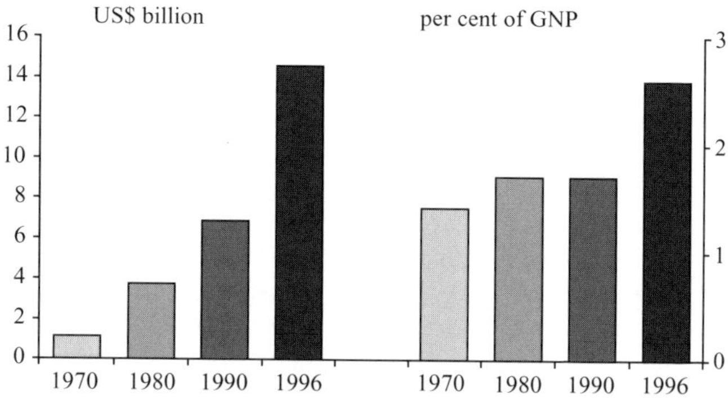

Figure 9.5 Net resource flows to South Asia, 1970–96
Notes: 1 Sum of net flows of long-term debt (excluding IMF), net FDI. and portfolio equity flows; that is excluding grants; 2 1996 figures are preliminary.
Source: World Bank (1997a).

Table 9.2 FDI flows to South Asia, 1980–5

	US$ million (annual average)	*per cent of US$ million flows*			
		Bangladesh	*India*	*Pakistan*	*Sri Lanka*
1980–6	190	0.2	37.0	41.7	21.2
1987–91	422	0.5	40.6	48.6	10.3
1992–5	1296	0.6	53.9	35.1	10.4

Note: US$ million column includes FDI flows to Bangladesh, India, Pakistan and Sri Lanka
Sources: IMF (b); for India: World Bank Data Base (1980–94); ADB (1997, table A 17).

Openness and improved attractiveness to foreign capital, especially FDI, seem to have helped better economic performance in South Asia. In the 1970s, when all major economies were fairly closed, the region failed to narrow the gap in per capita income between South Asia and more advanced economies; indeed the gap widened as South Asia reported a slow annual growth of per capita GDP of 1.3 per cent (ADB, 1989: table A2). By contrast, the region achieved a higher growth of per capita GDP than industrial countries in 1985–95 (2.9 versus 1.9 per cent; Figure 9.4). On the level of individual South Asian economies, too, openness seems to have supported economic development:

- *Bangladesh*, although considered to be more open than India (ERTI, 1996) attracted only marginal FDI inflows (Table 9.2). Nevertheless, economic reforms went along with higher growth of per capita GDP.[12] Economic reforms supported a stronger world-market orientation of Bangladesh.[13] Favourable export performance was largely attributable to soaring exports of clothing, and the country's clothing industry benefited greatly from the relocation of production from economies such as South Korea and Hong Kong. Korean companies, in particular, transferred managerial and technical knowhow to Bangladesh. FDI data tend to understate the engagement of foreign companies in the manufacturing sector of Bangladesh, as foreign involvement in the clothing industry is frequently of a non-equity type such as subcontracting.
- *India*'s share in FDI flows to South Asia in 1980–6 was less than half its share in the region's GDP and population (Table 9.2). India's FDI share increased significantly exactly when economic liberalization gathered momentum. At the same time, the ratio of exports to GDP that had remained stable at about 6–7 per cent throughout the 1980s increased to 10.6 per cent in 1993/4.[14] Per capita income growth rose to 4.2 per cent a year in 1992–7, compared to 2.8 per cent in 1987–91 (ADB, 1997).
- *Pakistan* is an exception in that openness was not associated with improved economic performance. This country had been the major

recipient of FDI within South Asia throughout the 1980s (Table 9.2). Absolutely increasing FDI flows in the 1990s notwithstanding, Pakistan's FDI share declined to 35 per cent in 1992–5. At the same time, per capita income growth declined from about 3 per cent in 1980–91 to slightly less than 2 per cent in 1992–7. It seems that FDI in Pakistan contributed less to world market orientation than elsewhere in South Asia. Pakistan clearly performed worst of the four economies under consideration in terms of gaining world export shares in 1980–96 (IMF b).

- *Sri Lanka* was the most successful in catching up with industrial countries between 1980 and 1995. This country was also most successful in attracting FDI. FDI inflows were exceptionally high, if accumulated inflows in 1980–95 are related to population in 1995.[15] Sri Lanka's reduced share of about 10 per cent of FDI flows to South Asia after 1987 (Table 9.2) was still more than three times as large as Sri Lanka's share of South Asia's GDP. Yet, Sri Lanka could possibly have achieved greater gains from openness if internal political conflict had not impaired its attractiveness to foreign capital. Political uncertainty seems to be a major reason for the rather unstable pattern of FDI inflows and economic growth.[16]

5.2 The risk involved

South Asia seems to have benefited from economic liberalization and greater openness towards international capital markets in recent years. However, as argued in Section 3, openness involves the risk of being affected by adverse capital-market developments. Current concerns are that the financial turbulence in East Asia may spread beyond the countries afflicted so far. Contagion may affect South Asia in two ways. First, the East Asian crisis may induce foreign investors to reconsider country risk in all emerging markets. This might cause a general shift from generous to restrictive investment behaviour in DCs; foreign investors would then retreat into the few remaining 'safe havens'. Second, South Asia's access to foreign capital may deteriorate if prolonged recession in East Asian problem countries leads China to renege on earlier commitments not to devalue the renminbi. In the case of a major devaluation in China, it would become more difficult for South Asian suppliers to penetrate markets in which China is a major competitor. Consequently, foreign investors would have weaker incentives to engage in export-oriented production in South Asia.

A detailed discussion of alternative scenarios concerning East Asia's future economic development and possible reactions of foreign investors, as well as a detailed account of the various factors shaping country risk in South Asia would be required in order to evaluate the significance of such fears. Section 4 suggested that financial market conditions in South Asian economies deserved particular attention. Space here prevents me from discussing more than two factors which, as previous crises reveal, are related to the issue of

Table 9.3 South Asia: structure of external financing and significance of short-term debt, 1995

	FDI	*Portfolio equity flows*	*Long-term debt*	*Grants*	*Short-term debt stock as per cent of international reserves*
	(per cent of net resource flows)				
South Asia[a]	15.3	31.8	38.2	14.7	29.3
Bangladesh	0.2	3.6	21.3	74.8	8.7
India	39.6	46.2	–2.8	16.9	22.1
Pakistan	16.3	29.0	47.2	7.5	128.0
Sri Lanka	10.0	9.7	52.8	27.6	25.6
All DCs[a]	38.5	16.1	34.5	11.0	70.2
East Asia[a]	52.6	11.1	33.9	2.4	48.4

Note: [a] Structure of external financing according to preliminary figures of 1996.
Source: World Bank (1997a).

sustainability of capital inflows; that is, the structure of external financing and vulnerability to a reversal of short-term capital flows.

An important caveat has to be kept in mind when interpreting the data presented in Table 9.3. Figures for individual South Asian economies refer to 1995, and hence it is almost impossible to assess the *present* risk concerning the sustainability of external financing.[17] Yet, Table 9.3 offers some interesting insights. First, FDI contributed significantly less to net resource flows to South Asia than to net resource flows to all DCs and East Asian DCs. This suggests that there is still substantial scope for South Asia to improve the sustainability of external financing, considering that FDI has typically been the most stable item of external financing when capital-market conditions were unfavourable. Second, South Asia as a whole compared favourably to East Asia and all DCs as concerns the significance of short-term debt stocks. International reserves would decline by less than 30 per cent, compared with 70 per cent for all DCs, even if the roll-over of short-term debt were to come to an abrupt and complete stop.

Third, Table 9.3 points to considerable differences between major South Asian economies in terms of external financing risk. The situation appears to be most critical in Pakistan. Short-term debt stocks exceeded international reserves, revealing Pakistan's high vulnerability to a reversal of foreign capital flows. Moreover, FDI and grants accounted for less than a quarter of net resource flows to Pakistan in 1995.

6 Summary and policy conclusions

It is beyond serious doubt that international capital markets tend to overshoot once profit expectations in emerging markets turn negative. Sudden shifts from enthusiasm to panic, associated with the herding behaviour of foreign investors, repeatedly prevented a 'soft landing' and exacerbated the social cost of economic and financial tension in DCs. However, overshooting is a phenomenon prevailing not only in international capital markets, but also in commenting upon acute crises. Some politicians, such as Malaysia's Prime Minister Mahathir, blame the messenger of bad news. Ignoring that international capital markets are reacting to changes in country risk, rather than being the cause of financial distress and currency crises, may have tremendous costs. To quote Krugman (1997, p. 34), 'Return to normalcy may be delayed for a long time if leaders start looking for villains instead of solutions'.

Some economists, too, have commented upon financial crises as if international capital markets do DCs no good. The evidence presented above is in strong conflict with the contention that openness of DCs towards international capital markets is exclusively in Wall Street's interest. Rather, open DCs have better opportunities than closed DCs to catch up economically with industrial countries. The recent experience of South Asia fits this picture. It follows that Wade and Veneroso's (1998) suggestion of closing the capital account, in order to avoid being at the mercy of volatile capital markets would be tantamount to *shooting oneself in the foot* because:

- The opportunity costs of closing the capital account may be large even for the high-saving East Asian economies afflicted by the current crisis. Capital transfers in the form of FDI provide benefits in terms of managerial knowhow, easier access to foreign markets and access to internationally available technologies, that is, factors that help to overcome the crisis and resume the process of catching up. Moreover, acquisitions by foreign investors limit the decline in asset prices. This implies that 'the mere potential for FDI may act as a stabiliser against the risk of domestic financial panics' (Krugman, 1998a, p. 9).
- DCs with rather low domestic saving rates are likely to suffer particularly high opportunity costs when closing the capital account. Compared to various East Asian economies whose domestic savings accounted for about 35 per cent of GNP in 1996, South Asia is in greater need to supplement domestic savings by foreign capital inflows. In 1996, domestic saving rates were in the range of 12–16 per cent in Bangladesh, Pakistan and Sri Lanka; with only India reporting a substantially higher saving rate of 27 per cent (ADB, 1997, table A7).

For DCs which do not want to forgo the benefits of capital inflows, the challenge is to reduce the risk of being affected by volatility in international capital markets. Recent crises offer some lessons in this respect (see Diehl and Schweickert, 1998). First, DCs can prevent speculative attacks on their currencies by adopting a flexible exchange-rate regime and, thereby, denying speculators a fixed target. Second, this task is more demanding for DCs using the exchange rate as a nominal anchor for internal stabilization purposes. International capital markets may question the credibility of the government's commitment to a particular exchange rate for various reasons. Third, it follows that DCs should avoid repeating the policy failures that caused previous crises, rather than blaming international capital markets for internal economic and financial problems.

Credibility must be ensured on several fronts. Speculative attacks are most likely if monetary and fiscal policy is inconsistent with a fixed exchange rate regime. However, it is not sufficient to avoid obvious macroeconomic inconsistencies. International capital markets may also turn their back on DCs, if rising real interest rates, high unemployment and low economic growth feed expectations that the government will change course and devalue in order to resolve internal economic problems.

Furthermore, the sustainability of external financing is at risk as long as major institutional weaknesses persist and domestic financial markets remain essentially unregulated. Financial institutions must be supervised effectively, prudential standards should be in line with international best practice and must be enforced, and governments must not create expectations that private sector liabilities are guaranteed. Effective regulation of domestic financial markets is essential particularly in the early phases of financial liberalization.

Finally, the structure of external financing matters for reducing the risk of a sudden reversal of capital flows. In order to avoid excessive reliance on short-term financing and improve the management of foreign debt, lenders and borrowers need timely and comprehensive information on outstanding liabilities. This calls for better data collection and data dissemination, both domestically and internationally. Among the different sources of capital inflows, FDI has typically proven to be the least volatile item. Hence, DCs should aim at a high share of FDI in overall external financing. The stabilizing properties of FDI help DCs in the midst of financial turbulence to limit the depth of the crisis. For other DCs, a strong reliance on FDI reduces the risk of contagion. All DCs attracting FDI have better chances to catch up economically with advanced economies since FDI provides for more than just capital.

Notes

1 Note that data for 1996 are still incomplete; for details, see Figure 9.2.

2 The subsequent data on net private capital flows to major emerging markets were released by the Institute of International Finance in February 1998, and are summarized in Quinlan (1998).

3 It is expected that capital flows to Latin America will decline by about US$15 billion in 1998. However, the projected inflows of US$75 billion to this region in 1998 would still be twice as high as inflows in 1995 (Quinlan, 1998).

4 According to IMF (a), equity securities accounted for 31 per cent of overall portfolio investment liabilities of all DCs in 1994–5; bonds and notes accounted for more

than two-thirds, whereas the contribution of money market instruments and financial derivatives to overall portfolio investment liabilities was marginal.

5 The constant share of South Asia in Figure 9.3 obscures the decline in this region's relative attractiveness in the early 1980s and later recovery, especially since 1991; see also section 5.

6 For a detailed discussion of the link between economic policy and attractiveness to foreign capital, see Gundlach and Nunnenkamp (1996) for an inter-regional perspective, and Nunnenkamp (1997) for a Latin American perspective.

7 Portfolio investment in Asian DCs jumped from US$8.3 billion in 1992 to US$28.2 billion in 1993; in the three subsequent years, inflows amounted to US$26.4, 27.5 and 36.6 billion respectively.

8 For detailed assessments, see Fischer and Schnatz (1996) as well as Langhammer and Schweickert (1995); see also IMF (1997b, box 1).

9 In addition, political uncertainty mounted in Mexico in 1994 as a result of political assassinations, social unrest and regional uprising.

10 The subsequent paragraphs draw on Diehl and Schweickert (1998), Krugman (1998b) and Nunnenkamp (1998a, 1998b).

11 Net resource flows to India fell from US$7.3 billion in 1994 to US$2.7 billion in 1995; however, debt flows turned negative and portfolio equity flows declined, whereas FDI flows doubled in 1995 (World Bank, 1997a).

12 Per capita income increased by 2.6 per cent, on average, in 1992–7, compared with 1.7 per cent in 1980–6 (ADB, 1989, 1997).

13 The ratio of exports to GDP more than doubled from 5.8 per cent, on average, in 1980–6 to 12.7 per cent in 1992–7 (IMF b).

14 More recent data are not available from IMF (b).

15 In per capita terms, FDI inflows into Sri Lanka amounted to US$57; Pakistan ranked second with US$26 (sources as in Table 9.2).

16 FDI inflows were at a low ebb in the mid-1980s, in 1989 and in 1995 (IMF b). Per capita income growth declined from 3.5 per cent, on average, in 1980–6 to 1.8 per cent in 1987–91, but recovered thereafter (ADB, 1989, 1997).

17 The structure of external financing may change significantly from year to year. For example, FDI accounted for only 8 per cent of India's net resource inflows in 1994; the share of portfolio equity flows and long-term debt amounted to 60 and 25 per cent, respectively, at that time.

References

ADB (1989) *Asian Development Outlook 1989* (Manila: Asian Development Bank).

ADB (1997) *Asian Development Outlook 1997 and 1998* (Oxford: Oxford University Press).

Calvo, G. A., L. Leiderman and C. M. Reinhart (1992) *Capital Inflows and Real Exchange Rate Appreciation in Latin America: The Role of External Factors*, IMF working paper 92/62. International Monetary Fund, Washington, DC.

Diehl, M. and R. Schweickert (1998) *Currency Crises: Is Asia Different?*, Kiel Discussion Papers 309, Institute of World Economics, Kiel.

ERTI (1996) *Investment in the Developing World: New Openings and Challenges for European Industry* (Brussels: ERTI).

Feldstein, M. (1994) *Tax Policy and International Capital Flows*, Bernhard-Harms-Lectures 16, Institute of World Economics, Kiel.

Feldstein, M. and C. Horioka (1980) 'Domestic Saving and International Capital Flows', *Economic Journal*, vol. 90, pp. 314–29.

Fischer, B. and B. Schnatz (1996) 'Stabilitätspolitische Probleme bei der Integration in die internationalen Finanzmärkte: Mexikos Weg in die Peso-Krise', in H.-B. Schäfer (ed.), *Die Entwicklungsländer im Zeitalter der Globalisierung*, Schriften des Vereins für Socialpolitik 245 (Berlin: Duncker & Humblot), pp. 13–39.

Gundlach, E. (1997) 'Openness and Economic Growth in Developing Countries', *Weltwirtschaftliches Archiv*, vol. 133, pp. 479–96.

Gundlach, E. and P. Nunnenkamp (1996) *Some Consequences of Globalization for Developing Countries*, Kiel Working Papers 753, Institute of World Economics, Kiel.

IMF (a) *Balance of Payments Statistics Yearbook*, Washington, DC (various issues).

IMF (b) *International Financial Statistics*, Washington, DC (various issues).

IMF (1997a) *International Capital Markets: Developments, Prospects, and Key Policy Issues*, Washington, DC. (November).

IMF (1997b) *World Economic Outlook: Interim Assessment*, Washington, DC (December).

Krugman, P. (1997) 'Latin Lessons for Asia', *Far Eastern Economic Review*, 25 September, p. 34.

Krugman, P. (1998a) 'Fire-sale FDI'. Massachusetts Institute of Technology, Cambridge, Mass. (internet version).

Krugman, P. (1998b) 'What Happened to Asia?' Massachusetts Institute of Technology, Cambridge, Mass. (Internet version).

Langhammer, R. J. and R. Schweickert (1995) *The Mexican Reform Process: Improving Long-run Perspectives and Mastering Short-run Turbulences*. Kiel Discussion Papers 255, Institute of World Economics, Kiel.

Mahathir, B. M. (1997) 'Asian Economies: Challenges and Opportunities', speech at the Annual Seminar of the World Bank, Hong Kong, 20 September (Internet version).

Montiel, P. J. (1994) 'Capital Mobility in Developing Countries: Some Measurement Issues and Empirical Estimates', *World Bank Economic Review*, vol. 8, no. 3, pp. 311–50.

Nunnenkamp, P. (1997) 'Foreign Direct Investment in Latin America in the Era of Globalized Production', *Transnational Corporations*, vol. 6, no. 1, pp. 51–81.

Nunnenkamp, P. (1998a) 'Dealing with the Asian Crisis: IMF Conditionality and Implications in Asia and Beyond', *Intereconomics*, vol. 33, no. 2, pp. 64–72.

Nunnenkamp, P. (1998b) 'Ursachen and Konsequenzen der Asien-Krise' (Causes and Consequences of the Asian Crisis), *Wirtschaftsdienst*, vol. 78, no. 3, pp. 135–8.

Quinlan, J. (1998) 'Global Capital Flows to Emerging Markets: How Asia Has Fallen', Morgan Stanley, New York, February (Internet version).

Sachs, J. D. and A. Warner (1995) 'Economic Convergence and Economic Policies', NBER working papers no. 5039, National Bureau of Economic Research, Cambridge, Mass.

UNCTAD (1997) *World Investment Report* (New York and Geneva: United Nations).

UNIDO (1996) *Industrial Development: Global Report 1996* (Oxford: Oxford University Press).

Wade, R. and F. Veneroso (1998) 'The Asian Financial Crisis: The Unrecognized Risk of the IMF's Asia Package', Russell Sage Foundation, New York (Internet version).

World Bank (1997a) *Global Development Finance* (Washington, DC: World Bank).

World Bank (1997b) *World Development Report* (Oxford: Oxford University Press).

10

Trade in the 2000s: New Rules, New Perspectives and New Priorities

Sheila Page
Overseas Development Institute, London

1 Introduction

Four trends can be identified in trade policy in recent years: liberalization, an increasing differentiation of treatment for different levels of developing country, a growing number of 'regional' agreements among countries, both developed and developing, and an expanding scope and strength of regulation. These have interacting and often conflicting effects on each other. The changes in treatment of developing countries must also be seen in the context of the increasing discussion of focusing help to developing countries on reducing poverty.

The identification of an export strategy with successful development is no longer as fashionable as in the 1980s, but clearly trade is one way of providing market incentives for developing country producers. Learning to seek new markets and meet external demand is part of development, and will have important effects on domestic efficiency, and probably also on the nature of domestic policies. Efficiency and scale benefits from trade may be more important for small and poor countries than for the more advanced: in these, domestic markets (and import competition) are less able to offer market incentives. But the Uruguay Round (UR) and proposals since have brought regulation into focus as the complement to liberalization. Although at first sight it can seem paradoxical, increased regulation is a necessary corollary of more open, more liberal markets, internationally and nationally. For a market-driven result to be seen as acceptable and 'fair', it is necessary that it be achieved by means that are regarded as fair, and this leads to the concern with 'process' as well as with 'products' in international trade, and to a perception of a need for rules to ensure that markets are efficient and fair.

Although much of the demand for rules in international negotiations came initially from the developed countries, they can be more useful for weaker countries (which cannot use unilateral trade policies). The history of the use of the World Trade Organization (WTO) dispute system and other new weapons available to it suggests that developing countries are increasingly learning to use rules. But there remains an inherent conflict: the rules have been made, normally, by the developed countries, at a late stage in their development, but an early one for those still developing. The developing countries must adapt to them, which may be complex, and must apply them during a stage of development where their predecessors were less controlled. This suggests new patterns of development, with greater certainty, but less freedom to choose the means.

What is the role of special trade rules for developing countries in this context? If trade offers special benefits for development, this would be an argument for giving tariff preferences an important role in assistance to developing countries, and, also, for giving developing countries greater freedom to use special incentives to increase the role of trade in the economy. An alternative argument would be that there are particular difficulties in exporting for new exporters. There are clear 'market entry' barriers for producers exporting for the first time, or with a new product, or to a new market. Developing countries are more likely, on average, to find themselves in this position, and therefore need a 'preference' over more experienced and often larger exporters. But there is a conflict between preferences and the other trends in international trade. As liberalization proceeds (by both developed and developing countries), every reduction in 'normal' tariffs reduces the potential size of preference margins, and it becomes increasingly necessary to think of non-tariff preferences to fit into the increased relative importance of non-tariff barriers. Differentiation among developing countries means that the less poor lose relative, and often absolute, preference margins. There are potential inconsistencies between differentiation on the basis of ability to use preferences, and differentiation by more fundamental measures of poverty or absolute need, or on the basis of other types of criteria such as governance, labour standards or the environment. Regional arrangements cut across preference levels, giving an increasingly complex trading regime.

This chapter explores how the trading environment for developing countries is changing, as a background for later discussion of how this affects their domestic development strategies. It will look first at general liberalization in the Uruguay Round and since; then at the changing role and new proposals for preferences. After a brief examination of the role of regions, it will consider the increased role of regulation and enforcement.

2 Liberalization

Tariffs on goods have been liberalized almost without interruption since the 1940s by the developed countries, although the increase in non-tariff barriers during the 10 years from the mid-1970s to the beginning of the Uruguay Round meant that net liberalization in that period is more doubtful. In contrast, it is primarily since the 1980s that the developing countries have liberalized. But from the point of view of individual countries what matters is the pattern for individual trading partners and commodities. Here, the contrast remains between liberalization of the most advanced manufactures and less liberalization of items like clothing, steel and shoes, found in industrializing developing countries, and also of some processing stages of raw materials (giving tariff escalation), with still little on agriculture. One important difference must be drawn between the GATT/WTO process of multilateral liberalization and the country or financial institution-led process of unilateral liberalization. The WTO process offers the prospects of bargaining and offsetting gains, and it also offers an international 'binding' of commitments: once bound, tariff cuts cannot be changed by individual countries without international permission. This gives greater certainty, not only for country governments, but for private exporters and importers.

A variety of studies have been done since the end of the Uruguay Round of its effects on developing countries, using partial equilibrium models to examine individual commodities in detail or a computable general equilibrium (CGE). The models in general have found that the major benefits went to the developed and the more advanced developing countries, because these opened their own markets more. But in terms of the benefits of securing access for export markets (the particular advantage of multilateral negotiations, as identified above), the major benefits have gone to Asian developing countries, partly because of the effects of removing the Multi-Fibre Arrangement (MFA) and partly because the other Asian countries gained access to the newly industrialising countries (NICs). The Overseas Development Institute's (ODI) estimates found that while all developing countries could expect an increase of 1.4 per cent in exports (once all effects had come through), the figures for Asia were 2 per cent, and for South Asia 4.6 per cent. Of this 4.5 per cent was from the MFA. Because of the way the two principal elements (agriculture and MFA) were to be implemented, effectively nothing was expected to happen in the first half of the implementation from 1995 to 2000.[1] Only after 2001 would effects come through, with the full effect at the final implementation, January 2005.

The distribution of these benefits depends principally, of course, on the products and the export markets of each country, but it also depends on how constrained market access was before the Round. The EU had given exemption from MFA to its associated countries under the Lomé agreement, and also to least-developed countries (including Bangladesh), although under a less favourable regime for rules of origin. It introduced special arrangements for the Eastern European countries. The USA had special arrangements for the Caribbean, and, since the UR, has allowed Mexican exports free access under NAFTA. Countries subject to these special arrangements did not gain from the Uruguay Round, and lost in relative terms, while those which were and remain most constrained have most to gain.

The major beneficiaries from the reforms of the MFA were therefore expected to be China, India, Pakistan, South Korea, Sri Lanka and Indonesia. This appears to be happening, with China in particular expanding very rapidly, followed by India, Pakistan and Sri Lanka. Bangladesh has also continued to expand rapidly because of low labour costs, and because it is still the only unconstrained exporter to the EU in South Asia.

The liberalization in the Uruguay Round illustrates the problems of the interaction of preferences and tariffs. It would be illogical to oppose general liberalization, especially as many of the unpreferred countries are still clearly poor and in need of better market access, many preferences are restrictive and limited to a few countries, and because the consumers of their products are also in many cases poor and in need of lower costs. But it means that preferences cannot be a stable concept.

The Round also left some unfinished business. Trade in services had been included for the first time, but achieved little more than the recording and binding of existing rules by all countries. Many services were omitted (all countries were required to include at least one service, but none needed to include all). The settlement may have been discriminatory against developing countries in that countries tended to give greater freedom of movement to professional labour (and to companies) than to other labour. The most frequently included services – tourism, business services and finance – also probably favour developed countries, although in some business services developing countries have been able to build up exportable services, for example in publishing and data processing. At the end of 1996, an initiative by the developed countries brought a major agreement on telecommunications, while financial services reached agreement finally by the end of 1997. This leaves on the Uruguay agenda the commitment to prepare for new agriculture and services negotiations in 1999, and reviews of the implementation of existing agreements, notably MFA, but also intellectual property.

The Uruguay Round also instituted regular ministerial meetings to provide the opportunity to put new items on the agenda, and eventually to open another Round. The first ministerial meeting in Singapore, in December 1996, dealt with several new areas: environment, labour standards, competition policy, investment, regional agreements, further advances on services, and government procurement. It also launched an initiative to improve trade access for the least-developed countries, as well as to assist them in meeting trade obligations. This continued the trend seen in the Round of the WTO extending its responsibilities into new areas. Although on labour the Singapore Declaration emphasized the role of the ILO, including labour in the statement was itself a demonstration of a WTO interest and potential role. On all the others, it established working groups, suggesting future WTO action.

3 Preferences

The present preferences[2] for developing countries stem from two sources: special arrangements for countries with historical ties or current political or security interest to particular developed countries, and a development-focused initiative in the 1960s which arose out of economic analysis of the difficulties of developing, primary-product-exporting countries in competing with developed countries.

Some colonies, and other developing (and developed) countries have had special relationships that have given privileged access. As the colonies became independent, some wanted to keep these special arrangements. In the European Community, the common external tariff meant that this had to become a more formal joint commitment, embodied in a series of conventions, most recently the Fourth Lomé Convention (1990–2000). This does not cover all ex-colonies of all members; in particular, the late entrants, the UK, Spain and Portugal, only brought in some of the countries with which they had had special arrangements. Some of the largest developing Commonwealth countries, including Bangladesh, India and Pakistan, were excluded, and all the developed members lost their special access. The Lomé Convention, therefore, is now applied to a collection of some of the countries with a special relationship to one or more of the EU members, and with income levels that vary widely. It covers all manufactured goods, including exemption from controls under the MFA, although the strict rules of origin limit foreign input and, therefore, particularly limit its usefulness for the smaller or less-developed countries. It covers most primary goods, but limits access on goods covered by the CAP, with special arrangements for 'sensitive' goods like beef, bananas, rum and sugar.[3] It is joined by different special arrangements between the EU and the Mediterranean countries (some now approach reciprocal free trade, or in the case of Turkey a Customs Union); with the Andean countries (to promote alternative exports to drugs); and with potential members in Eastern Europe (these will eventually be reciprocal). The USA and Canada have separate special arrangements for the Caribbean, and the USA for the Andean region, as well as other arrangements. In all these cases, the principal criterion for special trade access is a political or historical relationship, not the developmental need or poverty of the developing countries; the goods and countries excluded suggest an additional criterion of being not too competitive with the developed.

In the 1960s developing countries pressed for a right to differential treatment to be recognized as a legitimate modification of the MFN treatment under GATT. The initiative was led by the Latin American countries which did not have traditional forms of special access and whose economists had participated in the theoretical analysis which supported it. This was incorporated as Part 4 of GATT in 1971, and permitted developed countries to give more favourable treatment to developing country exports, as well as giving the developing countries more freedom to restrict their own imports for development (infant industry) or balance of payments reasons. The resulting Generalized System of Preferences allowed developed countries complete discretion on what products were included and the degree of preference, and to alter their schemes. In the last decade, the system has been modified by graduating countries which became competitive with developed countries (wholly or for particular products), by adding new groups of countries, notably South Africa and the former centrally-planned economies, and by introducing criteria on labour or human rights standards. Some developed countries have also offered differentiated preferences, for the least-developed and for other-developing. The EU scheme now divides products into four levels of preference, with additional special provisions for the least-developed. It currently offers free access to least-developed countries for most manufactured exports (including MFA goods, but with exclusions in leather, an important export for the least-developed) and most agricultural goods (with slightly more exclusions than under Lomé).

The Uruguay Round of GATT was the first to incorporate different requirements on the extent and timing of liberalization, with three tiers: developed, developing and least-developed, formalizing this emerging distinction. Of these, only the least-developed was formally defined. The agreement allowed the developing and least-developed groups more time to fulfil the requirements (and, in the case of the least-developed, some exemptions). It did not modify the existing provisions for general differential treatment of all developing countries by the rest of the world.

In 1996, the Director-General of the WTO proposed that developed countries give the least-developed duty-free trade access, 'bound' by commitment to the WTO (1996a). At the Singapore Ministerial meeting of the WTO in December 1996, a Plan of Action (WTO, 1996b) was adopted, and the meeting to implement this took place on 27–8 October 1997, jointly with the UN, UNCTAD, the ITC, the World Bank and the IMF. It has, however, become more modest in its goals for trade access and more oriented to technical assistance. The Plan has three parts: to improve the implementation of the measures for the least-developed in the Uruguay Round settlement; to assist in 'capacity-building in the area of trade', which seems to be interpreted broadly to include assistance in export diversification, as well as in taking advantage of existing markets; and finally market access, the originally proposed preferential access, but now with exceptions allowed. Both the technical assistance and the access sections asked more advanced developing countries to participate in helping the least-developed.

At the conference, most developed countries and some of the more advanced developing countries agreed to offer increased duty-free access to the least-developed. The EU confirmed its offer of April 1997, made in response to the WTO proposal (EC, 1997). The proposal is to give them the same access as Lomé countries, although in the end it found it politically difficult to extend the agricultural preferences in full. (It is also technically complex because these depend on tariff-quotas which are no longer included in GSP provisions.) This will add little to their present access to the EU, except on a few goods like leather. It noted the problems caused by the rules of origin and limitations on cumulation; these have recently been a problem for Bangladesh, one of the principal least developed exporters to the EU. Europe raised the possibility of cumulation within South Asia. The access excludes them from the special Lomé protocols on the sensitive products, beef, sugar, rum and bananas. The USA agreed to add 1700 products to the duty-free list of its GSP, restricted to the least developed, and has also proposed additional concessions for Africa. Morocco, South Korea, Thailand, Turkey and Egypt, among others, offering limited concessions on some goods. The effects have not yet been quantified.

The EU paper raised doubts about the feasibility of binding special concessions for the least-developed, and there has been no explanation yet of how this could be done to give a firm but temporary basis, or what criteria or procedures for graduation from least-developed status would be adopted. Preliminary reports on the conference suggest that the concessions will not be bound, but will be made on an autonomous and reversible basis, like the GSP.

The results of the Meeting on the Least Developed (WTO, 1997) were more detailed on the technical assistance part of the Plan. Each eligible country was encouraged, and assisted by one of the relevant agencies, to carry out a 'needs assessment'. This has led to some revival of interest in technical assistance for export promotion. This may be seen either as a way of avoiding giving 'concessions' on trade which can provoke protectionists, or a more realistic view of the limits of preferences in a world of low tariffs and too many special forms of regional and preferential area. The difficulties of cumulation suggest that concessions on rules of origin (the Lomé arrangements are much more generous than the GSP) could be another way of offering 'non-tariff preferences'.

Individual country initiatives on preferences, however, have also continued. As well as its participation in the Least-Developed Initiative, the EU is considering how to renew or revise its Lomé Agreement. The proposals range from improving the general GSP to the level of present Lomé access, thus moving entirely in the direction of non-discrimination, to altering the system into a series of FTAs between the EU and FTAs in each region of the world. The current proposal most likely to be adopted is to extend the present system for a further five years to 2005. It has also introduced increased preferences within its GSP for countries complying with some ILO and tropical forest conventions. The USA, which has been less committed to special provisions in the past (although it has had special arrangements for the drug exporting Latin American countries and for the

Caribbean) has launched a special initiative for Africa which would offer better access to African countries which undertake economic reforms and which open their own trade; the provisions on trade suggest that his could be to favour either general opening or FTAs with the USA.[4] The area which continues to lack special arrangements is Asia.

4 Regionalism

The importance of regionalism in the context of this chapter is as an alternative form of tariff liberalization and as a challenge to the regulation and the MFN principles of the WTO. The 1980s and early 1990s saw a number of new regional groups, and some revivals from the previous surge in the 1960s. Many of those announced and discussed have (so far) had little substance in terms of formal provisions on trade or investment. It is arguable that the growth of regions has, in part, depended on the general liberalization of trade. The motivation for the regions which is normally political or security, with economic regionalism seen as either a necessary part or a form of glue for the region. The lower the perceived costs (to protection) and the actual cost (in loss of tariff revenue and the real economic costs of trade diversion from the rest of the world), the more likely are these non-economic arguments for regions to prevail.

The 'real' regions, however, are having two effects. The first is on trade: large increases in the share of member countries' trade going within the region have been observed in the EU (and its association agreements with Eastern Europe), NAFTA, MERCOSUR (Argentina, Brazil, Paraguay, Uruguay), the Group of Three (Mexico with two members of the old Andean Pact, Colombia and Venezuela), Central America, the Caribbean and SAARC (Bangladesh, Bhutan, India, Maldives, Nepal, Pakistan, Sri Lanka). Other agreements with preferences, and therefore potential effects, but where none has yet been observed include ASEAN (in Southeast Asia). Trade is already increasing in the SADC (Southern Africa) region, although its Trade Protocol is still being negotiated.

The second effect has been on attitudes towards regions and their regulation within the multilateral system. The response was to strengthen the regulation of regions in the GATT. The relevant Article (XXIV) was reworded, to emphasize that regions had to cover substantially all trade, and could not remain forever in transition to this. This was to prevent regions based on diverting trade from others, at little cost to their own producers. The second step was to provide a more consistent way of examining new and existing regions. This was further strengthened by a new tool for examining all countries' trade policies, the Trade Policy Review Mechanism. The legal changes were reinforced by a change in attitude: countries have been more ready to require new groups to be examined carefully; the large number of regions means a larger number of countries feel themselves potentially affected by the regional trend, because of the precedent-setting and example effects; and, finally, the EU itself has drawn back from its enthusiasm for regions, putting more emphasis on preserving those that exist and requiring any new agreements to be WTO-compatible.

There is a clear potential conflict between preferences and regions, as most regions include countries at more than one preference level, and most preference regimes include members and non-members of regions.

5 Regulation

The Uruguay Round and subsequent changes by the WTO have extended regulation to new international flows and increased international accountability and control of national actions. Like trade before GATT, services had previously been considered purely national responsibilities (legally, although there was a range of international accords and private arrangements, notably in transport, communications and other traditional services). The Round brought provision of information on the controls which all countries exercise on at least some services, and the construction of a classification of services and of models of provision which will constitute, in the future, a negotiating framework. The introduction of the most-favoured nation (MFN) principle, with countries required to specify any exceptions from the beginning (at least for services which they included in their offers) moved away from special arrangements. As has happened with negotiations on goods in the half century since the founding of GATT, it is likely that services negotiations will become more standardized with greater experience and information. (The various formulas now used for cross-country tariff reductions were developed only in the more recent Rounds, and have no more economic validity than equivalent rules for services might have.) Services have thus become regulated, if not liberalized.

In its moves on standards and intellectual property, the Round moved into new principles of international regulation. The rules on areas like sanitary and phytosanitary standards for agricultural products specified general international standards which had to be used in most circumstances, except where a country could make a scientific case for its own rules. They also did not allow discrimination between imports and domestic production. This goes beyond the traditional GATT rule of most-favoured nation (no discrimination among importers) to national treatment (no discrimination between imports and home production) and minimum standards (international limits on national governments' behaviour).

Intellectual property was not treated as a trade issue in the past. It had its own international negotiations, through the World Intellectual Property Organization, or was subject to bilateral agreements. It was included in some regions, Europe and NAFTA. It was brought into the UR initially because of fears of exports of counterfeit goods, but pharmaceutical companies, especially in the USA, had long seen local production of their products, without the payment of licence fees and justified on national health grounds, as a serious cost to their potential trade. The agreement not only required countries to accept the substance of international conventions, but went beyond this to setting minimum legal and administrative procedural requirements to enforce these. Finally, by putting it under the WTO it opened the range of WTO dispute-settlement and enforcement mechanisms.

It is not clear how to measure the effect of the trade-related aspects of intellectual property rights (TRIPs) in normal trade-gain terms. It is pre-eminently a protective measure, the reverse of liberalization. It may provide incentives for invention, but it clearly favours those who are net exporters of high-technology goods over those who are net importers, and could have the effect of discouraging start-up production of such goods.

An interesting aspect of the services agreement (probably intended by the GATT technicians who devised it) was the way in which the emphasis was placed on regulating the supplier rather than the service, which has led to an argument that the services agreement is basically about investment. This leads, naturally, to an interest in extending investment regulation beyond services provision. The Singapore meeting, as stated, set up two working groups on this, but the more conspicuous initiatives in recent years have been the growth of bilateral investment treaties and the negotiations for a Multilateral Agreement on Investment (MAI) under the OECD. These had the aim of increasing regulatory certainty for investors (a parallel with the original aim of GATT for traders), but also of extending that to providing national treatment and minimum standards of treatment. At present, it seems unlikely that the MAI will succeed. The combination of the need to bring investment regulation into line with that of services and goods, the pressures from both developed and developing countries for a more regulated system, and the strong pressure to move from a complex set of bilateral treaties to a multilateral regime (again, as in the move to GATT for goods) suggests that some agreement will be reached, eventually in the WTO.

The environment, like intellectual property, has started to evolve its own regulatory mechanism. Under provisions similar to those for international standards, international environmental rules can take precedence over trade rules (although there is still uncertainty), but national rules cannot. The WTO has a Committee on the Trade and Environment, and is clearly trying to bring this regulation at least into consistency with, if not under, the trade regime.

On labour the moves are more contradictory, with conflict between those who want to bring labour under the WTO (where supervisory, dispute, and enforcement mechanisms already exist), and those who want to develop such mechanisms within the ILO and who regard labour as too broad an issue to be treated in terms of its trade-related aspects.

The desire to bring new areas into the GATT was always there, because it had a dispute-settlement mechanism, but that system has been greatly strengthened by the UR. Findings by the panels which act as tribunals are now binding, unless they are challenged on a point of law. Previously, acceptance depended on consensus, including by the defending country. There are also clear time limits. Since it came into force, the system has been extensively used, including by developing countries, and is a significant benefit to the less powerful trading countries. It is also a major contributor to more uniform treatment of countries: several of the cases have dealt with discrimination among importers, not simply non-compliance with provisions for imports or discrimination between imports and home production. Now, the awareness that the system exists and will be used is acting as a prior constraint, discouraging countries from adopting non-WTO-compliant rules (the EU documents on the reform of the Lomé system and recent papers on possible new special arrangements with other areas are all pervaded by requirements that any settlement be WTO consistent).

Another innovation of the Round was the Trade Policy Review Mechanism. The fact that there are now proposals to copy it if the ILO is given responsibility for regulating labour standards suggests that it is seen as successful, and it has certainly made a major contribution to detailed knowledge about countries' trade regimes. Unlike IMF reviews they are published, but unlike OECD reviews they are not subject to approval by the countries reviewed. Large countries are reviewed at two-year intervals, middle and smaller at four and six years. At first these were described as purely fact-finding exercises, which would not criticise policies or make formal findings that any were contrary to GATT rules. The first reviews accorded with the neutral model. But by the time second reviews were reached, the procedure had acquired acceptability and a reputation for usefulness. Clearly the GATT teams could not simply repeat the information in the first. The result was an increasingly critical and judgmental approach, reinforced by open discussions (included in the publication) of each report by the full WTO membership. Recent reports have moved increasingly from description of to comments on protective measures, and then to discussion of trade policies and their effects on growth and efficiency. The extension of WTO responsibilities has meant that the reports have also extended, to services, intellectual property, investment, and finally to a full review of the industrial and macroeconomic structure of the economies.

They provide both an enforcement mechanism (countries avoid being found in violation of rules) and evidence for the stronger enforcement through the dispute system. As the WTO (unlike other international organisations) has no direct powers of initiative, it can only encourage its members to enforce its rules through such a mechanism.

6 Conclusions

The international system is more liberal than in the past (with only a few exceptions like intellectual property). This has reduced the value of preferences, although efforts are being made to increase their value at least for the poorest countries. In general, preferences today offer much less assistance than the system devised in the 1970s. Partly encouraged by liberalization, regions have proliferated, and the interaction of general preferences, special preferences for least-developed countries, special preferences for countries favoured by individual developed countries, and regional arrangements might seem to threaten the multilateral system. This is, however, unlikely, principally because most tariffs are (or are expected to become) so low, but also because the significant regions and preference regimes are actually quite few in number, and for any individual developing country the system can look much simpler. There remain risks of distortions to internal development from products like foods or clothing where international constraints, and therefore preferences, are still discriminatory, but these have not increased since the UR, and may diminish.

Regulation has been greatly extended. Countries are more constrained to comply with international rules; there are more international rules, on more subjects; there are constraints on national laws; there is supervision of national enforcement of national legislation. All of these increase the certainty of both national and international regimes, for countries and also for traders and investors, but at the expense of individually designed country policies for development. What are the effects of this? One, of course, will be new types of national measure (just as non-tariff barriers replaced tariffs, and domestic subsidies replaced export subsidies), but the scope for evasion is increasingly limited, and the role of both official reviews like the Trade Policy Review and private information makes the sustainability of any new measures likely to be shorter. Ricupero (UNCTAD, 1997) defined

> the process and degree of a country's integration within the international trading system... [as] its ability to (a) identify and take advantage of trading opportunities, (b) conform to its multilateral trade obligations, (c) formulate and pursue development strategies within the framework of these obligations, (d) defend its acquired trade rights, and (e) set trade objectives and effectively pursue them in trade negotiations.

The innovations of the UR and the four years since it was completed have improved opportunities and probably improved the ability to defend rights, but increased the obligations to which countries must conform and made the framework more complex. The burden of participating in trade negotiations has increased in scope and in regularity. It becomes necessary to think about new forms of assistance to replace tariff preferences.

Within countries, governments have the advantage and disadvantage of 'ready-made' rules for standards, intellectual property, investment, environment, and potentially for labour. For traders and investors, consistent rules across countries add convenience to certainty.

The effect of broadening the WTO to include areas like intellectual property, environment and, perhaps, labour standards, may be profound for the international system. It not only goes beyond MFN to 'national treatment' and 'treatment which is considered satisfactory by the international community', it sets a precedent for extending the concept of 'trade-related' to cover any subject where some countries feel that others' principles or enforcement mechanisms are inadequate. This opens the way for a variety of new international issues or ones which already have their own international regulatory bodies to be brought under the WTO. It is not clear whether either the administrative or the political structure of the WTO can bear such a weight.

Notes

1 Because the conditions for the first two rounds of MFA liberalization (in 1995 and 1998) allowed countries to liberalize mainly quotas which were not in fact binding, it is only from 2002 that the now-constrained exporters will start to have major benefits.

2 'Preferences' is used here for agreements which are not intended to be fully reciprocal.

3 About '97%' of agricultural imports from the ACP are covered (EC, 1997), but this figure must be treated with caution as those not included are subject to high tariffs and/or quotas, so their value is necessarily restricted.

4 It should be noted that this initiative followed the EU signing agreements intended to lead to FTAs with Mexico and with MERCOSUR, the regional organization in South America. A non-economic explanation for both the US and the EU intervention outside their normal areas of interest would be to discourage too close ties with the traditional trading partner.

References

EC (1997) Communication from the Commission 'Improving Market Access for Least Developed Countries', April.

Hertel, T. W., C. F. Bach, B. Dimaranan and M. Will (1996) *Growth, Globalization, and Gains from the Uruguay Round*, World Bank Policy Research Working Paper no. 1614 (Washington, DC.: World Bank).

Hong, P. (1997) 'International Implications of the Uruguay Round Agreements – Summary of the Project LINK Studies', paper prepared for the workshop on The Impacts of the Uruguay Round Agreements Development, UNCTAD, 3–4 March, Geneva.

ILO (1997) 'ILO Governing Body to examine Declaration on Fundamental Rights', in *World of Work*, vol. 22 (December), pp. 14–15.

Maskus, K. E. (1997) *Implications of Regional and Multilateral Agreements for Intellectual Property Rights*, CIES Policy Discussion Paper no. 97/10 (Adelaide: Centre for International Economic Studies).

Page, S. and M. Davenport (1994) *World Trade Reform: Do Developing Countries Gain or Lose?* (London: Overseas Development Institute).

Page, S. (1996) 'Bilateral and Regional Trade Preferences under the WTO', paper prepared for Workshop on World Trade Organization, 26 June, Harare.

Rahman, M. (1997) 'Preferential Market Access under EU GSP Scheme and Bangladesh's Export Sector Performance: Evidence and Emerging Issues', paper presented at the conference on Trading Out of Poverty: The Future of EU Trade Preferences in Promoting Development, London, 22 April.

UNCTAD (1997) 'Analyzing the Impact and Dynamic Effects of the Uruguay Round and its Follow-Up on Developing Countries', report on a workshop convened by the Secretary-General of UNCTAD, 3–4 March, Geneva.

WTO (1996a) 'Singapore Ministerial Declaration', from the Ministerial Conference, 9–13 December, Singapore.

WTO (1996b) 'Comprehensive and Integrated WTO Plan of Action for the Least-Developed Countries', from the Ministerial Conference, 9–13 December, Singapore.

WTO (1997) Papers from the WTO–UNCTAD High Level Meeting on the Least-Developed Countries, October.

Part III

Adjustment and Poverty

11

Adjustment and Poverty in Asia: Old Solutions and New Problems

*Frances Stewart**
Queen Elizabeth House, Oxford

1 Introduction

Asia is a huge area, covering a great range of experience, so generalizations are often invalid. Nonetheless, it appears that the Asian adjustment experience was not accompanied by the sharp rises in poverty and general worsening of human well-being that occurred in other regions of the world – notably sub-Saharan Africa and Latin America. Indeed with a few blips and exceptions, poverty declined during adjustment in Asia. Recent events, however, seem to challenge this rather optimistic conclusion. This chapter first explores the apparently successful experience of past adjustment and explains why it differed so radically from that of much of the rest of the world; and, second, briefly considers the new situation, emerging problems for poverty and possible solutions.

In the next section I present a short overview of some of the likely connections between adjustment and poverty from a theoretical perspective. Section 3 reviews experience in Asian economies during adjustment (broadly during the decade following 1985). Section 4 analyses some implications for poverty of the financial crisis of 1997–8, and considers policies needed to protect the poor in the aftermath of the crisis.

2 Adjustment and poverty: what we might expect

The impact of adjustment on poverty is partly dependent on how we define poverty. Poverty is multidimensional and may be assessed and measured in many ways. One important distinction is between outcomes and inputs, where outcomes consist of measures of well-being (for example, longevity, educational achievements, ability to function in different dimensions, happiness and so on), and input measures are indicators of access to the resources needed to produce a desired outcome. While what matters, from

* I am grateful for very helpful research assistance from Emma Samman.

a welfare perspective, are *outcomes*, inputs are more immediately affected by policy and hence normally form the focus of an enquiry into the effects of adjustment on poverty.

Two types of input are key: first, *primary* (or *private*) income, that is income derived from the economic system, including employment and self-employment, subsistence production and income from assets; second, *secondary* (or *social*) income, derived from the state via social production of free (or subsidized) goods and services and income transfers, for example, unemployment benefits. (Private transfers – most often within families – can provide another important source of support.) Poverty arises when either primary or secondary incomes are inadequate to meet minimum needs.[1] The first type of poverty may be called private income poverty (PIP), and the second social income poverty (SIP). To a certain extent private income can substitute for social income (that is, with enough private income people can buy the services the state fails to provide), while generous state transfers can offset inadequacies in private income. But from an analytic perspective, the way adjustment affects poverty is different for PIP and SIP, so the two will be considered separately.

Adjustment policies broadly fall into three categories, with almost all packages containing elements of each of the three: first, deflation, consisting of rising taxation/cuts in public expenditure designed to promote credit restraine and reduce the budget deficit; second, switching policies (normally devaluation) designed to encourage resources to move into tradables; and third, measures of liberalization such as price decontrol, financial reforms, tariff liberalization, privatization, all intended to increase the role of the market in resource allocation. For shorthand we shall refer to these measures as deflation, switching and liberalization.

2.1 The impact of adjustment policies on PIP

2.1.1 Deflation

Demand restraint has unambiguously negative effects on PIP. Demand-reducing policies include cuts in government expenditure, rises in taxation, reductions in real wages and credit restraint. The policies cut into real incomes by reducing employment and real wages of those in employment and raising the prices of consumption goods, as indirect taxes are raised and prices liberalized.

Workers employed in the public sector are those most immediately affected by restraints on government expenditure and reduced real wages. But the credit restraints lead to cutbacks in the private sector, which also suffers from reverse multiplier effects as the public sector contracts. Wage restraints frequently apply to the large-scale private sector as well. The informal sector suffers as a consequence of the cutback in the formal sector from two directions: an increased labour supply as the formal sector contracts (or fails to expand in line with the expansion of the labour force), and reduced market outlets as formal sector markets diminish.

If demand is restrained by holding back consumption disproportionately, then one would expect the burden to fall more heavily on people with high propensities to consume – that is, lower income groups. Some policies are clearly designed to achieve a cutback in consumption – for example, policies to hold down money wages while allowing prices to rise, policies to reduce public sector employment, raise indirect taxes and reduce consumer subsidies. Devaluation also has the effect of reducing the real wage in the modern sector. Other policies tend to reduce investment, such as credit restraint, high interest rates, cuts in public sector investment. These policies also adversely affect wage-earners by creating unemployment, but to the extent that they lead to a fall in investment they allow current consumption to be higher.

Most of these negative effects are, at least in the first instance, *urban* and, particularly affect those employed in the formal sector. People in the rural sector are relatively insulated, especially, of course, those whose main activities are for self-consumption. But the many links between urban and rural sectors, via migration, markets and remittances, mean that some negative effects are felt there. The distributional implications and the effects on poverty levels depend partly on the initial location of poverty. This tendency for an *urban bias* in the adverse distributional implications of demand restraint is the counterpart of a previous urban bias in the location of modern sector employment. Since the switching policies also exhibit an adverse bias against the urban sector (see the next sub-section below), urban poverty is particularly likely to rise as a consequence of the adjustment package.

Some economists in the International Monetary Fund (IMF, 1986) have argued that the deflationary policies need not hurt the poor. Heller *et al.* (1988) for example, argue that there may be a negative short-run impact on the poor for two to three years, with falling output and employment following monetary contraction,[2] but that this may be offset in the longer run by positive consequences from supply-side policies for economic growth so there is 'no clear presumption that Fund-supported programmes adversely affect growth' (p. 16). Empirical evidence on this issue is ambiguous.

Moreover, it is argued that the programmes reduce inflation and this will help the poor: 'one expects the poor to benefit from reduced inflation because they typically pay most of the inflation tax' (Heller *et al.*, p. 15). The argument is that the poor lack assets which act as hedges against inflation and also hold a disproportionately large amount of cash because they do not have other means of exchange such as credit cards. The effects of inflation on the poor depend on whether the goods consumed by them rise in price more quickly than do other categories of goods; the extent to which the poor have assets which can act as a hedge against inflation; and on time lags between price and income increases for the poor. For each mechanism, the effects vary according to who the poor are. For example, subsistence farmers will be little touched by inflation, while urban workers could be badly hit unless their earnings keep pace. In general, debtors are likely to gain relative to creditors, and debtors can be expected to be poorer than creditors. A recent review by Sarel (1997) of 45 empirical studies found no evidence that the level, variability or the rate of change of inflation had a significant effect on the income distribution.

In summary, demand-reducing policies are likely to increase poverty in the short term, especially urban poverty, although they may not worsen income distribution.

2.1.2 Switching policies[3]

Switching policies aim to produce a change in the relative price of tradables. Devaluation is the main policy instrument used for switching (evidence from Polak, 1991, and the World Bank, 1990, shows it occurring in nearly all IMF programmes at the end of the 1980s and 85 per cent in a sample of World Bank SALs from 1981–8).

Assuming that the policies succeed in bringing about a real exchange rate change[4] with a rise in the price of tradables (T) relative to non-tradables (NT), the effects on income distribution and poverty depend: on the factor intensity in T and NT; on whether there is factor mobility between sectors; on the initial location of poverty; and on how prices are formed.

When the economy behaves according to neo-classical assumptions, with well-behaved production functions, complete factor mobility and competitive pricing, the well-known Stolper–Samuelson theorem applies and the effect of the devaluation will be to increase returns to the factor that is used intensively in T relative to that used intensively in NT. This apparently straightforward result does not, however, lead to simple conclusions concerning income distribution because of the heterogeneous and varied nature of T and NT, in terms of factor-intensity, in developing countries. Only where the tradable sector consists in relatively labour-intensive commodities will the switch lead to improved employment and wage income. This will not be the case where exportables consist mainly of mineral resources or agricultural products produced on large estates, or human-capital-intensive manufactures, especially if non-tradables consist largely of labour-intensive services. It is most likely to be the case where exports of labour-intensive manufactures increase.

The issue of factor mobility between sectors is key. If resources switch instantaneously, then full employment of resources can be assured. But if there is rigidity – with new projects requiring new investment which takes time as well as resources – there can be unemployment of labour and other resources in the transition, which is likely to increase poverty. With lack of mobility of factors, for example between the rural and urban sectors, exchange rate changes alter the terms of trade – normally in favour of the rural sector. This would tend to increase urban poverty, but might reduce rural poverty. A further qualification is needed for economies with sizeable oligopolistic sectors, where mark-up pricing is the norm. Heavily protected import-substituting industrial sectors are examples. In these sectors, devaluation will tend to reduce the wage-share and increase the profit share, worsening (normally urban) income distribution.

In summary, improved terms of trade between tradables and non-tradables would tend to improve income distribution where the poor are heavily concentrated in primary production – that is, in economies exporting agricultural products produced in a labour-intensive way by peasant producers, and also where labour-intensive manufactures form an important and price-elastic part of the economy and source of employment and income for the poor. The change in income distribution would be adverse where production of primary products is in large firms owned by the better-off, employing little labour (such as in mineral economies, or where mechanised large farms dominate export production). In countries with relatively large modern sectors, where policy changes lower the labour-share, then a worsening would be expected. This is likely to be the case with devaluation, wage restraint and inelastic demand for labour. Worsening may also occur as a result of increased differentials between those with more and those with less human capital, especially in middle-income countries where comparative advantage may lie with skilled rather than unskilled labour.

Applying these general principles to the various regions around the world, it seems that the Asian region, as a whole, is in a better position to secure poverty-reducing adjustment than other regions. In the first place, comparative advantage in most Asian economies lies in labour-intensive manufactures, given the low wages (arising from the heavy population pressure on land), the relatively high levels of human capital in the region and a fair amount of industrial experience. In contrast, the African region lacks industrial experience and human capital; and Latin America and the Caribbean have relatively high wages owing to their more generous land and mineral endowment. Secondly, with high rates of investment the Asian region is able to move resources into new areas relatively rapidly. The oligopolistic import-substituting industrial sector is also smaller in most countries, but there are exceptions – as, for example, the Philippines.

2.1.3 Liberalization

The impact of liberalization on income distribution and poverty depends on what the liberalization is *from*. If the prior situation is the stereotypical one, of an elite gaining privileged access to most resources (credit, employment, foreign exchange and so on) then a market solution would be likely to extend access to the poor compared with the prior situation. But if in the previous situation significant state benefits did succeed in reaching the poor, for example through employment schemes, credit allocation or food subsidies, then the more market-oriented solution may well deprive some of the poor of resources.

Contrast two models of the prior situation: (1) the model of a planned economy such as that intended by Nyerere or Nehru which incorporates the poor in production – through special credit schemes, employment schemes or production quotas – and in consumption – through free access to health and education, access to rationed food at subsidized prices, access to scarce imported inputs for medicines, and so on; and (2) the rent-seeking model of Krueger, Sahn and others, where all state interventions create rents which are monopolized by the elite. According to the first model, the poor will surely lose by liberalization; in the latter they will surely gain. Which model is right? Probably neither as most societies contain elements of both models, with some leaning to one rather than the other. Work on food subsidies by Cornia and Stewart (1993), has shown many cases where there is enough truth in model (1) for liberalization to worsen the position of the poor; similarly with government supported credit schemes, such as the Grameen Bank, or India and Indonesia's policies to force banks to lend a proportion of their resources to low-income borrowers which have led to such successes as the Self-Employed Women's Association in India and BKK in Indonesia. There are also cases where the prime beneficiaries of state interventions are the elite (for example, food subsidies in Morocco or Pakistan). Generalization is therefore not possible.

Evidence is accumulating, nonetheless, that liberalization tends to be unequalizing. For example, both the USA and the UK have seen sharp rises in inequality (after decades of Kuznets-type improvements as they sailed down the right-hand curve of the inverted U) with the liberalizing reforms of the 1980s. In Latin America, as Berry (1997) shows, there is strong evidence that import liberalization, in particular, has been associated with rising inequality. Privatization and the relaxation of restrictions on wage and salary differentials tend to increase inequality.

However, whether these reforms help or hurt the primary incomes of the poor, on balance, depends above all on the impact on the growth rate. If the growth rate rises, then adverse changes in income distribution may well be more than offset, while if growth declines the impact on the poor is almost invariably negative. Fields (1989) and Deininger and Squire (1996) have shown that in almost all cases, private income poverty is reduced with growth in GDP per capita, that is, growth is rarely immiserizing.

Thus the impact of adjustment policies on growth is key. We have already noted that deflationary policies tend to have a negative impact in the short term – hence the greater the deflationary element in the package, the more likely that falling incomes may follow. A second critical factor is the rate of investment; if this is high and sustained, then positive growth is likely. Some of the reforms tend to have a negative impact on investment, especially, as evidence from FitzGerald, Jansen and Vos (1993) and Serven and Solimano (1992) revealed, any cuts in public investment which tend to 'crowd-out' private investment. Investment is also likely to be sustained if external markets are growing and responsive to exchange rate changes.

The longer-run impact on growth is even more difficult to judge. Will the policies lead to sustained growth on the model of East Asia (or was government intervention essential for that success), or to moderate growth little different from the import-substitution era, as appears to be the case in most Latin America examples, or to prolonged stagnation, as in many African cases?

Empirical evidence has focused on the short to medium-term effects. Here the results are surprisingly weak – and highly dependent on who does the assessment. A summary of 23 investigations published in Stewart (1995, table 2.2) shows that the impact is very small, ranging from a small negative to a small positive effect on growth. If this is the case, then in the longer run the consequences for the poor do depend mainly on the distributional outcomes.

2.2 The impact of adjustment policies on SIP

What happens to SIP during adjustment is particularly important because (1) social income can adjust so as to compensate for losses in primary incomes (that is, the safety net function), or can compound these losses; and (2) parts of social income are important for building up human resources, especially educational access and nutrition, so that in the longer run PIP depends partially on what happens to SIP. Changes in SIP can be viewed as the outcome of changes in three ratios: the public expenditure ratio or G_E/Y; the social allocation ratio (where social expenditure includes health, education, water, sanitation, nutrition), or S/G_E; and the priority ratio, that is, the proportion of expenditure on the social sectors going to the poor, that is, S_P.

As noted, deflationary policies may raise taxation or cut expenditure or both, but typically there is some downward pressure on government expenditure, so G_E/Y can be expected to fall. The social allocation ratio is likely to fall too if part of the adjustment package is to raise interest rates and/or improve debt payments, so that debt servicing takes a growing proportion of government expenditure. Moreover, the liberalization package often involves a shift in responsibility for social services to the private sector, leading to a decline in state expenditure on the social sectors. In principle, those designing reform packages would intend to accompany such cuts with a rise in the proportion of state expenditure going to the poor, that is, an improvement in S_P. The net effect on the poor will depend on the balance of these changes, with the expenditure and social allocation ratio going in a negative direction, and, in principle, the priority ratio in a positive direction. However, raising the priority ratio is the hardest to achieve because it depends on successful targeting. Much evidence on targeted food subsidies and exemptions from user charges suggests that almost always many of the poor are left out. Consequently, as Cornia and Stewart (1993) and Creese (1990) showed, there was an improvement in S_P, but the coverage of the poor actually worsened.

Changes in the tax/subsidy system also tend to be unequalizing and to hit the poor. First, food and fuel subsidies are removed, sometimes to be replaced by targeted subsidies, nearly always of a lesser value. Second, tax reform typically reduces the role of direct taxation (which the poor rarely pay) and raises that of indirect taxation. Universal value-added taxes are paid to a greater extent by the poor, particularly if food is included.

The effectiveness of the social safety net in compensating for rising PIP depends on the institutional arrangements in place, and/or new ones that are introduced with the adjustment package. Where the arrangements in place are already fairly comprehensive – as for example in Costa Rica in the 1980s – they are able to be quite effective in protecting the poor during adjustment, but, as Stewart and van der Geest (1995) described, new arrangements specifically introduced for the crisis (as with many of the Social Funds that were developed in the late 1980s) almost always had low coverage in relation to need. This is partly because the concept of introducing a universal safety net sufficient to bring private incomes up to some poverty line is inconsistent with the philosophy of adjustment. An adequate safety net requires comprehensiveness of coverage, often associated with large-scale government works programmes. A universal food subsidy on basic foods is another helpful instrument. The implications for the design of safety nets are:

- large (albeit temporary) government expenditure at a time when the government is trying to introduce expenditure cuts;
- universal provision without means-testing at a time when targeting is in vogue; and
- government-financed projects at a time when private initiative is being promoted and government economic activity discouraged.

However, most social safety nets consist in project finance to be granted to privately organized activities – not surprisingly the end result is on a small scale and does not reach those most in need.

2.2.1 *Summary of expected consequences of adjustment policies for PIP and SIP*

The most important determinant of PIP is what happens to the growth rate. In the short term this depends largely on the extent of deflation relative to other adjustment policies and how far investment is sustained over the adjustment period. Aspects of the package are likely to improve income distribution in some contexts – notably if labour-intensive manufactured exports and peasant-produced agricultural products respond positively to the package. However, the general trend of the liberalization moves is towards rising income inequality, which might offset this effect. After-tax income distribution might worsen more as the tax system switches away from direct taxes to indirect, and towards reducing the marginal rates of income tax.

Adjustment policies also alter SIP, on the whole in a poverty-creating direction, though determined efforts to create effective safety nets and improve targeting have occasionally succeeded in reaching a high proportion of the poor. More often 'safety nets' are misnamed, or at least the safety they provide is not for the majority of the poor, but for the donors and politicians introducing the adjustment package who are able to convince themselves that effective protection policies are in place and hence there is no need for concern about the impact of the adjustment policies on the poor.

3 Experience in Asia: the 1980s and early 1990s

Asian economies were subject to less-intensive international financial institution (IFI)-sponsored adjustment packages than other areas, as their accumulated debt was substantially lower in relation to exports or GDP over the period and their current account deficits smaller as shown in Table 11.1. Nonetheless, most countries in the region had World Bank or IMF adjustment or stabilization loans at some time during the 1980–96 period. The principal exceptions, shown in Table 11.2, were Singapore, Indonesia, Taiwan and Malaysia.[5]

In examining the impact of adjustment on poverty empirically, three problems stand out. First, many economies followed some adjustment policies without actually having IFI backing or policy conditionality. This was especially important in the Asian region where a number of countries adopted their own subset of adjustment policies – including devaluation and import liberalization, for example – without formal IFI policy conditionality. Hence, in one way or another most countries in South, East and South East Asia can be regarded as 'adjusting' economies. But there is an important distinction between those countries adjusting on their own, which usually adopted adjustment policies selectively, and those which received IMF or World Bank finance associated with policy conditionality. In what follows we shall classify countries into those adjusting with IFI-support as IFI-adjusting countries, and the rest which include two categories – the 'own-adjusting category' and those which did not change their policies significantly. Taking five-year periods, 1981–5, 1986–90, 1991–6 we define IFI-adjusting countries as those that had IFI programmes during the sub-period. The South Asian countries were mainly IFI-adjusting. Thailand, the Philippines, China and South Korea also had IFI support for at least two of the three periods. Other countries in the region were at war (Afghanistan and Cambodia) or were socialist planned economies and as yet have undergone

Table 11.1 Contrasting conditions in Asia, Africa and Latin America, 1980–96

	Asia	*Africa*	*Latin America and the Caribbean*
Balance on current account as % of exports			
1981	−9.7	−23.8	−31.0
1986	−5.0	−18.5	−23.6
1990	+1.9	−5.8	−3.9
1996*	−3.2	−11.6	−12.8
Fiscal balance, % GDP			
1980	−3.4	−3.9	−0.6
1990	−2.9	−3.6	−0.8
1993	−2.9	−10.6	−0.1
External debt, ratio to GDP, %			
1980	15.9	35.7	27.3
1986	26.6	64.1	63.4
1990	30.2	68.4	46.5
1996*	28.2	68.7	41.4
Debt service ratio %			
1983	10.8	22.7	42.5
1990	16.3	22.5	24.5
1996*	8.1	14.8	30.0

* estimates.
Source: IMF, *World Economic Outlook* (various); United Nations, *World Economic and Social Survey 1997*.

Table 11.2 Dates of IMF programmes and World Bank structural adjustment loans in Asia 1980–97

	IMF Standby EFF SAF ESAF	*World Bank SALs*
Bangladesh	1979–80; 1980–3; 1985–7; 1987–9; 1990–3	none
China	1981; 1986–7	none
India	1981–4; 1991; 1991–3	1991
Indonesia	none	none
Korea	1980–2; 1983–5; 1985–7	1981; 1984
Laos	1980–1; 1989–92; 1993–7	1989; 1991; 1996
Malaysia	none	none
Mongolia	1991–2; 1993–7	none
Nepal	1985–7; 1987–90; 1992–5	1987; 1989
Pakistan	1980–6; 1988–91; 1993–7	1982
Philippines	1986–8; 1989–97	1980; 1983
Singapore	none	none
Sri Lanka	1979–82; 1983–4; 1986–8; 1989–97	none
Thailand	1981–3; 1985–7	1982; 1983
Vietnam	1993–7	1994

Source: World Bank, *Annual Reports*; IMF, *Annual Reports*.

little in the way of transition (Burma, Laos, Mongolia). Data are highly deficient for the last two categories, so the focus will be on East, SouthEast and South Asia.

The second well-recognized problem is that of the counterfactual. In principle any assessment should look at what happened compared with what would have happened without the adjustments. However, there is no completely satisfactory way of getting at the counterfactual. Comparisons of before and after in the same country or between countries with and without programmes provide some indication, but neither is satisfactory – the first because the prior situation might not have been sustainable, the second because countries which did not need IFI support were likely to have been in a better situation initially. However, what actually happened, without regard to the counterfactual, is of interest – especially to those who lived through the experience. If conditions got better for the poor during adjustment, then that is itself of considerable importance, whether or not they did so in comparison with some counterfactual. It is the fact that the actual position of the poor deteriorated in Latin America and sub-Saharan Africa in the 1980s that caused alarm and led to calls for 'Adjustment with a Human Face', not a comparison with a counterfactual. In our analysis we focus primarily on what actually happened in the two main categories of country.

Third, there is a problem of the lack of, or imperfect, data. The review that follows is based on readily available data, but it may well be incomplete and does not adjust for deficiencies in the data.

The basis for and measurement of the poverty estimates differ among countries and over time, so the comparisons and conclusions must be treated with caution. According to most indicators, poverty declined and social indicators improved in both IFI-assisted and other countries taking the period as a whole (Tables 11.3 and 11.4). But while national PIP rates declined in most countries from the early 1980s to the early 1990s, a rise in either rural or urban poverty rates was recorded in a significant number of cases over some part of this time. The data suggest that poverty rates rose significantly, that is by over 3 percentage points, in rural India, 1989/90 to 1993/4; urban Nepal, 1984/5 to 1995/6; rural Pakistan 1984/5 to 1994/5; urban Philippines, 1971 to 1985 (although early 1980s data are lacking); and rural Sri Lanka, 1979/8 to 1986/7. Note that all these countries are IFI-adjusting. Moreover, in each episode of rising poverty, an IFI programme was in place, as it was in the five cases, excluded above, where small rises of 3 or less percentage points in poverty were recorded.

There were also cases of IFI programmes associated with falling poverty – for example, the Korean, Bangladesh and Pakistan programmes of the early 1980s. But falls in both urban and rural poverty occurred in less than half the IFI programmes. In contrast, the 'other' category of countries (which includes only those termed 'own-adjusters' in this case, as there is a lack of

Table 11.3 Private income poverty estimates for Asian countries, 1980–95

Country	*IFI Programme between dates*[1]	*Date*	*Poverty rate %*		
			Rural	*Urban*	*Total*
Bangladesh	na	1981–2	74	66	73
	Y	1985–6	51	56	52
	Y	1991–2	53	34	50[2]
China	na	1981	24	11	20
	Y	1990	12	0.4	9
India	na	1977–8	55	34	43
	Y	1989–90	38	24	32
	Y	1992	48	25[3]	34
Indonesia	na	1980	28	29	29
	N	1987	16	20	17
	N	1990	14	17	15
	N	1993	na	na	8[4]
Korea, rep.	na	1980	9	10	10
	Y	1984	4	5	5
Malaysia	na	1980	37	13	29
	N	1987	25	8	17
	N	1989	19	7	15
Nepal	na	1979	61	55	60
	N	1984–5	43	14	43
	Y	1995–6[4]	44	23	42
Pakistan	na	1979	33	29	30
	Y	1984–5	26	25	26
	Y	1991	37	28	34
Philippines	na	1971	57	41	52
	Y	1985	59	45	54
	Y	1991	52	37	45
Sri Lanka	na	1978–9	26	20	23
	Y	1986–7	32	15	31
	Y	1991[4]	36	18	22
Thailand	na	1980–1	27	8	23
	Y	1988–9	29	7	2
	Y	1992	16	10	13
Vietnam	Y	1988	60	na	na
	N	1993	57	26	51

Notes: [1] Adjustment programmes include IMF Standby; SAF; ESAF; World Bank Structural Adjustment Loans; [2] poverty rate rose according to some estimates; [3] rate fell according to some estimates; [4] comparability of estimates questionable. na = not available.
Sources: Tabatabai (1996); World Bank (1997) *World Development Indicators*; World Bank (1998) *Human Development Report 1997*.

Table 11.4 Indicators of social poverty, 1980–95

Country	*Access to education, % of age-group not in school*				*% without access to*				*Infant mortality rate, deaths per 1000 live births*	
	Primary [1]		*Secondary*		*Health services*		*Safe water*			
	1980	*1993*	*1980*	*1993*	*1980*	*1993*	*1980*	*1994/5*	*1981*	*1995*
Bangladesh	38	0	82	81	20	26	59[4]	70	135	79
China	0	0	54	48	na	12	na	54	71	34
Hong Kong	0	0	36	na	na	na	na	0	10	5
India	17	0	70	na	50	na	na	37	121	68
Indonesia	0	0	71	57	64[3]	57	25[4]	37	105	51
Korea Rep.	0	0	22	7	na	0	7[4]	7	33	10
Lao PDR	0	0	79	75	na	na	na	56[5]	126	90
Malaysia	7	7	52	41	40[2]	12	na	10	30	12
Nepal	16	0	79	79	90	na	89	52	148	91
Pakistan	61	35	86	na	35	15	62	40	123	90
Philippines	0	0	36	21	na	29	34[4]	16	63	39
Singapore	0	0	42	22	0[2]	0	0	0	12	4
Sri Lanka	0	0	47	26	10	10	64[4]	43	43	16
Thailand	1	2	71	63	70	41	34[4]	19	53	35
Vietnam	0	0	58	65	25	3	59	62	97	41

Notes: [1] Under access to primary education; figures of zero children not attending school are given where gross enrolment rates exceed 100, but in fact as children out of the 'right' age group also attend primary and secondary schools, there may still be some children out of school even with gross enrolment rates over 100. [2]1985–7. [3]1980–6. [4]1983–6. [5]1990–6. na = not available.

Source: World Bank, *World Development Indicators 1997*; UNDP, *Human Development Report 1997*; World Bank, *World Development Report, 1983*; UNICEF, *State of the World's Children*, 1988, 1998a, 1985/7b, 1980/86c, 1983/86d, 1990–96.

data for the other 'other' cases), all showed falls in urban and rural poverty for each period. This is also true of Taiwan, omitted from the tables because of unavailable data.

When it comes to social poverty, countries in both groups reduced poverty according to almost all indicators (Table 11.4). The only possible exceptions were apparent worsening of coverage of safe water and health services in Bangladesh, safe water coverage in Indonesia and secondary education in Vietnam, but for the first two the data may not be comparable. Using reductions in infant mortality rates (IMR) as the single indicator of SIP, while all countries made improvements, the IFI-supported countries mainly did worse than the own-adjusting, with the exception of Sri Lanka, Korea and China as shown in Figure 11.1. On average the 1995 IMR was 46 per cent of the 1981 level for those without any IMF adjustment programmes, while the IFI-assisted countries rate fell to 55 per cent of the 1981 level.

Both groups of countries did well on poverty reduction compared with other adjusting regions – notably Latin America and sub-Saharan Africa. In both these regions, private-income poverty increased for the region as a whole over the adjustment years of the 1980s. Using Chen, Datt and Ravallion (1994) data for Latin America and the Caribbean, extreme poverty is estimated to have risen from 13.2 to 17.2 per cent between 1985 and 1990; for sub-Saharan Africa it rose from 31.7 per cent to 33.4 per cent. In contrast, in South Asia it fell from 36.8 to 33.3 per cent, and in East Asia extreme poverty remained constant at 4.9 per cent, while a higher poverty line showed a fall from 54.6 to 49.3 per cent.[16] In Latin America and sub-Saharan

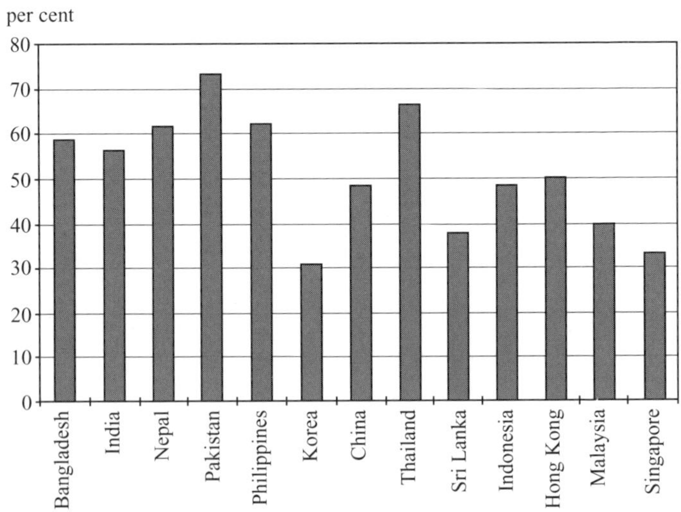

Figure 11.1 Infant mortality rate, 1995 as per cent of 1981

Africa, Stewart (1995) found that educational indicators had worsened in a number of countries, although both regions continued to show improvements in infant mortality rates in most countries, but the rate of improvement was less than that achieved in the Asian countries. The 1995 IMR of Latin America and the Caribbean was 65 per cent of its 1980 value, and for sub-Saharan Africa it was 80 per cent of the 1980 value, whereas for the adjusting countries in Asia, that is, the group of countries in Figure 11.1, it was 51 per cent. Hence there was relative success in both groups of Asian countries with respect to both PIP and SIP, and, despite some blips, overall rural and urban poverty rates declined for all countries over the 1980–95 period as a whole, with the possible exception of Pakistan.

The explanation for the relative success on poverty must lie, tautologically, in a combination of output growth and its allocation: for PIP the allocation concerns changing income distribution; for SIP it is a question of changes in the allocation of national income to social priorities. For any given allocation of private and social income the change in poverty depends on the change in per capita incomes.

For the 1980–96 period, average annual per capita incomes grew by 5.7 per cent. IFI-supported countries' rate was a bit less than that of the others, at 5.6 per cent compared with 6.4 per cent (Table 11.5). The rate for both groups was much greater than that experienced in other parts of the world; in sub-Saharan Africa income per head fell by over 1 per cent a year, and in Latin America it fell slightly during the 1980s and rose by about 1.5 per cent from 1990–5. The rate of growth of agriculture is of particular importance for success in reducing rural poverty, not only because of the direct earnings from agriculture, but also the rural non-agricultural linkages that result. Rates of growth of value-added in agriculture exceeding 3 per cent a year between 1980–95 – high enough to make a reduction in rural poverty probable – were experienced in China, India, Indonesia, Malaysia, Pakistan and Thailand, and Vietnam for 1990–5 (earlier data not available). This large difference in growth rates between Asia and other regions is more than sufficient to explain the differences in changes in PIP and SIP. This is confirmed by examining changes in the allocation of private and social income.

3.1 Private income poverty and private income distribution

In the Asian context – in contrast to Latin America and perhaps sub-Saharan Africa – one might expect adjustment policies to be associated with an improvement in income distribution, as labour-intensive exports expand and with them employment. As can be seen from Table 11.6, exports expanded spectacularly – by 15.4 per cent per annum among countries with IFI support (about double the rate of increase of the 'other' category). Moreover, the share taken by textiles, generally believed to be labour-intensive, was high: over 50 per cent for the IFI-adjusters in the 1990–5 period and 25 per cent for the others, in each case rising over the period

Table 11.5 Change in per capita income in Asian countries, 1980–96

Country	*Change in per capita incomes (%)*				*Rate of growth of value added in agriculture % pa*	
	1980–96	*1980–5*	*1986–90*	*1990–6*	*1980–0*	*1990–5*
Bangladesh	4.4	5.0	3.5	4.2	2.7	1.1
Bhutan	6.6	7.7	na	4.7	na	na
Cambodia	6.2	na	7.7	5.3	na	2.1
China	10.0	9.0	10.0	9.9	5.9	4.3
Hong Kong	6.8	8.4	7.0	4.8	na	na
India	4.8	3.8	6.3	4.9	3.1	3.1
Indonesia	7.0	6.8	6.0	8.1	3.4	2.9
Korea, Rep.	7.9	6.5	9.7	7.7	2.8	3.1
Lao PDR	5.4	na	4.1	7.6	na	na
Macao	6.6	9.5	7.3	5.6	na	na
Malaysia	7.1	7.3	4.6	8.9	3.8	2.6
Mongolia	2.5	6.7	5.5	1.7	2.9	na
Myanmar	3.0	5.7	−2.0	4.6	0.5	5.1
Nepal	4.3	3.1	4.9	4.9	4.0	1.5
Pakistan	5.9	6.7	6.4	4.7	4.3	3.4
Philippines	2.3	2.0	2.7	2.9	1.0	1.6
Singapore	7.8	8.6	6.0	8.7	−6.2	0.5
Sri Lanka	4.6	5.8	3.1	4.4	2.2	2.4
Thailand	7.7	5.4	9.1	9.4	4.0	3.0
Vietnam	6.3	na	4.7	7.7	na	5.2
Region average	*5.7*	*6.2*	*5.4*	*5.8*	*2.2*	*2.8*
IFI-adjusters	*5.6*	*5.5*	*5.9*	*4.5*	*3.3*	*2.6*
Others	*6.4*	*7.1*	*5.3*	*7.2*	*0.9*	*3.1*

na = not available.
Sources: World Bank (1997) *World Development Indicators* (CD-rom version); World Bank (1995) *World Tables*.

1980–96. Electronics – also labour intensive – formed a high and rising proportion of the 'other' country category. It was particularly high in Malaysia at nearly a third of exports, and accounted for over a quarter of exports in Singapore and Korea for 1990–5. Electronics formed a low proportion of the IFI-supported countries' exports at under 5 per cent for 1990–5.

Estimates for the labour-intensity of growth are provided by employment elasticities. These varied considerably, partly (but not wholly) reflecting the changing pattern of exports. There was high employment elasticity in Indonesia, 0.9 from 1981–92, while in the Philippines it was actually negative, −0.5. The typical employment elasticity for East and Southeast Asia was 0.5. In South Asia there was high employment elasticity in Bangladesh, 1.1, while it was 0.5 in Pakistan and only 0.3 in India. Estimates for employment elasticity come nearest to being an indicator of labour-intensive growth.

Table 11.6 International trade in Asian countries, 1980–96

Country	*% change pa 1980–96*		*% exports 1980–96*	
	exports $	*imports $*	*Clothing and textiles*	*Electronics*
Bangladesh	10.3	7.9	72.9	0.2
Bhutan	12.5	8.2	na	na
Cambodia	49.7	27.9	na	na
China	17.0	15.2	29.3	9.5
Hong Kong	15.2	15.8	33.5	15.6
India	9.1	6.4	27.5	1.6
Indonesia	5.7	10.7	11.7	2.2
Korea, Republic	13.6	13.3	21.2	21.2
Lao PDR	31.8	48.6	na	na
Macao	9.5	64.9	76.6	1.4
Malaysia	11.9	14.2	4.3	25.9
Mongolia	−3.3	−7.0	na	na
Myanmar	7.2	13.9	2.5	na
Nepal	12.8	10.3	65.8	0.2
Pakistan	9.1	6.3	72.6	0.1
Philippines	15.2	10.7	10.3	12.0
Singapore	10.1	11.8	4.0	24.1
Sri Lanka	15.9	6.9	31.6	0.6
Thailand	19.3	15.3	14.4	11.6
Vietnam	−0.8	14.7	5.5	0.2
Region average	*12.5*	*15.3*	*30.1*	*8.4*
IFI-adjusters	*15.4*	*13.6*	*35.1*	*5.7*
Others	*7.9*	*18.1*	*23.0*	*13.8*

na = not available
Sources: World Bank (1997) *World Development Indicators* (CD-rom version); Asian Development Bank, *Asian Economic Outlook*.

Defining labour-intensive growth as occurring where employment elasticities exceed 0.5, Bangladesh, Indonesia and Thailand qualify, and Sri Lanka in the latter part of the period. Korea, Malaysia, Thailand and the Philippines showed labour-intensive growth in the 1970s. Again this contrasts strongly with Latin America where the employment elasticity was negative in the 1980s.[6]

Rapid growth in employment depends on both output growth and its employment elasticity. Indonesia enjoyed high and labour-intensive growth – formal sector manufacturing employment is estimated to have grown by 11 per cent a year during 1981–92. In contrast, employment growth in India was only 0.6 per cent a year in manufacturing as output growth was sluggish and employment elasticity low. Korea and Malaysia experienced high manufacturing employment growth in the 1980s, at 5.8 per cent and 4.2 per cent respectively, even though their employment elasticities were not particularly high, while manufacturing employment in Bangladesh grew by only 2.6 per cent a year because slow output growth did not compensate for high employment elasticity. In general, the East and Southeast Asian countries which experienced fast employment growth also showed large falls in poverty rates and mostly improved income distribution. In contrast, manufacturing employment fell in the Philippines over the same period and poverty rose first and then fell. Using Muqtada and Basu (1997) data manufacturing employment grew more slowly in South Asia – by only 0.6 per cent a year in India from 1980–9 and by 2.6 and 2.3 per cent a year respectively in Bangladesh and Pakistan.

Aggregate formal sector employment, shown in Table 11.7, failed to keep pace with the growth in the labour force on average in IFI-supported countries for the first period, 1981–5, but exceeded the growth in the size of the labour force for the 'other' category for both periods and for the IFI-supported category in the 1986–93 period. However, Sri Lanka showed a very sharp change in direction. Excluding Sri Lanka, in the IFI-supported group employment fell just behind the growth in the labour force in the 1981–5 period and grew by 0.5 per cent more a year from 1986–93. This sluggish employment performance is probably partly responsible for the slow fall in poverty in these countries. Poverty fell fastest in the countries where employment grew most rapidly. However, even the slower growth countries

Table 11.7 Labour force and employment growth, selected countries

Countries	*Annual labour force growth, %*		*Annual employment growth %*		*Employment growth less labour force growth*	
	1981–5	*1986–93*	*1981–5*	*1986–93*	*1981–5*	*1986–93*
Bangladesh[2]	2.8	2.9	4.5		2.6	
India[2]	2.0	1.9	1.7		−0.2	
Pakistan	3.2	2.7	2.1	1.9	−1.1	−0.8
Sri Lanka	1.6	1.5	−4.8	12.1	−6.4	10.6
Indonesia	2.4	2.3	2.7	3.3	0.3	1.0
Malaysia	3.0	2.7	3.4	3.4	0.4	0.7
Thailand	2.5	1.9	3.0	3.2	0.5	1.3
Korea	2.7	2.1	1.8	3.4	−0.9	1.3
Hong Kong	2.1	1.9	2.6	1.3	−0.5	−0.6
Singapore	1.9	1.0	2.0	3.1	0.1	1.0
Philippines	2.5	2.5	3.5	2.3	−0.8	−0.2
Average, IFI-adj.[1]	*2.5 (2.6)*	*2.2 (2.3)*	*1.7 (2.8)*	*4.1 (2.8)*	*−0.8 (−0.2)*	*1.9 (0.5)*
Average 'other'	*2.4*	*2.0*	*2.7*	*2.7*	*0.3*	*0.7*

Notes: [1] Figures in brackets exclude Sri Lanka; [2] Bangladesh and India employment growth and employment growth less labour force growth refer to 1980–90.
Sources: ILO, *World Employment 1996/7*; Muqtada and Basu (1997).

compare favourably with Latin America in the 1980s, where employment fell by 0.8 per cent a year from 1981 to 1992.

The net effect of complex changes in patterns of production on private income distribution is shown in Table 11.8. But it must first be noted that the data are particularly unreliable in this area: both rich and poor tend to have their incomes understated, as they successfully evade government control –

Table 11.8 Income distribution in Asian countries (Gini coefficients)

Country	*Year*	*Rural*	*Urban*	*National*
Bangladesh	1981/2	0.350	0.410	0.390
	1988/9	0.370	0.380	0.380
China	1980	0.286	0.237	0.330*
	1988	0.364	0.300	0.376
	1995	na	na	0.451
India	1983	0.301	0.334	0.32
	1992	0.298	0.356	0.338
Indonesia	1978	0.361	0.381	0.348
	1987	0.260	0.320	0.321
	1993			0.317
Korea, Republic	1980	0.146	0.444	0.386
	1988	0.290	0.350	0.336
Malaysia	1979	0.482	0.501	0.508
	1984	0.444	0.466	0.480
	1989	na	na	0.445
Nepal	1984/5	0.292	0.371	0.301
	1995/6	na	na	0.367
Pakistan	1979	0.320	0.400	0.373
	1990/91	0.410	0.390	0.407
Philippines	1985	0.378	0.442	0.446
	1988	0.378	0.431	0.445
Sri Lanka	1980/1	0.400	0.440	0.410
	1985/6	0.430	0.500	0.437
Singapore	1982/3	na	na	0.420
	1987/8	na	na	0.410
Thailand	1981	0.437	0.427	0.453
	1988	0.443	0.456**	0.478
	1992	na	na	0.462

na = not applicable; * 1985; ** 1986.
Sources: Tabatabai (1996); World Bank (1997) *World Development Indicators*.

the poor by retreating to the informal sector and parallel markets, the rich by retreating to financial havens of various kinds. Taking the available data, it seems that income distribution worsened in half the cases (all IFI-assisted), showed little change in three and became more equal in three, including two 'own-adjusters' – Malaysia and Indonesia – as well as Korea (very much master of its own policies throughout most of the period). Hence it appears that on the whole IFI assistance was associated with worsening income distribution. All three countries where income distribution improved enjoyed both relatively rapid agricultural growth and high growth in manufacturing employment, a combination most likely to lead to improved income distribution and reduced private income poverty. In the case of Indonesia, the labour intensity of output was partly responsible, but this was not so in Korea and Malaysia, where the fast rate of output growth was responsible. Other countries which did less well on PIP (showing some worsening in income distribution and sluggish poverty reduction), such as India and Bangladesh, experienced much slower employment growth due to a combination of slower output growth and lower employment elasticities in the case of India, while in Bangladesh employment elasticities were high but output growth in both industry and agriculture was relatively slow.

3.2 Social income poverty and social income distribution

Government expenditure remained under 20 per cent of GDP over the period in both IFI-adjusters and 'others' – with the exception of a few high spenders – Bhutan and Malaysia. Expenditure ratios were lower than in Africa and Latin America – the average for all African countries was 27 per cent in 1990, and 23 per cent for Latin America. The proportion of government expenditure going to education in the Asian region on average rose from 10.5 to 12.3 per cent between 1980–90 and 1990–5. The proportion was higher and rose more among the 'other' category than the IFI-adjusters, where the ratio remained at 9.4 per cent throughout. The health allocation ratio also remained constant among the IFI-adjusters (at 4.5 per cent) and rose from 3.9 to 4.3 per cent among the others. Education plus health expenditure as a proportion of GDP remained constant among IFI-adjusters at 2.6 per cent and rose among the others from 3.4 per cent in 1980–90 to 4.2 per cent in 1990–5. Other regions of the world generally had higher social allocation ratios: both Africa and Latin America devoted about 20 per cent of their budgets to health and education in the 1980s compared with about 16 per cent for this region. In both regions, however, adjustment was associated with a cut in the share of government expenditure and of GDP going to the social sectors.[7] In Asia, Bhutan, Malaysia and Singapore have particularly high social spending (over 5 per cent of GDP), while Thailand and Sri Lanka increased expenditure to over 4 per cent of GDP on health and education by the end of the period.[8] Malaysia, Singapore and

Sri Lanka were among the best performers on IMR, but Thailand did poorly.

In summary, in Asia we observe little change in the expenditure and social allocation ratios during adjustment – avoiding the cuts experienced by other regions. But the most important difference from other regions was the rapid growth in per capita incomes, which meant that in real terms expenditure per head rose significantly in both health and education among adjusting and 'other' countries. Real expenditure per head on both health and education increased by two and a half times on average for the region. It increased both among IFI-adjusters and 'other' countries, education expenditure per head increasing substantially faster among the 'other' category, and health somewhat faster among the IFI-adjusters. Korea, Malaysia, Indonesia, Singapore and Thailand all at least tripled their expenditure on education per head. This is in strong contrast with other adjusting regions. In Latin America in the 1980s, real expenditure on health and education fell by about 6 per cent while in sub-Saharan Africa it fell by 10 per cent.

In conclusion, for both private and social income poverty, success in Asia was not, on the whole, due to improving the distribution of income, but to the rapid rate of growth of per capita incomes; as far as private income is concerned, in fact the distribution on balance worsened, while for social income it remained broadly unchanged. Since growth in incomes was such an important aspect of securing improvements in poverty rates during adjustment, it is necessary to consider briefly why the region was so successful in securing GDP growth.

The precise responsibility for the successful economic performance of East and Southeast Asian countries is, of course, a matter of controversy on which the debate continues to rage.[9] Both the high rate of investment and effective industrial policies appeared to play an important role, combined with appropriate macro-policies, that is, exchange rates and wage levels that maintained export competitiveness, and monetary and fiscal policies that were associated with only moderate levels of inflation. The adjustment programmes of the IFIs are partly consistent and partly inconsistent with this set of policies. On the one hand, their macro-policy advice on exchanges rate and fiscal and monetary balance are supportive of competitive exchange rates and moderate inflation levels. On the other hand, IFI policies are not good at securing sustained investment – and elsewhere have been associated with falling investment rates – since they often require high interest rates and restraints on public investment; in addition, IFI philosophy is quite inconsistent with an active industrial policy, directed credit and so forth.

The non-IFI group did somewhat better in poverty reduction than the IFI group because of their greater achievements with respect to economic growth. While it is not possible to attribute responsibility for the slower growth in IFI-assisted countries to the programmes – especially since some of the countries receiving IFI support had accelerated growth compared with previous decades – it does appear that countries without programmes were more successful in sustaining investment rates, a major element in generating high growth. The IFI-adjusters had a rate of investment of around 20 per cent of GDP throughout the period, a bit below that of other adjusting regions in 1980, although the rate did not fall significantly in contrast to the other adjusting regions (sub-Saharan Africa's investment ratio was 23 per cent in 1980 dropping to 19 per cent in 1995, and Latin America and the Caribbean recorded a rate of 25 per cent in 1980 falling to 20 per cent in 1995). The other countries in Asia experienced much higher investment rates (27 per cent in 1980–5 rising to 31 per cent in 1990–5). In addition, many of the 'other' adjusters had strongly interventionist industrial policies – which were ruled out by IFI programmes, even if in practice they did not succeed in eliminating industrial interventions in the countries they supported.

3.3 Social safety net programmes

The Asian success in reducing poverty was, as shown above, mainly a function of economic growth and the associated growth in employment, not social safety net programmes. Nonetheless, there clearly were a large number of programmes that would qualify as social safety nets throughout the region, many reaching large numbers of people. For example: public works programmes in Bangladesh and India; credit for low-income people in Bangladesh, Indonesia, Sri Lanka and parts of India; and food subsidy/rations/ price controls at various times in India, Pakistan, Sri Lanka and China. Some of these programmes were well targeted and extensive; others less so. There were also pension schemes for the low-income in a few areas: for example, Kerala has contributory welfare schemes for rural workers, and pensions for destitutes and handicapped persons, and some unemployment assistance; Tamil Nadhu has introduced low-level pensions for widows and the handicapped.

These programmes were, naturally, more extensive where economic growth was less successful in floating people out of poverty. In some cases, the adjustment process was associated with a quite dramatic unravelling of social safety nets – as in China and Sri Lanka. Downward pressure on public expenditure and the free-market philosophy encouraged the introduction of charges for health and education, and replaced general subsidies with narrowly targeted food subsidies, as in Sri Lanka. Hence while the social safety net programmes supported the poor in various respects, they almost never provided a comprehensive safety net, and were weakened rather than strengthened by the adjustment process. The poor relied primarily on traditional support systems, including the family and the informal sector for their survival. Success in reducing poverty became heavily dependent on sustaining growth in incomes and employment, given the limited coverage of social support systems.[10]

4 The social dimensions of the 1997–9 crisis in Asia

The 1997 economic crisis in Asia was different from previous crises, being a crisis of modernization rather than underdevelopment. It was the outcome of flaws in the apparently successful development of capitalism – of the lack of controls over international capital movements, the dependence on foreign capital (often short-term), the perhaps premature development of stock exchanges and inadequate regulatory and supervisory systems. These developments increased the potential for – and indeed actual – accumulation, but also raised these economies' vulnerability to fluctuations in confidence. IFI stabilization programmes, designed to re-establish confidence, were harsh in terms of their deflationary implications, as well as using the opportunity to insist on the introduction of more orthodox and less interventionist industrial policies. In the short term, the consequence was a significant reduction in output in some of the affected economies, and large falls in employment. In the longer term, the more orthodox policies may well lead to a lower growth rate.

In 1998 GDP contracted by 13.7 per cent in Indonesia, 9.4 per cent in Thailand, 7.7 per cent in Malaysia, 5.8 per cent in Korea, and 0.5 per cent in the Philippines. There were large reductions in employment in the modern sector, of some 20 per cent in Indonesia and Thailand. Although output growth generally recovered in 1999, with the exception of Indonesia where political problems prevented recovery, employment and wages lagged behind, and many people suffered severe hardship.

The reductions in employment did not hit the poorest sections of society in the first instance, though there were knock-on effects arising from the reduced dynamism of the formal sector adversely affecting markets in the rest of the economy. More serious, there were virtually no safety nets for the newly unemployed. The traditional systems that supported the poor in the past – the ability to retreat to subsistence production, close family links and support from the community – have been seriously weakened with the advent of a dynamic, modern, urban economy. Yet new social security systems suited to a modern industrial economy have not been put in place. The reliance on a growing economy which proved to be so successful in reducing poverty over the past twenty years had a severe drawback in making no provision for social security for the newly employed. Hence they will suffer severe hardship until some provisions are put in place. But a time of crisis is not a good time to introduce comprehensive support systems.

There was talk by the IFIs of the need to introduce some social safety nets. Yet the past record of safety nets IFIs have supported elsewhere has been extremely poor – in that the schemes have almost invariably reached only a fraction of those in need. Food subsidies have been narrowly targeted, missing the majority of the poor, while social funds and/or special credit schemes have typically covered an even smaller proportion.

A comprehensive support system would need to have some of the following features:

- Some provision, of one kind or another, to be available for *all* who wanted it, not limited in coverage by a pre-set sum of money.
- Support that took the form of public works employment; and/or provision of food; and/or financial (means tested) support. In the long run such support could be financed (or part financed) by an insurance scheme made up of workers and employers' contributions. But in the short run it would need to be financed by general taxation.
- Whatever the form it took, the level of support would need to be limited to an affordable amount (for example, set at the nationally defined poverty level). This would mean a large cut in income for the newly employed.

Support systems of this type, as shown in Cornia, Jolly and Stewart (1987), have been effective in adjusting countries elsewhere in the world – such as, Chile and Botswana. In the early 1980s Chile introduced open-ended public works schemes that were effective in reaching as many as wanted employment at the very low wages offered. Targeted health and nutrition schemes reached those most in need. These interventions were not enough to prevent a severe worsening in income distribution and rising PIP, as noted by Raczynski (1987) and Raczynski and Romaguera (1992), but did avoid the worst consequences of these changes for human indicators, such as health, nutrition and literacy. Botswana used employment schemes and food relief available to all who came forward in regions badly affected by drought. The need for support – in terms of numbers to be covered and duration of coverage – depends critically on what happens to the macro-economy, which is a further reason why deflationary policies should be avoided as much as possible, and a focus put on improved regulatory and financial systems to reestablish confidence in the system.

As far as social poverty is concerned, it is important that priority services be protected during cuts (primary health and primary and secondary education), and that charges for these services are not introduced, especially at a time when PIP is rising. Stewart (1995, ch. 8) describes how Indonesia provided a successful example of selective cuts which protected priorities in the early 1980s. While other adjusting regions were critized for cutting investment in the social sectors during the 1980s and preserving consumption, this was a sensible strategy to meet a short-term crisis, especially in the context of previous expansion of the system.

We have focused on East and South East Asia, regions hit by the recent crisis and which previously had got furthest in transforming their economies towards modern industrial economies combined with the disintegration of traditional support systems. The poverty in South Asian economies is greater in breadth and depth than in the economies of East and South East Asia. While, so far, adjustment policies have not led to any sustained rise in poverty in South Asian economies, if growth falls off there as a result of regional contagion there could be serious effects on poverty extending well beyond those newly unemployed in the modern sector. In that context, expansionary macro-policies that permit sustained economic growth, and meso-policies designed to protect priority sectors and safety-net expenditure, become of central importance.

5 Conclusions

The central conclusion is that Asian economies have been much more successful in reducing PIP and SIP during adjustment than other regions, a success which was greatest among those economies that adjusted on their own without the support of the IFIs. This success was due to the sustained growth in per capita incomes, not to a particularly egalitarian pattern of growth or to improved social allocation ratios. But dependence on economic growth has dangers when this growth is threatened. In that situation new policies are needed to protect the poor, in particular a comprehensive social support system.

Notes

1 There is much debate on how to define the 'poverty line' and how to measure the numbers who fall below it, to incorporate some indicator of the depth of poverty. This debate will not be considered here.

2 Heller *et al.* (1988) drawing on the conclusions of Khan and Knight (1985).

3 The issue of how the exchange rate affects income distribution has been explored by, among others, Krugman and Taylor (1978), Knight (1976), Demery and Addison (1987) and Kanbur (1987).

4 The more strongly organized groups are (for example, when there are strong trade unions), and the greater the degree of indexation, the more likely it is that a nominal exchange rate change will fail to bring about a significant real exchange rate change. The presence of lax monetary policy may also make it more likely that devaluation leads to internal inflation.

5 Also countries at war and socialist planned economies – such as Afghanistan, Cambodia and Burma.

6 The data come from Mazumdar and Basu (1997).

7 In the case of Latin America the fall in the expenditure ratio was slight, but there was a marked fall in the social allocation ratio.

8 It is important to note that data relate to central government; this may greatly understate expenditure in federal states (e.g. India).

9 See Amsden (1989); Wade (1990); World Bank (1993); Ranis (1993); special edition of *World Development* (1994); Lall (1996).

10 There were a few exceptional cases where support systems were more nearly universal in coverage – for example, the Noon Day Meals in Tamil Nadu, and food subsidies in Kerala and formerly in Sri Lanka. In Kerala, which has the best record for social support, 90 per cent of the population have ration cards. Each

individual acquired 70 kg of subsidized grain in 1991, compared with 6 kg in Uttar Pradesh. Malnutrition rates are the lowest in India despite the state having among the lowest per capita income (see Ramachandran, 1997).

References

Amsden, A. (1989) *Asia's Next Giant* (Oxford: Oxford University Press).

Berry, A. (1997) 'The inequality threat in Latin America', *Latin American Research Review*, vol. 32, no. 2.

Chen, S., G. Datt and M. Ravallion (1994) 'Is Poverty Increasing in the Developing World?', *Review of Income and Wealth*, vol. 40, pp. 359–76.

Cornia, G. A., R. Jolly and F. Stewart (1987) *Adjustment with a Human Face*, vols 1 and 2 (Oxford: Oxford University Press).

Cornia, G. A. and Stewart F. (1993) 'Two Errors of Targeting', *Journal of International Development*, vol. 5, no. 4, pp. 459–96.

Creese, A. (1990) 'User Charges for Health: A Review of Recent Experience', *Strengthening Health Services, Paper 1* (Geneva: WHO).

Deininger, K. and L. Squire (1996) 'A New Data Set Measuring Income Inequality', *The World Bank Economic Review*, vol. 10, pp. 561–91.

Demery, L. and A. Addison (1987) 'Stabilisation Policy and Income Distribution in Developing Countries', *World Development*, vol. 15, pp. 1483–98.

Fields, G. (1989) 'Changes in Poverty and Inequality in Developing Countries', *World Bank Research Observer*, vol. 4, pp. 167–86.

FitzGerald, E. V. K., K. Jansen and R. Vos (1993) 'External Constraints on Private Investment Decisions in Developing Countries', Centro Studi Luca D'Agliano/ Queen Elizabeth House, Development Studies Working Papers, no. 57.

Heller, P., A. L. Bovenber, T. Catsambas, K. Chu and P. Shome (1988) 'The Implications of Fund-supported Programs for Poverty', IMF Occasional Paper 58 (Washington, DC: IMF).

International Monetary Fund, Fiscal Affairs Department (1986) 'Fund-supported Programs, Fiscal Policy and Income Distribution', IMF Occasional Paper 46 (Washington, DC: IMF).

International Monetary Fund, *World Economic Outlook* (various years) (Washington DC: IMF).

Kanbur, S. M. R. (1987) 'Structural Adjustment, Macroeconomic Adjustment and Poverty: A Methodology for Analysis', *World Development*, vol. 15, no. 12, pp. 1515–26.

Khan, M. and M. Knight (1985) 'Fund-supported Adjustment Programs and Economic Growth', IMF Occasional Paper 41 (Washington DC: IMF).

Knight, J. B. (1976) 'Devaluation and Income Distribution in Less Developed Economies', *Oxford Economic Papers*, vol. 28, no. 2, pp. 208–27.

Krueger, A. (1974) 'The Political Economy of the Rent-seeking Society', *American Economic Review*, vol. 64, pp. 291–303.

Krugman, P. and L. Taylor (1978) 'Contractionary Effects of Devaluation', *Journal of International Economics*, vol. 8, pp. 445–56.

Lall, S. (1996) *Learning from the Asian Tigers* (London: Macmillan).

Mazumdar, D. and P. Basu (1997) 'Macroeconomic Policies, Growth and Employment: The East and South-East Asian Experience', in A. Khan and M. Muqtada (eds), *Employment Expansion and Macroeconomic Stability under Increasing Globalization* (London: Macmillan).

Muqtada, M. and P. Basu (1997) 'Macroeconomic Policies, Growth and Employment Expansion: The Experience of South Asia', in A. Khan and M. Muqtada (eds), *Employ-*

ment Expansion and Macroeconomic Stability under Increasing Globalization (London: Macmillan).

Polak, K. (1991) 'The changing Nature of IMF Conditionality', *Essays in International Finance*, no. 184 (Princeton: Princeton University).

Raczynski, D. (1987) 'Social Policy, Poverty and Vulnerable Groups: Children in Chile', in G. A. Cornia, R. Jolly and F. Stewart (eds), *Adjustment with a Human Face*, vol. 2 (Oxford: Oxford University Press).

Raczynski, D. and P. Romaguera (1992) 'Chile: Poverty, Adjustment and Social Policies in the 1980s', paper prepared for the conference 'Confronting the Challenges of Poverty and Inequality in Latin America', The Brookings Institution and Inter-American Dialogue, 16–17 July, Washington DC (Santiago: CIEPLAN).

Ramachandran, V. K. (1997) 'Human Development Achievements in an Indian State: A Case Study of Kerala' (Geneva: UNRISD), mimeo.

Ranis, G. (1993) 'Labour Markets, Human Capital and Development Performance in East Asia', background paper for the East Asian Miracle Study (Washington DC: World Bank).

Rodrik, D. (1994) 'King Kong meets Godzilla: The World Bank and the East Asian Miracle', CEPR Discussion Paper Series 944, Centre for Economic Policy Research, London.

Sahn, D., P. Dorosh and S. Younger (1997) *Structural Adjustment Reconsidered* (Cambridge: Cambridge University Press).

Sarel, M. (1997) 'How Macroeconomic Factors Affect Income Distribution: The Cross-country Evidence', *IMF Working Paper*, no. 97, p. 152 (Washington DC: IMF).

Serven, L. and A. Solimano (1992) 'Economic Adjustment and Investment Performance in Developing Countries: The Experience of the 1980s', in V. Corbo, S. Fischer and S. Webb (eds), *Adjustment Lending Revisited. Policies to Restore Growth* (Washington DC: World Bank).

Stewart, F. (1995) *Adjustment and Poverty: Options and Choices* (London: Routledge).

Stewart, F. and W. van der Geest (1995) 'Adjustment and Social Funds: Political Panacea or Effective Poverty Reduction?', in F. Stewart (ed.), *Adjustment and Poverty: Options and Choices* (London: Routledge).

Tabatabai, H. (1996) 'Statistics on Poverty and Income Distribution', International Labour Organisation, Geneva.

United Nations, *World Economic and Social Survey* (various years) (New York: UN).

Wade, R. (1990) *Governing the Market* (Princeton: Princeton University Press).

World Bank (1990) *Report on Adjustment Lending II: Policies for the Recovery of Growth* (Washington DC: World Bank).

World Bank (1993) *The East Asian Miracle* (Washington DC: World Bank).

12

Growth and Poverty during Adjustment: Lessons from Sub-Saharan Africa*

S. R. Osmani
University of Ulster, Belfast

1 Introduction

A great deal of work has recently been done on the impact of structural adjustment in sub-Saharan Africa. Although a great deal more remains to be done, especially in clearing up the factual basis of assessment, some lessons are already beginning to emerge. These lessons have a bearing not just for Africa, but for other developing regions as well. It may, therefore, be useful to draw some of these lessons while reflecting on the reform experience in South Asia.

The impact of structural adjustment on the poor has been hotly debated for the last decade or so. After years of complaint that the impact has been less than benign, a new view is emerging that adjustment is good for the poor after all, or at least it is not intrinsically inimical to them (Demery and Squire, 1996; Sahn, Dorosh and Younger, 1996; Sahn, 1996). This raises a number of questions. First, how valid is this emerging view? Secondly, even if its validity is granted one must ask: is adjustment sufficient for accelerated poverty reduction, or is it necessary to go further? Finally, if it is necessary to go beyond adjustment, will the broader strategy be compatible with the tenets of orthodox structural adjustment or will it be necessary to countenance some compromise? This chapter tries to address these questions, drawing on the experience of sub-Saharan Africa, but it will be argued that the debates surrounding these questions are also relevant to other regions.

Section 2 outlines the broad pattern of growth failure and poverty intensification in sub-Saharan Africa. Section 3 reviews the theory and the evidence on the impact of adjustment on poverty, while section 4 argues that a

*This chapter draws heavily on a research report (Osmani, 1998) prepared for the International Labour Office, Geneva. The author is grateful to the ILO, and in particular to Rizwanul Islam and Samir Radwan, for supporting this research.

broader strategy for accelerated poverty reduction calls not just for going beyond adjustment, but also for some attenuation of conventional adjustment programmes. Finally, section 5 summarizes the main conclusions.

2 Growth failure and poverty intensification in Africa

2.1 Poverty in Africa

Using the internationally comparable poverty line of 'a dollar a day' (in 1985 purchasing power parity), the World Bank (1997) estimated that 40 per cent of sub-Saharan Africans were poor. This represents a slightly smaller incidence of poverty compared to South Asia (43 per cent). But two features of sub-Saharan poverty are particularly disconcerting. First, the depth of poverty – that is, the extent by which the average income of the poor falls below the poverty line – is greater in Africa than anywhere else in the world. Second, the incidence of poverty has probably increased in sub-Saharan Africa in the last two decades, while it has fallen in the rest of the developing world.

Although there is no direct evidence on the trend in poverty in the majority of African countries, there is plenty of indirect evidence to suggest a worsening standard of living. For example, according to FAO estimates, the consumption of calories per head has declined from 2140 Kcal per day during 1969–71 to 2040 Kcal during 1990–2. Over the same period, the proportion of population without adequate access to food has increased from 38 per cent to 43 per cent, while this proportion has declined in the developing countries as a whole. In fact, according to FAO (1996) sub-Saharan Africa is the only region in the world where the proportion of people without adequate access to food has increased in the two decades since 1969–70. Furthermore, during the 1980s, life expectancy at birth has stagnated in this region, in contrast with all other developing regions where life expectancy has continued to improve. As a consequence of this secular deterioration in the living conditions of the poor, this region is also becoming increasingly vulnerable to periodic shocks due to wars, adverse climatic conditions and other hazards. This is one reason why famines and near-famine situations are becoming more frequent in this part of the world.

2.2 Growth and poverty

What lies behind this accentuation of poverty? In the 1960s and 1970s, development economists used to blame lopsided economic growth for increasing poverty. But the intensification of poverty in sub-Saharan Africa represents a different process; it has occurred as a consequence not so much of lopsided growth as of no growth at all. On average, real per capital GDP did not grow in Africa over the 1965–90 period, while in East Asia and the Pacific per capita GDP grew by over 5 per cent and in Latin America by about 2 per cent a year. During the 1980s, per capita GDP in sub-Saharan Africa actually declined – by 1.3 per cent a year, while the developing world as a whole enjoyed per capita income growth of 3.7 per cent. This deterioration continued in the 1990s; indeed the situation worsened in both absolute and relative terms – the decline in annual per capita income accelerated to 1.8 per cent during 1990–4.

Growth failure of such magnitude could not but result in the intensification of poverty. Only a spectacular improvement in income distribution could have prevented it; but this was unlikely to happen. In fact, such evidence as exists seems to suggest that distribution has, if anything, become more unequal in Africa in recent years (World Bank, 1995b). Any analysis of African poverty must, therefore, look into the causes of African growth failure. This does not mean, as will be argued later, that the solution lies in single-minded pursuit of growth to the exclusion of all other considerations, but it does mean that policies for growth revival must form an integral part of policies for poverty elimination in sub-Saharan Africa.

2.3 Growth failure and policy failure

In part, the stagnation of Africa's per capita income has something to do with its high rate of population growth. During 1965–90, population grew at close to 3.0 per cent per annum in sub-Saharan Africa as compared to an average of 2.2 per cent in the developing world. Thus, almost a full percentage point of Africa's growth shortfall (compared to the average for the developing world) is accounted for by its higher population growth.

The technique of growth accounting provides a starting point for understanding the reasons for growth failure. Between 1971 and 1991, total GDP grew by 3.4 per cent a year in sub-Saharan Africa as against 5.2 per cent in all developing countries (DCs) giving a growth shortfall of 1.8 percentage points. Collier (1997) estimated that one-third of this shortfall is accounted for by a slower rate of capital accumulation and two-thirds by slower productivity growth.[1]

This raises the question: why has Africa accumulated capital at such a slow pace and why has total factor productivity grown at a slower pace than elsewhere? In a sense, these questions lie at the heart of the continuing debate on whether structural adjustment of the kind advocated by the World Bank and IMF constitutes an appropriate response to the African crisis. Broadly speaking, the debate has centred on three sets of issues:

- To what extent does the root of the problem lie within Africa, and to what extent does it lie in the external economic environment, such as dwindling demand for Africa's export commodities resulting in a sharp decline in the terms of trade;
- Insofar as internal factors are responsible, how much of the blame can be attached to the failure of government economic policy as opposed to non-

economic factors such as civil wars, adverse climate, corruption, poor governance, etc.; and
- Insofar as bad economic policy is responsible, what exactly is the nature of this policy error?

The debate on these issues continues, but a dominant view has emerged which identifies a particular kind of policy failure as the villain of the piece. This is the so-called Bank-Fund view, the gist of which is that the problem lies in distorted price signals and unwise market intervention on the part of government. This view does not altogether deny the role played by external factors and internal non-economic factors, but it does attach a central importance to price-distorting policies.

For instance, while noting that external terms of trade declined and caused problems for Africa, this decline, too, is considered a case of distorted price policy because the effects of terms-of-trade decline could have been offset by exchange rate depreciation and elimination of export taxes. But this is a curious argument, because terms-of-trade decline must entail a loss of real income in the short run no matter what offsetting policies are adopted. Perhaps in recognition of this point, a second line of defence is offered by several World Bank documents, such as Easterly and Levine (1995) and World Bank (1994). They claim that Africa's growth shortfall cannot be explained by terms-of-trade decline because the extent of decline was no more severe for Africa than for the rest of the developing world. But the World Bank's own figures given in other documents contradict this, and show that between 1970 and 1992 the terms of trade declined by nearly 60 per cent for a group of ten countries in sub-Saharan Africa,[2] as against 35 per cent for four Southeast Asian countries (China, Malaysia, Philippines and Thailand) and a meagre 10 per cent for the East Asian tiger economies (Korea, Hong Kong and Singapore) (World Bank, 1995a, fig. 6, p. 16).[3]

As for internal non-economic factors, there is widespread recognition, reflected in World Bank documents, that these do play a large part in explaining Africa's growth failure. The study by Easterly and Levine (1995) brings this out most clearly. In cross-country growth regression using standard economic variables such as fiscal prudence, exchange rate policy, human capital, financial depth, and one non-economic variable to proxy for political stability, they found that the major part of African growth failure remained unexplained by these variables. The unexplained part, captured by the African dummy, accounted for 1.5 of the 2.3 percentage point difference in growth rates between non-African and African countries.[4]

It is questionable, therefore, whether Africa's woes are almost entirely due to bad economic policies. This is not to deny that policy failures did occur. The question is, where exactly did they occur?

3 Adjustment and poverty

3.1 The orthodox view

The orthodox Bank-Fund view holds that the most important policy failures in Africa took the form of distorting the price signal and stifling the market through excessive public intervention. The theoretical argument underlying this view is a simple one. The distortions created by misguided policies have tilted incentives against tradables – in particular, against the commodities in which Africa has some comparative advantage; as a result, production declined in the export sector in general and export agriculture in particular. This has retarded growth in two ways: first, by pushing production into sectors which do not enjoy comparative advantage and thereby causing an inefficient use of resources; and, second, by precipitating a foreign exchange constraint in the 1980s when capital inflow dried up and the terms of trade fell due to adverse external economic conditions. The argument further contends that while retarding growth, misguided policies also accentuated poverty because agriculture and the labour-intensive export industries – whose expansion was essential for helping the poor in the short run – suffered.

Based on this diagnosis, policy recommendations focused on the creation of an environment where resources would be allocated according to comparative advantage. This is the rationale of the Structural Adjustment Programmes (SAPs) that have been implemented across sub-Saharan Africa and in other parts of the developing world since the mid-1980s at the behest of the World Bank and the IMF. Although these programmes vary in detail from country to country, the core elements are common. These are: exchange rate depreciation, trade liberalization, inflation control, reduction (preferably elimination) of export taxes, and dismantling of agricultural marketing boards which served to keep producer prices artificially low. Each of these policies affects the economy in multiple ways, but all of them have a common effect which is of crucial analytical importance in the present context: they all work towards raising the real effective exchange rates facing the producers of tradables.

Since these exchange rates are alleged to have been kept artifically depressed in the past, it is expected that raising them towards their 'equilibrium' level would help to reallocate production according to comparative advantage, leading to higher growth and lower poverty. Higher growth will result from more efficient use of resources, while poverty will fall because reorganization of production according to comparative advantage in low-wage economies will boost the demand for labour – the most important asset owned by the poor.

3.2 How valid is the orthodox view?

Structural adjustment is thus claimed to be the right set of policies for both accelerating growth and reducing poverty. How valid is this claim? From a purely theoretical point of view, there was until recently a gap in the argument about growth acceleration. The neo-classical framework in which the theory of comparative advantage is couched allows one to conclude merely that the movement towards comparative advantage will yield a once-and for-all increase in real income owing to the more efficient allocation of resources, but it does not warrant the claim of a sustained increase in the growth rate (Corden, 1971). New growth theory has, however, come to the rescue in recent years by demonstrating the possibility that even a once-for-all gain can translate into a sustained increase in growth rate under certain conditions.

Even if new growth theory restores the theoretical consistency of the argument, there remain important empirical questions. Two kinds of question can be asked. First, are the underlying assumptions of the theory sufficiently valid in the context in which it is applied? Second, are the predictions of the theory borne out in fact? Both questions are examined below.

The fundamental assumption of the theory is that there exists sufficient flexibility in factor markets to bring about the desired reorganisation of production through the price signal. If the SAPs are implemented reasonably well, the immediate effect will be felt in the product market, that is, the relative prices of tradables will improve *vis-à-vis* non-tradables, assuming that the product market is reasonably flexible. Whether this change in relative price will actually promote a reallocation of resources towards the tradable sectors will depend crucially on how the factor markets respond to changes in relative product prices.

A number of case studies show that while structural adjustment in Africa has generally succeeded in moving relative product prices in the expected direction, factor markets have often behaved in the 'wrong' way.[5] For example, Ghana is said to have been one of the most successful reformers, and yet as Beaudry and Sowa (1994) show, in its post-reform period the tradable industrial sector experienced the lowest increase in real wages whereas the non-tradable transportation sector experienced the highest increase. Similarly, in Kenya urban employment has shifted more towards non-tradable service and professional sectors rather than towards tradable sectors, even though tradable prices have clearly improved (Milne and Neitzert, 1994). Another example is Malawi. A study of Malawi by Cromwell (1992) demonstrates that economic reforms succeeded in raising the real producer prices for export crops, especially during the early years of reform. The study concludes, however, that while the change in relative prices may bring benefits to the estate sub-sector – which has adequate access to land and capital resources to expand production – it will be of limited relevance to smallholders. The main problem is that the smallholder sector has little scope for diversification into labour-intensive crops, caused by the land constraint and poor access to other inputs.

In short, these studies demonstrate that while African factor markets are not entirely unresponsive to alteration in the structure of incentives, imperfections in those markets generally prevent changes in relative product prices from being translated fully into corresponding factor rewards. This means that even if reforms succeed in altering relative product prices in favour of tradables, the hoped-for effect on growth and poverty may not fully materialize.

Have the predicted effects on growth and poverty materialized? The answers given to this question are exceedingly diverse, ranging from extravagant claims on behalf of adjustment programmes to vehement criticism. This results from the methodological difficulties inherent in the evaluation of reforms. Some of the major difficulties arise because: (a) the reforms have not been implemented uniformly by all countries; (b) the reform programmes have several components, and it is not easy to devise an agreed aggregate index of implementation; (c) there may be long, variable and unpredictable lags before the effects begin to be felt; and (d) the reforming countries have been affected differentially by external factors (such as terms-of-trade decline) and internal non-economic factors (such as civil disturbance, war and droughts) in the post-reform period. Given these difficulties, neither before–after comparisons nor cross-sectional comparisons across countries can give unequivocal answers.

An additional problem in assessing poverty lies in the extreme paucity of good data. It is difficult to judge how poverty has evolved in the post-reform period because few African countries have comparable household survey data for two or more points in time. In the past decade, however, a handful of such surveys have become available under the auspices of the World Bank's Living Standard Measurement Studies. Comparable poverty estimates at two points in time are now available for at least six African countries – Côte d'Ivoire, Ethiopia, Ghana, Kenya, Nigeria and Tanzania. By using these estimates, Demery and Squire (1996), World Bank researchers, tried to shed light on the relationship between structural adjustment and poverty.

3.3 The Demery–Squire thesis

Demery and Squire (1996) followed the simple methodology of relating change in the magnitude of poverty to change in macroeconomic policy. They used the index of 'good' macroeconomic policy developed in World Bank (1994), 'good' being defined as conforming to the principles of orthodox structural adjustment, that is fiscal conservatism, low inflation and a realistic exchange rate. This index is a weighted average of three separate indices representing fiscal, monetary and exchange rate policies. A positive change in the value of the index between two points in time indicates improvement in economic policy. By this criterion, the policy environment worsened in Côte d'Ivoire but improved in the remaining five countries. It

Table 12.1 Macroeconomic policy and poverty

Country	*Survey years*	*Change in macro policy (weighted score)*	*Change in poverty (percentage points per year)*
Côte d'Ivoire	1985–8	−1.65	+5.30
Ethiopia	1989–94	+0.55	−3.60
Ghana	1988–92	+1.35	−1.95
Kenya	1982–92	+0.45	−0.28
Nigeria	1985–92	+1.79	−1.27
Tanzania	1983–91	+2.76	−1.83

Source: Demery and Squire (1996), table 6, p. 45.

can be seen from Table 12.1 that Côte d'Ivoire is also the only country for which poverty increased between the survey years, while in all other countries poverty declined. Thus, where the policy environment worsened poverty increased, and where the policy environment improved poverty declined. From this association, along with a detailed comparison of the experience of Côte d'Ivoire and Ghana, Demery and Squire (1996) concluded that poverty was more likely to decline in countries that improved their macroeconomic balances than in those that did not.

They further argued that the critical factor was economic growth, that is, good macroeconomic policies helped reduce poverty mainly by stimulating growth rather than improving income distribution. By decomposing the observed change in poverty between change in mean income and change in distribution, they found that the change in mean income was the major driving force behind poverty reduction. In fact, in some of these countries distribution became more unequal during the survey years, and yet poverty declined because the benign effect of growth on poverty was much stronger.

There are, however, a number of problems with the Demery–Squire conclusions. First, the claimed statistical association between policy and poverty is far from convincing. This association is based solely on the Côte d'Ivoire where the policy index worsened, and the other five countries where the policy index improved. What this comparison ignores, however, is the fact that during the period in question Côte d'Ivoire had adopted a draconian demand contraction policy to deal with its balance or payments crisis, as it was denied the option of exchange rate adjustment by its membership of the CFA zone. Strangulation of growth and exacerbation of poverty were inevitable consequences of the severe contraction of demand that followed. The comparison between Côte d'Ivoire and the other five countries reveals more about the adverse consequences of demand contraction than about the supposedly beneficial effects of structural adjustment.

A more valid procedure would be to leave out Côte d'Ivoire and compare the performance of the remaining five countries, none of which resorted to serious demand contraction. One could then ask: did poverty decline more in countries that improved their policy environment more? There are of course serious problems in answering this question satisfactorily; for example, the sample is far too small, and it is not clear that changes in the 'ordinal' index of policy can be interpreted as the 'extent' to which policy improved and so on. Yet, the figures in Table 12.1 fail to show any systematic relationship between the magnitude of change in the policy index and the magnitude of change in poverty. Thus, Ethiopia where improvement in the policy index was the least, except for Kenya, experienced the largest reduction in poverty; and Ghana enjoyed a larger reduction in poverty than Nigeria and Tanzania despite having a smaller improvement in the policy index.

Another set of problems relates to the nexus between policy and poverty proposed by Demery and Squire. They argue that better macroeconomic policies raised the real exchange rates facing producers of tradable goods, which helped restructure production according to comparative advantage, which in turn raised the efficiency of resource use and led to higher growth. Higher growth then translated into lower absolute poverty even if distribution became more unequal. They draw empirical support for this proposition mostly from the experience of Ghana, but a closer look at this experience appears to tell a somewhat different story.

Following the adoption of structural adjustment, poverty declined in Ghana by over 5 per cent in the five years between 1988 and 1992. As predicted by the orthodox view, the producers of export crops, many of whom were small farmers, saw their poverty decline by nearly 6 per cent. But it is noteworthy that producers of export crops accounted for only 7.5 per cent of the total poor population in Ghana, so their improved fortunes explained only a minuscule proportion of overall poverty reduction. The major factor was the fortune of food producers. They formed by far the major occupation group among the poor, accounting for 54 per cent of all poor Ghanaians, and their poverty declined by 7 per cent in the period under consideration. It is this, along with the fact that poverty of the next biggest group – the self-employed in the non-farm sector – also declined by about 5 per cent, that explains the overall reduction of poverty.

This raises the question of exactly how reforms helped these groups. For the Demery–Squire thesis to be valid, it has to be shown that relative price changes brought about by macroeconomic reforms did the trick. As Sarris (1994) noted, relative food prices actually declined in Ghana from the inception of structural adjustment to about 1987, and remained trendless thereafter. While relative prices for the products of the non-farm self-employed are not available, it can safely be assumed that insofar as many of them are engaged in non-tradable service activities, there is no reason to expect any improvement in their product prices following structural adjustment, which is deliberately biased against non-tradable sectors.

Thus the experience of the two major groups whose improved fortunes accounted for by far the major part of overall poverty reduction in Ghana seems to deny the nexus between policy and poverty postulated by Demery and Squire. It is true that growth revived and poverty declined in Ghana following structural adjustment, but for different reasons. This issue will be discussed in section 4.

3.4 Model simulations

In view of the problems associated with 'before and after' comparisons, some researchers, for example Sahn (1996) and Sahn, Dorosh and Younger (1996), adopted a modelling approach, comparing the 'with reform' scenario with the counterfactual 'non-reform' scenario as well as alternative policy scenarios, holding other things constant. The effects of trade and exchange rate reforms were studied for four countries – Cameroon, Gambia, Madagascar and Niger – with the help of computable general equilibrium (CGE) models. In model simulations, the economies were subjected to a terms of trade shock, combined with a decline in net foreign capital inflows. Two alternative policy responses were considered: full adjustment in the real exchange rate through trade liberalization and import quotas.

Model simulations demonstrated that trade reform is the superior alternative in terms of the impact on both growth and poverty, but the difference was not spectacular. For example, liberalization raised GDP by only 1.25 per cent in Gambia and Madagascar, and by less than 1 per cent in Cameroon and Niger. The effect on poverty was similarly muted. Under liberalization, the real incomes of the rural poor rose by 7.4 per cent in Cameroon, 4.5 per cent in Madagascar, and 2.8 per cent in Gambia and Niger.

Apart from these evaluations of trade reforms, the studies reported in Sahn (1996) and Sahn, Dorosh and Younger (1996) also undertook evaluations of fiscal and agricultural reforms in selected African countries – some with the help of models, some without. The overall conclusion of this set of studies was that removing distortions generally improved income distribution and raised the incomes of the poor, albeit marginally. These findings thus reject the proposition that economic reforms are inherently harmful to the poor or that the poor bear a disproportionate cost of adjustment. This is not so to say, however, that there are no losers from adjustment. There are, but they happen to be mostly the non-poor, such as public-sector workers or traders who had privileged access to scarce foreign exchange. Besides, most of the decline in incomes that followed from reforms was the result of elimination of rents, rather than of demand contraction as generally assumed. In practice, interventions were not pro-poor although in theory and in intent they were when first implemented.

However, as Sahn (1996) notes in his concluding observations, while macroeconomic and sectoral policy reforms associated with structural adjustment are generally not anti-poor, they are by no means a sufficient condition for either growth or long-term poverty alleviation, because, as we have seen, the effect on both growth and poverty were marginal. This point is made explicitly by Sahn, Dorosh and Younger (1996), who concluded that adjustment policies in Africa 'mostly redistribute real incomes in a way that is marginally beneficial to the poor', and 'While adjustment policies are not a threat to the welfare of most of Africa's poor, it is also true that these policies have not generated rapid economic growth and as a result they have not contributed substantially to poverty reduction' (p. 741).

4 Beyond adjustment

Obviously, it will be necessary to go beyond structural adjustment and devise a long-term development strategy in order to make any appreciable impact on Africa's growth and poverty. As Sahn, Dorosh and Younger (1996) have rightly observed, 'Adjustment policy does not negate the need for a sound development policy' (p. 742). The crucial question is, however: are the tenets of adjustment, as currently implemented, wholly consistent with the requirements of an appropriate development strategy for Africa? To ask this question is not to imply that it was a mistake to adopt adjustment programmes in Africa in the sense that Africa might have been better off without them. Clearly, the countries that have adjusted well have done better at reviving growth and on the whole they have done so without exacerbating poverty, and possibly even by reducing poverty a little. But, as noted above, the impact on both growth and poverty has been marginal. So the question arises, if attempts are to be made to accelerate the pace of poverty reduction, will it be necessary to compromise with some aspects of adjustment policy as it is currently conceived? Are there trade-offs between the dictates of structural adjustment and the imperatives of accelerated poverty reduction? So long as it is not claimed that structural adjustment is both necessary and sufficient for accelerated poverty reduction – and nobody claims that, not even the World Bank and the IMF – these questions will have to be faced.

4.1 'Win–win' policies?

A complacent view seems to be emerging in certain quarters that no such trade-off may need to be countenanced: while adjustment may not be sufficient, it is claimed to be entirely consistent with the requirements of accelerated poverty reduction. This view has been most forcefully articulated in the World Bank's (1997) attempt to analyse the African crisis. This document acknowledges that while growth is important it will not do simply to maximize growth – it will be necessary to adopt pro-poor patterns of growth to reduce African poverty. It then identifies what it calls 'win–win' patterns of growth which, if pursued, will bring poverty down rapidly without entailing any sacrifice of growth, and without conflicting with the tenets of structural adjustment.

This so-called 'win–win' pattern of growth is to be based on three sets of policies:

1 macroeconomic policies that achieve stabilization and provide incentives for employment-creating production, for both domestic and export markets;
2 sectoral policies that encourage employment of the poor and improve social services;
3 rural development, including strategic rural infrastructure, agricultural research and extension, pro-poor public expenditure patterns, and pro-labour investment policies.

The first set of policies is clearly the macroeconomic stabilization–adjustment package currently in vogue; the other two involve various sectoral and other disaggregated policies. It is not explained, however, how these three sets of policies can be compatible with each other without involving any trade-offs – it is merely asserted that they are.

According to the World Bank's own assessment, its adjustment-lending to Africa has not been particularly pro-poor. For example, World Bank (1997) notes that only about 30 per cent of its pro-growth lending during 1990–2 was likely to benefit the poor directly, either through stimulation of labour-intensive growth or better prices of agricultural products. There is an implication here that it should have chosen its pro-growth projects to be also pro-poor at the same time. But the other possible interpretation is that such 'win–win' opportunities were simply not available in plenty – trade-offs rather than 'win–win' may be what one confronts more frequently in real life. We shall illustrate this point from the experience of sub-Saharan Africa, and show that the requirements of sustained growth and accelerated poverty reduction may in some cases be incompatible with at least two tenets of conventional adjustment programmes, namely, a conservative attitude towards inflation and export-bias.

4.2 Inflation control versus investment push

Consider the example of Ghana, once renowned as the 'star pupil' of structural adjustment. Ghana was one of the earliest reformers of sub-Saharan Africa, and one of the most successful, until recently. It carried out almost all the elements of the standard adjustment package and was rewarded generously in terms of a huge inflow of official development assistance. There was, however, one blot – it failed to rein in inflation; in fact inflationary pressure worsened in Ghana following adjustment. The numerous evaluations of Ghana's reforms almost invariably point this out as a sign of partial failure.

It is arguable, however, that far from being a sign of failure the emergence of inflation was a sign of precisely how Ghana engendered its growth revival, with a consequent reduction in poverty. The standard view claims that Ghana achieved better growth by tilting the real exchange rate in favour of tradables, which in turn brought down poverty (Demery and Squire, 1996). But as noted in section 3, this view does not quite fit the facts. The most impressive decline in poverty occurred not among the producers of the primary export crop, cocoa, but among the producers of non-traded food crops and rural non-farm products. This does not suggest a case of export-led growth. It seems more likely that Ghana enjoyed an all-round upsurge of growth fuelled by an investment boom, financed partly by sharply increased inflows of foreign aid and partly by fiscal expansion. Ghana's fiscal expansion in the post-reform period has sometimes been presented to counter a criticism of adjustment policy that it tends to be contractionary, but fiscal expansion was the stimulus that was at least partly responsible for reviving growth; inflation was an inevitable byproduct in the short run.

If Ghana had tried to be not just a 'star pupil' but an 'ideal' one by clamping down on fiscal expansion at the first sight of inflation, it would have sacrificed some growth and with it some poverty reduction as well. This shows that at least one tenet of structural adjustment – namely rigorous control of inflation – may not always be compatible with growth and poverty reduction. Of course, inflation has its costs, but this is exactly where the trade-off comes in. How great is the cost? The orthodox view underlying the Bank-Fund type of adjustment programme holds that it is quite big, entailing a negative effect on growth. In support of this view, World Bank (1994) reported cross-country growth regressions purporting to show the negative effect of inflation on growth, but these regressions have been convincingly criticized by Mosely, Subasat and Weeks (1995), whose own regressions contradict the orthodox view.

Nobody denies that runaway inflation can cause serious damage, but, with a few exceptions, African inflation has hardly been excessive. For example, in the 1970s, before the crisis of the 1980s, the average inflation rate in sub-Saharan Africa was just over 10 per cent, only marginally higher than the 9 per cent inflation rate that prevailed in East Asia and the Middle East and

Table 12.2 Inflation rates in developing regions: 1970–90 (per cent).

Region	*1970–9*	*1980–90*	*1970–90*
Sub-Saharan Africa	10.44	13.25	11.99
Latin America	15.32	24.16	19.97
South Asia	7.42	8.63	8.00
East Asia	9.19	6.47	7.75
Middle East & North Africa	9.19	11.55	10.05

Source: Serven (1997), table 2, p. 37.

North Africa (Table 12.2). The rate accelerated slightly to 13 per cent in the 1980s, near the 12 per cent rate that prevailed in the Middle East and North Africa but nowhere near the 24 per cent rate that rocked Latin America. Sarel's (1996) growth equations show that there is a significant non-linearity in inflation's effect on growth: below about 8 per cent inflation did not harm growth. There is of course nothing sacrosanct about the figure of 8 per cent; different methodologies and data sets may suggest different thresholds. The point, however, remains that there is no ground for presuming that relatively low rates of inflation have a significant cost in terms of growth.

Much depends, however, on exactly what is being purchased for the price of inflation. Even a 5 per cent rate of inflation may be thoroughly undesirable if it arises from financing completely unproductive expenditure. What did Ghana purchase? It purchased a massive programme of investment on infrastructure, especially rural roads which played a crucial role in promoting all-round growth and in bringing about a broad-based reduction of poverty.

The importance of Ghana's investment on rural infrastructure can be seen from the performance of its food market. It was widely feared in Ghana that market liberalization, undertaken as part of structural adjustment, would cause suffering to the poor by raising the price of food. But Alderman and Shively (1996) have demonstrated that food prices actually declined after liberalization, as marketing margins fell with the unleashing of competition. Falling marketing margins enabled food producers to receive a higher price for their products even as the consumer price fell, thus benefiting both producers and consumers. Alderman and Shively interpret this as proof that market efficiency improved as a consequence of reform, but it was not simply because of liberalizing reforms: the development of rural infrastructure played a critical role. Many other African countries have undertaken market liberalizing reforms in the agricultural sectors, but few achieved Ghana's level of success, primarily because complementary investment in rural infrastructure was lacking.

According to Goletti and Kheralla (1997), transport costs sometimes constitute as much as 50 per cent of the operating costs of traders in rural Africa. In this situation, liberalization alone cannot induce large numbers of private traders to enter the market, especially as the market is so thin because of low purchasing power and a large geographical dispersion of the population. In Malawi, for instance, when as part of liberalization the parastatal marketing board ADMARC reduced its operations in areas with low trading and poor infrastructure, the private traders also shied away from those areas for the same reasons. As a result, ADMARC was forced to reopen its markets in some of these areas. In Madagascar, for the same reasons, government monopoly has been replaced by private geographic monopolies (Goletti and Kheralla 1997).

Ghana avoided this trap precisely because it was bold enough to undertake a massive programme of infrastructure investment, undaunted by the emergence of inflation. Without this, marketing margins would not have fallen, in spite of liberalization; the happy congruence of higher producer prices and lower consumer prices would not have occurred, leading to the congruence between higher growth and lower poverty.

4.3 Investment allocation: pro-export bias?

A second set of trade-offs arises on the question of prioritization of investment between and within sectors. The basic argument here is in two parts: first, it is a mistake to assume that once relative prices are set straight private investment will flow automatically in the right direction – public investment will have to be planned and targeted in order to relieve the most important bottlenecks; and, second, when it comes to planning and targeting public investment, it may sometimes be necessary to violate some of the tenets of conventional structural adjustment.

On the first point, it is readily recognized by everyone that governments must ensure a secure legal and institutional framework and a stable political environment in order to attract private investment – getting prices right is not enough. The point being emphasized here goes deeper than that; it argues that African governments need to do more than merely provide an enabling environment – they have to induce and guide private investment through careful targeting of public investment.[6] In economies ridden with market imperfections, the private sector will simply not invest unless complementary public investment is made in order to remove specific bottlenecks. Empirical evidence from sub-Saharan Africa gives strong support to this view that well-directed public investment tends to 'crowd-in' private investment[7] (Taylor, 1988, p. 51).

The need for well-directed public investment can be illustrated by considering the case of sub-Saharan African sectoral reforms in agriculture being implemented as part of structural adjustment. Between 1980 and 1995, privatization (withdrawal of state agencies from grain pricing and marketing activities) and liberalization (the relaxation of regulatory controls on private marketing) took place under aid-conditionality in over 20 African countries (World Bank, 1994; Donovan, 1996). The effects of these reforms continue to be hotly contested. Much donor-supported research finds support for an upsurge in agricultural productivity following reforms (Block, 1994; Sahn and Sarris, 1991; USAID, 1993; World Bank, 1994). But some critics have raised doubts about the general validity of these claims for the region as a whole (for example Cornia and Helleiner, 1994; Mosely and Smith, 1989; Staatz and Ba, 1996).

In an attempt to resolve these controversies, a group of researchers at Michigan State University have recently carried out a comprehensive analysis of reforms in seven countries drawn from Eastern (Kenya and Ethiopia), Western (Mali, Senegal and Burkina Faso) and Southern Africa (Zimbabwe and Zambia). Their principal finding (Jayne, *et al.*, 1997, p. 12) was that,

> Although there is some evidence that output marketing reforms have been associated with increases in land and labour productivity at the aggregate level in the countries studied, it appears that much of these increases are due to shifts in crop mix and the geographical location of production rather than the intensification of existing farming systems.

In other words, while pricing and marketing reforms have done their job by reallocating resources wherever possible, they have hit the limit of what can be achieved through static reallocation. There is no sign yet of sustainable increases in productivity growth for the millions of semi-subsistence rural households that cannot move and have limited capacity to change their crop mix.

Therefore, 'A remaining challenge is how to translate the one-time gains from changing crop mix and location into more sustainable ongoing productivity gains for individual crops', especially for coarse grains (millet, sorghum, and maize) which constitute most of the area cultivated by African farmers (Jayne *et al.*, 1997, p. 16). What is needed is a set of supportive measures that include public investment in infrastructure and agricultural research. In a similar vein, another comprehensive study of input market reforms in sub-Saharan agriculture (Goletti and Kheralla, 1997, p. 32) concluded that:

> Market reforms have apparently improved the distribution system of agricultural inputs and outputs, but have been unable to increase the effective demand of farmers for modern inputs that could lead to substantial increases in production and productivity. Unless market reforms are complemented by institutional reforms in rural finance and [the] extension system, and by improvement in infrastructure, the smallholder farmers are going to be left out of the reform process, or, at most, be affected only marginally.

Irrigation, as well rural roads, is another important area of public investment. While reforms do not generally seem to have accelerated the adoption of modern technology, there is one exception in Madagascar where both the cultivated area and yield of irrigated rice (not of rain-fed rice) have improved: in general, the rain-fed highlands have not benefited from reforms, but the irrigated Lac Alaotra has (Goletti and Kheralla, 1997). As for agricultural research, analysis in the region has shown high pay-offs from such research (Oehmke and Crawford, 1996), yet both national and donor funding for technology development are dwindling. A complacent view seems to be held that seed-fertilizer technologies already exist that can double or triple farm yields in Africa, but as Jayne *et al.* (1997, p. 17) observe: 'there remains a dearth of research on the profitability and riskiness of those technologies under current input and output market conditions or those foreseeable under alternative sustainable input and output marketing arrangements.'

The problem of course is that the scope for public investment is severely constrained by budgetary resources. There is a need to prioritize – to decide which crops and which groups of farmers to target in the immediate future. Here again possible trade-offs arise between growth and poverty and between the dictates of structural adjustment and those of long-term productivity growth. The logic of structural adjustment urges bias towards export crops, but it is by no means clear that in terms of technological possibilities and expected growth of demand these provide the best option. Nor is it clear that they are always the best option for accelerated poverty reduction.

Recent household surveys indicate that while the majority of rural poor in Africa derive their livelihood from agriculture, only a small proportion do so from export crops. Thus, the rural poor derive 70–80 per cent of their income from agriculture in Côte d'Ivoire and Tanzania, 60–70 per cent in Ghana, 50 per cent in Malawi, and 40–50 per cent in Madagascar. But only in Côte d'Ivoire do export crops contribute a large share of agricultural income of the rural poor (45 per cent).

One must therefore wonder whether according higher priority to the export sector is compatible with the goal of accelerated poverty reduction. Of course, just because the poor are relatively less-dependent on the export sector does not mean that the export sector should receive lower priority. Indirect effects operating through product and factor markets must also be taken into account. There are in fact a few studies that have tried to assess the relative priority of different sectors by considering both direct and indirect effects within a general equilibrium framework. Dorosh and Haggblade (1996) have done so for Madagascar. They considered three options – investment in cocoa (main export crop), in paddy (main food crop and an important import item), and in formal manufacturing – and found that investing in paddy was the best strategy for both growth and distribution. The study on Zaire by Kone and Thorbecke (1996) also demonstrated the superiority of promoting agriculture (not primarily export-oriented) over both mining (the chief export sector) and manufacturing.

It is not being claimed that this conclusion can be generalized for the whole of Africa, or the developing world. There may well be cases where according priority to the export sector is indeed the best strategy from the point of view of both growth and poverty reduction. The point, rather, is that the opposite is also possible, and that when this possibility arises doctrinaire adherence to the precepts of structural adjustment would be a folly.

5 Summary and conclusions

Conventional wisdom parades Fund-Bank type structural adjustment as the growth-enhancing strategy *par excellence*. It also claims that growth of the kind promoted by adjustment is intrinsically beneficial for the poor. A careful analysis of the African experience suggests, however, that the effect of adjustment on both growth and poverty has been only marginally beneficial. The effect on growth has been marginal because, although adjustment does improve allocative efficiency, that alone is not sufficient to generate sustained growth. The effect on poverty has been marginal, partly because the effect on growth has itself been marginal and partly because various market imperfections have prevented the poor from benefiting fully from growth.

The strategy for accelerating poverty reduction must, therefore, go beyond adjustment. This is true as much for Africa as for the rest of the developing world. How compatible such a broader strategy will be with the requirements of conventional adjustment is an important issue. A view seems to be emerging that although adjustment may not be sufficient for either sustained growth or accelerated poverty reduction, it is both a necessary component of and perfectly compatible with the broader strategy. In this chapter, I have argued against this view. While not suggesting that structural adjustment should be thrown overboard, I have pointed out that it may be necessary to compromise on some tenets of conventional adjustment.

In particular, extreme fiscal conservatism and inflation phobia should be given up for the sake of market-augmenting types of public investment, and a doctrinaire bias towards the export sector may have to be abandoned in favour of import substitution and the non-traded sectors while deciding priorities for investment allocation. This is not a counsel for indulging in reckless inflation or rampant protectionism, but a plea for pragmatism. If opportunities arise for accelerating growth and reducing poverty rapidly through public investment that results in moderate inflation, and through an allocation of investment that accords priority to non-export sectors, it would be wrong to ignore them in the name of adhering to the doctrine of adjustment. This chapter has shown that such opportunities can and do arise in Africa; no doubt they can arise elsewhere as well. These opportunities should not be missed, for the sake of the poor everywhere.

Notes

1 Collier further argues that the slower rate of capital accumulation is in part accounted for by a higher rate of capital flight from Africa compared to other developing regions.

2 These are: Cameroon, Côte d'Ivoire, Ghana, Kenya, Mali, Senegal, Tanzania, Zaire, Zambia and Zimbabwe.

3 It is also interesting to note that there is a curious asymmetry in the manner in which the problem of terms-of-trade decline is treated as between pre-reform and post-reform periods. The fact is that the terms of trade continued to decline in the post-reform period, but unlike the pre-reform decline the post-reform decline is readily seen as an exogenous event over which internal policy had no control. This exogeneity argument is in fact frequently invoked while explaining why many

adjusting countries failed to generate adequate growth; no allowance is made for the proposition that the effect of terms-of-trade decline could have been offset by correct policies (see World Bank, 1995b, p. 35). One wonders why 'sauce for the gander' is not 'sauce for the goose'!

4 Exactly what lies behind the African dummy remains an open issue. Easterly and Levine themselves point to ethnic fractionalization and contagion of troubles from neighbouring countries. But Sachs and Warner (1996) put a lot of blame on the geography of Africa, while Collier (1997) blames the extreme riskiness of investment caused by adverse non-economic factors.

5 For a detailed discussion of the relevant evidence, see Osmani (1998).

6 The plea for not sacrificing productive public investment at the altar of structural adjustment has been made forcefully by, among others, Griffin (1996), Weeks (1997) and Stewart (1991 and 1995).

7 This is not to deny the validity of the commonly held view that misguided public investment can and does 'crowd out' private investment.

References

Alderman, H. and G. Shively (1996) 'Economic Reform and Food Prices: Evidence from Markets in Ghana', *World Development*, vol. 24, no. 3, pp. 521–34.

Beaudry, P. and N. K. Sowa (1994) 'Ghana', in S. Horton, R. Kanbur and D. Mazumdar (eds), *Labor Markets in an Era of Adjustment*, vol. 2, EDI Development Studies (Washington, DC: The World Bank).

Block, S. A. (1994) 'A New View of Agricultural Productivity in Sub-Saharan Africa', *American Journal of Agricultural Economics*, vol. 76 (August), pp. 619–24.

Collier, P. (1997) 'The Marginalisation of Africa in the World Economy' (mimeo), Centre for the Study of African Economies, University of Oxford.

Corden, W. M. (1971) 'The Effects of Trade on the Rate of Growth', in J. N. Bhagwati, R. W. Jones, R. A. Mundell and J. Vanek (eds), *Trade, Balance of Payments and Growth* (Amsterdam: North Holland).

Cornia, G. A. and G. Helleiner (eds) (1994) *From Adjustment and Development in Africa: Conflict, Controversy, Convergence, and Consensus* (London: Macmillan).

Cromwell, E. (1992) 'Malawi', in A. Duncan and J. Howell (eds), *Structural Adjustment and the African Farmer* (Oxford: James Currey in association with Overseas Development Institute).

Demery, L. and L. Squire (1996) 'Macroeconomic Adjustment and Poverty in Africa: An Emerging Picture', *World Bank Research Observer*, vol. 11, no. 1, pp. 39–59.

Donovan, G. (1996) 'Agriculture and Economic Reform in Sub-Saharan Africa', AFTES working paper no. 18, Africa Technical Department (Washington, DC: The World Bank).

Dorosh, P. and S. Haggblade (1996) 'Growth Linkages in Madagascar: Implications for Development Strategies', in D. E. Sahn (ed.), *Economic Reform and the Poor in Africa* (Oxford: Clarendon Press).

Easterly, W. and R. Levine (1995) 'Africa's Growth Tragedy: A Retrospective, 1960–89', working paper no. 1503, Policy Research Department (Washington, DC: The World Bank).

FAO (1996) *The Sixth World Food Survey* (Rome: The Food and Agriculture Organization).

Goletti, F. and M. Kheralla (1997) 'The Slow Response in Input Markets and Input Use: A Five African Country Comparison', paper presented at the XXIII Conference of the International Association of Agricultural Economists, 10–16, August, Sacramento, CA.

Griffin, K. (1996) 'Macroeconomic Reform and Employment: An Investment-Led Strategy of Structural Adjustment in Sub-Saharan Africa', Issues in Development, discussion paper no. 16 (Geneva: International Labour Office).

Jayne, T. S., J. M. Staatz, M. T. Weber, S. Jones and E. W. Crawford (1997) 'Agricultural Policy Reform and Productivity Change in Africa', paper presented at the XXIII International Conference of Agricultural Economists, 10–16 August, Sacramento, CA.

Khan, A. R. (1997) 'Reversing the Decline of Output and Productive Employment in Rural Sub-Saharan Africa', Issues in Development discussion paper no. 17, Development Policies Department (Geneva: International Labour Office).

Kone, S. and E. Thorbecke (1996) 'Sectoral Investment Priorities for Renewed Growth in Zaire', in D. E. Sahn (ed.), *Economic Reform and the Poor in Africa* (Oxford: Clarendon Press).

Milne, W. J. and M. Neitzert (1994) 'Kenya', in S. Horton, R. Kanbur and D. Mazumdar (eds) *Labor Markets in an Era of Adjustment*, vol. 2, EDI Development Studies (Washington DC: The World Bank).

Mosely, P. and L. Smith (1989) 'Structural Adjustment and Agricultural Performance in Sub-Saharan Africa, 1980–87', *Journal of International Development*, vol. 1, no. 3.

Mosely, P., T. Subasat and J. Weeks (1995) 'Assessing Adjustment in Africa', *World Development*, vol. 23, no. 9, pp. 1459–73.

Oehmke, J. F. and E. W. Crawford (1996) 'The Impact of Agricultural Technology in Sub-Saharan Africa', *Journal of African Economies*, vol. 5, no. 2, pp. 271–92.

Osmani, S. R. (1998) 'Growth, Labour and Poverty in Sub-Saharan Africa: Going Beyond Adjustment' (mimeo), a report prepared for the Development Policy Department (Geneva: International Labour Office).

Pearce, R. (1992) 'Ghana', in A. Duncan and J. Howell (eds), *Structural Adjustment and the African Farmer* (Oxford: James Currey in association with Overseas Development Institute).

Radwan, S. (1997) 'Towards Full Employment: Egypt into the 21st Century', Distinguished Lecture Series, Egyptian Center for Economic Studies, Cairo.

Sachs, J. D. and M. Warner (1996) 'Sources of Slow Growth in African Economies', Development Discussion Paper 545 Cambridge, Mass.: Harvard Institute for International Development.

Sahn, D. E. (ed.) (1996) *Economic Reform and the Poor in Africa* (Oxford: Clarendon Press).

Sahn, D. E., P. Dorosh and S. Younger (1996) 'Exchange Rate, Fiscal and Agricultural Policies in Africa: Does Adjustment Hurt the Poor?', *World Development*, vol. 24, no. 4, pp. 719–47.

Sahn, D. and A. Sarris, (1991) 'Structural Adjustment and the Welfare of the Rural Smallholders: A Comparative Analysis from Sub-Saharan Africa', *World Bank Economic Review*, vol. 5, no. 2.

Sarel, M. (1996) 'Nonlinear Effects of Inflation on Economic Growth', *IMF Staff Papers*, no. 43, pp. 199–215.

Sarris, A. H. (1994) 'Household Welfare During Crisis and Adjustment in Ghana', *Journal of African Economies*, vol. 2, no. 2, pp. 195–237.

Serven, L. (1997) 'Uncertainty, Instability and Irreversible Investment: Theory, Evidence and Lessons for Africa', Policy Research Working Paper no. 1722 (Washington DC: World Bank).

Staatz, J. M. and M. Ba (1996) 'Fostering Agricultural and Food System Transformation in Africa', Michigan State University Policy Synthesis no 13, East Lansing.

Stewart, F. (1991) 'Are Adjustment Policies in Africa Consistent with Long-Run Development Needs?', *Development Policy Review*, vol. 9, pp. 413–36.

Stewart, F. (1995) *Adjustment and Poverty: Options and Choices* (London and New York: Routledge).

Taylor, L. (1988) *Varieties of Stabilisation Experience*, WIDER Studies in Development Economics (Oxford: Clarendon Press).

USAID (1993) *Africa: Growth Renewed, Hope Rekindled: A Report on the Performance of the Development Fund for Africa, 1988–1992*, Office of Development Planning, Bureau for Africa (Washington, DC.: USAID).

Weeks, J. (1997) 'Macroeconomic Policy for Employment and Incomes, with Reference to Africa South of the Sahara', papers in Jobs for Africa Programme (Geneva: International Labour Office).

World Bank (1994) *Adjustment in Africa: Reforms, Results and the Road Ahead* (New York: Oxford University Press).

World Bank (1995a) *Labor and the Growth Crisis in Sub-Saharan Africa*, Regional Perspectives on World Development Report 1995 (Washington, DC: World Bank).

World Bank (1995b) *The Social Impact of Adjustment Operations: An Overview*, report 14776, Operations Evaluation Department (Washington, DC: World Bank).

World Bank (1997) *Taking Action to Reduce Poverty in Sub-Saharan Africa*, Development in Practice Series (Washington, DC: World Bank).

Part IV

Sustainability of Reforms

13

Sequencing and the Sustainability of Economic Reform in India

*John Toye**

Institute of Development Studies, Sussex and UNCTAD

1 The timing of adjustment: the big bang versus gradualism

The adoption by India since 1991 of a set of structural adjustment policies has posed once again the question of how to *time* the policy changes that economic reformers try to implement. In the early 1990s, two different approaches to this question of timing were debated. On one side of the argument were the advocates of the 'big bang' approach. They said that comprehensive stabilization and liberalization measures should be introduced immediately at the start of the reform process and implemented as fast as possible. They were the advocates of speed and stealth in a top-down style of reform. The classic example of this is the reforms carried through by Lescek Balcerowicz in Poland in 1990–2 (Rodrik, 1996, p. 34; Williamson, 1994, pp. 153–77). The supporters of the big bang in Eastern Europe and the former Soviet Union were influenced by unacknowledged political considerations. They detected a very brief window of opportunity to demolish the economic structures that underpinned state socialism, before disillusion with 'capitalism' set in: for example, see the speech of J. Sachs in Williamson (1994).

On the other side of the argument were the advocates of gradualism. They pleaded for the stretching out of the reform measures over a longer time period, reasoning that this would ease the pain of the adjustment process, allow time to develop a political consensus in support of the reform process and thus make it more politically sustainable. To this plea, the 'big bangers' retorted that any procrastination would add to the total costs of adjustment and would, contrary to the rationale for gradualism, make the whole adjustment process *less* politically viable, by allowing opponents of reform time to marshal their forces of political obstruction.

The discussion here will focus first on the problem of the timing of reforms, and in sections 2 and 3 on what welfare economics and political

* Comments of participants were most helpful in revising the original paper, especially those of Deepak Nayyar.

economy each contribute to its resolution. It is suggested that both of these contributions are partial, but are mutually compatible within the framework of critical path analysis (CPA). In section 4, the Indian economic reforms are re-examined with the CPA method in mind. Section 5 concludes with a consideration of whether, and for what reasons, the use of the CPA method for the management of reform sequences needs to be qualified.

Turning first to the issue of the timing of adjustment reforms, it is important to note that neither the 'big-bangers' nor the gradualists had much to say about the problem of the optimal sequencing of reform measures. The 'big bangers' urged the necessity of the *simultaneity* of all reforms, be they stabilization or liberalization measures. By definition, this is a denial of the need for any kind of *sequencing* of reforms. On the other hand, the advocates of gradualism assumed that all reforms would be costly in welfare terms and that, without democratic consensus-building, they would be politically destabilizing. This led them to ask simply for *more time* for reform, without considering whether the reform timetable that was already in place could be rearranged to better effect. Fortunately, by the 1990s, awareness of the problem of optimal sequencing of structural adjustment policies had grown more widespread. So also had an awareness of the difficulty of resolving it.

Suppose that one were to think of the implementation of a set of structural adjustment policies as a very large project, composed of a myriad of interrelated activities. Suppose one were then to ask oneself how this very large project could be managed in the most efficient way. The thought occurs: is not this a familiar problem in operational research? If this is so, and the analogy between the management of economic reforms and the management of a very large project – whether physical or institutional – is sound, it would imply that a solution to the sequencing problem might be found by applying an operational research method. The method in question is CPA.

Let us now explore the economic reforms/large project analogy more closely. The difficulty of efficiently managing any large project arises because of certain characteristics of the interrelationships of the many discrete activities that are involved in the completion of the project (MacCrimmon, 1987). The three key characteristics are:

- *There is a precedence ordering of some activities* Although some of the activities may be able to be undertaken simultaneously, others will have to follow a required order or sequence in time. Thus even when there is only one way to perform an activity and when the completion time is known for certain, there is always a problem of determining when an activity can begin.
- *There is uncertainty about the duration of activities* The completion time of some activities can be known with certainty, but the completion times for many others are uncertain. Unexpected negative shocks will delay the

completion of some activities, while favourable shocks may advance completion dates for others. However, because of the order of precedence that does apply to *some* of the activities, not all delays and speed-ups of particular activities are equally significant (or 'critical') for the completion time of the entire project.

- *Activities have alternative designs that are more costly* There may be only one way to perform some activities, but for others there may be more than one way to achieve the intended outcome. Since, under assumptions of rational behaviour, the option that minimizes cost would have been chosen first, other options will have higher resource costs. Nevertheless, it may be worthwhile to incur the extra costs of the re-design of activities that are critical, because of the difference that they make in shortening the completion time of the entire project.

Thus, managers of very large projects need to know which activities are critical in the above sense. For that purpose, a CPA is undertaken. CPA requires that all the activities of the project must first be specified, along with the minimum time needed for them, and then they must be placed in their order of time precedence. The critical path of operations is the longest path through the entire network.

The idea of the CPA method can be used as a heuristic device to reconsider the question of the sequencing and sustainability of structural adjustment programmes. Much of the existing literature on this question is cast in terms of one or the other of two quite distinct approaches, as for example, Kanbur (1995). One of these is welfare economics, which is concerned with how changes in economic policy affect the welfare of individuals, groups and thus society at large. The other is political economy, which examines how those who stand to gain or lose from the policy changes will react or fail to react by organizing themselves to operate in the political process. The argument being made here is that, within the larger framework of the CPA method, the insights of welfare economics and of political economy can become complementary.

To date, unfortunately, they have usually been seen as conflictual. What frequently happens in the debate over economic reforms is that the welfare economists try to demonstrate that the reforms will increase welfare. Having done so to their own satisfaction, they then urge governments to implement them forthwith, wringing their hands and shaking their heads if governments fail to do so. For their part, the political economists see that the reform agenda creates political conflict and power struggles, and infer from this either that economically desirable reforms are politically infeasible, or that politically feasible reforms are economically undesirable, for example because of a presumed negative impact on the poor.

Since these battle-lines are so familiar, it may be more profitable to try to avoid them. Let us ask instead what welfare economics and political economy each have to contribute to the analysis of economic reform when it is viewed as a very large project, whose management requires the minimization of the duration of its 'critical path' in the face of a variety of stochastic shocks. In the next section, the potential contribution of welfare economics is considered from this perspective. This is followed in section 3, by a discussion of the potential contribution of the political economists.

2 What does welfare economics say about the sequencing of reforms?

What does welfare economics teach us about the sequencing of policy changes, in particular measures of stabilization and liberalization? The lessons are surely not very abundant. Furthermore, the main difficulty of the search for relevant lessons lies deep in the entrails of economic theory, which in many of its manifestations simply abstracts altogether from the dimension of time. Many of the great economic theorists of the past have struggled to incorporate a time dimension into fundamental economic theory, and with limited success (Currie and Steedman, 1990). As a modern development economist, Stern (1989, p. 21) has noted, 'Our theories . . . do not provide us with a satisfactory analysis of timing and sequencing. That is not a subject which can be analysed very easily and it is not one on which economic theory has progressed very far.'

The standard starting point in welfare economics is the economic theory of the second best. This begins with Pareto's theorem that a general equilibrium of markets brought about by freely adjusting prices maximizes economic welfare (assuming that the existing distribution of assets and income is optimal). This is because, in general equilibrium, no further welfare improvements are possible by means of reallocating resources. It is no longer possible to make any one better off without at the same time making someone else worse off. If this is so – and if the underlying distributional assumption is also accepted – an economy without any constraints to impede the emergence of a general equilibrium must be preferable to an economy where such constraints (often called 'economic distortions') do exist, and where therefore there are barriers to welfare improvements. But this logic does not also prove that any single move towards the ideal undistorted economy also increases welfare. Eliminating one distortion while leaving others in place may reduce welfare rather than improving it.

It is easy to see intuitively why this is so. One distortion may be counterbalancing the effect of another distortion. In this case, if one is removed, but not both, the economy may become more distorted rather than less distorted as a result. It is also easy to see how the theory of the second best is related to the advocacy of the 'big-bang' approach to adjustment. Only when *all* distortions are swept away *simultaneously* does economic theory appear to guarantee that the result will be welfare-improving. However, it is very important to ask 'what kind of a guarantee is this?' It is hardly a reassuring one, once we have read the small print. The reason is that the theory of the second-best also lacks any time dimension. It rests on a static comparison of a disequilibrium situation with an ideal equilibrium, ignoring both the dynamic path of transition and the time that such a transition takes to complete. Advocates of the 'big-bang' approach therefore actually rely on a further assumption, namely that the process of equilibration is instantaneous, or at least so rapid that the problem of the path of transition can be neglected. This assumption is embedded in, for example, the monetary approach to the balance of payments developed at the University of Chicago, and applied with disastrous welfare effects by Chicago-trained economic policy-makers who were guiding the Chilean economic adjustment process between 1976 and 1981.

The theory of the second best does, however, have a particular relevance to the question of appropriate sequencing of structural adjustment, when this term is defined to include both the stabilization and the liberalization of the economy. As already discussed, the theory analyses the welfare implications of different moves from disequilibrium to a general equilibrium of markets, and especially the different welfare implications of the removal of microeconomic distortions all at once or piecemeal. The results of this analysis are, as just mentioned, inconclusive, and of no help to the policy-maker concerned with the sequencing of economic adjustment measures. However, one aspect of the theory is relevant here. It is that the theory of the second best, like all developments of general equilibrium theory, analyses microeconomic welfare problems on the assumption of macroeconomic stability. The validity of all its theorems relies on the assumption that a stable level of general prices has already been achieved, by some form of monetary policy, so that the relative prices that consumers and producers face are defined in real and not merely nominal terms.

This feature of the theory of the second best suggests that to embark on a programme of economic liberalization or deregulation before taking measures to stabilize macroeconomic imbalances is a wrong order of precedence, in that it will not produce the desired welfare results. So welfare economics does after all have *something* to contribute to establishing an order of precedence for the package of policy changes. If one were to write any rules of precedence for policy changes, Rule No. 1 of adjustment sequencing would be that macroeconomic stabilization must be started first, if there is serious macro-instability. Rule No. 1(a) is that, until stabilization measures have reached the target values for the fiscal and balance of payments deficits, liberalization measures should be pursued only to the extent that they are consistent with achieving these stabilization targets.

At the beginning of the adjustment sequence, policy-makers will almost certainly face a trade-off between the pursuit of macroeconomic stabilization objectives and the pursuit of their liberalization objectives. For example, the liberalization of foreign trade often involves the lowering or removal of tariff barriers to imports, which will reduce customs revenue for imports and *ceteris paribus* increase the size of the fiscal deficit. Again, the liberalization of the financial system usually has the effect of raising the rate of interest on government debt, and thus *ceteris paribus* increasing government expenditure on debt interest, and thus widening the fiscal deficit. This suggests that tariff reductions and financial liberalization should not start until stabilization targets have been hit.

All is not gloom, however. Some liberalization measures contribute positively to reaching the stabilization goals. For example, the imposition of a hard budget constraint on public enterprises has the effect of reducing public expenditure, and *ceteris paribus* also reducing the fiscal deficit, by eliminating those budgetary subsidies that financed previous public enterprise losses. Again, the replacement of quantitative restrictions by tariffs of equivalent protective effect, which is a necessary preliminary action for trade liberalisation, increases customs duties and reduces the fiscal deficit *ceteris paribus*. Further, the reduction of the rates of export taxes can be expected to switch some exports back from illegal channels to legal channels of export where the tax will be levied. If previously a substantial proportion of exports has been smuggled out, the net effect of the reduced rate of tax and the additional volume of exports that has switched to exiting by legal channels could be an increase in revenue, and *ceteris paribus* a reduced fiscal deficit. So certain liberalization actions provide a positive reinforcement to stabilization. The aim of policy-makers has to be to allow the economy to benefit from the benign interactions between liberalization and stabilization, and to minimize the effect of the malign interactions. This implies Rule No. 1(b): advance in the sequence of liberalization measures those that reinforce stabilization goals, while holding back those that will make stabilization more difficult.

Before considering this further, let us state Rule No. 2, that stabilization measures themselves have an appropriate sequence. Since monetary policies are often inadequate on their own to the task of stabilization, they need to be complemented by fiscal and exchange rate policies. When this is so, the sequencing of fiscal deficit reduction and exchange rate devaluation is itself important. If, for example, the fiscal deficit has not been reduced sufficiently and is still causing inflation at a higher rate than the weighted average rate of the country's trading partners, a devaluation will not be effective. Further devaluation will soon be required. This situation does not constitute a restoration of macroeconomic stability. Apart from other consequences, expectations of repeated devaluations will deter inward foreign investment and provoke speculative outward capital movements. These will be attempted illegally if capital controls are in place, and legally if they are not. So, adequate reduction of the fiscal deficit must precede a devaluation if the latter is to be stabilizing in its effect.

When macro-stabilization has been given its appropriate priority and reduction of the fiscal deficit is the instrument chosen for this, then care must be taken about precisely how the deficit is reduced. Whether revenue raising is to be preferred to expenditure reduction, or both are to be employed, will depend on the initial conditions of the economy when an adjustment process begins. About this policy choice there can be no general rule. In some economies the economic crisis will already have driven public expenditure down to sub-optimal levels, while in others it will be bloated public expenditures that caused the crisis in the first place, and will therefore need to be pruned back. In that case, liberalization measures that lead to public expenditure reductions will be of special importance.

If the deficit is to be reduced by the reduction of public spending, the cuts should not be arbitrary, either in the form of a reduction of *x* per cent in all expenditures or reductions only in categories like the purchase of supplies and equipment, which are the paths of least resistance. Such arbitrary cutting merely introduces new distortions that reduce the productivity of the public sector's service provision. Rather the least productive areas of service provision have to be identified and closed down in their entirety. What should remain are those areas of expenditure that act as the most positive incentive to domestic and foreign private-sector investment. Good economic infrastructure (transport, telecommunications, electricity, water) and good social sector services (health, education, social security) will have the desirable incentive properties.

If tax revenue is to be raised rather than public spending reduced, the first step on the road to trade liberalization, the conversion of quantitative restrictions on imports into equivalent tariffs, can be taken early on, because, as already noted, it has its own additional stabilizing effect by raising customs revenue. Trade liberalization proper does not occur until some tariffs are reduced. Once this happens the benign interaction arising from tariffization of quantitative restrictions is succeeded by the malign one of tariff reductions that lower tax revenue. Since many countries in need of adjustment rely quite heavily for revenue on taxes on foreign trade, this malign effect can be powerful if replacement revenues are not quickly mobilized in addition to the new revenues that will be required to reduce the fiscal deficit. Where to find both replacement and additional revenues? The new taxes should be broad-based, levied on domestic economic activity and themselves non-distorting in their economic effects. These criteria point clearly in the direction of a value-added tax.

As well as these qualitative requirements for expenditure reductions and revenue increases, the reduction of the fiscal deficit should meet a quantitative target. This target will depend on a judgement of how large a deficit can be financed on a sustainable basis, by domestic or foreign borrowing or through the inflation tax. Once the fiscal deficit is being brought down to a sustainable level, by means of the right type of revenue expansions or expenditure cuts, it is prudent to embark on the decontrol of essential imports which will be needed if firms are to be able to respond to a devaluation, or to a process of exchange rate liberalization which usually is accompanied by a devaluation – either all at once or by means of a crawling peg. Since infrastructural bottlenecks are likely to constrain the export supply response, foreign aid should be sought at this point for rehabilitation projects. One final preliminary action is needed before liberalization proper is begun. The extent and timing of future trade liberalization should be announced. It is most important to give a clear advance warning before liberalizing the trade current account. This gives a limited time to firms operating in protected industries either to improve their competitiveness, or to diversify their assets into other activities that will not be damaged by the removal of protection. It also warns new foreign investors against getting locked into industries in which profits can be made only if existing levels of protection continue.

The debate about the order of precedence of liberalization measures *once the economy has been stabilized* centres on the order in which domestic financial markets, factor markets (including labour markets), goods markets, foreign trade and capital markets are deregulated. The need for a successful sequence of liberalization measures is well understood by some, and economists have tried to solve the problem by considering short-term, medium-term and long-term effects of such measures (Nayyar, 1996). The order of financial/factor/goods/foreign trade/capital markets is the sequence which seems to represent the consensus view. However, this consensus does not rest on much formal welfare economics. Rather, it has arisen from the observation of the results of what have in effect been experiments in different practical settings. Thus the debate is likely to continue as different types of interaction between liberalization measures are highlighted by experience and subsequently analysed.

Here I can only give some flavour of this essentially pragmatic discussion. The objective of the 'project' of structural adjustment is not merely to kill off those forms of economic activity that have been induced artificially by subsidies, distorted prices and uneconomic lending and investment. This should be no more than preliminary to releasing resources for the growth of new economic activities that make better use of the resources thereby released. Only if this actually happens will economic growth take place. For success, a strong domestic supply response to the changed prices is imperative. But, evaluation studies of structural adjustment, as for example, Taylor (1988), have discovered that the supply response to devaluation is often inhibited because the banking system is unable to supply the quantities of credit that are needed by firms as working capital. As is also well-established, this credit constraint is far more severe for small enterprises which are unable to offer the banks any collateral security against failure to repay. Small enterprises include small farms in the rural areas which might otherwise invest in high-yielding varieties and fertilizer, as well as small businesses in urban areas which might otherwise be able to upgrade their existing technology, or even just meet their start-up costs. Provided that the environment is not fraught with risks so high that they deter investment, much of the success of the structural adjustment project hangs on the health or otherwise of the banking system as a point of access to credit for sound borrowers. Are the banks still encumbered with bad debts and managed by the same staff whose lending decisions incurred those bad debts, or has its balance sheet been cleaned and its management turned over to people who will lend solely on considerations of expected returns? Further, are there good microfinance institutions functioning for borrowers who cannot provide collateral? If so, are they using operating procedures which succeed in minimizing, in the absence of collateral, the risk of non-repayment?

The answers to these questions vary greatly as between Asia and Africa. Bangladesh and Indonesia have had mass credit-based rural development programmes in place since the 1970s, that have reached millions of households. Unlike some other similar programmes, for example in India, their repayment record has been good. This has been assisted by devices like granting discounts to those who repay on-time, profit-related bonuses for staff and repayment-related incentives for neighbours who act as character referees. Repayments are collected at short intervals at the borrower's house, and the borrower is encouraged to open savings deposits and required to place one-twelfth of the loan in an insurance fund (Mosely, 1994). When financial intermediation for small borrowers is widespread and well-organized, inhibitions about retrenchment of public sector workers are greatly eased. Equally clearly, they need to be in place before it is realistic to make progress on labour market reforms. Further, if this sequence is followed, the economy will be well-placed to ensure that all the advantage of a liberalization of the goods markets is not captured entirely by foreign exporters and investors.

Thus the reform of labour and other factor markets should follow financial sector reform, but precede trade liberalization. The rationale for this sequence is that, if deregulation of labour markets has the effect of reducing formal sector employment, credit should be available on market terms to permit the expansion of informal self-employment. This shift, in turn, is an essential prerequisite for a strong domestic supply response, once trade barriers are removed and foreign firms are allowed to compete in previously protected domestic markets.

The liberalization of the capital market is placed at the end of the sequence, for various reasons. The underlying assumption is that controls on the capital market are at least partly effective, and that some capital, either domestic or foreign is retained in the country 'unwillingly'. If capital market controls are abandoned before the domestic credit market is liberalized, some of the unwillingly held capital will exit, in search of the higher market interest rate which can be found abroad. This flight of capital will be reinforced to the extent that the domestic currency carries a significant risk of devaluation. If capital market controls are abandoned before the exchange rate is stabilized, capital will flow out even after domestic and foreign real interest rates have been equalized, since savers are able to take an almost costless, and often self-fulfilling, gamble that the domestic currency will be devalued.

The financial crisis that began in Thailand in July 1997 exhibited a particular variant of the latter scenario. Several Asian countries had followed policies of fixing the exchange rate of their currency to the US$. This meant that they accepted for themselves the whole of the foreign-exchange risk of borrowing abroad as a method of attracting foreign investment. At the same time they maintained or moved to an open capital account. While confidence lasted, all was well. Once the spectre of devaluation was raised in Thailand, other countries with fixed exchange rates had no defence against speculative attacks on their currencies, unless they could turn to a lender of last resort, as Hong Kong could turn to China. These events have underlined the importance of addressing sequencing issues in the liberalization of the capital account.

If the liberalization of the capital account accompanies the reform of foreign trade, capital inflows may succeed in the short run in pushing up the real exchange rate and permitting resource inflows into the non-traded goods sector which later have to be reversed (Falvey and Kim, 1992, p. 913). This is what happened in Chile from 1976 to 1981. Although there are some welfare arguments for small partial capital account liberalizations during trade reform, the bulk of the capital account liberalization is best left until the trade reform is already well-advanced.

In countries such as Chile, where the range of reforms has been wide, empirical analysis suggests that malign interactions will arise from adopting the wrong order of precedence in stabilization and liberalization, and constitute a major risk to the success of the adjustment project. This risk has been described as 'policy inconsistency'. It undermines the credibility of any structural adjustment programme. Once credibility has been lost, economic actors change their behaviour in ways which make the programme fail, even if previous political opposition to it was being successfully contained.

This discussion of the order of precedence of economic reforms indicates that welfare economics can be used to deduce some simple rules that give stabilization priority over liberalization measures, except in those cases in which the latter reinforce the move towards the stabilization targets. More loosely related to economic theory and more informed by lessons of experience are some 'rules of thumb' for sequencing the liberalization measures themselves, once stabilization targets have been met. (For the sake of clarity it should be emphasized here that meeting stabilization targets is a continuous process, given the existence of stochastic shocks from both internal and external sources, and not something that ever is or can be achieved once and for all). It is reasonable to argue that the economic reform project does have an order of precedence among at least some of its activities. This must throw doubt on the utility of the 'big bang' approach, while also showing the limitations of the gradualists' banner, if all it says is 'More Time!'

3 Political economy and the critical path of economic reform

If welfare economics throws some light on the interdependences in time of the manifold activities of the economic reform project, what is the contribution of political economy? Political economists of economic reform attempt to cover a very broad spectrum of adjustment issues, including the following:

- Theories that attempt to explain, by focusing on 'urban bias' or 'rent-seeking behaviour' or 'patrimonialism', why failures of economic performance should be interpreted not as a series of individual mistakes, but as a syndrome that causes widespread economic distortion (Toye, 1994, pp. 22–6).
- The precise combination of circumstances under which countries initially embrace the structural adjustment agenda, including the role of economic crises, the emergence of new forms of leadership and changing paradigms of development ('the rôle of ideas').
- The dynamics of the relationship between the government of the adjustment country and the international financial institutions that make it loans conditional on policy changes (for example Mosely, Harrigan and Toye, 1995).
- The ability of different types of political regime to initiate and sustain the project of structural adjustment. One question under this heading is whether it is necessary to have a ruthless authoritarian government to discipline the interest groups that benefit from a distorted economy.

Fascinating as all these topics are, and the findings of different researchers who have enquired into them, they are not pursued further in what follows. In this chapter special attention is focused on political economy analyses that illuminate the uncertainty that affects the duration of reform activities, and also the possibilities for redesigning activities that lie on the critical path so that the original timetable of the reform project can be adhered to.

This is quite convenient, and fits in well with the choice of India for our case study. In the case of India, the answers to the first four questions are sufficiently clear. It is enough to state that:

1 India had built up by 1991 an economy that grew only moderately fast, with a large and largely unprofitable state enterprise sector and extensive controls over the private economy.
2 After the foreign exchange crisis of 1991, the Indian government decided to make a new and more strenuous effort both to stabilize and to liberalize its economy, for whatever reasons.
3 In this effort, the international financial institutions have played only a minor part, because they do not have the leverage to be able to pressure the Indian policy-makers.
4 India has been and will continue to be a democracy, so that counterfactual comparisons of what might happen under an authoritarian regime are of academic interest only.

The political economy question that is most relevant in India's current situation is that of the management of the reform process. How can a democracy which has begun a historic break with its past development strategy carry that project through to a successful conclusion?

The political economy of the *implementation* of economic reforms is concerned with identifying the gainers and losers from particular reforms, and examining whether, to what extent and with what effect, each group engages in political action to advance or defend its interests. The standard approach is first to define a discrete set of interest groups, such as large farmers, the landless, industrialists, small entrepreneurs and so on, including politicians and bureaucrats as having their own interests to advance. Then their existing income sources are specified, and the impact of individual economic reforms on their income flow is estimated. It is assumed that the political preferences of each group are governed by the effects of reforms on their own incomes, and so their support or opposition for reforms is read off from this 'pocket-book politics' assumption. In fact, because the poorer groups who tend to benefit from liberalization are politically weaker than the richer groups, who tend to lose as a result, the political economy of the pocket-book draws the conclusion that economic reforms will tend to be blocked by a veto coalition.

If the problem of implementing economic reforms is rethought from the perspective of CPA, what new insights do we gain? It is that the political economy of the pocket-book has to be modified in the light of considerations of timing. If all the activities involved in the economic reform project were systematically enumerated, the variation with respect to their normal duration would surely be very considerable. Reform activities could indeed be placed along a spectrum, running from those whose normal duration is very brief indeed to those whose normal duration is very long. What is it that accounts for this extreme variation? The time normally required for a given reform activity depends on a number of factors. In particular, it depends on the following variables:

- The extent of the *technical consensus* on the design of the reform activity. Is there a clear agreement among the relevant specialists about how the activity is to be done? Lack of consensus will lengthen normal duration.
- The *amount and current availability of detailed information* required to satisfy the technical criteria in practice. If, for example, complex economic calculations have to be done, is the relevant data to hand, or will it have to be collected first? Unavailability of relevant detailed information will lengthen normal duration.
- The *number and variety of actors* who need to cooperate in order for the reform activity to be implemented. How many individuals, ministries, NGOs and other agencies have to collaborate together to achieve success? The more people and institutions have to collaborate, the longer will be the normal duration.

Because of the operation of these three tendencies, it has become commonplace to contrast the quick reforms of altering interest rates and exchange rates, which can be done by a few individuals in a single ministry, with the long drawn out reorganization of tax systems or sectors such as agriculture, education or health.

It seems to be the case that the longer the normal duration of a reform activity, the greater the likelihood that gainers and losers will be able to mobilize politically in support of their own interests. They will both have more time to try to penetrate the deliberate opaqueness of government policy, and more time to mobilize their respective constituencies. However, the potential losers will be more politically active than the potential gainers, an observation about reform first made by Machiavelli in *Il Principe*. So the longer the normal duration of a reform activity, the more time the potential losers will have to initiate blocking actions, such as strikes, legal challenges and parliamentary filibusters. This means that the longer is the normal duration of a reform activity, the more uncertain is the actual time duration of that activity, and, indeed, the more uncertain is its final outcome.

Because an economy is an interdependent system, economic policies have to be consistent, including the consistency between macroeconomic measures and microeconomic measures of all kinds. It was argued in section 2 that policy consistency has a time dimension, formally so between stabilization and liberalization, and more pragmatically so within the different measures of liberalization. The consistency requirement clearly becomes progressively more difficult to fulfil as more and more sectors are included in the liberalization process. In response to this difficulty, Rodrik (1990) has suggested that there is a trade-off between the range or scope of liberalization and the sustainability of structural adjustment. He judges the latter to be more important than the former, so he recommends deep liberalization in only one or two sectors, rather than a wide-ranging liberalization that could destabilize the entire reform process.

Governments can lose a great deal of political capital, defined as legitimacy and credibility, in such set-piece contests. This makes governments wary of provoking them in the first place, especially if the existing situation is providing reliable flows of political benefits. The CPA perspective, however, suggests that there is an alternative to delaying the start of reform activities that seem difficult, or back-tracking towards the pre-reform position when opposition manifests itself. In contrast with this passive or reactive approach, the political contest over activities that lie on the critical path could be actively managed. There are ways to do this, for example by designing into the reform activity greater compensation for those who lose from it. This would call for greater resources, and thus would lower the initial benefits arising from the implementation of the activity. Nevertheless, provided the compensation given to losers was of a one-off nature (and therefore partial) and was effective in reducing the additional implementation delay imposed by the political contest, it would be preferable both to avoiding the contest by doing nothing, and to entering the contest and then simply allowing it to take its course.

4 Some sequencing problems of economic reforms in India

The Indian economic technocrats, led by Dr Manmohan Singh, set out on the adjustment path late relative to many other developing countries. This in itself was a significant initial handicap. The existing strategy of planned, state-led industrialization had already been in place for nearly forty years. This continuity implied a strong sociopolitical institutionalization of the old planning strategy. Enough time had elapsed for coherent managerial elites to form in the public sector, along with unions representing relatively privileged public sector labour. In addition, the private sector that had grown up with the stimulus of protection and survived with the aid of state sector credit had not been clamouring for economic liberalization (Waterbury, 1992; pp. 183–4, 187). Although some efforts of liberalization had been made in the 1980s, they had had a very fragile political base, and Manmohan Singh's position was hardly more secure as the Finance Minister of a minority government led by the Congress Party, which had itself consructed the old economic order in the days of its political dominance. Against this background, what has been achieved, though flawed, is nevertheless rather remarkable.

The fiscal and foreign exchange crisis of 1991 gave the liberalization agenda a fresh opportunity. The initial position of the economy was that the foreign exchange reserves were extremely low, the country's international credit rating was low, inflation was high at 12 per cent and the current account deficit stood at US$9 billion, or 3 per cent of GDP and 40 per cent of exports (Cassen, Joshi and Lipton, 1993). The fiscal deficit was deteriorating, although not unmanageable. From the perspective of reform sequencing, the unsustainable macroeconomic position meant that stabilization was the need of the hour and was rightly given top priority. From the outset of the reform process, however, the economic reformers within the government voiced a clear commitment to two other policy objectives, market liberalization and improved distribution, that is, poverty reduction and increased equality of incomes. Outside the government, only a minority were persuaded as to the desirability of liberalization and, for historical reasons already mentioned, there were strong interest groups that possessed the potential to mobilize powerful opposition to pro-market reforms.

The central government's record of controlling its deficit has been mixed, and the figures are set out in Table 13.1. They show that a strong start was made in deficit reduction, but that the process was allowed to go into partial reverse in 1993–4. By October 1993, the government's borrowing requirement had ballooned to even higher levels than in 1991 and the fiscal deficit rose to 7.5 per cent of GDP for 1993/94. This was a significant departure from the initial plans of fiscal control as an essential condition supporting the reform process. The government achieved 20 months of belt tightening, but relented in the 1993 budget in an attempt to draw the economy out of recession.

Efforts to cut the budget deficit had met with social and political resistance. By 1991, subsidies had grown to be about 10 per cent of central government expenditure. The central government managed to prevent spending on subsidies from growing between 1991 and 1993, but it had not been able to make significant reductions. In particular, there had been strong public opposition to the removal of fertilizer subsidies. In July 1991, fertiliser prices were subject to a 40 per cent increase, but this was scaled back to 30 per cent. The controlled price of urea was actually reduced by 10 per cent. In June 1993, the government reintroduced a temporary subsidy on non-nitrogenous fertilizer as a result of pressure from farmers and industry and to cushion the impact of decontrol. The government was also forced to drop plans for the immediate price decontrol of urea. Subsidies for fertiliser

Table 13.1 India: central government deficits, 1990–1 to 1995–6 (per cent of GDP)

Type	*1990–1*	*1991–2*	*1992–3*	*1993–4*	*1994–5*	*1995–6*
Revenue	3.5	2.6	2.6	4.1	3.6	3.4
Fiscal	8.3	5.9	5.7	7.5	6.5	5.9
Primary	4.3	1.6	1.3	2.9	1.8	1.1

Notes
1 Revenue deficit = revenue expenditures – revenues.
2 Fiscal deficit = revenue deficit + net capital expenditures.
3 Primary fiscal deficit = fiscal deficit – disinvestment receipts – gross interest payments.
Source: GOI Economic Survey data.

(as for basic foodstuffs) have maintained their share of GDP. The government has had more success in reducing budgetary support to the state-owned enterprises, and this has contributed to such contraction of the fiscal deficit as has been achieved.

The high precedence to be accorded to financial sector reform in the liberalization activities of the structural adjustment project was acknowledged by the government when it commissioned the Narasimham Report in 1991. In its wake, moves to prepare the financial system for liberalization have been made. In order to strengthen a fragile banking structure, more adequate accounting standards and stricter measures of bank supervision and regulation have been established. At least Rs57 billion in capital has been injected into state-owned banks to help them provide for previous bad debts. The size of the funds that banks must lend at a lower than market interest rate to the government has been reduced from 35 per cent of bank deposits to 25 per cent. In addition, the complex system of administered interest rates has been greatly simplified, and only a few rates remaining regulated.

At the same time, government borrowing from banks and the Reserve Bank of India has increased rapidly. A combination of this, recession in 1996–7, high rates of interest, bank caution over the new accounting methods and the capital adequacy ratios has resulted in depressed lending to industry. Despite the lower interest on government debt, banks still find its zero risk attractive. Overlooking the importance of adequately reducing government borrowing before financial liberalization has led to a credit squeeze on the private sector. The government still appears keen to press ahead with reform in the financial sector. Cash reserve ratios are to be further reduced and the regulations, which limit competition between banks, are to be eased. However, with a continued high fiscal deficit, financial reform objectives will be difficult to achieve. The difficulty is that:

> The inconsistency between tight monetary and loose fiscal policy could lead to spiralling fiscal deficits...Fiscal consolidation is now essential for the success of further interest rate liberalization.
>
> (Joshi and Little, 1997; p. 131)

There are also two political roadblocks ahead that have not been tackled. One is defended by the recipients of directed credit at concessional interest rates, notably the better-off farmers and small-scale industrialists. Since recovery of these loans is very poor, they are often *de facto* transfers and hence highly prized. Apart from the recipients, local politicians also have a vested interest in opposing change, since their ability to influence these credit allocation decisions is a way of buying future political support. There is also a major obstacle in the way of improving the general efficiency of the banking system – the bank unions, who are likely to fight all government measures designed to reduce the current overstaffing or introduce mechanization.

The bank unions are but one example of a whole array of public sector unions that are opposed to job losses in their enterprises. Employment in the organized sector of the economy constitutes only 8.4 per cent of the total Indian labour force, and in 1991 public sector employees accounted for 71 per cent of all employment in the organized sector. Thus they have privileged pay, status and conditions compared with the rest of the working population. But on average their productivity is lower than workers in the private organized sector. The arguments for the retrenchment of labour in the public sector are well known:

> Preserving existing unproductive jobs may in fact damage the interests of new entrants into the labour market. The jobless may be fewer with reform than without. Further, the money that is used to protect unproductive jobs could be gainfully used to create several times more jobs.
> (Venkata Ratnam, 1997, p. 50)

Nevertheless, the government has stopped short of undertaking the labour market reforms that would make large public sector redundancies possible. No specific changes were planned to remove barriers which restricted labour mobility. Regulations which constrained adjustment of the workforce and placed limits on firms' ability to liquidate assets and close plants were not dismantled. The fact that financial liberalization has not yet created a competitive credit market must be one factor in the government's unwillingness to proceed with labour market reform.

India's Eighth Five-Year Plan highlighted the need to address the problem of loss-making state-owned enterprises, and indeed this need had been the theme of a number of high-level official reports in the 1980s, from committees chaired by Mohd. Fazal (1980–2), L. K. Jha (1983–4) and Arjun Sengupta (1986). In the early 1990s, leaving aside the oil sector, three out of four state-owned enterprises (SOEs) were making losses. The method chosen to tackle the problem was restructuring or revitalizing sick public sector enterprises by means of Memoranda of Understanding, which granted greater operational autonomy in exchange for a reduction in budgetary support. Non-viable enterprises were to be closed. The National Renewal Fund was set up with a corpus of Rs20 billion to ensure that the costs of technical change and modernization would be alleviated by the provision of safety nets, retraining and redevelopment. The Sick Industrial Companies Act was amended in December 1991, and 40 chronically sick public sector enterprises were referred to the Bureau for Industrial and Financial Reconstruction for rationalization or closure. However, as of 1997 no closures had taken place.

The government has continued to deny any intention of retrenching public sector workers. The necessary changes to labour laws that still require all enterprises to obtain prior government approval for closure, lay-offs and retrenchments have not been undertaken. Steps were taken to strengthen the National Renewal Fund by the allocation, in 1992–4, of an additional Rs10 billion from World Bank IDA loans, plus some of the proceeds of disinvestment of public sector undertakings. But the Fund has been used mainly to pay some of the costs of voluntary retirements within the central public sector.

There was an initial awareness within the authorities of the importance of holding down budgetary support to the SOEs in order to help to reduce the fiscal deficit at a reasonably early stage of the reform process. This was right from the sequencing viewpoint, and it was also implemented successfully as indicated in Table 13.2. The share of SOE resources derived from budgetary support fell markedly in the first three years of the reform period. This proportional fall reflected an actual cash fall in the relevant years.

Yet simultaneously there was also a recognition of the importance of avoiding opposition from powerful trade unions and of calming anti-reform sentiments within the public. Since the SOEs were able to persuade the state-owned banks to take up the large unsubscribed portion of their public bond issues, and since government disinvestment rarely exceeded 20 per cent of the equity, there was little real pressure for change. The composition of the SOE boards and their management practices carried on much as before. Privatization was not an explicit policy objective, although that has now changed with regard to the telecommunications industry. The virtual ban on compulsory redundancy remains in place as a tacit acknowledgement by the government of the strength of the public sector trade unions.

The severe balance of payments problem of 1991 was corrected rapidly, largely through an initial 19 per cent devaluation and a reduction in imports. This success paved the way for the start of trade and exchange rate reform. After a spell with a dual exchange rate, the 1993 budget made the rupee fully convertible – which amounted to a further 9.2 per cent devaluation. There was a sharp reduction in import tariffs on a range of goods such as cars, televisions, refrigerators, air-conditioning, tea and coffee. The maximum

Table 13.2 Resources of public sector enterprises, 1990–1 to 1993–4 (percentage of total by source)

	1990–1	*1991–2*	*1992–3*	*1993–4*
Budgetary support	27.1	23.5	17.9	13.8
Internal resources	38.2	40.8	44.0	40.4
Extra-budget resources	34.7	35.6	38.1	45.8
Total	100.0	100.0	100.0	100.0

Note: Totals do not always add to 100 due to rounding.
Source: Adapted by the author from Venkata Ratnam (1997), p. 53, table 3.3.

tariff rate was cut from 110 per cent to 85 per cent. Trade reform has continued, with the peak tariff rate reducing from 85 to 65 per cent. More recently, in the 1997–8 budget, a peak rate of 40 per cent has been indicated, with an average of 22 per cent. But India still has relatively high levels of protection, and a variety of different tariff rates which encourage demarcation disputes. The negative effect of tariff reduction on customs revenue is now beginning to be felt. Customs revenue fell by 4.5 per cent between April and November 1997. Now, domestic entrepreneurs are complaining that they are being exposed to external competition too soon, particularly before reforms in the credit and labour markets have gone far enough to allow them to compete effectively. This may result in a political backlash.

Uncertainty about what will happen next must be a deterrent to both domestic and foreign investment. The reforms of the regulation of industry, which looked very dramatic because the previous licence-permit requirements were so extensive, are (and can only be) permissive in character. Greater private sector participation in industries once reserved for the public sector is now permitted. Foreign direct investment is now discouraged less than previously, allowing greater scope for expansion and diversification by foreign subsidiaries. All this is welcome, and necessary, but will not generate enough private investment in the right sectors on its own, while uncertainty continues to cloud the prospects of further trade and financial sector reforms.

Now the advent of the BJP and its allies to government brings forth a new scene, and new 'owners' to the economic reform project. Like most of the main Indian political parties, the BJP has declared itself in general terms to favour the liberalization of the economy. But, as a nationalist party, it has made some hostile noises towards foreign investment, and is unhappy with some of the implications of India's membership of the World Trade Organization. Its big business backers will expect a long transition towards the full blast of international competition. At the same time, the BJP may be more radical in tackling some of the vested interests in the public sector that the Congress and United Front governments were unwilling to touch. But these declared preferences may or may not get translated into action depending on the whims of the BJP's assorted coalition partners: they, too, are part-owners of the project, and will have their say on if, and how, it is completed.

5 Conclusion: implications and issues for the future

The CPA perspective has various implications for an understanding of the Indian economic reforms. In the first place, it confirms the view that launching reforms that come later in the order of precedence *before* reforms that come earlier in the precedence order are consolidated does little to advance completion of the whole process. The 'premature' reforms at best tend to run into the sands, and at worst can be positively damaging. In particular, failure to bring the budget deficit under control has a far-reaching effect on the sorts of liberalization that are feasible. There is a sense, not altogether paradoxical, in which India has tried too much reform, rather than too little. It has tried too much of the wrong kind, temporally speaking, and not enough of the right kind.

Second, there has been a clear difference between the successful implementation of reforms that rest on a technical consensus, have low information requirements and involve few actors, like the deregulation of private industry and investment, and others with the opposite features such as the reform of state enterprises. The Indian experience amply confirms the view that there are 'difficult' types of reform which can be blocked by veto coalitions.

Third, there has been no attempt at the imaginative redesign of reforms when they have run into opposition. The reaction to opposition encountered has been to retreat partially to the pre-reform position, rather than to devise a form of temporary compensation that would allow the reform to proceed, but at a higher cost. This is seen clearly in the matter of the partial reinstatement of the fertiliser subsidies. The Indian tactics to date have been neither those of speed and stealth ('the big bang'), nor those of slowness and consensus-building ('gradualism'). Instead, they have been a combination of slowness ('a series of little bangs, not always in the right order') and stealth. Since the resort to political action depends upon the degree of transparency of the political system, the government can baffle some opposition simply by increasing the opaqueness of its policies. Successive Indian governments since 1991 have advanced by stealth, but only when the opportunity to do so seemed to offer itself (Jenkins, 1998). The disadvantage of such tactics is that they preclude the active rallying of support constituencies. The result is that the real alignment of political forces on either side becomes rather hard to detect, both by the combatants and by observers.

These tactics have brought what began in India as a broadly successful economic strategy, that since 1992–3 has raised the historic growth rate by 2 percentage points, down to a very slow pace of implementation. The interest of the CPA method is that it highlights the tactics of active management, not just to sustain the reform process – that is, to prevent reversals of stabilization and liberalization – but to accelerate the pace of its implementation. The Rodrik (1990) view that a relaxed fiscal stance and deep reforms in one or two sectors would make the adjustment process politically sustainable over the longer run has proved correct in the Indian experience. The Indian reform project is still just about alive; it has never been officially declared defunct. However, it could have been, and could still be, moved forward by a larger injection of political imagination and tactical ingenuity.

The best prospect for achieving this is to devise schemes to compensate losers in ways that do not negate all the benefits of reform, but only reduce them initially. This was already being urged when India was starting its reform process (Mosely, Harrigan and Toye, 1995, vol. I. It is still being urged (Joshi and Little, 1997, pp. 193–4). The reasons why governments have not tried harder to fashion compensation schemes for losers in order to allow politically blocked reforms to go ahead remains one of the unsolved mysteries of the political economy of structural adjustment (Rodrik, 1996, p. 39).

The CPA method is a rational action paradigm. It has a clarity and a precision that makes it a useful framework for thinking about the problems of implementing a programme of economic reforms. However, is one valid objection to it that it is an overly rational approach? Does it require a degree of rationality that is unsuited to the actors of the real world, imperfect as they are and it is? Is the concept of the rational actor too utopian in practice?

It certainly takes an effort of the imagination to see a government as a rational actor. Although ideally all government actions are fully coordinated and government action is therefore unitary in character, in practice this is hardly ever true. Within any single Ministry, there is usually a struggle taking place to control the policy agenda. Different government departments pursue objectives that conflict to some extent: for example, some want to spend while others want to control expenditure. In federal countries, conflicting objectives are often found between central and provincial levels of government. Thus, even within those areas where the government can exercise control, policies are at least partially inconsistent. Inter-level inconsistency is more pronounced in federations or confederations, like India, where the powers of different levels of government are constitutionally entrenched. Indeed, this fact has proved to be the stumbling block so far to aspirations to replace a number of existing Indian taxes with a value-added tax.

Policy consistency is thus hard for governments to achieve across all the bodies that in some sense constitute 'government' at a point in time. Across time, inconsistency creeps in as personnel change, as ministers, prime ministers and governments come and go. Some grand projects are simply stopped in their tracks and what survives is only phase one of a project that was never completed. Others evolve over time in ways that the original designers did not envisage, or would not have approved. It is easier to detect these abortions and elisions in the physical environment than in the institutional landscape, but they can be found there, too. It is hard to maintain the rationality of the structural adjustment project, when its original owners (if it was lucky enough to have any) disappear from the political scene and are replaced by others who may have a different overall agenda to pursue.

Nevertheless, the fact that governments are not (and perhaps never can be) rational actors does not dispose of the need for a rational action paradigm in government. Those within governments who are economic reformers are in constant tension with others who are not, and their relative power rises and declines, giving rise to the external impression of a lack of policy consistency. The beleaguered economic reformers need to have their own understanding of rational action if their cause is to make progress. The method of critical path analysis is a tool at their disposal.

The issues that arise from this for future policy are the following:

1 Is there a single order of precedence among reform policies that is generally valid, along the lines explored above? If there is more than one, what are the factors that create the need for a different order of precedence? Do they include the initial conditions of the economy and the precise content of the reform package? Is the order of precedence of reforms something that itself needs to be, or can be, customized by a country?
2 Can the concept of a 'normal duration' for a reform activity be operationalized? How strong is the empirical backing for the claim that normal duration is a function of technical consensus, the amount of relevant detailed information and the number of institutional actors involved?
3 Have any countries already made use of a CPA-type method in planning their reform programme? If so, what was the outcome? Did the experiment include the use of partial compensation of opponents of critical reform activities? If so, what was the outcome?

While the India case study is helpful in raising and illustrating these issues, a number of comparative case studies across different regions and different types of economy would be needed in trying to resolve them.

References

Cassen, R., V. Joshi and M. Lipton (1993) 'Stabilization and Structural Reform in India', *Contemporary South Asia*, vol. 2, no. 2.

Currie, M. and I. Steedman (1990) *Wrestling with Time. Problems in Economic Theory* (Ann Arbor: University of Michigan Press).

Falvey, R. and C. D. Kim (1992) 'Timing and Sequencing Issues in Trade Liberalization', *Economic Journal*, vol. 102, no. 413.

Jenkins, R. S. (1998) 'Democratic Adjustment. Explaining the Political Sustainability of Economic Reform in India', D. Phil. thesis, University of Sussex (mimeo).

Joshi, V. and I. M. D. Little (1997) *India's Economic Reforms 1991–2001* (Delhi: Oxford University Press).

Kanbur, R. (1995) 'Welfare Economics, Political Economy and Policy Reform in Ghana', *African Development Review/ Revue Africaine de Développement*, vol. 7, no. 1.

MacCrimmon, K. R. (1987) 'Critical Path Analysis', in J. Eatwell, M. Milgate and P. Newman (eds), *The New Palgrave. A Dictionary of Economics* (London: Macmillan).

Mosely, P. (1994) 'Development Economics and the Underdevelopment of Africa', Inaugural Lecture at the University of Reading.

Mosely, P., J. Harrigan and J. Toye (1995) *Aid and Power. The World Bank and Policy-based Lending*, 2 vols (London: Routledge).

Nayyar, D. (1996) *Economic Liberalization in India. Analytics, Experience and Lessons* (Hyderabad: Orient Longmans).

Rodrik, D. (1990) 'How should Structural Adjustment Programs be Designed?', *World Development*, vol. 18, no. 7.
Rodrik, D. (1996) 'Understanding Economic Policy Reform', *Journal of Economic Literature*, vol. XXXIV, no. 1.
Stern, N. (1989) 'Prices in Planning', *China Programme No. 1*, London School of Economics, STICERD Development Economics Research Programme.
Taylor, L. (1988) *Varieties of Stabilization Experience* (Oxford: Clarendon Press.).
Toye, J. (1994) 'Structural Adjustment: Context, Assumptions, Origin and Diversity', in R. van der Hoeven and F. van der Kraaij (eds), *Structural Adjustment and Beyond in Sub-Saharan Africa* (Oxford: James Currey).
Venkata Ratnam, C. S. (1997) 'Adjustment and Privatization in India', in R. van der Hoeven and G. Sziraczki (eds), *Lessons from Privatization. Labour Issues in Developing and Traditional Countries* (Geneva: International Labour Organization).
Waterbury, J. (1992) 'The Heart of the Matter? Public Enterprise and the Adjustment Process', in S. Haggard and R. R. Kaufman (eds), *The Politics of Economic Adjustment* (Princeton NJ: Princeton University Press).
Williamson, J. (ed.) (1994) *The Political Economy of Policy Reform* (Washington DC: Institute for International Economics).

14

Missing Markets or Missing Institutions? The Sustainability of Policy Reforms

*Willem van der Geest**

European Institute for Asian Studies, Brussels

1 Four generations of adjustment programmes

When adjustment policies were introduced in the early 1980s, the general opinion expressed by the international financial agencies and Ministries of Finance of the countries concerned was that it was a short-term process which would improve the situation of the country and its workforce. There was therefore no room for social concerns. However, in the mid-1980s, this perception changed: Structural adjustment programme (SAP) agreements were renewed at various times in most countries. Moreover, the programmes ventured beyond short-term stabilization. The social consequences of the programmes became increasingly visible, and two areas of particular concern have been:

- The macroeconomic and fiscal policy frameworks adopted under structural adjustment yield negative results for public investments, and therefore employment creation and public sector employment levels were reduced, and conditions of work worsened;
- The limitations and possible negative distributional consequences of shifting from broadly targeted social measures (such as food subsidies) to narrowly targeted social safety net programmes.

Since the early 1980s, four generations of adjustment policies, as discussed in van der Geest and van der Hoeven (1999, ch. 1) could be distinguished as follows:

1 The first generation of adjustment programmes aimed at stabilizing the economy after internal or external shocks. The major thrust of these

* The author acknowledges his close and fruitful collaboration with Rolph van der Hoeven.

programmes was to utilize the same instruments as industrialized countries had been applying since the 1950s to combat a balance of payments deficit. Key measures included containing fiscal deficits by reducing government expenditure; making real interest rates positive; applying wage restraint to public sector workers and, as far as possible, private sector workers as well; and a real devaluation of the currency to stimulate exports and discourage imports. Reliance on these policy instruments characterized the programmes of the early 1980s which were also designed – especially in Latin America – to deal with the growing debt crisis, typified by the problems in Mexico in 1982.

2 A second generation of adjustment programmes, introduced in the mid-1980s, dealt more explicitly with the issues of growth and capacity. These adjustment programmes were introduced because policies merely emphasizing stabilization in the economy did not succeed, in most cases, in bringing about growth – at best the balance of payments gap was reduced. As a consequence, several countries with stabilization programmes were caught in a vicious circle of slow or negative growth, and large debt service payment. This inhibited consumption and investment growth and compressed imports. Fairly early in the 1980s, it was realized that adjustment programmes would only succeed if they took into account concerns for growth beyond merely attempting to stimulate the export sector through devaluation. Initially it was thought that growth could be stimulated by liberalizing the economy. Restrictive policy regimes were perceived to have created distortions in product, capital and labour markets which hampered growth. Later, more attention was given to investment and increasing productivity, as it became clear that the liberalization of markets when stabilization policies were carried out meant that growth opportunities were delayed. At best, stabilization laid the basis for improved growth in the future, but estimates of the turnaround of the economy were extended from 1–2 years in the early 1980s to 4–8 years in the later the 1980s.[1]

3 A third generation of adjustment programmes started to focus explicitly on social concerns. In response to UNICEF's plea for 'Adjustment with a Human Face', the World Bank introduced its 'Social Dimensions of Adjustment' programme in 1988. This introduced the notion of social safety nets and compensatory programmes in order to help or to compensate those groups whose living standards were adversely affected by the adjustment policies, and who faced a decline in living standards either through a decline in government services or because of increased unemployment. Since the 1990s, most adjustment programmes contain some form of social safety net, although there is still discussion on whether these provide the poor and those most affected by adjustment programmes with sufficient tools to overcome poverty on a sustainable basis.

4 A fourth generation of adjustment programmes is intended to deal not only with the effects of adjustment on people and institutions, but also to include people and institutions as actors in the process, thereby promoting consultation and participation. The reasons for renewed attention to consultation and participation were that adjustment programmes had been designed mainly by central banks, ministers of finance and international agencies, based on the earlier concept (especially during the first generation) that adjustment would be a 'quick fix', setting countries back on the track towards sustained growth. However, when adjustment programmes included concerns for growth and social development, the drafting of the Policy Framework Papers was still dominated by those responsible for stabilization. Not only were those responsible for development and social policies left out, but mature associations and representative institutions such as chambers of commerce, manufacturing associations and trade unions were also excluded from the policy reform process.

The Bretton Woods Institutions are currently trying to apply the third generation of adjustment policies, often combining growth-oriented programmes with so-called compensatory programmes. Various World Bank policy statements have acknowledged the need to move to the application of the fourth generation of programmes. However, as they themselves readily admit, this will be difficult.

It is argued here that sustainable reforms will require the formulation of adjustment programmes along the lines of this 'new' fourth generation – where consultative and, in some cases, representative institutions are part of the process of policy design in order to get agreement on the implementation of the reforms. This fourth generation approach is more likely to generate outcomes acceptable to future decision-makers and hence avoid the pitfalls of non-implementation, stop–go approaches and policy reversals.

2 Sustainable processes of policy reforms

Our understanding of the sustainability of policy reforms draws on the more general discussion of sustainable development. A recent analysis summarizes some of the many definitions of sustainable development processes and notes that there is fundamental disagreement amongst analysts.[2] However, the following three working rules (Markandiya, 1994) have proved useful in defining sustainable development. First, there is the issue of *equity* – that is, the greatest emphasis must be given to assisting low-income households in the preservation of their resource base for the future; second, there is the issue of *efficiency* – obtaining the greatest incremental value addition from any given input. Third, there is the issue of *resilience* – that is, the capacity of a system to maintain its structure and pattern of behaviour in the face of external disturbance. Systems lose their resilience if they become highly susceptible to internal or external shocks.

These three working rules can provide a working definition of sustainable reform processes. If economic reform processes are perceived as highly inequitable it is most unlikely that the supporting coalitions will be stable. Further, policy reforms which do not produce tangible outcomes in terms of better economic performance are unlikely to be supported, and to continue to invest analytical capacity and decision-making time into reform processes which have weak or zero responses can not easily be justified. Last but not least, if the post-reform economic system is significantly less resilient than before, and has become highly susceptible to shocks (such as currency and stockmarket instability), the likely support for these reforms is diminished. As the recent experience of Indonesia (Simanjuntak, 1998) and other South-east Asian countries shows, much of the reform-induced growth may be lost overnight.

Hence, sustainable reforms are those where the changed set of policies is consistent with the equity objectives of the society – distribution-improving development; where the resulting economic system remains resilient – ability to absorb shocks; and where the resources required to execute the policy reform have a short 'pay-back' period – net growth gains.

3 Missing markets and missing institutions

Let us restate the 'market' view of the impact of policy reforms as follows: the responses to a change in the set of economic circumstances are transmitted by signals of these changes which are observed by the economic actors allocating labour, capital and other scarce resources. In response to the changed signals they would tend to reallocate their resources, or adopt different pricing rules for them, or perhaps a combination of both. For example, the lowering of a real exchange rate relative to that of other competing economies means that export opportunities and volumes for that particular economy would tend to improve. Indeed, this reasoning focusing on action–response sequences characterizes most of economic thinking and is fundamental to the analysis of *both* the standard as well as heterodox adjustment models.

However, often these expected responses to a set of policy reforms do not materialize or are merely very small. This is often described as a case of low or zero elasticities. Although this provides us a with a useful descriptive indicator, it does not in any sense explain the processes which may or may not be taking place.

The 'missing market' view would tend to argue that if in response to the change in the incentive structure the new opportunities are not captured or realized, it is because in the chain of markets required for this reallocation or re-pricing there is a market 'missing'. For example, increasing the production of a particular export commodity may require various types of skilled labour, some of which are not available within the economy. In that case the 'missing' factor prevents the increase of production of the commodity. Hence there is no visible output response, even though the policy reform has effectively changed the economic incentive structures. In such a case the missing market 'explains' the absence of the response. If policy reforms go without responses the process is not sustainable or even feasible – the inputs to the process do not yield any tangible outputs.

The 'missing market' view tends to go further by arguing that the absence of the responses is not merely an expression of the limits of the resource base of a particular economy, but also points to the debilitating influence of existing regulations which hamper the responsiveness of economic actors. The 'missing market' view tends to argue that the limited responses to economic reform and liberalization can only be overcome through further and more sustained liberalization and deregulation.[3]

The 'missing institutions' argument, advanced here, does not in itself disagree with the analysis that responses to policy reforms are weak because reallocations and different pricing rules are not forthcoming. However, it explains this by noting that the preconditions for generating such market-based reallocative processes may simply not have been fulfilled. It argues that a variety of institutions which enable markets to function efficiently are not in place. The absence of such institutions, or their poor functioning, is the reason for the weak response to reform.

The difference between the two approaches is one of diagnosis and remedy. In particular, the policy conclusion that a better response to liberalization processes can be realized through intensifying the reform measures is not readily accepted. It is instead argued that the institutions which enable actors to respond to reform need to be created or strengthened. In the missing institutions viewpoint the weak or non-functioning institutions tend to create opportunities for 'super-profits' accuring to scarce factors or monopolized processes of production; this tends to accentuate the distribution-worsening impact of the liberalization sequences.

In a narrow sense, 'institutions' are often regarded as synonymous with organization, that is defined primarily by physical and administrative structures. In a broader sense, it refers to a set of 'rules of the game' or perhaps conventions, habits and rituals. Economic analysis tends to favour the broader definition. However, to use a generic definition of institutions as 'rules of the game' has the problem of rendering the concept all-inclusive and perhaps meaningless. Virtually everything is an institution: markets, behavioural patterns such as risk-taking, any type of organization and so on. A hybrid definition of 'institutions' as 'rules of the game' defined by organized processes which are accountable and verifiable seems more appropriate. In this sense a 'market' is not an institution, but market regulations may be. Policies themselves are not institutions, but policy decision-making bodies are.

The motives for forming an institution are manifold but the economic aspects include gains of specialization, reduction of risks through pooling and sharing, as well as economies of scale and scope. Hence, 'missing institutions' are the absence of 'rules of the game' which have been formulated in an organized and transparent way.

The institutional life-cycle may be compared to those characterizing human life: genesis and birth; childhood followed by adolescence; maturity followed by old age; and, at some point in perhaps a distant future, death and demise. A 'mature' institution is characterized by a well-defined set of procedures to define its rules and activities and to account for these in a transparent way. Most interest group associations would, in principle, be mature institutions, provided they have a well-defined membership and an agreed procedure for appointing leadership. For example, corporations listed on a stock exchange should be expected to be 'mature'. However, young associations representing 'new' interests may be less than mature if their procedures are not yet well-defined. Hence, the 'missing institutions' view is not merely that institutions would be non-existent; it may also be that institutions are in a young, untried and untested phase. Or, alternatively, institutions may be near-demise or moribund. In a comparative sense one may argue that South Asia has a greater density of institutions than sub-Saharan Africa, although it would be too hasty to conclude that the South Asian institutions are therefore 'mature'.

4 Missing institutions: some findings for sub-Saharan Africa

The benefits of sub-Saharan Africa's economic reform programmes cannot be ignored. For example, the sub-Saharan Africa growth rate reached 4 per cent in 1995, a sharp contrast with the sluggish performance of 1.4 per cent over the period 1991–4. Positive per capita income growth has been realized in 31 countries out of 42 during fiscal years 1992–4. In the earlier five years, only 15 to 20 countries obtained positive growth. World Bank economic forecasts project a further acceleration of growth. Nevertheless, competition for financial resources, investment, technology and trade has intensified in recent years and is likely to intensify further.

One important indicator of the social and distributional impact of these programmes is the impact on employment, as earnings from labour and self-employment constitute the primary stream of income for most households. Van der Geest and van der Hoeven (1999) in an analysis of the impact of adjustment on employment showed that the informalization of the African economies has been accelerating during adjustment. The growth rate of employment in the formal sector (widely defined) tended to be below that of the influx of new job-seekers onto the labour market – implying that the formal sector's share of total employment was decreasing. However, in some countries the problem is rather more acute as the level of employment continued to decline in absolute numbers during adjustment; limited employment creation in the private sector was less than the loss of jobs in the public sector.

Formal wage employment declined in relative as well as absolute terms. The changes in public sector employment from some selected case studies (Kenya, Malawi, Tanzania, Uganda, Zambia and Zimbabwe) illustrate the decline of public employment levels – in absolute as well as relative terms – during the 1990s, in contrast to the increases during the 1970s and the 1980s. Private sector formal wage employment levels also declined during the 1990s, except for Kenya where there was a small increase. Hence, the decline of the share of formal employment in the total labour force was not only due to the rapid growth of the labour force; the public and private sector employment decline in absolute terms accelerated this decline as well. In terms of changes of the employment structure, the relative shares between the public and the private sectors remained quite stable, except for Tanzania. In Kenya and Zambia approximately half of formal sector employment was in the public sector, whereas for Uganda and Zimbabwe these percentages were of the order of one-fifth and one-third respectively. In Tanzania the private sector has increased in importance since 1985.

In summary, the overall impact of adjustment on employment creation is ambiguous and depends critically on the initial conditions under which these programmes started. In the slow-growing economies, the employment effects of adjustment are likely to be negative. Even where there is positive economic growth, it was found – for example in Kenya – that the expansion of the informal sector employment was a lateral one, with the same level of activities carried out by more people (slow or negative TFP growth). While comprehensive sectoral and firms' data on labour productivity are not available, it would seem that labour productivity may have declined during the adjustment period.

Real wage levels have declined significantly during the adjustment period, as the bargaining powers of trade unions were constrained by government policies, the high levels of unemployment and underemployment, and the overall weak macroeconomic environment. It is clear that inflation tends to erode average non-agricultural earnings quite sharply, hence the need for macroeconomic stability is also imperative from the point of view of the wage-earner.

Organizations representing employers and employees across the region have developed different perspectives on these employment and labour market impacts. SAPs have received both support and opposition from key employers or manufacturing organizations across the region, and their reactions varied with different components of the programmes. For example, there was strong support for the removal of restrictions on access to foreign exchange, as well as for removal of various types of price control, while there has been intensive lobbying against a number of aspects of trade liberalization. It has been argued that import liberalization led to a massive increase in imports, and calls were made for the protection of domestic producers. Employers also campaigned for the relaxation of redundancy laws to enable employers to declare workers redundant without too much bureaucracy. They argued that some of the components of structural adjustment were adversely affecting the volume of their operations and their profits, which made the restructuring of their workforces inevitable.

In recent years, the trade unions have put forward their views on SAPs – a good example is the *Beyond ESAP* project of the Zimbabwe Congress of Trade Unions (1996). The trade unions have also started to develop closer links with the informal sector, particularly through developing informal sector skills.

Table 14.1 summarizes the agenda issues for 'fourth generation' adjustment programmes. For each of these agenda points the specific objectives as well as the mode of implementation will need to be spelled out, together with the implications for governments and international development agencies, including the Bretton Woods Institutions. Indeed the African debates have noted the limits of consultation, in particular as some economic policy

Table 14.1 Perspectives on selected policy reforms in east and southern Africa

Policy reforms	*Supportive of present implementation*	*Seeking alternatives to present implementation*
A. Import liberalization	Consumer organisations Manufactures (raw material)	Employers (finished products) Manufacturers (finished products) Trade unions
B. Devaluation	Employers (export-oriented industry) Manufacturers (exporters) Trade Unions (export industries)	Trade unions (non-export sectors) Employers (importers) Manufacturers (importers) Consumer organizations
C. Removal of price controls	Employers Manufacturers	Consumer organizations Trade unions
D. Privatization and retrenchment	Employers Manufacturers	Trade unions
E. Relaxation of redundancy procedures	Employers Manufacturers	Trade unions

Source: Summarized from a series of seminars in Kenya, Tanzania, Uganda, Zambia and Zimbabwe; and van der Geest and van der Hoeven (1999).

decisions are to be taken in confidence because the decisions taken influence market stability directly (for example on issues of devaluation or a central bank's reserve management). However, it may be argued that most of the adjustment policy issues are structural in nature and the decision-making process can be more transparent.

A second set of issues relates to who will be consulted about what and when. The issues of inclusion/exclusion as well as the possible modes of consultation are intensively debated amongst academic analysts and policy-makers in sub-Saharan Africa. In particular, what are the criteria for inclusion/exclusion? Are consultations to be based along traditional lines of the tripartite structures, with the dangers of involving organization in a state of terminal decline, or should it be driven by the newly-emerging interest organizations such as, for example, chambers of commerce, manufacturing associations, informal sector associations or consumer organizations? What constitute criteria for exclusion; for instance, are only national organizations to be included, or regional and/or sectoral institutions as well? Other issues concern the public nature of the organization (as distinct from private profit-oriented organizations), the size of the membership, the sources of its funding, and so forth. The most desirable frequency and timing of consultative and monitoring processes (say at each budget, or at the time of a new PFP) is yet another issue. Finally, the best strategy to *institutionalize* the adjustment policy consultation is also contested; is it to be driven by government invitations or through the membership of national councils or institutes (with a secretariat)?[4] The next section will examine some of the debates surrounding the implementation of adjustment programmes in Bangladesh.

5 Missing institutions: issues facing Bangladesh

Many institutions have functioned well in Bangladesh, particularly those appointed to oversee the execution of large infrastructure projects. The building of the Jamuna Bridge provides a good example. The 4.8 kilometre bridge, which was overseen by an agency created by ordinance in July 1985, was built in four years. The original plans, approved by the World Bank, were modified following intense public discussion in favour of a scheme to allow for both domestic and international rail traffic as part of a future trans-Asian route. The agency also survived major political change and challenges to the legality of separate development levies imposed to cover one-third of the domestic building cost (Centre for Policy Dialogue, 1997b). Institutions in charge of economic rather than physical management, however, performed less well.

A comparison of policy intentions as expressed in the 1985 Third Five-Year Plan, and actual policies, shows the Government of Bangladesh's (GOB) execution to have been weak with frequent policy reversals. Van der Geest

(1996) assessed these changes in policy intentions both *ex ante* and *ex post* using a multisectoral applied general equilibrium model of the Bangladesh economy. This allowed policy intentions and expected outcomes to be compared with actual policy implementation and realized outcomes – identifying areas of weak implementation.

A major area of weakness was found in the prioritization of the allocation of investment from public resources. Public investment increased by less than intended, and the planned relative increases in allocation to agriculture intended to improve food security failed to materialize. In 1989–90, although nearly one-quarter of the Adjustment Development Programme (ADP) was allocated to agriculture, primarily for water and flood control, this level was no higher than in 1984–5.[5]

Taxation, particularly of income, was a second area of weak implementation and policy reversal. Higher income tax receipts as a share of GDP had been anticipated from the urban and rural high-income groups. However, at the end of the plan period the contribution of direct taxes on income and land to domestic public resources, as well as non-tax revenues, fell far short of the stated targets – reaching less than 3 per cent compared to the targeted 4.6 per cent.[6] Another area of weakness was in the food and income support measures, reflecting a reduction in the committed statutory rationing, which benefited urban and rural formal households, especially military and civil-service households.[7] Meanwhile, 'flexible' rationing for the landless and small and medium farmers, together with the informal rural and urban households, grew to over US$ 200 million by the end of the plan. Subsidies on procurement to these farmers remained limited, while the fertilizer subsidy was to be abolished. In line with policy intentions, statutory rationing declined to 65 per cent of the initial volumes, and modified rationing was phased out. Food-for-work distribution expanded by some 20 per cent, whereas relief distribution, though variable, rose well above the 1984–5 base year level. However, the resources effectively reaching the low-income target households were well below target.

In summary, the three types of policy slippage – direct taxation of high-income earners; food-based transfers to low-income households; and public investment priorities – may be presumed to have had negative distributional consequences. Second, the resilience of the Bangladesh economy to external shocks is likely to remain low while the focus of public investment remains largely dominated by external sources of finance. Third, this low resilience is itself a consequence of the failure to achieve the modest domestic resource mobilization targets.

The financial sector, particularly the institutional aspects, was the major area of policy reform during the 1990s. The recommendations from a number of policy studies were introduced in the mid-1980s, and underpinned by new financial legislation and technical assistance.[8] The main measures, discussed in greater detail in the Centre for Policy Dialogue (1998), were to:

1 privatize the government-owned commercial banks;
2 allow the entry of both domestic and foreign private banks;
3 liberalize interest rates;
4 introduce market-based instruments of financial control;
5 relax directives covering credit allocation;
6 remove restrictions on the banks' activities; and
7 introduce improved managerial and operational tools.

Notwithstanding these reform proposals, the state of the formal financial sector continued to deteriorate; the reforms appear to have provided a sharper definition of the problems, but no clear solution. As Hossain and Rashid (1997) concluded '...financial institutions are operating with huge unrecoverable loans. They are in distress and technically insolvent. Loan recovery efforts have so far produced little success. Political interference in loan distribution is continuing' (pp. 260–1). The banking sector continues to be dominated by the four nationalized banks (NCBs), with 14 commercial banks (PCBs), six foreign banks and three specialist financial institutions.[9]

'Classified' loans continued to increase during the reform period, implying an accumulated debt-in-default of US$3 billion (taka 122.4 billion) in mid-1997, and the share classified as 'bad' and irrecoverable, as distinct from just 'dubious', rose to about three-quarters. This was particularly serious as the provisions for bad debt made by the banking sector were only about half of the stipulated minimum requirement. Lastly, a growing incidence of 'insider lending' in the private commercial banking sector was observed, especially after supervision of the nationalized sector had been intensified. Major stockholders and directors of these private banks had used their influence to channel loans to enterprises they (partly) owned – violating the banking laws on inter-group lending and risking the funds of their depositors.

From the institutional aspect these reforms can be separated into two parts: first, a new set of 'rules of the game', and, second, a reorganization to ensure the reforms could be implemented and sustained. A critical pre-condition for the sector's stability was the autonomy and independence of the Bangladesh Bank.[10] However, complementary organizational reform, including a clear separation between the banking division of the Ministry of Finance and the management operations of the NCBs and PCBs was also needed. Thus, a diagnosis of the financial sector reforms in terms of 'missing institutions' would stress the weaknesses in the regulatory system, not merely a weak market response. This institutional weakness is transmitted through the system in various ways, including 'insider lending', and severe liquidity constraints following the provision for bad debts instead of relending to new investment projects.

The 'missing institution' argument is, perhaps, most salient in the aftermath of the stockmarket crash in Bangladesh. Soon after the June 1996 elections, which had created an expectation of fast growth, the stockmarket soared by about three and a half times, only to crash in December 1996, reaching an all time low at one-sixth of the peak value. The losses were largely sustained by small middle-class investors who had entered the market gripped by bullish expectations and had little to fall back on. On 4 April 1997, the *Financial Times* reported that the arrest had been ordered of 36 leading brokers for '...allegedly manipulating share prices'. It was also reported that domestic trading houses unilaterally cancelled trade from foreign investors, who had borne losses of some US$ 20 million.

Information-disclosure remains sensitive. This is one reason why self--regulation – the dominant mode of regulation – was not and cannot be expected to be effective. It is easier to establish whether the proper procedures are in place than whether they are followed. External supervisors find it difficult to detect improper conduct where internal management is involved, as appears to have been the case in the Dhaka stock exchange crisis. Nevertheless, there is a need for an external regulatory body in which both investors and market-makers are involved. It appears that in Bangladesh a situation was created that faciliatated undetected opportunities for share-price manipulation. As in the case of the Bangladesh Bank, the independence and autonomy of the Stock Exchange Commission remained in jeopardy.

It appears from the examples of policy reform that the institutional set-up was inadequate to cope with the potential impacts of the reform process. The failure of these reforms was not so much because of 'missing markets', but rather because of the 'missing institutions' of market regulation. The impact of these reforms was that they could not be sustained – as shown by the absence of new investors in the stock exchange, or the threat of a formal sector banking crisis. Without well-functioning institutions the reforms appear to have increased inequity without reaping the efficiency gains from capital market development and improved financial intermediation.

6 Conclusion

Adjustment programmes have been around for nearly two decades and are still the subject of intense debate and scrutiny. We have distinguished four generations – with the last still under construction. This was characterized by a different approach to the process of adjustment policy design. Our main argument has been that a greater emphasis should be placed on the *political* process of decision-making as a way of ensuring an appropriate policy focus. This represents a move away from a tradition of a *technocratic* process of decision-making. In a number of countries this had been practised by the APEX ministries (finance, planning and economic development and the central bank) often with tacit support of the Bretton Woods institutions. The latter approach has jeopardized the credibility of the adjustment programmes because of the absence of institutions with a legitimate interest in the policy reforms – such as enterprise councils and business associations. It has led to repeated policy reversals, to stop–go approaches and to incomplete implementation of the programmes, reducing the sustainability of the reform process. In this sense 'institutions' have been missing in the reform processes, as the cases of Bangladesh amply demonstrates.

Sustainable reform processes were defined as those which were: distribution-improving; increasing resilience, and efficiency-enhancing. These three criteria need to be judged against a counterfactual of the likely performance of the economy in the case of absent or different implementation of the reforms. It is unlikely that such a demanding set of criteria can be realized without regular analysis of a programme's impact as well as consultation or dialogue with a wide variety of economic actors whose operations are directly concerned prior to and during programme implementation.

Notes

1 The International Monetary Fund, for example, introduced an Enhanced Structural Adjustment Fund (ESAF) for poor countries, which allowed them to receive support for three years with repayment over ten years, compared to the regular credit tranches reimbursed over one to two years.
2 An important issue is the level of aggregation. Are development processes sustainable if they permit a bequest of a resource base to future generations, with a total value at least equal to the present resource base? Or should a more disaggregated view be taken to preserve certain specific components of the present resource base for the future?
3 The 'missing market' view would also seek to explain the persistence of monopolies or the emergence of new monopolies within a reforming economy as the consequence of inadequate market development. This view has been expressed in the analysis of reform processes in both sub-Saharan Africa by Collier (1995).
4 The National Economic Development and Labour Administration Council (NEDLAC) in South Africa set up specifically to consider economic adjustment issues was considered a useful model by the Zimbabwe trade union movement (ZCTU) (1996).
5 For sectoral allocations see World Bank (1994, p. 203).
6 World Bank (1995, pp. 179 and 201–2).
7 Subsidized food grain sales by statutory rules to priority groups and through modified food rationing were distinct from free relief distribution and food-for-work schemes.
8 The technical assistance was to the Bangladesh Bank and various vital pieces of legislation were introduced, such as the Financial Loan Court Act 1990; the Bank Companies Act 1991; the Financial Institutions Act 1993; the Securities and Exchange Commission Act 1993; and the Bankruptcy Act 1997.
9 The NCBs had about 3500 branches, four times as many as the PCBs.
10 The Bangladesh Bank should by statute aim to achieve three objectives: low inflation through monetary policy; reserve management to limit exchange rate volatility; and supervision of the banking sector to prevent loan default and delinquency. As an organization, it should be strictly independent of the banking division of the Ministry of Finance and its governor(s), and a board of directors

should be appointed with statutory responsibility enshrined in the Constitution (Centre for Policy Dialogue, 1998, p. 136).

References

Brownbridge, M. and C. Kirkpatrick (1998) 'The Lessons of the Asian Crisis for Financial Sector Regulation and Policy', paper presented at the 15th Sino–European Conference, Taipei, Taiwan, 13–16 December 1998.

Centre for Policy Dialogue (1996) *Experience with Economic Reform. A Review of Bangladesh's Development 1995* (Dhaka: University Press).

Centre for Policy Dialogue (1997a) *Growth or Stagnation? A Review of Bangladesh's Development 1996* (Dhaka: University Press).

Centre for Policy Dialogue (1997b) *Quality of Public Investment in Bangladesh* (Dhaka: University Press).

Centre for Policy Dialogue (1998) *Crisis in Governance. A Review of Bangladesh's Development 1997* (Dhaka: University Press).

Collier, P. (1995) 'The Marginalization of Africa', *International Labour Review*, vol. 134, no. 5.

van der Geest, W. (1996) 'Distribution-Improving Development Policies for Bangladesh: Applying the Equilibrium Framework', unpublished PhD thesis, University of Cambridge, UK.

van der Geest, W. and R. van der Hoeven (1999) *Adjustment, Employment and Missing Institutions in Sub-Saharan Africa* (Oxford: James Currey).

Goodhart, C. (1998) 'An Incentive Structure for Financial Regulation' in *The Emerging Framework for Financial Regulation* (Financial Market Group, London School of Economics, London).

Hossain, A. and S. Rashid (1997) 'Financial Sector Reform', in M.G. Quibria (ed.), *The Bangladesh Economy in Transition* (New Delhi: Oxford University Press, and Dhaka: University Press).

Markandiya, A. (1994) 'Policies for Sustainable Development', FAO Economic and Social Development Paper, no. 121 (Rome: FAO).

Quibria, M. G. (1997) *The Bangladesh Economy in Transition* (New Delhi: Oxford University Press, and Dhaka: University Press).

Simanjuntak, D. (1998) 'Reconstruction of the Indonesian Economy, Roles for Development Cooperation', paper presented at the Clingendael Institute conference on EU–Indonesia relations, The Hague, 25–6 October.

UNCTAD (1995) *The Least Developed Countries 1995 Report* (Geneva: UNCTAD).

World Bank (1994) 'Bangladesh: From Stabilisation to Growth', Report No. 12774-BD (Washington DC: World Bank).

World Bank (1995) 'Bangladesh: Recent Economic Developments and Priority Reform Agenda for Rapid Growth', report no. 13875 – BD (Washington DC: World Bank).

Zimbabwe Congress of Trade Unions (1996) *Beyond ESAP* (Harare: ZCTU).

Part V

Lessons from the East Asian Crisis

15
The Asian Crisis: Causes and Policy Lessons

*Azizul Islam**
UN ESCAP, Bangkok

1 Introduction

For many years East and Southeast Asian countries received universal acclaim as the fastest growing economies in the world. Their remarkable achievement in sustaining a high rate of economic growth over a long period was significantly fostered by focusing on active participation in the globalization process. This focus enabled them to take advantage of the increasing opportunities for trade and for access to external capital and technology. However, participation in the globalization process is fraught with certain risks. Unless adequate precautionary measures are taken, these risks can have a debilitating impact on national economies. During the second half of 1997, several East/Southeast Asian economies fell victim to some of the pitfalls associated with closer integration with the international economy. The most seriously affected were Indonesia, Malaysia, the Philippines, the Republic of Korea and Thailand. Two of them – Indonesia and Thailand – will most likely record negative GDP growth in 1998. The other three will suffer a drastic deceleration. Their prospects in the near future remain uncertain.

In this chapter we analyse the causes underlying the upheaval that gripped those five economies more or less simultaneously, and draw policy lessons from this experience for other countries aspiring to participate in the globalization process. Section 1 provides a glimpse of the policy context in which the crisis occurred and its depth; section 2 analyses the underlying causes; section 3 highlights the policy lessons; and the chapter ends with some concluding observations.

* This chapter draws heavily on chapter III of the *Economic and Social Survey of Asia and the Pacific 1998* drafted by the author, with valuable research support from Abul, Hashem and Prabowo. I am grateful to Janet Farooq for helpful comments. The views expressed do not necessarily reflect those of the United Nations.

2 The policy context and the evolution of the crisis

The policy context

The crisis occurred against the backdrop of policy reforms aimed at greater integration with rapidly increasing trade in goods and services and flows of foreign direct investment (FDI) and other private capital at the global level. The policy initiatives taken by East and Southeast Asian countries to promote exports and attract FDI have been elaborated in some recent publications by the United Nations Economic and Social Commission for Asia and the Pacific (UN ESCAP, 1995, 1997) and will not be repeated here. Suffice it to mention that the rewards of these initiatives were reaped in the form of a substantial increase in the export/GDP and FDI/GDP ratios as shown in Table 15.1 in most of these economies.[1]

During the 1990s, financial sector reforms were intensified, and the various elements of reform can be grouped into several major areas: reduction of barriers to entry; deregulation of interest rates; relaxation of directed credit requirements; promotion of new financial markets and instruments; and liberalization of the external dimension of the financial sector. The focus here is on the latter. With some variation among countries, liberalization permitted local citizens and foreign residents to open accounts with commercial banks either in national or foreign currencies; the banks to extend credit in foreign exchange in the domestic market; non-bank private sector corporations as well as financial institutions to borrow abroad; foreigners to own shares listed by national companies in domestic stock exchanges; the sale of securities in international stock and bond markets by national companies; the sale of domestic monetary instruments, such as central bank bills and treasury bills, to non-residents; greater freedom of entry to foreigners into the domestic banking sector; and the establishment of offshore banks which were also allowed, in some cases, to borrow abroad and lend domestically.

Table 15.1 Ratios of exports and FDI to GDP

	Exports (%)		*FDI (%)*	
	1980–84	*1990–95*	*1984–89*	*1990–94*
Indonesia	25.8	23.9	0.5	1.3
Malaysia	48.1	77.4	2.4	7.8
Philippines	15.6	20.4	1.0	1.5
Republic of Korea	30.0	25.5	0.4	0.3
Thailand	18.5	30.5	1.3	1.7

Source: UN–ESCAP, *Economic and Social Survey of Asia and the Pacific 1997*, table III. 4, p. 89 and table IV. 6, p. 151.

Indonesia abolished most remaining restrictions on foreign equity ownership in the early 1990s to allow 100 per cent ownership in most industries. Foreign investor participation in the domestic stockmarket was limited to 49 per cent of the total shares of a company, but that restriction was lifted recently. Non-residents have been permitted to establish joint-venture securities firms with residents, foreign banks are permitted to establish joint ventures with domestic banks, and the ceiling on foreign commercial borrowing by banks was removed in a series of reforms in the late 1980s. Since 1992, domestic firms have been permitted to list up to 30 per cent of their equity on foreign stock exchanges.

Since 1987, Malaysia has permitted non-residents to wholly own companies that export at least 80 per cent of their output, and has allowed foreign firms to issue corporate bonds in the domestic securities market since 1989. Portfolio investment by foreign investors is limited to 30 per cent of the listed shares of any one company. From the late 1980s, the operation of foreign securities companies has been permitted and investment trust funds have been established to promote foreign participation in the local stockmarket. The country set up an international offshore financial centre in 1990.

In the early 1990s, the Philippines virtually eliminated restrictions on current account transactions and sharply reduced limitations on inward and outward capital flows. Exporters can now retain 100 per cent of their foreign exchange earnings; there are no limits on foreign exchange purchases; and foreign investors can repatriate capital without requiring prior approval of the central bank. Since 1994, the entry of foreigners into the banking sector has been greatly eased. They can purchase equity in an existing bank or establish new joint-venture banks with local residents.

In the Republic of Korea, virtually all restrictions on direct investment by non-residents were lifted, and from 1992 foreign investors were permitted to invest directly in the stockmarket, albeit with restrictions on the total equity holding in any one company. At the same time, domestic institutional investors were allowed to invest in foreign securities. Capital account liberalization was accelerated in 1995, focusing primarily on the deregulation of outflows. For example, for the first time domestic residents were allowed to hold overseas deposit accounts.

Thailand permits banks and businesses to borrow offshore in foreign currencies, to open domestic financial institutions and instruments to foreign participation, and permit the operation of branches or affiliates of foreign institutions. Since 1991, Thailand has permitted 100 per cent foreign ownership of firms that export all their output. In terms of portfolio investment, foreign investors are permitted to hold up to 49 per cent of the total shares of a listed company. In 1993, the Bangkok International Banking Facility (BIBF) was launched, permitting commercial banks to carry out various international lending and investment banking operations. Forty-five banks were awarded a BIBF licence by mid-1996; these banks are also allowed to accept deposits in foreign currencies from non-residents and lend such funds to both residents and non-residents.

2.1 The evolution and the depth of the crisis

In chronological order, Thailand was the first country to experience the turmoil in 1997. The Thai currency, the baht, came under speculative attack in February and May 1997, and initially official foreign reserves were sold to defend the currency. In the process, the reserves fell from about US$39 billion in January 1997 to US$32 billion in June 1997. In addition, the Bank of Thailand sold over US$23 billion of its reserves on the forward market. This rapid depletion of reserves forced the Bank to announce a float of the baht on 2 July 1997.

In parallel, the weakness of the financial sector became starkly manifest. A case in point was the Bangkok Bank of Commerce Ltd., the control of which was taken over by the Ministry of Finance in May 1996 after it reached the brink of insolvency owing to high levels of sub-standard debt and inadequate provision for capital as well as loan loss. This was followed by the collapse in early 1997 of Finance One Public Co. Ltd. one of the largest finance companies in the country. As confidence in the financial system waned, borrowers faced increasing difficulties in rolling over short-term debt, outflows from finance companies as well as commercial banks intensified and selling pressure on the stock exchange increased. Developments in the stockmarket and in the currency market fed upon each other. Fifty-six of the country's 91 finance firms had to be closed. The country was forced to conclude an agreement with the International Monetary Fund (IMF) for a US$17.2 billion rescue programme in August 1997.[2] In the first quarter of 1998, the central bank had to take over four more commercial banks.

Indonesia suffered major exchange-rate weakness beginning in August 1997. This led first to the floating of the currency outside its previous trading band supported by high interest rates; then, as pressure on the rupiah remained intense, the government decided to seek help from the IMF in October 1997. A US$40 billion programme was arranged, with approximately one-fourth to be contributed by the IMF and the remainder made up of commitments from various other sources, including US$5 billion from Indonesia itself in the form of contingency reserves. Sixteen banks, thought to be unsound, were ordered to close.

Malaysia also suffered from the backlash of currency and stockmarket weaknesses that plagued Indonesia and Thailand. The government had to bring in measures to reduce the current account deficit, primarily by cutting down on planned infrastructure expenditure and deferring other large investments. These included the Bakun hydroelectric dam, a new international airport in the northern state of Kedah, and the Linear City project near Kuala Lumpur. In addition, current government expenditures were to be reduced, while privatization, stockmarket listings and rights issues were to be frozen for the time being because of stockmarket weakness. A package of austerity measures announced in December 1997 included an 18 per cent reduction in government spending and the postponement of all mega projects not yet started.

The Philippines was also not immune from the upheaval. The initial response to the attack on the peso was a combination of intensified US$ sales and several upward adjustments in interest rates. This strategy did not prove effective in arresting the peso slide, but caused the depletion of reserves. It was, therefore, decided in July 1997 to widen the band within which the peso could float. Since then, several measures have been put in place to restrict foreign exchange trading (for example, the maximum amount the banks could sell over the counter was reduced); to decrease liquidity (for example, the banks' liquidity reserve requirement was raised); and to strengthen the financial system (for example, a regulatory limit was placed on bank loans to the property sector). Several austerity measures were announced in December 1997, among them the shelving of all new capital projects and a 25 per cent cut in spending by government agencies, corporations and local authorities.

Following a similar attack on the currency and large financial outflows, the Republic of Korea was forced to seek assistance from the IMF. An agreement was concluded in December 1997, involving an overall assistance package of US$57 billion, the largest bail-out ever arranged by the IMF. The amount is being contributed jointly by the IMF, the World Bank, the Asian Development Bank and several developed countries. By the end of January 1998 ten merchant banks had closed down and the country had to enter into a debt-rescheduling agreement with creditors.

The most visible manifestations of the crisis are the drastic depreciation of exchange rates and the dramatic fall in stock market indices. The depth of the crisis can be gauged from the data in Table 15.2.

Table 15.2 Exchange rates and stock market indices

Country	*Exchange rate in US$*		*Stock market index*	
	25 June 1997	*30 December 1997*	*30 December 1996*	*30 December 1997*
Indonesia	2432	5570	637	401
Malaysia	252	389	1238	589
Philippines	264	405	3171	1869
Republic of Korea	888	1635	651	376
Thailand	253	470	832	366

Source: *The Economist*, various issues.

3 The underlying causes

A number of factors combined to cause the crisis, and the important ones that can be identified with the benefit of hindsight are discussed below.

3.1 The rising current account deficit

One of the causes that triggered the crisis was the deterioration in the current account of the balance of payments in all the affected countries shown in Table 15.3. The magnitudes of the deficit differed, ranging from 3.5 per cent of GDP in Indonesia to 8 per cent in Thailand by the end of 1996. But the deficit increased in all cases with the exception of Malaysia, where during 1993–5 it was much higher than in the previous three-year period. The most rapid deterioration took place in the Republic of Korea, where the deficit averaged less than 1 per cent during the period 1993–5, but reached 5 per cent in 1996.

The deterioration in the current account balance was caused mainly by the slowdown in export growth, which was particularly sharp in 1996 (see Table 15.3) and persisted in many cases through 1997. A slackening in export demand, in major exports, such as electronic goods, was partly responsible for the sharp export slowdown in 1996. To some extent it reflected the deceleration in global trade. An important reason, however, was the gradual erosion of the competitiveness of the region's export industries as a result of rising domestic costs, especially wage costs. There was also a tendency for real exchange rates to appreciate (see Figure 15.1) as the nominal exchange rates with the US $ were held stable while domestic inflation rates tended to exceed those of major trading partners, including the USA. The realignment of currencies of the other countries also had an effect on the appreciation of real effective exchange rates. At the same time, new competitors emerged both within and outside the region to encroach on the markets for the labour-intensive products of some countries.

Table 15.3 Changes in dollar value of exports and current account balances

Country	*Annual percentage change in US $ value of exports*			*Current account balance as percentage of GDP*	
	1993–5	*1996*	*1997*	*1993–5*	*1996*
Indonesia	10.2	9.7	8.9	−2.2	−3.5
Malaysia	21.9	6.2	3.2	−6.5	−4.9
Philippines	21.7	16.7	24.0	−4.2	−4.7
Republic of Korea	18.1	4.2	0.3	−0.8	−5.0
Thailand	20.1	−1.2	2.3	−6.3	−8.0

Note: Figures for 1997 refer to the first half of 1997, annualized growth rate.
Sources: UN ESCAP Secretariat calculations; based on UN (1997); ADB (1997); IMF (1997a); UN (1997b).

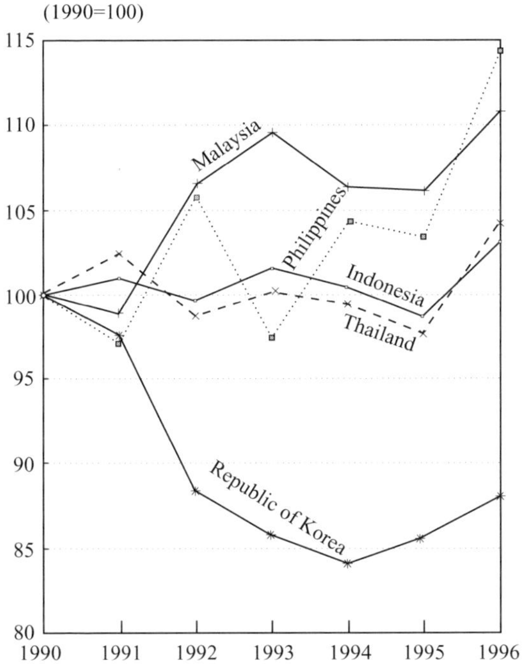

Figure 15.1 Selected South East and East Asian countries, index of real effective exchange rates, 1991–6.
Note: Index of real effective exchange rates defined in terms of foreign currencies per unit of domestic currency; a rise in the index implies a fall in competitiveness.
Source: United Nations, *The World Economy at the Beginning of 1998* (December 1997b).

3.2 Developments in the capital account

The rising current account deficit naturally had to be financed by capital inflows, and private flows are the dominant component in most countries of East and South East Asia. In these countries, FDI has been and remains an important component of total capital inflows. However, portfolio investments and the credit component, including banking flows, clearly showed rising trends. In the Republic of Korea, net portfolio flows rose from an average of 2 per cent of GDP in 1990–2 to 2.8 per cent in 1995–6. During the same periods, they rose from −0.1 per cent to 2.3 per cent in Indonesia; from 0.1 to 2.6 per cent (1995) in Malaysia; and from 0.2 to 2.2 per cent in Thailand. Similarly, in the Republic of Korea banking and other inflows rose from 1.4 per cent of GDP in 1990–2 to 2.6 per cent in 1995–6. In Indonesia, this component of capital flows recorded a significant increase between 1993 and 1995, reaching 1.2 per cent of GDP in 1995. In Malaysia, the Philippines and Thailand, non-FDI private inflows as a proportion of GDP kept rising, reaching an average level of 9 per cent of GDP in Thailand in 1995–6. In Malaysia and the Philippines they remained at around 5 per cent of GDP during 1993–5.

These substantial capital inflows took place not merely to finance the deficits in the current accounts of the balance of payments, but often also as a result of investors seeking profit opportunities in capital markets, which were expanding fast and entry to which was recently made easier. At the same time, a significant structural change was taking place in the international financial markets. The rapid institutionalization of savings in developed countries led to a huge accumulation of resources in pension and mutual funds. The growing institutionalization of savings and the participation of institutional investors in international markets boosted the purchase of emerging market securities as a means of diversifying their portfolios.

Many countries in the region pursued a policy of relatively high interest rates in order to maintain a stable exchange rate. The prevailing differential between the relatively high domestic interest rates and international interest rates, together with the liberalization of policies noted earlier, was a further lure for capital inflows, while stable exchange rates minimized currency risks. The volume of total inflows often exceeded current account financing needs and added to official reserves. The rising level of reserves, despite the deteriorating trend in the current account deficit, is shown in Table 15.4.

The above factors gave rise to a rapid build-up of the stock of foreign debt (see Table 15.5), a large part of which was not hedged against currency risks. Between 1992 and 1996, the increases were about threefold in the case of Malaysia, the Republic of Korea and Thailand, and about twofold in the case of Indonesia and the Philippines. It should also be noted that a high proportion of the stock of private debt was of a short-term nature. In 1996, this ranged from 50 per cent in Malaysia to 67.5 per cent in the Republic of Korea. A high proportion of short-term debt contains the risk of a sudden reversal and crisis owing to adverse expectations with respect to either the exchange rate or the health of the financial sector, or both.

Table 15.4 International reserves (US$ billions at year end)

Country	*1993–5*	*1996*	*mid-1997*
Indonesia	12.4	18.3	20.3
Malaysia	25.5	27.0	26.6
Philippines	5.7	10.0	9.8
Republic of Korea	26.2	34.0	34.1
Thailand	29.9	37.7	31.4

Source: IMF (1997a).

Table 15.5 Stock of debt to foreign private creditors, 1992–7

	Total (US$ billions)						*Short term (per cent of total)*[a]					
	1992	*1993*	*1994*	*1995*	*1996*	*mid-1997*	*1992*	*1993*	*1994*	*1995*	*1996*	*mid-1997*
Indonesia	28.4	30.5	34.2	44.5	55.5	58.7	60.5	61.7	61.8	61.9	61.7	59.0
Malaysia	8.5	13.0	13.5	16.8	22.2	28.8	48.1	56.8	48.8	47.2	50.3	56.4
Philippines	6.9	5.8	6.5	8.3	13.3	14.1	45.7	40.8	47.4	48.8	58.2	58.8
Republic of Korea	38.7	41.2	56.5	77.5	100.0	103.4	71.4	70.8	71.1	70.0	67.5	67.9
Thailand	23.0	29.6	43.4	62.8	70.1	69.4	69.0	72.1	71.0	69.4	65.2	65.7

[a] Up to and including one-year maturity.

Source: Bank for International Settlements, *The Maturity, Sectoral and Nationality Distribution of International Bank Lending*, various issues.

Mention should also be made of the relevance of the utilization of capital inflows which financed the deficit. The sustainability of the deficit becomes questionable when foreign resources are used for the purpose of consumption or for investments which yield low returns, or investment in non-tradables such as land, buildings and infrastructure which generate returns in local currency, but repayment has to be made in foreign currency. To some extent this happened over the last few years in the countries which came under attack, as explained later.

3.3 Deficiencies in dealing with capital inflows

3.3.1 Fiscal policy

One policy response for dealing with capital inflows could be to pursue a contractionary fiscal policy so as to reduce the potentially inflationary impact. However, there are inherent limits to the use of fiscal policy as an instrument for dealing with capital inflows. Government tax and expenditure policies are determined primarily by medium- or long-term development considerations, rather than short-term fluctuations in capital flows. The countries experiencing large capital inflows from private sources typically have a more liberal policy regime governing the operations of financial sector institutions, which are allowed to set their own credit policies as was the case in East and Southeast Asian countries. Consumer credit is frequently made readily available by financial institutions during periods of heavy capital inflows. This factor may also constrain the effectiveness of fiscal policy in curtailing aggregate demand.

The affected countries cannot be considered to have pursued profligate fiscal policies. In fact, all of them have had a budgetary surplus in recent years. However, it is noteworthy that in 1996 the surplus declined in Malaysia, the Philippines, the Republic of Korea and Thailand, and only in Indonesia increased from 0.4 per cent of GDP in 1995 to 0.8 per cent of GDP. The implication is that fiscal policy was not used for dealing with capital inflows. In fact, it is most likely that the deterioration in the fiscal balance in the majority of the affected countries was one of the factors that contributed to adverse market sentiment and the 1997 crisis.

3.3.2 Monetary policy: sterilization

The sterilization policy, implemented by monetary authorities, aimed at insulating the domestic economy from the effects of capital inflows by targeting two macroeconomic variables simultaneously: the prevention of nominal exchange rate appreciation, and the reduction of the domestic money supply. This sort of intervention has been the most common policy response in countries facing sharp increases in private capital flows in the region. In order to avoid the exchange rate appreciation induced by capital inflows, monetary authorities often resorted to intervention in the foreign exchange market by selling local currency for foreign exchange.

The instruments used to sterilize the possible adverse consequences on money supply growth following the increases in foreign reserves varied across countries at different points of time, but mostly involved open-market operations, increases in reserve requirements, and a shift of government deposits and funds from the banking system to the central bank. The intensity of sterilization operations varied across countries.

In most countries, sterilization has not been an effective tool of monetary control, and domestic credit expansion has remained high. The increases in interest rates induced by the sterilization operations attracted further foreign capital. This underlines a fundamental contradiction in financially open economies, where attempting to control both the exchange rate and the inflation rate proves a futile and costly exercise in the medium term. Indeed, the experience of most of the economies indicates that short-term interest rates rose as sterilization efforts progressed, whereas in the absence of sterilization domestic interest rates would be expected to decline with the inflow of foreign capital. Even with the easing or cessation of sterilization, interest rate spreads have tended to remain high, attracting further inflows of short-term capital. Under a less liberal capital account regime, even if open-market operations were to result in a high interest rate regime, domestic borrowers would be constrained from accessing funds overseas.

The increase in short-term interest rates as a result of sterilization can discourage long-term investment demand as the cost of capital rises, while returns on less risky assets such as government paper become more attractive. Sterilization, therefore, may have had the unintended effect of changing the composition of capital flows away from the long term to short term.

The unintended effects of sterilization may take other forms and be magnified when the financial sector is weak. With rising interest rates, financial institutions tend to become less stringent in evaluating credit risks and expand short-term operations without careful assessment of the trade-offs between risks and returns. Their institutional capacity may thus become overstretched and they may quickly run into serious problems with non-performing loans. With inadequate loan–loss provision or capital reserves, public confidence in financial institutions may weaken, leading to large withdrawals and a precipitous crisis. To some extent this is what happened in the affected countries, as explained later.

3.3.3 The exchange rate policy

Another policy response to capital inflows would be to allow greater flexibility in exchange rates. This would imply an appreciation in nominal exchange rates during periods of large inflows and depreciation during periods of outflows. The underlying rationale is that the flexibility in exchange rates would introduce some uncertainties that might discourage purely speculative and highly reversible inflows. It also allows the monetary authorities a greater degree of independence in exercising control over monetary aggregates as they become relatively free from preoccupation with the stability of the exchange rate.

There are, however, a number of reasons why countries may wish to maintain a stable exchange rate. First, the prevention of appreciation in the nominal exchange rate is often a policy priority with a view to maintaining the competitiveness of exports. Second, there is apprehension that once the currency is allowed to float, it may become highly volatile inhibiting both trade transactions and capital inflows. Such a situation arises particularly because of the lack of development of deep markets for managing currency risks. Third, a stable exchange rate may be an effective anchor against inflation in the domestic economy. Fourth, a government's ability to maintain a stable exchange rate may be viewed as an indicator of its policy credibility, which can help to maintain confidence in the economy.

However, as discussed in Bensaid and Jeanne (1997), a fixed or highly stable exchange rate regime is inherently vulnerable to speculative attacks, particularly when there are expectations that devaluation is likely. Several factors can cause an expectation of devaluation in the market, and these may be related to fundamental problems of an economy such as loss of export competitiveness or deteriorating current account or fiscal balance; political events; or actions of some strategic market participants, for example major hedge-fund operators. Once expectation of devaluation sets in, speculators are aware that a government's willingness or ability to defend the exchange rate is subject to several limitations. The intervention in the foreign exchange market is bounded on the upper side by the stock of accumulated international reserves. Efforts to prevent devaluation by raising domestic interest rates impose certain costs on the economy, including an increase in public debt obligations, a collapse of the property market, and a dampening impact on the level of economic activities in general. Speculators recognize that these costs cannot be sustained indefinitely and may therefore persist with their attacks. In the end, the governments or monetary authorities may win if they are ready to endure the high cost, as happened in Hong Kong, China where the authorities recently permitted a drastic increase in interest rates in order to defend the exchange rate; they were also, of course, backed up by a high level of foreign exchange reserves. But in the affected countries, it was the authorities who were forced to succumb.

3.3.4 Financial sector weaknesses

In an economy characterized by a relatively liberal financial sector regime, the currency crisis and the financial sector crisis become closely intertwined. A recent empirical study by Kaminsky and Reinhart (1996) has shown that in many cases the simultaneous occurrence of the two crises had their common origin in the deregulation of the financial system. The interaction between the exchange rate collapses and runs against the financial intermediaries works in both directions. Expected devaluation, for the reasons noted, changes the return profile of investment for foreign investors and increases the perceived benefits of early withdrawals, thereby causing a significant drain on the financial intermediaries and a fall in capital markets. On the other hand, the withdrawal of funds from financial intermediaries and repatriation outside the country causes a depletion of reserves and forces a devaluation of the currency. A withdrawal may be prompted by many considerations, including expected devaluation, opportunities for better returns elsewhere, doubts about the viability of financial intermediaries in the light of their asset and liability portfolios, and worries about potential changes in rules governing capital markets.

There is no doubt that a part of the explanation for the crisis lay in the weaknesses inherent in overstretched operations by the financial institutions. In Thailand, the total assets of the principal domestic financial institutions, excluding the Bank of Thailand, expanded from US$96 billion in 1990 to US$290 billion in 1995, and those of the commercial banks from US$71 billion to US$200 billion. During the same period, the foreign liabilities of the Thai commercial banks went up from 6 per cent of their total liabilities to 23 per cent, and those of the non-bank financial institutions from about 5 to 7 per cent. In 1987, foreign liabilities of the commercial banks constituted a mere 1.5 per cent and of non-bank financial institutions only 0.1 per cent of their total liabilities.

In Indonesia, domestic credit as a proportion of GDP rose from less than 50 per cent in 1990 to 54 per cent in 1996. The corresponding figures for Malaysia were 78 and 93 per cent; for the Republic of Korea 57 and 65 per cent; and for Thailand 70 and 99 per cent.

There is some evidence that the rapid credit expansion was associated with some degree of misallocation. In Thailand, for example, total advances to manufacturing expanded ten-fold between 1985 and 1996, but credit to the real estate sector increased 22-fold during the same period. The stock and the property markets in Thailand, as well as in the other countries, shot up rapidly since 1989–90, with growing foreign portfolio investments partly the reason for the explosive growth in the stockmarket.

The persistent oversupply in the property market and the downward pressure on its prices negatively affected the financial sector with its substantial exposure to the property market. A downturn in the stockmarket had started in 1993–4, and assets pledged against loans depreciated rapidly with the decline in both these markets. Failure of businesses to repay their borrowings from the financial institutions exposed the vulnerability of those institutions as a large proportion of their credit advances became bad debts. By the first half of 1997, non-performing loans as a proportion of total loans increased rapidly, from about 13 per cent in the Philippines to nearly 20 per cent in Thailand; in 1996, these proportions stood at less than 5 per cent in all cases, with the exception of Indonesia where it was close to 9 per cent. The financial institutions did not even have effective legal recourse to foreclosures to recover defaulted loans because of weaknesses in the legal systems, in particular inadequate bankruptcy laws or cumbersome procedures for their enforcement.

These institutions, in turn, had difficulty in repaying their sizeable foreign obligations. Export slowdown, falling property and stock values, and the increasing revelation of accumulated bad debts of financial institutions ultimately shook investors' confidence and triggered large-scale capital flight. Domestic currencies came under pressure, and initially the central banks tried to defend their value by using available reserves. Their efforts, however, did not succeed and they had to give up when they started to suffer a serious loss of reserves.

3.3.5 The role of foreign market players

The point can be made that foreign creditors were substantially responsible for sowing the seeds of the crisis. The outstanding credit from the foreign private sector was almost entirely contracted by the private sector in the borrowing countries. These transactions were, therefore, the result of the evaluation of risks and returns by foreign private creditors. The underlying economic causes discussed earlier should have acted as a warning signal for discriminating creditors; yet overall bank lending to Asian developing countries, including the ones in crisis, proceeded unabated in the first half of 1997 as described in *The Asian Wall Street Journal* (1998). This can be viewed as an instance of market failure, but not the first in recent history. It has been argued that the Latin American debt crisis of the early 1980s owed its origin partly to the failure of proper risk assessment and the poor ability of transnational banks to evaluate creditworthiness (Dillon *et al.*, 1985; *The Economist*, 1982).

Having sown the seeds of the crisis, the market players played a role in aggravating it. In a world of integrated financial markets, investors such as mutual funds or hedge funds tend to look upon a region or a sub-region as a single market. The problems confronted in one country may prompt them to pull out of the whole region or sub-region in a herd reaction. Thus, following the problems in Thailand, many short-term investors pulled out of the markets of Southeast Asian countries and the Republic of Korea more or less at the same time. Investors overreacted in a panic-stricken manner, even though all these countries had had some strong economic fundamentals immediately prior to the crisis. In 1996, all the countries had high rates of saving, exceeding 30 per cent, with the exception of the Philippines; budgets were in surplus; foreign exchange reserves were rising; and inflation was moderate at less than 7 per cent, except in the Philippines where it was 8.4 per cent. Besides, despite the common weaknesses among the affected countries in terms of the economic indicators discussed earlier, there were considerable differences. To illustrate this, the current account deficit as a proportion of GDP in Indonesia in 1996 was less than half that of Thailand, its exchange rate was more flexible, and it had a smaller volume of foreign private debt. Similar observations apply to the Philippines. As for Malaysia, the current account deficit as a proportion of GDP was a little higher than that of Indonesia and the Philippines, but considerably lower than that of Thailand, and its stock of foreign private debt was higher than that of the Philippines, but less than half of that of Indonesia and a third of that of Thailand.

4 Policy lessons

4.1 Short term

For any country facing a crisis created largely by debt to foreign private sources or other short-term inflows, the first priority is to limit the outflows of foreign exchange. This can be accomplished through several means, which include roll-over of short-term debt, rescheduling of debt repayment and renegotiation of terms of loans. Some restrictions can be imposed on transactions with non-residents; among these are restrictions on transfer of funds by foreigners after selling local stocks or bonds, the imposition of a ceiling on bank loans to foreign residents, and restrictions on the purchase of foreign exchange by residents.

From the perspective of preempting the emergence of a future crisis attributable to external capital inflows, short-term measures may be aimed at reducing inflows and/or influencing the composition of such flows in favour of long-term flows. One measure might be a non-remunerated reserve requirement (to be deposited with the central bank) on liabilities in foreign currency arising from borrowing by firms. The reserve requirement can be varied with the maturity of the loan, the percentage of the requirements declining with the increasing length of the maturity. Another might be an explicit tax on inflows with variation across assets as well as across maturity. The tax can either be imposed on the domestic debtors, for example on a local firm issuing bonds abroad, or on the foreigners, for example those investing in the stockmarket. It is also possible to impose quantitative capital control measures, such as prudential limits or prohibition on non-trade-related swap activities, offshore borrowing, ceilings on banks' foreign currency liability or on the sale of short-term money market instruments to foreign residents.

Some of these policies were, in fact, implemented at different points in time during the 1990s by several countries of the region, including Indonesia, Malaysia, the Philippines and Thailand, as well as by some countries in Latin America, such as Chile, Colombia and Mexico. A recent review of these experiences, by Reinhart and Dunaway (1996), concluded that in the short run, policy measures of this kind can be effective in reducing the volume of inflows and in changing the composition of flows towards longer maturity. However, the longer the inflows persist or the longer the measures remain in place, the less binding are the controls as market operators find ways to circumvent them.

4.2 Medium to long term

4.2.1 National policies

1 *The choice of policy target and instruments* In countries with a large degree of openness to capital account transactions, governments have to ensure that policies are compatible and avoid serious conflict of objectives, such as aiming simultaneously at a stable exchange rate, financial openness and independence in executing monetary policy, the so-called 'impossible trinity' (Frankel, 1996). Investors, creditors and speculators sensed such an inconsistency in policies in the region – policies which had kept exchange rates rather inflexible and maintained open capital accounts. This combination permitted domestic currencies to become overvalued in real terms, an increase in current account deficits and a rapid rise in external indebtedness (encouraged by high domestic interest rates) with a high proportion of short-term maturities. Governments are thus faced with a difficult choice between stabilizing the exchange rate with a fixed parity or within a relatively narrow band, or alternatively pursuing a monetary policy for domestic stabilization irrespective of the consequences to the exchange rate. Finding the most appropriate mix of policy instruments to ensure both internal and external stability in a dynamic setting is not an easy task.

   Governments have to choose carefully and flexibly any one target, such as nominal or real effective exchange rate, interest rate and monetary aggregates and then adopt a combination of instruments to pursue that target. In this context, particular mention should be made of the role of foreign exchange reserves. Typically, the level of reserves maintained by developing countries is some multiple of the average monthly import bill. With open capital accounts, the level of reserves should additionally take into account the likely outflows associated with capital account transactions by the private sector.

   It is important that once the choice of a target is made, the instruments, typically administered by different agencies of governments, are devised and applied in a coordinated manner. The choice of a target as well as the mix of instruments (such as fiscal, monetary, trade-and capital-account-related measures) may vary among countries and at different points of time in an individual country. The assistance of independent think-tanks could be extremely useful in making these choices.

2 *Strengthening the financial sector* The crisis has revealed particularly serious weaknesses in the financial sectors of the affected economies. The

weaknesses relate not only to the operations of the individual financial institutions but also to the regulatory and supervisory regimes governing them. On the one hand, the intermediating entities appear to have been unaware of, or unable to gauge correctly, the underlying risk of many of the investment and lending decisions taken; on the other hand, they did not have the capital strength to absorb the losses that subsequently occurred. Supervisory and regulatory bodies also appear to have been lax in carrying out their functions effectively, whether in the matter of banking regulation or capital market supervision, but particularly in allowing a lack of transparency to flourish.

One policy implication is that countries should move gradually in financial liberalization and opening. In addition to strong economic fundamentals, a sound financial sector is an essential pre-condition for the liberalization of the capital account (Fischer, 1997). Governments should establish a proper regulatory framework and effective implementation of that framework. Equally important, proper accounting, auditing and disclosure requirements need to be in place.[3] In particular, rules regarding non-performing loans and adequate provisions of capital with appropriate risk weights should follow international standards. Legal lending limits to insider borrowing should be established and rigorously enforced. The rules regarding consolidation of financial reports of financial and other companies with extensive cross-holding and interlocking of ownership between them need to be formulated and implemented. Foreign exposure of financial institutions as well as other corporate entities have to be monitored. In their absence, any business or company evaluation and analysis will rest on poor financial data – either biased or meaningless – and, in effect, financing decisions rely heavily on investors' confidence which can be very fragile and volatile. The rigorous efforts to restore the soundness of financial institutions should be complemented by appropriate support to debtor enterprises in the real economy that are fundamentally sound, but currently facing liquidity problems. Also important are competition policies to restrict improper business practices in both the financial and the real sectors.

Governments have a critical role in establishing proper supervisory and regulatory bodies. They should consider the viability of an integrated supervisory framework for the financial sector as a whole. There is a growing trend worldwide to adopt such an integrated framework, the recent cases being in Japan, Malaysia, the Republic of Korea, the UK and (to some extent) India. The main rationale for this is that many banks, non-bank financial institutions and securities and insurance firms engage in a widening variety of financial transactions in different financial markets, both directly and indirectly. In the existing supervisory framework, each separate body supervises only one type of financial institution. The supervisory body or bodies thus tend(s) to be ill-equipped to monitor the total financial activities of institutions and the risks involved, and hence to enforce prudential standards. A related issue is the role of the central bank in financial supervision. Governments may consider assigning the supervisory functions to a separate autonomous body, leaving the central bank with the sole conduct of monetary and exchange rate policy. Such a separation of functions has occurred in a few countries.

3 *Coping with risk in financial transactions* Both the increasing array of financial instruments available and the globalization of financial markets make it imperative that public and private operators have access to, and actively use, hedging instruments for managing their risk. Risks include unanticipated changes in prices, interest rates and exchange rates and so forth. These can be managed or counterbalanced to a large degree through hedging techniques on forward or futures markets. However, most countries in the region do not yet possess active financial forward or futures markets, and those which do exist are very thin, with few active participants. The recent exaggerated swings in currency markets bear testimony to this. The development of viable financial risk management markets would require not only having an adequate supervisory mechanism in place, but also providing training for and access to a wide spectrum of participants including business enterprises, investors, financial institutions and so forth. Both UNCTAD and the World Bank have put programmes in place to assist countries in this area. The countries should avail themselves of these programmes. The wider (in terms of different types of participants) and deeper (in terms of number of transactions per day) a market, the more robust is its price formation and the less the price volatility. More specifically, it can be claimed that a well-functioning forward or futures market for a currency is a necessary adjunct to a currency float, particularly for commercial transactions of various sorts, and its existence should lead to smoother variations in the exchange rate over the longer term.

In opening up the financial sector to new entrants, both domestic and foreign, governments should take into account how much competition can be allowed. Too much competition can erode profit margins, encourage the financing of highly risky projects and eventually lead to the failure of some institutions and a crisis.

4 *Reducing the savings – investment gap and the current account deficit* The recent crisis has also brought into sharp focus the unsustainability of a substantial and prolonged savings – investment gap. This is reflected in the current account deficit and creates problems, particularly when the deficit is financed by private sources. Hence the need for giving greater attention to raising the level of domestic savings if high levels of investment are to be sustained. One of the options that countries with already high savings rates may have to consider in the future is to settle for lower levels of investment and lower rates of economic growth. Meanwhile,

efforts should be continued to increase domestic savings, to whatever extent is possible, through such measures as a wider coverage of insurance services, pension systems and provident funds. Stricter supervision of the credit practices of commercial banks and financial institutions may have the desirable effect of curtailing consumption credit and raising domestic savings. In this context, it should be noted that the efficacy of the interest rate policy as an instrument to encourage savings is rather constrained in a country with an open financial sector, as a large differential between the domestic and foreign interest rates tends to bring about an upsurge in short-term inflows and sow the seeds of instability.

Finally, countries will have to persist with efforts to enhance their export competitiveness through technological upgrading, improvements in the quality of human resources and increases in the domestic value-added component of exports, including the reduction of import intensity. The underlying rationale is to ensure that legitimate import requirements are primarily financed by export earnings, rather than short-term private credit.

4.2.2 International and regional cooperation[4]

1 *Should there be an international debt strategy?* The problems of the external sector management currently being faced by the countries affected by the recent crisis are not without precedent; a very similar problem confronted several developing countries in Latin America in the early 1980s. Following the inception of the Latin American debt crisis in 1982, the initial strategy towards solving the problem, particularly by creditor countries, was aimed at normalizing the relationship between debtors and creditors through a combination of economic adjustment by debtor countries and negotiated financial relief. The strategy was based on the notion that the problem was one of liquidity, not solvency. The transnational banks joined crisis containment operations and accepted additional incremental exposure so as to protect existing assets, especially by way of enabling debtor countries to sustain current interest payments. The financing modalities provided debtor countries with some financial relief through lower interest rate spreads, reduced fees, extension of maturities and provision of some new money. The negotiations, conducted on a case-by-case basis for particular debtor countries, were orchestrated by private bank steering committees in consultation with the World Bank, IMF and the governments of the creditor banks' home countries. This coordinated case-by-case approach received official endorsement under the Baker Plan in October 1985. However, the approach faced a mounting challenge owing to the failure of the international banking community to provide new money on the scale hoped for, and progressive deterioration in the economic conditions in indebted countries. A large outflow of resources

caused by heavy debt-servicing requirements in combination with enforced austerity measures had a strongly negative impact on the debtor countries' investment, growth, consumption and other indicators of economic and social welfare. In consequence, there was a major shift in the strategy towards dealing directly with the debt problem. This was embodied in the Brady Plan announced in March 1989, which represented a change in emphasis from the maintenance of the stream of debt-servicing payments to explicit debt reduction through, *inter alia*, the exchange of old debt for new collateralized bonds at a discount, or for new par value bonds with reduced interest rates.

In the context of the current Asian crisis, only the Republic of Korea has so far succeeded in striking a debt-rescheduling deal with creditor banks. The implementation of the deal is voluntary and there are uncertainties as to how many creditors will actually join it. A more general issue is that a case-by-case approach is usually a time-consuming process and imposes high economic costs on the debtor countries in the interim. In fact, in the case of the Latin American countries it took seven years before the creditor community accepted the need for debt reduction. There are also inequities in the present system. Foreign creditors typically enjoy an explicit or implicit seniority in their claims (IMF, 1997b). In the event of a crisis, governments are often in a hurry to reassure these creditors that all their claims will be met. The burden of adjustment falls almost entirely on the domestic debtors. Besides, no one can guarantee that the debt crisis will not recur in the future. These considerations point to the need for the revival of the discussion on an international debt strategy, an idea which seems to have dissipated with the resolution of the Latin American debt crisis.

2 *The need for global governance of financial flows* The globalization process that has been characterized by occasional imbalances and sizeable disruptions in financial markets brings the issue of market stabilization to the fore. While speculative activities can be useful in correcting imbalances between national or regional markets, thus promoting global efficiency in the longer run, there is a valid concern that these activities may impose unacceptably high short-run costs. Hence, there is a case for considering a mechanism for global governance of international financial flows comparable with that in the area of trade. Its components could include the establishment of an international bankruptcy mechanism[5] as well as the setting up of a new institution, alongside a reorganized IMF and World Bank, to overcome the inadequacies in supervising and regulating financial institutions and markets.

A further policy option could be to try to slow down adverse consequences of speculation by taxation ('putting sand in the wheels of international finance'). The Tobin tax proposes to levy a small globally uniform tax applied to spot transactions on foreign exchange with the twin objectives of deterring speculative flows as well as allowing greater autonomy to national monetary policy. So far, the idea of the tax has remained academic, but many practical problems notwithstanding, there is a case for giving more serious attention to the proposal (Haq *et al.*, 1996).

3 *Some thoughts on regional cooperation* The need for greater regional cooperation beyond the periodic meetings among central banks in the region has been felt more urgently in the wake of the recent financial crises. So far there has not been much progress on the proposed Asian Fund, but the establishment of a regional scheme to supplement the IMF deserves consideration. In November 1997, a 14-nation meeting in Manila drew up a scheme called the Manila Framework which was later endorsed at the APEC Summit in Vancouver, Canada. Ideas were subsequently floated on converting or swapping some of the outstanding debts of the most indebted countries for bonds to be underwritten by the Asian governments as well as the Asian Development Bank (ADB). More recently, a proposal has been mooted to make use of regional currencies in intraregional trade transactions so as to reduce the demand for foreign currencies. These proposals need to be seriously examined in order to arrive at a consensus on regional responses that could be in place well before the region is hit by another crisis.

Greater regional cooperation is also needed to address the issues of financial sector regulation, the establishment of common prudential standards for the industry, and development of systems to provide early warning against the appearance of risks. Governments in the region could also explore the feasibility of the establishment of an insurance scheme dealing with cross-border financial claims. It should be noted that for FDI there exist multilateral schemes administered by the World Bank and the International Finance Corporation providing coverage against certain types of risk. Many developed countries also have national schemes.[6]

Financial market instability has been partly aggravated by perceptions of weaknesses in the financial institutions as well as other corporate entities and the lack of reliable relevant information regarding their operations. This has arisen partly from differing standards of regulation, the lack of information regarding assets and liabilities, and the variability as well as inadequacy of standards of corporate accounting, auditing, disclosures and corporate governance generally. It would appear, therefore, that arrangements capable of generating and transmitting more accurate, transparent and timely information regarding the build-up of significant financial risks within a particular jurisdiction would be very useful for the authorities in another jurisdiction.

Serious consideration could also be given to some common training facilities for accrediting accountants, auditors and regulators. Some common standards on licensing of stockbrokers, financial intermediaries and so on could also lead to more cross-border listing of securities or regional issuing of bonds, so directly enhancing the depth and breadth of these markets.

Much of the current crisis can be traced to doubts regarding the ability of countries to service their foreign liabilities, especially short-term debts. Doubts arose as market operators appeared to be unaware of the true extent of the affected countries' indebtedness, principally because short-term debts had not hitherto been included in the official debt data. All economies need to make substantial improvements in this area by providing comprehensive and timely debt information to counter the deleterious effects of rumour and speculation. Governments could cooperate in setting out common definitions, information requirements and reporting procedures and in establishing a system for sharing information.

5 Concluding observations

The central message is that the currency crisis and the financial crisis which gripped the East and Southeast Asian economies had their common origin in the liberalization of financial sector policy regimes encompassing both internal and external dimensions. No judgement is expressed on the desirability or otherwise of such liberalization *per se*. Each country has to make its own choice based on an objective assessment of the benefits and the risks of liberalization.

However, we emphasize that an essential precondition for liberalization of capital account transactions, in addition to strong macroeconomic fundamentals, is the establishment of a sound financial sector. This requires an effective regulatory and supervisory framework which should include such elements as auditing, accounting, reporting and disclosure requirements; limitations on interlocking interests between financial institutions and other corporate entities; and ceilings on foreign exposure. Moreover, the authorities responsible for the supervision of the financial sector must have the capacity to monitor and enforce compliance.

Macroeconomic management becomes extremely complex with open capital accounts and the cost of policy mistakes can be very high. The complexity arises largely because of the impossible trinity:

- pursuit of a highly stable nominal exchange rate;
- open capital account; and
- independence in executing monitoring policy to achieve domestic objectives, such as containing inflation.

Consistency of policy targets and instruments should, therefore, be always ensured.

Given the large volume of international flows of short-term capital the speculative movement of which is not determined exclusively by economic fundamentals, national policies alone are unlikely to be adequate to eliminate the risks of volatility. Hence, there is a need to develop a system of global governance to deal with such flows. There are also several areas in which regional cooperation could contribute towards mitigating the risks. We have made some proposals in these respects, all of which require more systematic examination.

Finally, two caveats should be mentioned. First, we have dealt exclusively with the financial dimension of the crisis; space did not permit any consideration of the implications for the real sector of the economy in terms of loss of output and employment and the resultant social discontent. Second, we have limited discussion to the economic analysis of the causes underlying the crisis, and have not delved into the political economy dimensions of economic management embodied in such concepts as nepotism, corruption or crony capitalism cited by some analysts as explanatory factors.

Notes

1 Note that Indonesia's export figure for the early 1980s is somewhat distorted by the inclusion of oil, the price of which boomed during the 1970s. A better indicator of its export performance is the growth of export of manufactures, the share of which in total exports increased from 2 per cent in 1980 to 53 per cent in 1993 (World Bank, 1997, table 15, p. 242). In the Republic of Korea, the export/GDP ratio seems to have stabilized around 30 per cent during the 1980s and 1990s; this ratio was less than 15 per cent in 1970. Also note, that, up until recently, the Republic of Korea has been relatively restrictive towards FDI except in some preferred sectors such as automobile and electronics.

2 For a brief description of the conditionalities imposed by the IMF on the various countries and a critique thereof, see UN ESCAP (1998).

3 UNCTAD has developed a set of internationally recognized accounting norms and offers technical assistance in this area; General Data Dissemination System (GDDS) and Special Data Dissemination System (SDDS) being organized by the IMF in order to improve the coverage, integrity and quality of data on various sectors of the economy, including the financial and external sectors, are also important initiatives.

4 Most of the proposals contained in this section have been floated in one forum or another; their pros and cons require more detailed examination. They have been put together here with a view to encouraging further discussion.

5 The importance of action in this area was highlighted a few years ago by the United Nations; see United Nations (1992).

6 For a review of the types of risk covered and the criteria of coverage, see United Nations Centre on Transnational Corporations (1992).

References

Asian Development Bank (ADB) (1997) *Key Indicators of Developing Asian and Pacific Countries* (Oxford: Oxford University Press).

The Asian Wall Street Journal (1998) 'Banks Continued Lending to Asia in First Half of 1997', 5 January, p. 6.

Bank for International Settlements (various years) *The Maturity, Sectoral and Nationality Distribution of International Bank Lending* (Basel: Bank for International Settlements).

Bensaid, B. and O. Jeanne (1997) 'The Instability of Fixed Exchange Rate Systems when Raising the Nominal Interest Rate is Costly', *European Economic Review*, vol. 41, no. 8, pp. 1461–78.

Dillon, K. B. *et al.* (1985) *Recent Developments in External Debt Restructuring*, IMF occasional paper no. 40, Washington DC.

The Economist (1982) 'Bottomless Debt', 11 December, p. 12.

Fischer, S. (1997) *Capital Account Liberalization and the Role of the IMF* (Washington DC: International Monetary Fund).

Frankel, J. A. (1996) 'Recent Exchange-rate Experience and Proposals for Reform', *The American Economic Review, Papers and Proceedings of the Hundred and Eighth Annual Meeting of the American Economic Association*, vol. 86, no. 2, pp. 153–8.

Haq, M. and I. Kaul, and I. Grunberg (eds) (1996) *The Tobin Tax* (New York: Oxford University Press).

International Monetary Fund (1997a) *International Financial Statistics* vol. L, no. 12 and table no. 92165 (Washington DC: IMF).

International Monetary Fund (1997b) *International Capital Markets: Developments, Prospects and Key Policy Issues* (Washington DC:, IMF), p. 40.

Kaminsky, G. L. and C. M. Reinhart (1996) *The Twin Crises: The Causes of Banking and Balance of Payments Problems*, International Finance Discussion Paper, Washington DC, Board of Governors of the Federal Reserve System.

Reinhart, C. M. and S. Dunaway (1996) *Dealing with Capital Inflows: Are there Any Lessons?* (Helsinki: United Nations University, and World Institute for Development Economics Research).

United Nations (1992) *World Investment Report 1992* (New York: UN).

United Nations (1997a) *Monthly Bulletin of Statistics* vol. LI, September, (New York: UN).

United Nations (1997b) *The World at the Beginning of 1998* (New York: UN), December.

United Nations Centre on Transnational Corporations (1992) *Foreign Direct Investment, Debt and Home Country Policies* (New York, UN).

UN ESCAP (1995) *Sectoral Flows of Foreign Direct Investment in Asia and the Pacific* (New York: United Nations).

UN ESCAP (1997) *Economic and Social Survey of Asia and the Pacific 1997* (New York: United Nations).

UN ESCAP (1998) *Economic and Social Survey of Asia and the Pacific 1998* (New York: United Nations).

World Bank (1997) *World Development Report 1997* (New York: Oxford University Press).

16
Learning from East Asia's Woes

John Williamson
World Bank, Washington DC

1 Introduction

For almost two decades East Asia was held up as a role model for developing countries, by economists in general and by those from the World Bank in particular. Since last July the region has been engulfed by a severe economic crisis, and innumerable sages have emerged from the woodwork to proclaim that the miracle was really a mirage, or that the region's problems are the penalty it has to pay for deviating from free market orthodoxy, or that the crisis is a deliberate act of sabotage of the region's progress by the West. In this chapter we offer an interpretation of the crisis that will allow us to assess the validity of such claims, and then proceed to ask how other developing countries, particularly those of South Asia, should respond to the crisis.

2 A crisis that surprised

No one foresaw a crisis of the character and severity that has engulfed East Asia. True, some of us worried that Thailand was taking a risk in committing itself to the defence of a fixed exchange rate (defined in terms of a single currency, which resulted in large cycles in the effective exchange rate as the dollar went on its roller-coaster) given that a massive current account deficit had developed, but we never imagined that the ensuing crisis might result in a devaluation of almost 50 per cent, or a fall in the stock market of over 40 per cent, or that output would decline by 8 per cent. Still less did it occur to us that a Thai crisis would result in rapid and widespread contagion. And if we had asked ourselves who would be likely to suffer from any contagion that might occur, we surely would not have selected as the likely victims the other East Asian countries, who boasted just about the strongest 'fundamentals' in the world, at least as we have been accustomed to thinking of fundamentals (in terms of macroeconomic variables like the fiscal balance, inflation, savings, investment and growth).

3 Common features of victims

For several months I think most of us were quite unable to detect a pattern in which countries fell victim to the crisis. We were relieved that no South Asian country succumbed in a serious way; we were also surprised because all the countries of South Asia are weaker than those of East Asia in terms of what we have been accustomed to thinking of as the fundamentals. But gradually a pattern emerged. With one partial exception, all the victims had three things in common:

- strong asset prices in the years preceding the crisis;
- large exposure to the international markets, including a large stock of short-term debts denominated in foreign exchanges;
- a weak financial sector, notably banks of dubious solvency because of a large volume of non-performing loans.

It is not too difficult to understand why a country with those three features should suffer contagion from the Thai crisis (whose initiation, I have argued, can be understood as a conventional exchange rate crisis). The Thai crisis raised questions about the sustainability of asset prices in any country whose economic situation appeared to resemble that of Thailand. Similarly, the Thai demonstration that exchange rates could depreciate severely caused a rush for dollars on the part of those with uncovered positions in foreign exchange, especially if these were short-term, which rapidly precipitated the very depreciation that agents were trying to insure themselves against. This depreciation weakened the balance sheet position of most companies with foreign exchange exposure (the exception being firms heavily engaged in exporting), which reinforced the asset price declines, and thus further undermined the solvency of the financial sector. These crises have been dubbed 'new-style crises', in contrast to old-style or conventional balance of payments/exchange rate crises.

Countries (such as those of South Asia) that exhibited only the last of the three features listed above, namely a weak banking system, were not vulnerable to a new-style crisis. But it would be a mistake to draw too much comfort from this; they remain vulnerable to old-style crises, and indeed their vulnerability to such a crisis may well have been increased by events in East Asia, notably the devaluations, which have reduced the competitiveness of South Asian exports.

4 Explaining East Asian vulnerability

To say that the countries engulfed by the crisis were those with high asset prices, that had heavy exposure to the international financial markets, and that had weak banking systems immediately poses the question: how did countries get into this situation? It seems to me that there were at least three policy mistakes that contributed to creating the vulnerability in most or all of the victim countries.

The first, and the one highlighted by the most elegant piece of theorizing to have been spawned by the crisis so far (Krugman, 1998) is the provision of explicit or implicit guarantees of the liabilities of financial intermediaries without the creation of a system of financial regulation and supervision adequate to restrain the moral hazard which such guarantees create. If the creditors of financial intermediaries believe they have no need to check the solvency of those to whom they are entrusting their assets, while the owners of the financial institutions believe that their losses will be socialized while they will reap the full benefits of the profits the institutions may make, they will have an incentive to undertake investments that are excessively risky from a social point of view. In the absence of a functioning system of regulation and supervision to restrain that moral hazard, the banks can be expected to acquire too many risky assets. That temptation may be expected to be particularly strong in the aftermath of financial liberalization, when bankers have been told it is their social duty to lend to those whom they judge it advantageous to lend to, and when they have not yet had the experience of a collapse to warn them against imprudent lending.

Guarantees without adequate regulation and supervision might go a long way towards explaining the weakness of the banking system, and they might go some way towards explaining how the prices of risky assets began to boom, but they certainly cannot explain how countries acquired a large exposure to the international financial market. To explain that, one needs also to recognize the second policy error, which was the premature liberalization of the capital account of the balance of payments. It was this which allowed foreign as well as domestic wealth-holders to respond to the attractive (because presumed to be largely risk-free) returns offered by financial intermediaries, and thus provide the financial resources that in many cases powered asset price booms – booms that for a long time seemed to validate the excessively risky lending that was being undertaken. And in the process, of course, the countries acquired their large exposure to the international markets. I take the East Asian meltdown as decisive evidence showing the wisdom of the Tarrapore Committee (1997) in having argued that Indian capital account convertibility needs to be preceded by the establishment of a liberalized, well-supervised, domestic financial system. And I concede that a part of the blame for the East Asian crisis can legitimately be laid at the door of those in the West (including in the international organizations) who pushed for rapid, unconditional and complete liberalization of capital account transactions.

While one can offer a complete explanation of the East Asian crisis in terms of those two policy errors, there is surely a third factor that contributed to the weakening of the banking systems in most or all of the victim countries. This is 'crony capitalism', the favouring of particular enterprises controlled by the friends or relatives of the politically powerful. One of the ways in which the cronies received favours was in terms of access to credit, which weakened the banks when the cronies either were unable to repay or chose not to repay because they knew that their political patrons would defend them against the sanctions that are normally imposed on defaulters.

5 Interpreting the crisis

If this is indeed how the East Asian meltdown developed, what does that imply for the sorts of claims mentioned at the beginning of this chapter? Was the miracle a mirage? Was the disaster a consequence of deviating from the free market? Did the West sabotage the miracle?

Surely the miracle was no mirage. Per capita incomes rose faster in Korea and Thailand between 1970 and 1995 than in any other countries that started with a comparable level of income (see Table 16.1). According to one estimate, poverty in Indonesia fell from some 58 per cent in 1971 to just 8 per cent in the early 1990s, surely the only time in history that a country has lifted half of its population out of poverty in a couple of decades, and dramatically superior to South Asia's reduction of perhaps 20 percentage points (from a similar figure to that of Indonesia in 1971 to perhaps 35 per cent in the early 1990s). Suppose that poverty doubles in Indonesia as a consequence of the crisis, which is surely an extreme assumption; it would still be less than half that in South Asia, even though poverty rates in the two regions were similar a quarter of a century ago. The miracle involved building productive assets and teaching people how to make good use of them, and those investments and skills are not going to evaporate because of a

Table 16.1 Comparative growth rates of per capita GNP, 1970–95[1] (US$)

Country	*1970*	*1995*	*Change (%)*
Côte d'Ivoire	270	660	144
Ecuador	290	1390	379
Egypt	230	790	243
Ghana	250	390	56
Korea	270	9700	3493
Morocco	260	1110	327
Philippines	220	1050	377
Thailand	210	2740	1205
Zaire	240	120	–50

Note: [1] Comparator countries are those with a population over 10 million and per capita GNP between $200 and $300 in 1970.
Source: World Bank Yearbook (various years).

financial crisis, no matter how severe. The miracle was real, and the people of those countries will again benefit from the assets that were built up when the crisis passes, as it will.

Can one explain the collapse by governments forcing their populace to save or invest or export too much, or otherwise distorting the market? One can argue that there was some over-saving, especially in Singapore – but Singapore is hardly at the eye of the storm. On the contrary, its over-saving enabled it to build a financial position so strong that it was able to weather the storm with rather little damage. Advocates of the over-investment thesis seem unable to agree whether the problem was too much investment in non-tradables (golf courses and shopping centres) that would not yield foreign exchange to service the debts that had been taken on, or too much investment in tradables so that they were satiating the world market. The latter version is quite implausible: most of the countries were importing more than they were exporting, and thus supporting rather than detracting from world demand. The former version is much more persuasive – but it amounts to saying the governments had let their former dedication to macroeconomic discipline, notably a competitive exchange rate, slip. And yes, crony capitalism had introduced distortions.

Did the West sabotage the miracle because it was jealous of the progress being made by a bunch of upstarts? The saboteurs were supposedly the speculators, who are presumed to have been responsible for causing the devaluations that initiated the crisis. No one can reasonably deny that the speculators were the proximate cause of the Thai devaluation (though it is not at all clear that they were responsible for the subsequent devaluations). The question is whether one believes that speculators act in response to a perception that prices (in this case exchange rates) are out of line with the fundamentals, thus presenting them with an opportunity to profit when the authorities are forced to face the facts, or whether they have the ability to make money by forcing a price away from its equilibrium level. This was the contention that Milton Friedman (1953) first challenged with his attempt to demonstrate that destabilizing speculation must be unprofitable (you make money by buying low and selling high, not vice versa). While I am among those who do not find this argument definitive in the context of a floating exchange rate (Williamson, 1993), basically because of the possibility that stop-loss traders provide a source that can be milched almost systematically by traders who follow chartist rules (Krugman and Miller, 1992), the equivalent argument in the context of a managed exchange-rate system relies on governments being forced by the speculators to change their macro policies in a way that will validate the speculation (Obstfeldt, 1995). So far attempts to find instances where speculators have induced validating changes in government policies have failed. (I see not a shadow of evidence to support any wider charge that the West in general consciously set out to disrupt the economic progress being made in East Asia; on the contrary, most Western economists fell over themselves in trying to prove that the economic progress that they welcomed and admired was a consequence of the East Asian countries adopting their particular policy preferences.)

Is there any alternative interpretation at a similar level of generality that is suggested by the analysis in the preceding sections? I propose that we think of these countries as having been seduced by their own success into overconfidence and thence carelessness. They had lived so long without a macro crisis that they had forgotten the penalties of letting the exchange rate become uncompetitive, as well as the necessity of reacting with overwhelming force and determination when introducing a policy package designed to resolve a crisis. Contrast Brazil's reaction to a speculative run in November 1987 with the initial dilly-dallying in Thailand, Indonesia and Korea. They had enjoyed such a long boom that they mistook a speculative bubble in the asset markets for a natural market reward for success. They had profited by liberalizing their economies, and did not realize the lesson learned in South America in the early 1980s, that a necessary counterpart to financial liberalization has to be the institution of adequate regulation and supervision. The West told them that liberalizing international capital flows was a part of growing up, and they took the advice without questioning. Their poor had benefited spectacularly despite the favours bestowed on the cronies, so it did not seem particularly dangerous to allow the cronies ever bigger favours.

6 Policy responses

I shall frame my lessons with a particular view as to how the South Asian countries should respond, although most of the things that I say apply also to other developing, or even in some cases developed, countries.

6.1 Avoidance of an old-style crisis

Since the South Asian countries exhibit only one of the three factors that precipitated the new-style crises in East Asia, I do not see much reason to fear similar crises in South Asia. However, the danger of an old-style crisis, one in which a balance of payments deficit precipitates a run on the currency, has been increased by the troubles of East Asia. The major factor here is the increased competitive pressure from East Asian countries following their massive devaluations, reinforced by the fall in demand for South Asian exports caused by the recessions in East Asia but somewhat attenuated by the weakening in the prices of primary commodities (notably oil) which are imported by both East and South Asia. The appropriate policy response is a tightening of macro policy, notably a more austere fiscal policy (including a reduction in quasi-fiscal deficits) and, if not necessarily an immediate depreciation, then certainly a greater willingness to allow the exchange rate to respond promptly to signs of a deterioration in the external accounts.

6.2 Continue to pursue a South Asian miracle

Just about every country in South Asia has in recent years set itself the goal of a major acceleration in its growth rate, inspired by the example of East Asia and its demonstration that rapid economic progress is possible if the policy stance is appropriate. Perhaps the most tragic consequence of the East Asian crisis would be if it dissuaded other countries from learning from the truly impressive achievements of East Asia over the past 30 years or so. There is no reason to believe that the policies that most economists hold responsible for nurturing the miracle of high and sustained growth with a reasonably egalitarian distribution of its fruits – macroeconomic stability, until 1997; high savings rates (aided by an early demographic transition); investment in education, beginning at the primary level; providing the private sector with a reasonably level playing field; export orientation; neutrality on industry versus agriculture; or even industrial policy (if you believe that was a factor) – were those that induced the crisis. On the contrary, it was the recent departures from those policies – the risks with macro stability involved in borrowing too much abroad and stabilizing the exchange rate rather than making sure it remains competitive, the failure to follow through from the successes in primary education by equivalent attention to secondary education, the violations of neutrality involved in growing preferences to the cronies – plus the sudden embrace of capital account convertibility, that set the stage for the crisis. With the exception of the growth of crony capitalism (and the neglect of the environment, though that is another story), pre-1990 East Asia remains a role model to be emulated.

6.3 Pre-empt new-style crises

While achieving a couple of decades of East Asian rates of growth should be the primary objective of economic policy in South Asia, it is obviously desirable to avoid that growth being interrupted at some point in the future by the emergence of a new-style crisis. This demands avoiding those mistakes bred of over-confidence that have laid East Asia low in recent months. First, while it is probably undesirable to avoid all guarantees of bank liabilities, it is essential that any that are issued be accompanied by good regulations (requiring transparent accounting, capital requirements at least up to the international norm, prohibitions on connected lending, a legal system that exacts sanctions if loans are not serviced conscientiously, and so forth) which are enforced by a competent and motivated body of supervisors. Second, it suggests that countries should eschew dogmatic commitments to capital account convertibility, and retain some ability to require financial actors to maintain a reasonably balanced currency position, and to make it expensive for domestic agents to borrow abroad short-term, as Chile and Colombia do. Third, it argues the need to abandon crony capitalism once and for all.

7 Concluding remarks

When this chapter was written, in February 1998, I had started to hope that the countries of East Asia were beginning to emerge from the crisis. That hope proved premature, especially with regard to Indonesia, but at the time of revision in October 1998 the hope looks more secure, unless the crisis goes into a second round as it ripples further around the world. Even so, the costs of the crisis have been so massive that it is of obvious importance for other countries to learn how to avoid similar disasters in the future. South Asia certainly needs to learn that – but it needs even more to learn how to grow in the way that East Asia did for the preceding quarter century.

References

Friedman, M. (1953) *Essays in Positive Economics* (Chicago: University of Chicago Press).

Krugman, P. (1998) 'What Happened to Asia?' MIT (http://web.mit.edu/krugman/www/DISINTER.html).

Krugman, P. and M. Miller (1992) 'Why Have a Target Zone?', *Carnegie-Rochester Conference Series on Public Policy*, no. 38 (June), pp. 279–314.

Obstfeldt, M. (1995) 'International Currency Experience: New Lessons and Lessons Relearned', *Brookings Papers on Economic Activity*, no. 1, pp. 119–211.

Tarrapore Committee (1997) *Report of the Committee on Capital Account Convertibility* (Mumbai: Reserve Bank of India).

Williamson, J. (1993) 'Exchange Rate Management', *Economic Journal*, vol. 103, no. 1, pp. 188–97.

World Bank *Yearbook* (various years) Washington, DC: World Bank.

Part VI

Comments: Beyond Adjustment and Emerging Issues

17

South Asia and the World Economy: Challenges Ahead

Nurul Islam
International Food Policy Research Institute, Washington DC

1 Background

South Asia faces the twenty-first century with several challenges. First, it has to complete the economic reforms, including stabilization, trade liberalization and output/input market reforms already undertaken at different paces and sequences in individual countries in South Asia. Second, simultaneously with domestic reform it must integrate effectively into an evolving, dynamic world economy that combines dual trends towards globalization and regionalism. Third, the process of integration will take place in an external economic environment which presents opportunities and constraints different from the ones faced by the high-performing East Asian countries in the past. The central theme underlying the ongoing economic reforms is that state intervention in economic activity in South Asia was greatly overextended in the past. While the need for public intervention to correct market failure is recognized, there is an ongoing controversy as to what constitutes market failure under specific circumstances, and whether public intervention can successfully correct such market failure and whether government failure may not exceed, in some instances, market failure. In the resolution of such an argument in particular instances judgment plays a crucial role.

2 Liberalization of financial markets

One important challenge South Asia faces, while integrating with the world economy, is how to respond to the globalization of financial markets. Until recently, South Asia has been heavily dependent on official development assistance (ODA). Given the stagnant or even declining level of overall ODA and increasing competition from aid recipients in Africa and among the transition economies, the share of South Asia will fall. Private capital flows will assume increasing importance. The relevant question in this context is how fast the domestic financial market should be opened up to the free flow of external funds, including the unrestricted participation of foreign financial institutions in the domestic market. South Asia did not experience the East Asian type of financial crisis in the last few years, as it did not open up the capital account for the free flow of funds. While it avoided the losses imposed by such a crisis, it suffered, it may be argued, from a limited access to external financial flows that contributed so significantly to the past East Asia's growth.

The emerging consensus among the international community seems to be that the liberalization of external capital accounts should be 'orderly and gradual'. It should be accompanied or preceded by the development of efficient domestic financial institutions, both banks and non-bank financial institutions, supported by an adequate domestic capacity for their regulation and supervision. At the same time, internationally recognized and accepted (i) banking supervision standards, (ii) accountancy standards, and (iii) bankruptcy laws have to be introduced and effectively enforced. This will contribute to increased transparency and predictability in the relationships between borrowers and lenders – both national and international – a feature that in many instances was said to be missing in East Asian countries. Reforms in these areas will greatly facilitate the task of risk assessment on the part of external investors. In practice, however, the growth of efficient financial markets and strong regulatory and supervisory mechanisms takes time – sometimes a long time. South Asia currently suffers from serious shortcomings and inefficiencies in the domestic financial market; the progress of reform to date is slow. Even in the presence of properly functioning and efficient financial markets, the case for temporary control on short-term capital flows to reduce their high degree of volatility is increasingly accepted by many analysts and policy-makers (UN, 1998). The circumstances under which such controls should be imposed, including the mechanisms, nature and duration of such controls are, however, still under debate in the Bretton Woods institutions. The lessons of experience of Malaysia in respect of controls on capital movements introduced in 1998 would be worth serious examination.

Foreign direct investment (FDI) (as distinguished from foreign portfolio investment) has demonstrated much less volatility in the short run and a greater long-run perspective. South Asia has greatly liberalized its regulations relating to FDI. However, following other developing countries, they compete in offering various fiscal, credit, and financial incentives to attract FDI. There is a strong case to move towards a harmonization of various incentives by individual South Asian countries to attract FDI. This competition frequently results in a loss of government revenues and an increase in public expenditure and adds to the excess profits of the FDI attracted by low labour costs or advantages in specific natural resources such as oil/gas exploitation or power generation.

3 Prospects of export growth and new world trade rules

The growth in external trade in South Asia depends predominantly on the expansion of labour-intensive manufactured exports and their future prospects in the world market. The recent East and Southeast Asian crisis, resulting in a fall in real wages, may prolong the competitive pressure of exports of labour-intensive manufactures from East Asia. Added to this will be the increasing competition from (a) the economies in transition – such as Eastern Europe, China, Vietnam, and (b) the African continent. Unlike the East and Southeast Asian countries in the past, South Asia will not be able to use the instruments of targeted trade, exchange rate, and credit allocation policies to promote exports, irrespective of the controversy regarding the efficiency or otherwise of such measures in the short run (Srinivasan, 1994). In any case, the rules of the World Trade Organization (WTO) and the economic policy reform agenda undertaken by the South Asian countries under the auspices of the international donor community severely limit such options. In order to take advantage of external market opportunities, South Asia needs to concentrate on productivity growth, through cost-reducing innovations including improved infrastructure and human capital formation. It has been estimated that the worldwide implementation of the Uruguay Round holds out prospects of about 9 per cent increase in exports from South Asia, of which 98 per cent of the gains are to be derived from manufactures, particularly garments (World Bank 1992). The abolition of the Multi-Fibre Arrangement (MFA) quota restrictions will favourably affect South Asia's textile and garment exports; the higher the growth in productivity in this sector, the higher will be the increase in exports and in real incomes. However, the different countries in South Asia would gain in varying degrees depending on (a) how restrictive the MFA quotas are currently in respect of their exports, (b) the division of exports between quota and non-quota countries, and (c) the relative rate of growth in productivity.

As South Asia proceeds to accelerate the process of diversification of exports, natural-resources-based as well as non-traditional exports such as horticultural exports, it is likely to face new constraints. The principal constraints relate, first, to environmental standards; and, second, to labour standards that must be met in the production of exports. The incorporation of these standards in trade rules is going to be an important theme in the course of the forthcoming WTO negotiations to start in 2002 (Schott, 1998). In the meantime, the introduction of improved environmental standards by the bilateral and multilateral financing institutions in their lending programmes and projects is also under way. The labour-intensive raw material processing industries such as leather, textiles (jute and cotton) and sugar cause a pollution of water and air. The adoption of measures to counter such effects may add to the costs of production, unless new technology is more efficient, and thus adversely affect any cost advantage in export markets.

One set of environmental standards relate to the sanitary and phytosanitary standards (PSP) that affects the exports of food or horticulture, fisheries or livestock products. The current WTO agreement has already incorporated PSP standards that affect cross-border trade flows and the mechanisms exist such as the joint WHO/FAO Codex Alimantarius Commission to set international PSP standards for food and agricultural products. Though the harmonization of international standards based on scientific criteria for many products is underway, the scope of judgment in setting such standards cannot be ignored; after all, science often sets the margin or determines the boundaries within which the setting of precise standards becomes a matter of judgment and of international negotiations. The latter is necessary to ensure their acceptability by all nations. At the same time, there is scope for disputes among trading partners in the interpretation and implementation of such standards as evidenced by recent disputes between the USA and the European Union (EU). Thus, it is important that South Asian countries effectively participate in the international forums, where such standards are debated and formulated, and attempt to bring to bear the considerations that are relevant to South Asia. Also, the South Asian countries need to build up adequate technically trained personnel and institutional capacity for interpreting, applying and enforcing these standards.

Among the new issues that are likely to affect the international trade regime in the coming years is the employment of child labour in South Asia. The developed importing countries concerned that this use of child labour confers on them a competitive disadvantage in low-cost manufactures, advocate the use of trade restrictions on such imports; increasingly they tend to make the grant of the generalized system of preferences (GSP) for developing countries conditional on the ban of child labour in export industries; and their trade unions press the multinationals to terminate the subcontracting arrangements with enterprises in developing countries that use child labour. Also, there is a movement to 'label' such products so that consumers would buy commodities that are labelled as not using child labour. In recent years, South Asia has been confronted with the threat of trade barriers on such exports as garments, carpets or shoes. In Bangladesh, in response to protests from importers, the trade unions and other human rights activists in the USA, an arrangement between USAID, the ILO, the government and the garment factories has been worked out to provide financial assistance in order to send the child workers in the garment factories to school. In any case, in the future in order to expand exports of low cost labour-intensive manufactures, the South Asian countries will be required to abandon the use of child labour in the export sector and concentrate on improving operational efficiency to reduce costs – more so, in view of increasing competition from other developing and transitional economies. Moreover, they would be required to enforce the ban on the use of child labour in export processing zones (EPZ) (Islam, 1994).

4 Regional trade liberalization in South Asia

Along with the movement towards global trade liberalization, there has been a proliferation of regional trade agreements or various types of regional economic cooperation agreements around the world. Whether the liberalization of trade and economic cooperation on a regional basis supplements and helps accelerate the process of global liberalization or slows it down and detracts from its benefits remains a matter of debate. The tentative consensus in the WTO seems to be that it depends on the particular circumstances of each regional agreement, that is, how outward-looking it is or whether it is accompanied by a reduction or increase in trade barriers with the third or non-partner countries; whether regional trade liberalization is across the board or selective (the latter increasing 'trade-diversion' effects); whether it is accompanied by a 'deeper integration' such as the liberalization of capital flows, including FDI and labour migration, and so on. The main trading partners of South Asia, that is, Europe and North America, are grouped in regional trade and economic cooperation agreements, that is, the EU and the NAFTA. The East and Southeast Asian countries have groupings of their own, such as the ASEAN and the emerging APEC which includes their developed-country trading partners – North America, Japan, Australia and New Zealand.

Official statistics for inter-regional trade among South Asian countries show that it was no more than 4 per cent of total trade in 1996. India has a consistent surplus in trade balance with all countries. Individual countries have a greater share of their total trade with the East and South East Asian countries than they have among themselves. The share of intra-regional South Asian trade in total trade in 1996 ranged from 18.2 per cent in the case of Nepal and 12.5 per cent for Bangladesh to 2.4 per cent in the case of India. The share of intra-regional exports in total exports in 1996 ranged from 11.2 per cent in the case of Nepal and 4.8 per cent for India to 1.7 per cent in the case of Bangladesh, whereas the share of intra-regional imports in total imports ranged from 21.4 per cent for Nepal and 17.7 per cent for Bangladesh to 8.5 per cent in the case of Sri Lanka and 0.45 per cent for India. For South Asia as a whole, the share of intra-regional exports in total exports was 4.0 per cent, and that of intra-regional imports in total imports was 3.6 per cent. As against them, the share of exports to East Asia in total exports of South Asia was 41.4 per cent, and that of imports from East Asia in total imports was 39.3 per cent.

Liberalization of trade in South Asia would open up possibilities of specialization and economies of scale on the basis of a regional market, based on each member country's advantage in natural resources and labour costs, even though gains are likely to be greater for the smaller economies such as Bangladesh and Nepal rather than for the continental economy of India. The opportunity to base their operations on the basis of a regional market would provide an added incentive to multinationals and foreign direct investment to locate in the region. Regional trade liberalization will legalize the illegal trade which is currently quite substantial – almost equal to the volume of legal trade in the case of the India–Bangladesh bilateral trade – and save the loss of customs revenue.

However, the gains will be more equitably shared among all the members, if intra-regional trade liberalization is accompanied by (a) a liberalization of capital flows and technology, (b) trade in electricity, gas, and other goods or inputs that are non-tradable globally but tradable among contiguous countries, and (c) cooperation in the exploitation and use of water resources – a very significant factor in the future growth of the region's agriculture and in the solution of flood control and environmental problems. Moreover, the cheap and efficient transit facilities for Nepal and Bhutan through India and Bangladesh to the world market, and similar facilities for India through Bangladesh to north-eastern India will contribute to the economic growth and welfare gains in Nepal and Bhutan, in one case, and in the northeastern states of India on the other. An expansion of joint Indo–Bangladesh investment in Bangladesh oriented partly, if not predominantly, towards the northeast Indian market will further promote equitable growth, peace and stability in north-east India.

The South Asian Association for Regional Cooperation (SAARC), created in 1985, has not progressed much in reality – even though there is a formal commitment to proceed towards free trade by 2005, if not by 2000. The South Asia Preferential Trade Agreement (SAPTA) initiated in 1995, has not made much headway, limited as it has been so far to liberalization mainly in respect of items of trade in which the member countries do not and are not likely to compete with each other; thus leading to minimum trade creation. In view of India's more diversified economic structure and a higher level of technological and managerial development, the smaller members are apprehensive that liberalization will have adverse effects on their import-competing sectors and will greatly enlarge the current trade deficit – which each of them has with India. In any case, there is a strong case for India, the biggest and more developed trade partner, undertaking a faster and a higher rate of trade liberalization *vis-à-vis* the other countries, especially in relation to Nepal and Bangladesh. The latter are the least-developed countries in South Asia, and are in any case, under WTO rules, eligible for enlarged access to markets in other developing countries on a preferential basis that is not likely to be offset by reciprocal and equivalent trade concessions. The offsetting advantages to India, for example, from such concessions are more likely to accrue from such areas of cooperation as the joint exploitation of natural resources like water, trade in gas and electricity, transit facilities, and capital investment in other member countries. Further, an acceleration of economic growth through trade with and investment in neighbouring countries is likely in the long run to provide a large market for Indian exports as well as to discourage the emigration of unskilled labour to India.

In conclusion, South Asia as it enters the twenty-first century faces a dynamic and evolving external economic environment, both regionally and worldwide, governed by new rules and conventions regarding trade, technology and capital flows. This will present opportunities as well as constraints. The role of the public management of economic policies will be significant but will change in character and content compared with the past, and will require not less but greater skill and expertise.

References

Islam, N. (1994) 'Asia and the World Economy', in A. Abdullah and A. R. Khan (eds), *State, Market, and Development: Essays in Honour of Rehman Sobhan*, ch. 5 (Bangladesh and India: University Press Ltd and Oxford University Press).

Schott, J. J. (ed.) (1998) 'Launching New Global Trade Talks: an Action Agenda', Special Report no. 12 (Washington, DC: Institute for International Economics).

Srinivasan, T. N. (1994) 'Preferential Trading Arrangements in South Asia: Theory, Empirics, and Policy, South Asia Region' (Washington, DC: World Bank), draft.

UN Committee of Development Planning (1998) *Report on the Thirty-second Session* (4–8 May 1998) (New York: United Nations).

World Bank (1992) *World Development Report 1992* (New York: Oxford University Press).

18
Monitoring the IMF

Koichi Hamada
Yale University

In the summer of 1997, I visited a small village near Lilongwe, the capital of Malawi. I was one of the evaluators of the IMF's Enhanced Structural Adjustment Facility (ESAF), a concessional loan programme to low-income countries, and I travelled to several sub-Saharan countries. The village emerged from the vast horizon painted on the backdrop of a beautiful sunset. Women of the village with their barefoot children surrounded a big round heap of manure. They complained, 'We need to use manure for producing maize because subsidies for fertilizer were stopped thanks to the IMF policy'. The IMF stabilization policy often recommends the removal of subsidies on the grounds that subsidies distort the price mechanism and worsen the budget deficit. Such a policy in Malawi affected the lives of villagers in the absence of necessary transition policies. On the occasion of presenting our paper to the IMF six months later, I recollected what a great chasm existed between the oval table in the Executive Assembly Room there and the oval-shaped heap of manure in Malawi.

The transmission of IMF policies to recipient countries can be described as follows: the IMF is a top-down, hierarchical organization. The guideline for policy agreement, the Policy Framework Paper (PFP), is often drafted almost totally in Washington, only to be filled in with actual numbers when it reaches the recipient country. Like a caravan whirling sand in its wake, the IMF mission stays just for a few weeks, collects (sometimes makes up!) data, negotiates the programme, and fills in the PFP. I sympathize with mission members who have to work out programmes, torn between Washington's plan and the appeals of the recipient government.

The IMF mission group is dispatched to a recipient country with guidelines based on the 'Washington Consensus' – policy prescriptions based on free market principles and monetary discipline. The current influential generation in the Fund was educated at the peak of the orthodox price theory's popularity, when a monetary approach to the balance of payments was in vogue. Those theories are sound in many cases, and the Mundell–Fleming framework is still effective in making policy advice to a country with some degree of wage–price inertia. However, this type of traditional analytical tool should be supplemented by incorporating new developments in economics, such as the explicit account of inter-temporal choice, and the economics of incomplete information that can deal with reputation, commitment and default. New developments are studied in the Research Department but do not seem to be sufficiently applied in field operations.

Consequently, a uniform menu following the 'Washington Consensus' is applied to many countries. During the Asian crisis, regardless of existing macroeconomic conditions such as budget or balance of payments deficits, the same austere prescriptions were applied. The IMF may have closed too many banks in Indonesia; the adjustment process for individual countries was not taken into account. The manure scene in Africa is an illustration of the disregard for the adjustment process.

Throughout the IMF, multiple layers of monitoring networks exist. The executive committee is supposed to monitor the Secretariat of the IMF. Among executive committee members, major countries, guided by their own national interest like helping lenders of the same nationality, attempt to influence the decisions of the IMF through the board of directors meetings and other informal channels of influence. Allegedly, the IMF is an institution dominated by European influence just as the World Bank is dominated by Americans. Once this influence is in place at the executive level, the next channel is for those high-ranking members to motivate staff members at the next level. The bureaucratic process can be readily studied at the IMF.

The next layer is the process by which the IMF monitors national economies receiving its aid and concessional lending. This negotiation is seen as a game of incomplete information. Borrowers report on their current economic situation and deliver or promise policy changes. Lenders find it difficult to know which parts of these promises are true. The network of monitoring extends beyond the narrow jurisdiction of the IMF. How does the network around the IMF interact with the network around the World Bank? The whole process of monitoring in the IMF is an experimental ground for the theory of economic policy-making developed by Avinash Dixit and others. The process is a succession of surveillance of situations by the IMF, the promise to deliver by recipient countries, the imposition of conditionality by the IMF that may be excessively strict, possible betrayal by recipient countries, followed by a reassessment of the situation. Taking Japan as an example, let me illustrate the processes of monitoring and influence. In terms of human capital, Japan's involvement in the IMF is tenuous, and in general Japan has kept a low profile in world politics since the Second World War. At the beginning of 1992 there were 30 Japanese employed in the IMF out of a total 1700 employees. This is less than 2 per cent of total employees and the percentage is much lower than the relative financial contribution of Japan (around 7 per cent). At the World Bank, the ratio of

Japanese professionals to the total employee population is even smaller – about 1 per cent.

Moreover, the majority of Japanese employees at the World Bank and the IMF are on leave from the government, central bank or related institutions in Japan. Some of them are working in a transitional or stopgap position in Washington while waiting for the next important position at home. Aside from the relative ratio of employees, Japan's position in these international institutions is generally not conspicuous.

There are at least three reasons for Japan's low profile in the international institutions. The first is her reaction to the Second World War; Japan, like Germany, maintained a passive attitude in international politics after the war. Subsequently, Japan has acted as a 'generous uncle' in the world community. The second reason for Japan's low representation in the IMF is her lack of international leadership and entrepreneurship. Japanese education overemphasizes memorizing and calculation. Students are taught to conform to conventional ideas and not to express independent, creative ideas. I have taught both Tokyo University students and Yale students. Students at both universities are well-trained intellectually; the critical difference between them is that Yale students feel free to voice their independent opinions. It is hard for young Japanese employees in the international organizations to cope with the culture of debate and persuasion. Everywhere politics exists but without rhetoric and persuasive power one cannot even approach the political arena. The third reason for a low profile is the difficulty that Japan has in taking the initiative in international action. Japan's quota in the IMF is always limited to protect European and American dominance. This, despite the fact that Japan has provided additional funds (this is apparently not limited!) to the IMF to finance various rescue operations for troubled countries. Difficulty in taking the initiative, coupled with a lack of human capital and with latecomer disadvantage, necessitates that Japan take the easier position of being passive.

The alternative was for Japan to build its 'own' international organization. In September 1997, in Hong Kong, Japan launched a plan for the Asia Fund. According to the theory of monitoring mentioned above, it was natural for a government that found the existing international institutions inadequate for its purposes to attempt to build a new one. The US Treasury, as well as high officials in the IMF, expressed strong antagonism to Japan's proposal. Stanley Fischer, Senior Vice-President of the IMF, said that the Asia Fund could undermine the authority and effectiveness of the IMF itself.

We should separate the economic logic from the ideology and from the defence of privileged position in examining the opposing opinions. The defence of privilege is a reflection of the fact that a rival institution might reduce the effectiveness of the existing institution as well as the power of nations that have dominant influence on it. The downside to establishing another institution such as the Asia Fund may include the following:

1. As international monetary stability and credibility in the exchange market are public goods, it is more economical and less confusing to produce them via a single institution;
2. The IMF itself creates moral hazards and easy attitudes in borrowing countries, and two or more institutions will aggravate this tendency; and
3. Japan lacks financial entrepreneurship, as exemplified by the recent financial turmoil.

Accordingly, the Asia Fund may not be able to contribute much to the world or Asian welfare, and could become the vehicle by which Japanese officials are provided with 'amakudari' (golden parachutes).

To respond to point 3 is difficult, but as to point 1 one can argue that a substantial part of the IMF's activity is not the supply of public goods. Concessional lending like the ESAF as well as the relief finance to financially troubled Asia and CIS countries has the nature of private goods. Therefore, point 1 is only partially right. As for point 2, if the present situation creates excessive moral hazards, that is the problem of the IMF itself. Ideally, a second competitive fund might mitigate the degree of moral hazard; if the world needs additional loans, even the extension of loans with the same degree of moral hazard might be desirable.

When certain countries have a dominant influence in an institution, or if they have biased motives to steer the institution, an outsider country has every reason to seek to build another one. Competition in institution-building is one source of innovation. Therefore, the Asia Fund plan should be studied carefully. It should not be dismissed simply because of opposition from the American or other governments in an effort to protect their own interests.

In general, we need to study the incentive system of networks around the IMF, the World Bank and other international institutions. Proper monitoring of IMF activities is essential as well as proper monitoring by the IMF of recipient countries. The IMF should incorporate current theory of economic science into its operations as well as in its research. Both cooperation and competition among international monetary institutions are required in order to improve the incentive mechanism within the monitoring networks in the world economy.

Reference

Ken-ichi, and Izumi Ohno (1993) *The IMF and the World Bank* (Tokyo: Nihonhyoron-sha) in Japanese.

19
Convertibility and the Asian Crisis

Deepak Lal
University of California, Los Angeles

The Asian crisis has come as a godsend to the dirigistes of South Asia many of whose intellectual gurus were assembled in Dhaka for the IEA conference. What has become clear from their papers and the discussion here is that their main concern now is to prevent the opening of the capital account of the balance of payments in South Asian countries. This remains the last shibboleth of the old dirigiste consensus on development.[1]

Two major concerns were expressed about convertibility and the free capital movements this entails. The first relates to the volatility of these flows, and thence of national income in countries without any controls on capital. This is an ancient worry of the Third World, earlier expressed as the purported adverse effects on growth of the export instability engendered by primary product exporting countries' integration into the world economy. In Lal and Myint (1996), a 25-country study covering the period since the Second World War found no statistical evidence that volatility of growth rates affected long-run growth performance – a conclusion that agreed with the numerous studies on the effects of export instability on growth. Thus, Hong Kong has had one of the most volatile growth rates amongst developing countries, and India one of the most stable – but the long-run growth performance of Hong Kong puts that of India to shame.

The second concern is that the Asian tigers lost their stripes once they opened up their capital accounts, and South Asia would be wise not to follow suit. To appraise this argument we need to discern the causes of the Asian crisis. These were threefold, in my view.

The first cause was the *quasi* fixed exchange rate regime in many of the countries. It is becoming increasingly clear that in a world with a globalized capital market only two exchange regimes are viable: a fully floating exchange rate or a rigidly fixed rate as in the currency board of Hong Kong. The reason, as Lal (1994) makes clear, is that these are the only ones which allow automatic adjustment to external and internal shocks without any need for any discretionary action by the authorities. In a world which requires instantaneous response to the actions of a highly decentralized but integrated world capital market mediating these shocks, the authorities do not have the time or the means to obtain the requisite information to deal with these shocks in a centrally planned manner. They often end up by being the problem rather than the solution if they try to manage their exchange rates in this volatile and unpredictable world economy, leading to serious misalignments of the real exchange rate. An automatic adjustment mechanism is therefore preferable to a discretionary one.

The second cause of the Asian crisis was a systemic flaw in the 'Asian' model of development. A central feature of this model – as seen most clearly in Korea but presaged by the development of Japan – is a close linkage between the domestic banking system, large industrial enterprises and the government. Thus in Korea, the government channelled subsidized credit to the *chaebol*, whose performance was then subject to fulfilling explicit export targets. These *chaebol* like the *zaibatsu* in Japan were government creations to deal with a perceived problem of 'agency' faced by newly-industrializing countries. These find that, once they have to move from the simpler manufactures which can be produced by family-owned enterprises to the more complex manufactures requiring large and lumpy capital investment, they have insufficient agglomerations of private wealth for enterprises to remain owner-managed. To overcome the ensuing 'agency' problem when ownership and management were separated and domestic capital markets underdeveloped, they adopted three routes: the political creation of concentrations of private wealth by encouraging state-subsidized family conglomerates, as in Korea and Japan; by putting such industries in the public sector, as in Taiwan and India; or by encouraging direct foreign investment, as in Singapore.

The Korean and Japanese route can be fairly effective, as the export targets used to monitor the performance of the favoured groups offered subsidies of cheap credit through the banking system, which cannot be corrupted by the actions of local mandarins, who have no way of effecting foreign sales of the favoured conglomerates. However, this artificial creation of agglomerations of private wealth is not essential, as the success of Hong Kong, as described in Lal and Myint (1996, ch. 3), relied on the natural forces of growth; and whose performance as judged by the efficiency of investment is the highest amongst the Gang of Four.

The real danger, however, in the Korean way of dealing with this 'agency' problem is that by making the banking system the creature of the government's will, it creates tremendous moral hazard in the domestic banking system. The banks have no incentive to assess the creditworthiness of its borrowers or the quality of the investments to be financed by their loans, because they know that no matter how risky and overextended their lending, they will always be bailed out by the government. This can lead in time to a mountain of bad paper and the *de facto* insolvency of a major part of the banking system, as happened in both Korea and Japan – not to mention the corruption that is inevitably involved in this type of development.

The third cause of the crisis was that the problem of moral hazard for the domestic banking system created by this 'Asian' model was aggravated by the actions of the IMF and the entrance of foreign bankers as lenders in the newly-liberalized capital markets. Of the three types of capital flows that can be distinguished – direct foreign investment, portfolio investment and bank lending – the income and foreign currency risk of the first two types is shared by both the lender and the borrower, as the 'investments' are denominated in domestic currency. By contrast, foreign bank loans are usually denominated in US dollars and the interest rate is linked to the London interbank offered rate (LIBOR). This means that if faced by a shock which requires a devaluation, the domestic currency burden of the foreign bank debt rises *pari passu* with the changing exchange rate. If the debt is incurred by the private sector, this rising debt burden need pose no problem for the country for, if the relevant foreign banks run, the borrowers can always default on their debt.

Now enter the IMF. Ever since the 1980s debt crisis, the foreign banks faced by a default on their Third World debt have argued that this poses a systemic risk to the world's financial system, and asked in effect for an international bail-out to prevent this catastrophe. The IMF has been more than willing to oblige. For since the era of the Bretton Woods adjustable-peg exchange rate regime – which the IMF was set up to manage – ended with President Nixon's closing of the gold window in the early 1970s, the IMF has resembled a character in Pirandello's play *Six Characters in Search of an Author.* The debt crisis of the 1980s provided one such play, the rocky transition of the Second World from plan to market a second, and the Mexican and Asian crises a third. The IMF has increasingly become the international debt collector for foreign money centre banks.

The IMF in recent years has, thus, generated serious moral hazard in foreign bank lending. With the increasingly confident expectation that they will be bailed out via the IMF no matter what the quality of their lending to Third World countries, foreign banks have no incentive to act prudently in their foreign lending. When this international moral hazard is coupled with the domestic moral hazard associated with the politicized domestic banking systems of the 'Asian' model – as in Korea – a disastrous witches' brew was created. Foreign banks lending to domestic banks which know they will be bailed out will over-lend, leading to risky investments and an eventual debt crisis for the country.

With measures to remove the domestic moral hazard being widely adopted in the region, the international moral hazard arising from the IMF's operations remains. What is to be done? The best solution would be to shut down the IMF; its original mandate ended with the Bretton Woods exchange rate system. But it is unlikely that the IMF will be shut down. The ideal way to deal with volatile foreign bank lending is for local central banks to ensure that all such borrowing is suitably hedged. If they lack the requisite capital markets for such hedging, they might consider a second best 'control' on such capital flows. This would lay down that all such loans must be denominated in *local* currency. By raising the costs of such borrowing this would be equivalent to a market-determined tax on such flows. Second, it would mean that the foreign banks would have to share in the foreign exchange risk, and in times of contagion instead of running they might pause and refinance their potentially viable borrowers.

Extending the same policy to the IMF would mean that this 'bank''s short-term loans should also be denominated in *local* currency. As one major aim of Fund programmes is to stabilize the currency, their success would now be judged by an honest balance-sheet item – the value of the payments it receives compared with the loans made in US dollars. If the programme were successful it would make a foreign currency profit on its lending, if not, a loss. This would also mean that the benighted taxpayers of the borrowing countries would not have to bear a rising foreign-currency-denominated debt burden because of the past and continuing folly of their rulers.[2]

Beyond this limited and 'market'-based control of short-term capital flows there is no need for any other controls. Moving to full convertibility of their currencies and maintaining exchange rate flexibility would allow the undoubted gains from integration in the world economy to be reaped. This remains the unfinished business for South Asian governments, who should disregard the siren voices of the dirigistes at this conference, whose current panaceas are as flawed now as in the past.

Notes

1 An accessible account of the various guises the dirigiste dogma has taken since the Second World War will be found in Lal (1997).

2 The argument that the IMF is needed as a lender of last resort is fallacious. There are two functions such a lender has to perform, as set out in the famous Bagehot rules. First, it should be able to create high-powered money quickly to lend to *solvent* banks to prevent a liquidity crisis. Second, it must be able to distinguish between good and bad 'paper', and thus judge the soundness of the institutions to which it is extending liquidity, the insolvent ones being liquidated. The IMF is incapable of doing either. This is well-argued in Schwartz (1998).

References

Lal, D. (1994) *The Repressed Economy*, Economists of the 20th century series, ch. 6 (Cheltenham, Glos.: Edward Elgar).

Lal, D. (1997) *The Poverty of 'Development Economics'*, 2nd revised expanded edition (London: Institute of Economic Affairs).

Lal, D. and H. Myint, (1996) *The Political Economy of Poverty, Equity and Growth – A Comparative Study* (Oxford: Clarendon Press).

Schwartz, A. (1998) 'Time to Terminate the ESF and IMF', *Foreign Policy Briefing, no. 48*, Cato Institute, Washington DC (26 August).

20

Development-oriented Economic and Social Reforms vs the Neo-liberal Agenda in South Asia

Amiya Kumar Bagchi
Centre for Studies in Social Sciences, Calcutta

Thanks to the propaganda blitz of the neo-liberal establishment, the phrase structural adjustment has become a part of the naturalized language of every economist, journalist, politician and educated layman. Yet it does not signify something as definite or as unambiguous as the 'sun', a 'mango' or a 'chair'. Which structure are we talking about? Is it the economic structure as given by an input–output table for a country, or the structure of incomes and occupations as in the Clark–Fisher scheme of classification between the primary, secondary and tertiary occupations, or the structure of industries as between capital-intensive and labour-intensive sectors, or as between high-technology and traditional sectors? If it is none of these, is it the set of regulations governing economic activities, or the associated pattern of incentives motivating such activities? What do we mean by 'adjustment'? Is there a universally optimal pattern of regulations and incentives applicable to all countries? If not, then what is the 'adjustment' supposed to fit? Whose convenience must the 'adjustment' be directed to?

These are all very elementary questions, but I find that few policy documents emanating from government sources, or from such august bodies as the IMF and the World Bank, ever care to raise such questions, let alone try to answer them. The same comment applies to the associated phrase 'economic reforms'. The advocates of economic reforms do not specify what they are supposed to comprise. It is far more obvious, in their lexicon, what they are not supposed to include. They rarely if ever include basic social reforms. Lip service is paid to the need to address so-called 'social sector' issues, such as literacy, health and so on. But they are mostly treated as an appendage to economic reforms, and public resources are to be devoted to them only if the kitty contains a surplus after meeting the fiscal deficit targets, and targets of tax-cutting all round. In many cases the economic reformers assume that the reforms will lead to the desired social sector improvements as a by-product of the changes wrought by the reforms.

For the sake of rendering the meanings of the various phrases more transparent, and aligning them with the usage of social reformers and advocates of equity and democracy, it is useful to distinguish between different kinds of reform in society, economy and governance styles in a typical less-developed country, which fits the reality of virtually all the SAARC members.

The first and the most important area of reform is that of social relations and the architecture of governance in such a country. In a typical region in a South Asian country the majority live in rural areas, and these areas are dominated by landlords, petty and big. By using their position in rural society and extending their influence through open and clandestine networks to the towns and the seats of power, they manage to acquire a large proportion of the surplus produced by the land, and the rents distributed through public channels in the form of subsidies, lucrative contracts and franchises of various kinds. These landlords also have a strong foothold in the bureaucracy through kinship ties. The landlords, thus, not only grab too large a fraction of the investible surplus of society but directly interfere in the working of all kinds of markets, including the markets for labour, land, its produce, water, fertilisers and credit. They also actively obstruct the access of the poor not only to decent incomes, but also to public channels of education, healthcare and credit. Anybody who is really interested in the long-term prosperity of South Asia and a decent standard of living for the majority of its population has to find the means of abolishing or drastically curtailing landlord power. The instruments for achieving this may vary across regions, but according security of tenure to cultivating peasants and preventing the landlord from grabbing the lion's share of the revenue and public patronage are essential steps. (For an analysis of 'rent-seeking' from a non-neoclassical standpoint, see Bagchi, 1993, 1998.)

In densely populated countries with extreme differences in wealth and power between the rich and the underprivileged, land reform has to be combined with the creation of democratic institutions from the village up to the level of governance of the whole country. Local public institutions are needed to provide a framework for speeding up advances in education, healthcare and public infrastructure. Given the steepness of interest rates and the scarcity of credit for the poor in these societies, local-level democratic institutions can also help to provide credit on reasonable terms to the poor. The success of the Grameen Bank in Bangladesh may seem to contradict the necessity for grassroots democracy. It may even be contended that in a landlord-dominated society of largely illiterate peasants and workers, so-called grassroots democracy will play into the hands of the rich and may interfere with the working of a Grameen Bank type of institution. But this argument only underscores the critical importance of combining procedural, electoral democracy with substantive democracy by reforming the social relations such as those between the landowner and the peasant (through the elimination of non-cultivating landlords), the literate and the illiterate (through the spread of literacy), men and women (through the equalization of men's and women's rights in marriage, work and education) and employers and workers (through the elimination of deployment of private or illegitimate state power by the former against the latter). If such reforms are not effected, a Grameen Bank will serve mainly as an adjunct to the existing power structure and a palliative for the ills of poverty and illiteracy rather than as the empowering institution it could be under the alternative scenario.

Moving from these issues of social and political reform, an 'economic reformer' can then turn to the reform of the domestic real economy and the financial sector. The agenda of such reforms will vary from country to country. Productivity-raising transformation requires a substantial rise in the share of industry in national income and employment. In the case of a country in the first stage of industrialization, economic reforms may involve, among other things, the adoption of policies for raising the educational and skill levels of workers, selective (and terminable) protection of infant industries and skills, and the encouragement of research and development by public authorities and private business. The line between public and private ownership or control of assets, between subsidies and tariffs and quantitative restrictions on foreign goods, will have to be drawn keeping the needs of the country in question, and this line will shift over time depending on conjunctural circumstances. The placing of these lines, and the intensity and duration of public support will often involve controversy, and lead to mistakes particularly in countries with what might be called semi-feudal social and incentive structures. But putting all such countries on the Procrustean bed of structural adjustment can kill both promising and terminally-ill industries, and no lusty infants can be conjured up from beneath that bed.

In cases in which domestic industry has become unduly cartellized, and lack of competition thwarts efficiency and growth, there may be a justification for allowing import competition in a selective manner; forcing such industries to become net foreign-exchange earners may also be an effective disciplining device. It is only after the domestic economy has been deregulated and energized in such a deliberate fashion that the question of liberalizing the foreign-trade regime across the board can be tackled without harming the incomes and employment of poor economies. Today, the European Union (EU) stands as a protagonist of free mobility of capital, finance and manufactured goods (but not of labour or agricultural produce) and is seen as the enemy of state patronage for industry and agriculture in the less-developed countries. There is little difference between the stances of the USA and the members of the EU in this respect.

However, apart from the long history of protectionism in all the European countries during the early period of their industrialization, even in the period since 1945, the European nation-states played a critical role in providing protection to agriculture on a stupendous scale, and patronage for strengthening the competitiveness of the manufacturing sector. It is only after the controllers of European economies judged that they had acquired sufficient prowess to claim equality with the USA and Japan in most respects that they embarked on the path of external liberalization of their economies (Milward, 1992; for a brief analysis of the political economy of restricted versus free trade regimes, in Europe and the USA, see Bagchi, 1992). But integration of the European economies for the sake of protection of their respective national economies took precedence over opening up to the rest of the world.

Whether internal industrial policy reform should also be accompanied by reforms in the domestic financial sector depends on how the latter functioned in that particular economy (Rodrik, 1992). One of the most misleading and theoretically unsound doctrines that has infested the profession is the idea propagated by R. I. McKinnon and E. S. Shaw that low interest rates and directed credit are always a sign of so-called 'financial repression'. These instruments had served in many countries of Europe and Asia to encourage long-gestation but productive investment projects which might otherwise be eliminated by the market, and to build up the bargaining power and productivity of particular sectors and the people employed in them who were discriminated against by a capital market riddled with asymmetric information, as discussed by Calomaris and Himmelberg (1994) and Stiglitz (1994). The literature advocating the freeing of interest rates and the ending of directed credit has been driven by the profoundly mistaken idea that capital and money markets can clear through the operation of unregulated competition just as the market for vegetables or for eggs clears from day to day or week to week (Bagchi, 1990; Wade, 1990).

In many DCs, of course, the cheap credit was misused by private businessmen to systematically milk the public exchequer and defraud depositors. However, this laxity was itself partly encouraged by the doctrine that the governments in DCs have no higher duty than enabling private businessmen to make as much profit as possible, while paying as little as possible in the way of taxes. Most of the non-performing assets of banks in India have accumulated because of the delinquency of rich borrowers rather than the default of poor peasants and small businessmen availing of the priority-sector loans. I suspect that a similar situation holds in Bangladesh and Pakistan.

The proponents of financial-sector liberalization want more than the deregulation of interest rates on loans and deposits of formally organized banks (in India, Pakistan, Bangladesh and Nepal, of course, interest rates in the informal credit market have always been free of regulation, and generally usurious). The financial liberalization agenda also comprises the unification of money and capital markets, the lifting of controls on capital issues, and the unification of domestic and global capital markets through the free mobility of capital into and out of the country concerned. An addendum to the neo-liberal agenda is the development of a market for firms through deregulation of mergers between firms and takeovers of one firm by another.

This agenda elevates the Anglo-American model of the firm and the arm's-length relationship between banks and firms above all the other patterns of corporate governance as the ideal to be achieved by all countries, including DCs with weak capital and money markets (Bagchi, 1997). Such a valorization flies in the face of the evidence that, not only in South Korea and the People's Republic of China, but also in Japan, Germany and France, 'relationship banking' and a highly restrictive regime for takeovers and mergers of firms led, in the postwar period, to higher rates of investment and growth than in the USA and Great Britain. An international market for firms is almost certain to lead to the takeover of many of the most promising 'infants' in the manufacturing, infrastructure and service sectors of the DCs.

The liberalization agenda of the Washington twins places far greater emphasis on the deregulation of external trade and payments than on the stimulation of competition within the domestic economy. The abolition of quantitative restrictions on virtually all commodities, and a drastic reduction of tariffs on imports and subsidies for exports, were made mandatory for countries applying for IMF assistance to tide over external debt problems. All these measures have now become part of the agreement leading to the emergence of the World Trade Organization. The WTO agreement insists on freeing virtually all controls on the international movement of goods and foreign investment. But it has remained silent on the mobility of labour and imposed a far more restrictive regime on the exploitation of inventions and international transfer of technology than had been current in the period up to the end of the 1980s. Under the so-called trade-related investment measures (TRIMs) of the WTO, the LDC governments have already been deprived of any power to discriminate between foreign and domestic investors. Under the proposed Multilateral Investment Guarantee Agreement (MIGA), the state is to be made responsible for protecting the property of all foreign investors absolutely while being deprived of even the kinds of regulatory measures it can impose on domestic firms.

There has been some rethinking among orthodox economists about the desirability of pushing forward the agenda of full capital account convertibility (CAC) in LDCs. In India and many other LDCs, radical economists had been arguing for a long time that full CAC and the ability of domestic firms to borrow unlimited amounts in international capital markets is a recipe for disaster. In spite of these arguments, the high-powered CAC committee appointed by the Reserve Bank of India had recommended in 1997 that India should make a transition to CAC by the year 2000. Fortunately for India, the Southeast Asian crisis which erupted in July 1997 with Thailand suffering an unsustainable capital outflow and with a major banking crisis on its hands, which then spread to Indonesia and South Korea and threatened to engulf Malaysia as well, showed up the dangers of CAC (Bagchi, 1998;

Wade and Veneroso, 1998). It has been argued that the crisis could have been averted if there had been proper monitoring of the financial system and the inflows and outflows of capital. However, such monitoring would have implied putting some curbs on CAC. In fact, the Asian economies which have so far been able to withstand the destabilizing effects of the Asian currency crisis are the People's Republic of China (PRC), and Taiwan, and Hong Kong, which is now part of the PRC. These economies had large balance of payments surpluses, large foreign exchange reserves, and various implicit or explicit controls over movements of capital across their borders.

Large foreign exchange reserves are by themselves no guarantee against destabilizing outflows of capital from an LDC or a country in transition from a command economy to a free market. The most spectacular cases of such destabilization even with large foreign exchange reserves are Mexico in 1994–5, Russia in 1998, and Brazil in 1998–9. If poor economies with no strong political backing from, say, the USA or the EU want to avoid a traumatic balance of payments crisis they must build up a credible record of balance of payments surpluses, the retirement of foreign debt and the building-up of foreign exchange reserves out of their own resources (and not principally on the basis of inflows of foreign capital). If these conditions are not satisfied, then when an exogenous event causes a large balance of payments deficit, the currency will be judged to be overvalued by foreign investors and/or domestic agents holding their assets in foreign currency (such holdings are now widespread in Russia, and most of the large Latin American economies), and the country will suffer unsustainable capital outflows.

The South Asian economies have in the past had a large inflow of foreign resources through the earnings remitted by their citizens working in the West Asian oil-producing countries. For India, Pakistan and Sri Lanka these earnings generally far exceeded net foreign-aid inflows and net foreign capital inflows taken together. These resources were squandered, especially in India and Pakistan, by the profligacy of the government and the rich. The latter refused to invest enough in the economy and build up the competitiveness of their enterprises. Nor have the governments been able to tax the rich enough to be able to balance their budgets. The main effect of so-called 'fiscal austerity' (to the extent it has been practised at all) has been to abridge social sector expenditure and public capital formation. Apart from harming the improvement of the health, education and living standards of the poor, this style of austerity damages the competitiveness of the economy.

The open invitation to transnational corporations (TNC) and foreign capital to enter virtually all sectors of the economy is triggered by this failure of domestic competitiveness and investment. But the increasing penetration of TNCs into LDCs means an acceleration in the process of creeping liberalization. As this penetration grows, the import bill on account of global sourcing by TNCs increases, and foreign exchange outflows on account of profits, fees and other service charges exacted by TNCs go up, the threat of eruption of unsustainable balance of payments looms larger, and the pressure for allowing CAC also increases. Thus, disallowing CAC while carrying out the rest of the neo-liberal agenda is not a credible stance in the long run.

The external liberalization of the economy in South Asia has not been simply the effect of the pressures exerted by the IMF, the World Bank, the USA or other powerful external actors. The investment failure and tax evasion on the part of the rich and the governments complacently acquiescing in such defaults have played an equally important part in measures of liberalization that harmed the interests of the economy and the ordinary people of these countries. One of the most glaring examples of the activities of the rich, and a permissive government conniving in those activities, is the huge volume of gold imports into India. The liberalizers' wisdom was that permitting gold imports into the economy in an unrestricted fashion would choke off such imports, for, according to them, it is the margin between domestic and international prices arising out of restrictions on gold imports that drives these imports. In fact, since 1992 when such imports were permitted in the payment of a nominal duty, they have increased by leaps and bounds. It has been estimated by the World Gold Council that the quantity of gold imported into India in 1997 was 737 tonnes, an increase of 45 per cent from 507 tonnes imported in 1996 (RBI, 1998, p. VII–7). In terms of quantity, gold imports in 1998 will probably be three times the amount imported in 1991 or 1992. Gold has become the second largest item of import into India and will account for the major part of the expected balance of trade deficit of about $14 billion in 1998. It is to be noted here that the value of gold in real terms, whether measured in foreign currency or Indian rupees, has depreciated almost continuously during the last decade. Such a large locking-up of scarce foreign exchange resources by the risk-averse, tax-evading rich in India (and probably in other parts of South Asia) shows up the socially unproductive character of the behaviour of a major section of the wealthy community.

I cannot pretend to carry out a thorough analysis of the pitfalls of the neo-liberal agenda. This agenda proves to be particularly counterproductive in South Asia when tested against the requirements of economic growth and social and political equity, because the basic social and economic reforms for laying the foundations of a sustainable, equitable growth process have not been carried out. The semi-feudal structure of the society has been preserved, and in many cases reinforced, through state inaction, and action favouring the landlords, traders and other rent-seekers. The same regulators who had loyally operated various kinds of controls have, by and large, turned into vociferous advocates of the neo-liberal agenda without disturbing the social bases of rent-seeking, the use of illegitimate private power and socially damaging asset-holding propensities. I hope that the discussion of economic and social reforms will discard the agenda set by yesterday's semi-feudal regulators turning into today's semi-feudal liberalizers and turn to the real agenda for action.

References

Bagchi, A. K. (1990) 'The IMF View of International Economic Policy and the Relevance of Sraffa's Critique of Economic Theory', in K. Bharadwaj and B. Schefold (eds), *Essays on Piero Sraffa: Critical Perspectives on the Revival of Economic Theory* (Delhi: Oxford University Press), pp. 494–515.

Bagchi, A. K. (1992) 'On the Political Economy of the Choice of a Trade Regime', Silver Jubilee Paper no. 13, Brighton, Institute of Development Studies, University of Sussex.

Bagchi A. K. (1993) '"Rent-seeking", New Political Economy and the Negation of Politics', *Economic and Political Weekly*, vol. 28, no. 34, 21 August, pp. 1729–36.

Bagchi, A. K. (1997) 'Economic Theory and Economic Organization, I, a Critique of the Anglo-Saxon Theory of Firm Structure', occasional paper no. 165, Centre for Studies in Social Sciences, Calcutta.

Bagchi, A. K. (1998a) 'Local and Global Monopolies and the Prospects of Global Democracy', in D. Nayyar (ed.), *Economics as Ideology and Experience: Essays in Honour of Ashok Mitra* (London: Frank Cass), pp. 96–124.

Bagchi, A. K. (1998b) 'Growth Miracle and its Unravelling in East and South-east Asia: Unregulated Competitiveness and Denouncement of Manipulation by International Financial Community', *Economic and Political Weekly*, vol. 33, no. 18, 2 May, pp. 1025–42.

Calomaris, C. W. and C. P. Himmelberg (1994) 'Directed Credit Programmes for Agriculture and Industry', Proceedings of the World Bank Annual Conference on Development Economics, 1993 (Washington, DC.: IBRD) pp. 113–37.

Milward, A. S. (1992) *The European Rescue of the Nation-State* (London: Routledge).

Reserve Bank of India (RBI) (1998) *Report on Currency and Finance 1997–98*, vol.1 (Mumbai: RBI).

Rodrik, D. (1992) 'The Limits of Trade Policy Reform in Developing Countries', *Journal of Development Economics*, vol. 43, no. 1, pp. 5–38.

Stiglitz, J. E. (1994) 'The Role of the State in Financial Markets', Proceedings of the World Bank Annual Conference on Development Economics, 1993 (Washington, DC.: World Bank) pp. 19–52.

Wade, R. (1990) *Governing the Market: Economic Theory and the Role of Government in East Asian Industrialisation* (Princeton, NJ: Princeton University Press).

Wade, R. and F. Veneroso (1998) 'The Asian Crisis: The High-debt Model versus the Wall Street–Treasury–IMF Complex', *New Left Review*, no. 228, March–April, pp. 3–24.

Index of Names

Subject Index